KU-271-864

THE PIG AND THE SKYSCRAPER

CHICAGO: A HISTORY OF OUR FUTURE

———————◆———————

MARCO D'ERAMO

Translated by Graeme Thomson

FOREWORD BY MIKE DAVIS

VERSO

London • New York

This edition first published by Verso 2002
© Verso 2002
Copyright © Graeme Thomson 2002
Foreword © Mike Davis 2002
First published as *Il maiale e il grattacielo* ("Universale Economica" edition)
© Giangiacomo Feltrinelli Editore Milan 1999
All rights reserved

1 3 5 7 9 10 8 6 4 2

The moral rights of the author and the translator have been asserted

Verso
UK: 6 Meard Street, London W1F 0EG
US: 180 Varick Street, New York, NY 10014-4606

Verso is the imprint of New Left Books
www.versobooks.com

ISBN 1 85984 624 6

British Library Cataloguing in Publication Data
A catalogue record for this book is available from the British Library

Library of Congress Cataloging-in-Publication Data
D'Eramo, Marco, 1947–
[Maiale e il grattaciolo. English]
The pig and the skyscraper / Marco d'Eramo ; translated by Graeme Thomson ;
foreword by Mike Davis
p. cm.
ISBN 1-85984-624-6
1. Chicago (Ill.)–Description and travel. 2. D'Eramo, Marco, 1947–Journeys–Illinois–Chicago.
3. Chicago (Ill.)–History. 4. Chicago (Ill.)–Social conditions. 5. Capitalism–Social aspects–
Illinois–Chicago. I. Thomson, Graeme. II. Title
F548.52.D47 2001   977.3′11–dc21   2001046573

Designed and typeset by Steven Hiatt, San Francisco, California
Printed and bound in the USA by R. R. Donnelley & Sons Co.

Contents

Foreword

by Mike Davis

On 11 July 1995, the National Weather Service warned Chicagoans that Mother Nature was about to turn temperatures to "broil." A potentially deadly heat wave was rapidly engulfing the Midwest with Chicago near its epicenter. The next day, as thermometers punctually exploded, anxious residents sacked appliance stores of every last fan and air-conditioner in Cook County. It was a rational panic, since in the week to follow access to artificial cooling would all too often become the difference between life and death.

Chicago, of course, is notorious for its extreme weather: Moscow in the winter, Calcutta in the summer. Nothing taller than the Sears Tower stands between the mid-continent metropolis and the North Pole in one direction, and the tropical Caribbean in the other. In January super-chilled air avalanches southward, while in July the Mississippi Valley becomes a vast duct for torrid air being sucked northward. In Chicago folklore, if the icy blast of the "Hawk" don't kill you, then summer's suffocating heat will.

By 1995, however, city government had put very different valuations on the political liabilities of extreme cold and heat. Winter blizzards are a direct threat to commerce and profit, cutting off the Loop from its suburban commuter belt and paralyzing O'Hare, the nation's most important air hub. Voters who are famously tolerant of political corruption are at the same time ruthless in their expectations about wintertime municipal services. Keeping the snow ploughs at work, accordingly, is a classic test of political kingship in Chicago. When Mayor Bilandic badly fumbled snow clearance during a major blizzard in 1984, he was promptly evicted from office.

Sweltering summer heat, on the hand, seldom disrupts the flow of goods or the comfort of the air-conditioned middle classes. Although extreme heat is a more lethal health hazard than cold in Chicago, its victims are traditionally old, very poor and majority Black. Their deaths, moreover, are only controversial when mortality reaches epidemic proportions: the last instance being the smoldering summer of 1955. Thus forty years later, the city was massively geared up to battle winter storms but had no emergency plan for dealing with a protracted heat wave. Vulnerable groups without air-conditioning were expected to cool themselves with cheap fans or open fire hydrants. A few "ordinary" heat deaths would hardly constitute a crisis. What ensued between 13 and 20 July, however, was carnage on the scale of a double jumbo-jet crash at O'Hare. An estimated 733 Chicago residents, according to a study in the *Annals of Internal Medicine,* perished in the brick ovens of their tiny SRO rooms and dilapidated Southside tenements. Although city officials would monotonously invoke the hand of God (who turned up the thermostat to 106 degrees in the shade on 13 July), a science panel of the National Oceanic and Atmospheric Administration insisted in 1996 that given the Weather Bureau's accurate advance warnings, "many, if not all, of the heat-related deaths associated with this event were preventable."[1]

Prevention, however, would have required prompt recognition of urgency. Yet, even as heat deaths soared into the three figures, City Hall's attitude was lethargic if not callous. Marie Antoinette indeed would have recognized a kindred spirit in Chicago's own hereditary monarch. "It's hot," said Mayor Richard M. Daley. "It's very hot. We all have our little problems but let's not blow it out of proportion. ... We go to extremes in Chicago. And that's why people like Chicago. We go to extremes."[2]

---

1   S. Changon et al., "Impacts and Responses to the 1995 Heat Wave: A Call to Action," *Bulletin of the American Meteorlogical Society* 77:7, pp. 1497–1506; CNN, "Chicago Braces for Another Scorcher," 29 June 1995; and National Weather Service, Public Affairs Office, "Many Heat Deaths Preventable," 1996 (cites Disaster Survey Report from NOAA).

The extremes during that long hot July week included the partial breakdown of Commonwealth Edison's generators (leaving several areas of the city without air-conditioning), and a "water war" as police battled desperate inner-city residents who attacked fire hydrants with "acetylene torches, sledgehammers, power drills, and saws to generate a flow of water." Meanwhile, as ambulances raced futilely from one hospital to the next, heat stroke victims were dying by the scores for lack of available emergency room staff. Half of the hospitals in Chicago shut their doors at some point to additional heat casualties.

On the edge of the Loop, the chief medical examiner frantically assembled enough refrigerator trailers to handle the overflow of corpses from the city morgue. The bodies of nearly 300 heat victims were delivered to the morgue on Saturday; 240 on Sunday. "At the height of the heat wave's destructiveness," writes Eric Klinenberg, "ten large trucks, along with a traffic jam of ambulances, police wagons, and fire department vehicles used to deliver bodies from around the city, television and radio vans, and health workers' cars crammed the area surrounding the morgue, forming a parade of death so enormous, so surreal, that it semmed impossible to believe that this was happening in the center of the city."

In his study of the political ecology of the 1995 heat disaster (which can be read as a brilliant epilogue to *The Pig and the Skyscraper*), Klinenberg shows how mass mortality was concentrated amongst isolated aged African Americans in the poorest sections of the South Side and Westside ghettos. Hundreds of lives might have been saved, he argues, if the Police Department had activated specially designated "community policing" units to warn and, if necessary, evacuate at-risk senior citizens. But the younger Daley and his satraps stuck to the official dogma that it was primarily the responsibility of the elderly poor themselves to seek whatever relief was available.

Their inability to do so, and the city's failure to rescue them, Klinenberg concludes, is "a sign and symptom of the new and dangerous forms of marginality and neglect endemic to contemporary American big cities and notably severe in Chicago." As the Weather Bureau and numerous medical researchers have acknowledged, there was very little, if anything, "natural" about the fate of the 733 victims

---

2   Quoted in Eric Klinenberg, "Denaturalizing Disaster: A Social Autopsy of the 1995 Chicago Heat Wave," 1999 draft version. All following quotes are from the draft.

of Chicago's worst disaster. What happened in July 1995 might be better understood, Klinenberg suggests (quoting Friedrich Engels), as "social murder."

There were, of course, no homicide indictments. The *Chicago Tribune,* which had excoriated Bilandic for his missing snow ploughs, preferred to overlook Daley's responsibility for "our little problem" of hundreds of dead senior citizens. Nor did the remnants of the city's once mighty civil rights and Black power movements force a confrontation over the racial politics of the heat disaster. In the end, most of the dead were simply shoved into a mass pauper's grave, and Chicago avoided any embarrassing debate over the radical social vulnerability that made such a hecatomb possible. The *ancien régime,* into whose cancerous heart Harold Washington had tragically failed to drive a silver stake, went back to its chief (and most lucrative) preoccupation: polishing the image of a Downtown renaissance, a Chicago reconquered for conventioneers and suburbanites.

This white-lie Chicago – where dead bluesmen, gangsters and industrial ruins supply romantic tourist ambience – is only the latest of the fantastic facades behind which ancient class and racial politics continue to be carried out with exemplary greed and brutality. It is no accident that so many martyrs of the Left – from Albert Parsons to Fred Hampton – are buried in Chicago. If Chicago is the most comfortable big city in North America, it is also the most ruthless. It wipes no sins from New York's or Los Angeles' souls to point out that neither ever hung the leadership of the local labor movement (the Haymarket Martyrs), machine-gunned scores of peaceful strikers (the Memorial Day steel massacre), or summarily executed the head of the local Black Panthers (Fred Hampton).

Marco d'Eramo brings a fresh, exhilarating and distinctly Italian perspective to these old battlefields. Eschewing the monographic approach of the famed Chicago School, he has had the audacity to attempt to grasp the whole in world-historical perspective. His Chicago is capitalism without a g-string. Here, where the bison recently grazed, "social murder" has always been part of the epic conflict by which capitalist modernity has defined itself. Like the hardboiled novels of Nelson Algren, the blues laments of Muddy Waters, or, for that matter, Brecht's *St. Joan of the Stockyards, The Pig and the Skyscraper* takes the Windy City straight up, no chaser. The effect is bracingly dialectical. *Das Kapital,* after all, was only a theoretical outline: the unexpurgated history of Chicago is the real thing.

PART ONE

1

Arrival in Chicagoland

You expect the city of Al Capone – but what you find are pleasant boulevards coursing up and down between the neoclassical buildings of the 1893 World's Columbian Exposition. The novels you read in school described Chicago's slaughterhouses; instead, you see awe-inspiring skyscrapers. The city center unfolds, an architectural miracle that is to twentieth-century urban planning what Venice must have been in the fifteenth century.

You were thinking of a land-locked city plumped down in the American heartland, but instead you find yourself in a maritime metropolis. To an Italian, the word *lake* evokes mountain pools or the ponds of Roman castles; a fair-sized lake, for example, would be Italy's Lake Garda or Switzerland's Lake Zurich. What Chicagoans refer to as *Lake* Michigan is what we would call a *sea*: its boundless expanse stretches as far as the eye can travel, covering a surface area of some 60,000 square kilometers (150 km by 400 km) – roughly the size of the Adriatic Sea. Storm waves crash against the breakwaters, sending clouds of spray as far as Lakeshore Drive, which looks more like a seafront road than an urban expressway. The metropolitan area of Chicago appears to have arranged itself along Lake Michigan, a strip of almost 200 kilometers running from the state of Wisconsin (north of Illinois) south to Indiana. If Gary, Indiana, is already part of "Chicagoland," it won't be long before this immense coastal urban sprawl subsumes Milwaukee as well.

During winter, the ice of Chicago holds everything in its grip: skyscrapers, parks, the endless suburbs of single-family houses. In the more exposed coastal areas, waves that normally beat against the shore appear frozen in midsurge, like a series of overlapping steps, oblique slabs of bluish slate streaked with white that veer steeply down to the lake. Off the quays, the ice has sculpted chairs for those who fish, sitting with their lines dangling into holes in the lake's surface. The authorities advise not to eat fish caught off the urban lakefront more than once a week and to steer clear of the bigger (hence older) fish that have probably eaten more than their fill in the polluted waters. Inhabitants pay no heed to such warnings, however – not surprisingly, considering that all of the city's drinking water comes from the lake.

More than any other maritime city, Chicago finds itself blasted by winds; its nickname, the Windy City, finds its way even onto the sides of school buses. Pedestrians brace themselves against gusts that are violent enough to uproot traffic lights. The TV weather forecaster gives two temperatures: one for the air and the other for the wind (a bit like giving summertime temperatures for under the sun and in the shade). While the air temperature might be ten below, the corresponding windchill could drop to as low as minus thirty. Glacial winds arrive from the Northwest, from Alaska and the Arctic, sweeping across the great Canadian plain to descend upon Chicago. With winds and winters like these, the city's elevated urban transit system is left exposed to icy blasts. Those who use it do so at their peril. Here, as elsewhere in the United States, you are punished for not using – or for not having – a car.

By the time spring comes, the sidewalks are already littered with café tables. With the slightest hint of warm weather, out come the bathing suits and halter tops. In summer, city dwellers descend in droves on the beaches, as on the great European lidos – Glifada in Greece or San Sebastián in Spain. Many of them go in for a dip. In 1919, the first great urban race riot broke out on the beach, when a young Black man was killed for having swum beyond the invisible waterline that separated Black bathers from whites. During summers, the lakeside parks come to life, playing host to blues festivals, open-air concerts, barbecues, picnics, improvised volleyball games, evening promenades and cruising. On weekends, the lake's pale blue swath is dotted with a myriad of white sails.

It is this *sea* that makes the social geography of Chicago so anomalous. In other cities of the interior United States, such as St. Louis, the wealthy tend to inhabit the west side, where fresh winds ensure a ready supply of pure air, while the poor are shoved to the polluted eastern zones, where the air arrives fully "processed" by the combined forces of industrial and human contact. (In London and Paris, too, the *haute bourgeoisie* have tended to settle in the west, leaving the east to the working classes.) In Chicago, the sea of Lake Michigan instead creates an insuperable barrier to the east, while the land stretches out flat as a pool table for hundreds of miles to the north, south and west. The most affluent quarter of the city thus lies along the shores of the lake, with the dividing line running north to south rather than east to west as in other cities.

The southern side of the city has always been associated with the combined stench of slaughterhouses, factories, lard refineries and other industrial plants specializing in the rank and malodorous: oil refinery and steelwork chimneys bar the horizon all the way to Gary, on the Indiana state border, pumping thick plumes of multicolored smoke, from orange to bluish gray, into the sky. The southernmost part of Chicago is also where many of the city's ghettos are located.

Meanwhile, immediately to the north and south of the business district are the quays and wharfs with their fleets of yachts and pleasure cruisers. There's even an airport for private aircraft and a port for seaplanes. The Gold Coast, the city's most chic quarter, is one of the richest residential areas in the entire United States. Also extending along the lakeside is Michigan Avenue, Chicago's main drag, whose nickname, "Boul Mich," is the same as Parisians use to refer to the Boulevard St. Michel. The section of Michigan Avenue just north of the Chicago River is known as the Magnificent Mile because of its boutiques and mansions.

To the west, toward the interior, a mere stone's throw from the Magnificent Mile, you can still see the Cabrini-Green housing projects. The inhabitants here are African American; the average family income is forty times lower than the Gold Coast's, and an eight-year-old child might be killed by a stray bullet on the way to school. So close to paradise, Cabrini-Green has become such an embarrassment that the Chicago housing authority has decided to tear down at least the high-rises. But Chicago is not two cities, one lavishly resplendent and the other squalid and depressing. There is only one Chicago, with its innumerable avant-garde theaters; its Vietnamese, Afghan and Peruvian restaurants; its mythic blues and jazz clubs; its gangs and its housing projects.

Eight years of uninterrupted prosperity have reshaped the city's urban geography. Some of the old eyesores have been demolished and replaced by dainty little townhouses. The University of Chicago is in the midst of gentrifying the area next to its campus, where once stood an old flea market. Yet still you see children happily romping in the mire while the roadside lies littered with heaps of tires and dark bodies buried in layers of "walking sleeping bags," images that bring to mind the streets of Lucknow or Kanpur in Uttar Pradesh. Inhabitants of this modern metropolis – and of the richest and most powerful country on Earth – can be seen digging around in the trash, plunging their heads and upper bodies into garbage cans. "Certain wild creatures, male and female, are to be seen about the countryside, grimy, livid, burnt black by the sun, as though tethered to the soil which they dig and till with unconquerable tenacity; they appear to have articulate voice; and when they stand upright they show an human face; they are, in fact, men; at night they creep back into dens where they live."[1] It was thus that some three centuries ago the French moralist and writer Jean de La Bruyère described the peasants of his time, never imagining how uncannily similar to them some of the denizens of Chicago would turn out to be.

The Chicago campus of the University of Illinois is just one of the city's seven institutes of higher learning, with their plethora of Nobel and Pulitzer Prize winners. "In contrast to New York, San Francisco or Los Angeles," says James Weinstein, founding owner and editor-in-chief of the biweekly publication *In These Times* and one of the key figures of the American Left, "Chicago provides you with a reality check – in other words, here you get an idea of what real America is thinking, you're deep in the heartland." Indeed you are – more so than if you were in Des Moines or Omaha, basically parodies of cities. Chicago still boasts a civic center (you can actually find newsstands selling daily papers, an institution absent even in other big US cities such as Denver). Here you have buses – and a

---

1   This famous passage from La Bruyère's *Caractères* (sect. *De l'homme,* para. 128) is cited by Erich Auerbach in *Mimesis: The Representation of Reality in Western Literature* (1953), Princeton, N.J.: Princeton University Press, 1968.

subway – but at the same time, you're in front-lawn America, a relatively small center surrounded by the infinite reaches of single-family suburbia.

Speak to a feminist from a well-heeled neighborhood, to a Trotskyist from the Chicago historical society, to a journalist champion of the issues of the Third World – the kind of people you might think to be far from the conformist script of the American Dream – and you will find that each gushes with boundless love for this city. Dig a little deeper, and you'll find the most disparate motives for such zealous devotion: the vitality of the city's unions, its alternative culture, its Black cultural galaxy. Yet even from this supposedly anticonformist minority oozes that quintessentially American, quintessentially capitalist ideal, that the ultimate human aspiration is to own a single-family dwelling, separated from neighboring dwellings by a lawn, but still to be able to enjoy the various urban amenities: concerts, theaters, restaurants, cinemas. Chicago represents the ideal of a city that is both *'burbs* (pleasant to live in) and bustling metropolis (good for going out).

Chicago also helps to answer another question that everyone asks him- or herself after living for some time in the United States (or so historian Wolfgang Schivelbusch told me): "When and how was it that European immigrants stopped being Europeans and started being *Americans*? What is it that has made them so imperceptibly, yet clearly, different in their way of living, dwelling, even picking up a fork?" Or rather, as Werner Sombart wrote in his curiously titled 1906 book, *Why Is There No Socialism in the United States?*

> What has Nuremburg in common with Chicago? Nothing, except the superficial characteristic that in both places many people relying for their sustenance on supplies from outside live concentrated next to one another. In matters of spirit there is no resemblance. The former is a village-like, spontaneous formation, while the latter is a real city artificially set up according to principles of rationality, in which (as Tönnies would say) all traces of *Gemeinschaft* ("community") have been extinguished and pure *Gesellschaft* ("society") has been established. However, if in the old Europe the city takes after the countryside (or rather has done till now) and has brought the character of the latter to itself, in the United States, on the contrary, the flat countryside is basically only an urban settlement that lacks cities.[2]

---

2 Werner Sombart, *Warum Gibt Es in den Vereinigten Staaten Keinen Sozialismus?* (1906). Eng. trans. *Why Is There No Socialism in the United States?,* White Plains, N.Y.: International Arts and Sciences Press, 1975, p. 8.

Chicago expresses the truth about the United States for yet another reason. In Europe, capitalism is masked – *bridled,* you might say – by the legacy of its history: in France, by the tradition of the nation-state; in Italy, by the church; in Britain, by the nobility. For us, capitalism encounters an obstacle in the form of an already-stratified tradition, fossilized customs, prejudices that are ocean-deep.

In the United States, you can instead feel capitalism in all its naked force, in the subversive power it has to uproot entire lives from the mouth of the Mekong or the Indus Delta and set them down in decidedly chillier climes. You can see the capacity of capital to mold every single element of people's lives, whether their way of moving around, of dwelling, or even of eating. Palate, touch, sexuality: the thumbprints of capitalism are everywhere. Not by chance did Werner Sombart, writing in 1906, begin his book with these words:[3] "The United States of America is capitalism's land of promise. All conditions needed for its complete and pure development were first fulfilled here. In no other country and among no other people was capitalism favoured with circumstances that permitted it to develop to the most advanced state."

In this sense, too, Chicago is without doubt the most American of US cities. No other place in the world can boast the kind of fanatical belief that you find in this city in capital's liberatory potential and in the religion of capitalism. If the United States is capitalism's land of Canaan, then surely Chicago is its Jerusalem.

One good example of Chicago's capitalistic ethos, the city's Art Institute, is among the largest and finest art museums in the world, thanks to the patronage of Chicago's butchers and delicatessen owners. Here, however, the patrons do not limit themselves to simply having their names engraved on a plaque next to the works of art, as in other museums. If you're looking for a particular work by a particular artist in this museum (say, Edward Hopper's *Nighthawks*), you might as well go home, because the pictures here are organized according to who donated them, not who painted them. In one room, you might find a Hopper, a Picasso and a Utrillo by the kind donation of Mr. X, while ten rooms down are gathered paintings donated by Mr. Y, including a Matisse, a Lichtenstein and … another Hopper. Thus it is that distant epochs, different genres, and artists who have nothing to do with one another are all subsumed and reunited under the aegis of the

---

3 Ibid., p. 10.

patron. And so it goes: the subject of the art museum is not the artist or the art itself, but the donor.

One last point: It cannot be denied that Chicago wants to be, and is, a lovable city. Along with America's most corrupt politicians, its most vicious gangs and its most ruthless capitalists, you will also find here the country's most generous grassroots organizations. Here, for example, Jesse Jackson started out on the campaign trail. And from under the trees of Lincoln Park, near the limpid blue lake, squirrels stare right at you, their little heads cutely inclined. Puff jowled, their tails glistening in the sun, they rub at the white fur of their bellies, as though anticipating the nuts you will hold out to them.

2

The Tracks of Tomorrow

Considering the brief history of this city, it's amazing to think that it has become one of the world's megalopolises in less than 170 years, already settled into a somewhat wizened maturity. Yet even now, the archaeology of the city's capitalist expansion – which brought Chicago in under fifty years from a village of two hundred inhabitants to its unassailable position at the end of the nineteenth century as the world's greatest commercial "republic" – can still be traced. Indeed, Chicago at that time was a "railroad republic," the modern equivalent of the maritime powers that once held sway over the medieval world. What proves so unsettling, however, isn't so much Chicago's history as the questions that history raises. In no other city is the extent to which capitalism has itself been a "railroad," not to say a "railroaded," phenomenon so evident. Just as in no other city does one realize the extent to which the concept of the railroad has shaped our notion of communism.

We might label as "railroad" the kind of communism that aims to impose a program for the national economy as rigorous and inflexible as a national railway timetable, the very prototype of centralized planning. This kind of communism follows a revolutionary "schedule," having various stages mapped out with the same precision as a timetable used to chart a train's movements (stops, arrivals, departures, switches) and having a similarly high level of command and meticulous control. In this context, the communist government might be considered a kind of omniscient "social divinity," ever mindful of the current positions of all of its social subjects (its trains and their cars, passengers and cargoes). The system works according to an established plan, allocating resources to the various sectors of society and the different zones of the country in relation to their presumed needs, just as the railways might allocate X locomotives and Y cars to line Z in month K. It is a system with a Gosplan that equates economic flows with the goods and passengers streaming along the railway lines in a sort of human hydrodynamics; that designs its social infrastructures as metaphorical bridges, viaducts and tunnels; and whose chain of command falls into a neatly structured hierarchy of station masters, conductors, engine drivers and linesmen. The idea is that equality means rendering the early-morning mass of workers more or less indistinguishable when they, like the railcars in which they travel, are no longer separated into first, second and third classes. Rather the people are "of a single class," an indistinct, sluggishly drifting fog of humanity. Living in a communist-governed society can thus be like traveling on the public railways: in both cases, you are merely a passenger.

Railroad capitalism, by contrast, had the effect of wiping out entire herds of buffalo and turning cities black with coal dust. Mountains were gutted of their secret hoards of iron ore, forests cut down to provide wood for fuel, as-yet-unsettled land already rife with speculation. Just as hundreds of thousands of workers from India were deported to Africa, the Chinese were imported as laborers into North America. (Many of the railways in both Africa and North America have by now succumbed to the ravages of rust, but the Indians and Chinese remain, human communities washed up by the tide of history.) The idea was that progress was a train (the "engine of the economy") and that civilization extended only as far as the sighting of its latest puff of steam.

This was a railroad capitalism; the railway lines made sense only in that they made possible the connection of crowded stations, centers of high population density. Between these urban centers, the train establishes a hierarchy of importance, expressed by the number of lines crossing a given town. A suburban-line train may pick up just a few passengers each time it stops at a particular outlying station, only on condition that it drops them off at a central terminal where the population density is high. Here, in this high-population area, are the big factories and offices where people work, the centralization of the workplace, the "scale economy." In Chaplin's film *Modern Times,* the masses of workers pouring out of the subway in a silently bleating flock defined the title as much as did the factory production line. This, too, was one of the faces of railroad capitalism.

Considerable study has been done on the absurdities of Soviet central planning's distribution system. It wasn't Stalinism, however, but American "railroad capitalism" that forced a Wyoming cattle rancher to dispatch his live steers two thousand kilometers by train to Chicago to have them butchered there, rather than to have them quartered in nearby Cheyenne. This capitalism on rails, still active in Europe, now seems only a distant memory in the United States. Like the temples of a forgotten cult, the stations have become ancient monuments one visits but no longer worships in. Shops have sprung up where ticket offices once stood, while platforms have become pedestrian walkways. St. Louis Central Station is now a mall; those who approach the station in Memphis, Tennessee, after dark do so at their own risk.

With the vanishing of the railroads, it now seems in the United States as though a type of "car capitalism" has taken over, geared more to the individual and family and more akin to the station wagon than to an endless chain of train cars. This form of capitalism is more flexible in terms of control, freed from the idea of a timetable, yet its surveillance structures and chain of command are even more efficient because the flexibility renders them less ossified and more rational: the center gains in its capacity to control what it loses in formalism.

"Car capitalism" produces a radical decentering and derailment, not simply in terms of control, logistics and organization of labor, but in the fabric of people's daily lives, in our very notion of civilization. With cars and trucks, areas of extremely low population densities – areas that would no doubt have been isolated in the railroad world – can be linked. This four-wheel capitalism has radically distorted our century-old image of the city by permitting the interlinking of suburban zones previously connected only by, for, and via the center, making possible a metropolitan area with no metropolis, no city center and no downtown, an area no longer with a periphery around a center, but rather self-centered. The civic ideal is no longer "urbanity" but rather "suburbanity": in contrast to Europe, in the United States the term *suburb* has positive connotations. In this new border-land between city and country, the greatest human aspiration is to own and live in a single-family house with a garage, surrounded by a lawn that separates you more effectively than any wall from your neighbors, who are, of course, equal to you in every respect, down to their lawns and garages. Underpinning this world of graceful, tree-lined suburbs – the social diaspora spread out in gardens and charming walkways – is the fact that the "capitalism on wheels" of single-family houses exacerbates racial and class segregation, pushing US society toward implosion and possibly complete internal disintegration.

It was in Chicago that railroad capitalism was to unfold in all its raw power, forging entire peoples, shaping cultures, uprooting and deporting millions of lives. The city, in fact, offers unequaled opportunity not only for studying the monuments of this capitalism, but for exploring the phenomena it has generated. Here you can analyze the waves of migrants abandoned by the railroads on the banks of Lake Michigan and chart the rise and fall of the city's businesses and industries. Because the epoch of railroad capitalism is definitely over, the study of Chicago is already a distinct species of archaeology: an archaeology of modernity.

Yet the deeper you dig, the more questions you begin to ask yourself. The slenderest worm of doubt wriggles its way into your mind: And then? And now? And tomorrow? And *which* tomorrow? You look for traces of the future, for clues that seem to lead somewhere. A report from Chicago is already something more, something akin to an archaeology of the *future,* in fact. Such anxiety about the future was already, nearly a century ago, clearly present in Sombart's mind when he asked himself why, given that the socialist movement was itself a product of capitalism, this most capitalist country of all – the true Mecca of capitalism – had not generated its own form of socialism: "Will the future social structures of Europe and America turn out the same or different? Is America or Europe the 'land of the future'?"[1]

Although the railroads are no longer central to Chicago's economy, "Chicago-land" remains one of the most powerful among "nations": if its railway terminals were once the most travel-worn in America, this honor today goes to the city's airport, O'Hare. In the falling to ruins of entire quarters, in the bankruptcy of once-

---

1 W. Sombart, *Why Is There No Socialism in the United States?*, p. 24.

Trains at the Illinois Central's Randolph Street Station, 1893. Courtesy Chicago Historical Society.

potent financial dynasties, in the brutal contrasts between luxury and misery, stunning beauty and appalling squalor, Chicago is living proof that there is no such thing, nor has there ever been such a thing, as a design of capital. There is only a logic of capital, a logic that is highly singular, illogical to the end, and yet at the same time solid as iron.

In vain, you scour Chicago's horizon for a sign of Grand Central Station, once the most crowded railway terminal on earth. You pan right from the vertiginous heights of the Sears Tower (at fifteen hundred feet, the world's tallest skyscraper from 1976 to 1996), away from the endless expanse of Lake Michigan toward the zones to the west and south of the city center, the no-man's land of Chicago's ghettos. There, among the ruined buildings, you see nothing but desolate freight-yards, deserts of rust furrowed by a web of corroded rails carrying the occasional interminably long freight train (from eighty to one hundred freight cars) in from the Iowa corn belt or the mines of Utah. In mountain regions, four diesel locomotives are needed to pull these trains, each more than a mile long: there are virtually no electrified lines in the United States. Even the names of the companies, seen in countless Westerns, have a decidedly nineteenth-century ring to them: Northern Pacific, Chicago, Burlington and Quincy, Northwestern, Illinois Central – as though the railroads had yet to cross the frontier of the *fin de siècle*. Nonetheless, these companies, through their capital- and profit-driven logic, would transform an isolated village of two hundred people into one of the most powerful urban sprawls on the planet, the largest lumber market and grain-trading center not only in America but in the entire world, the city Upton Sinclair dubbed "the slaughterhouse of the universe."

First of all, consider the question of capital: to a continental European born after the war, railways are linked to the idea of the state or, better, to the nation, in the sense that you can have German, French and Italian railways. Unimaginable, however – at least until recently – was the idea of two different railway companies operating in the same country. Just as a legitimate monopoly on violence and repression define the modern state, so too were the railways a state-run monopoly in postwar Europe. When Europeans think of public railways having competition, we generally mean competition with private car transportation, not with other railway companies. By contrast, the railways in the United States have always been private, just as roads were private during the first half of the nineteenth century: you could use them only if you paid an exorbitant fee (a tollbooth, the so-called turnpike point, marked a city's limits). In the early days of railroads, when locomotives shuttled along at a snail-like pace, the carts and stagecoaches that traveled the wood-paved toll roads offered greater speed and security than did the trains.

It was natural that the railroads in the United States would be private, just as the riverboat companies had been before them: curiously, the only industry sector in Europe still to follow the nineteenth-century model of American capitalism is that of shipping companies, owned by magnates such as Aristotle Onassis and Niarchos. In the United States, a whole genealogy connects train and paddle steamer. Steam power made its appearance first with Robert Fulton's ferryboat, and only later with the locomotive. The same New York– and Boston-based companies that had constructed the canal networks also built and held sway over the railroad lines.

This riverboat connection was even to influence the way railway cars were designed. Railway cars in Europe were built to resemble carriages (hence the name we generally give them) – with closed compartments that contained two facing bench seats, each sitting three to four people, in the manner of a stagecoach. The cars in the United States were more like a ship's passenger decks, having a single open space with many rows of seats placed one in front of the other and a central gangway running between them. The prototype of the American sleeper car was designed and built in 1859 by George Mortimer Pullman, one of Chicago's most notorious and aggressive industrialists, in imitation of riverboat sleeping cabins.[2] American millionaires made it a point of honor to buy themselves the most luxurious train they could lay hands on, just as today's big money-makers flex their muscles on fabulous yachts. In this way, they might feel that they were traveling on "a ship on rails," their very own land-going pleasure cruiser.

Like the ship, the train was a private world unto itself, with it own rules and its own unit of measure. Every railroad had its own gauge (the distance between the rails and therefore between the car wheels): the Erie Railroad had a six-foot gauge, while in the South, five feet was more common; the New England and Northern companies, meanwhile, showed a marked preference for the English gauge of four feet, eight inches. The difference in gauges meant that cars built for one line could not be used on another.[3] Even *time* was privatized. The extent to which the railways have modified our perception of time almost challenges belief, in fact. Before the advent of railways, at least on terra firma, the flow of our lives was marked by the quarter hour. In town or in the countryside, it didn't matter if you were a few minutes late: the stagecoach would wait, the boat wouldn't leave you stranded on the dock. If you were late by only half a minute, however, you would certainly miss the train. Train travel was responsible for the nineteenth-century boom in pocket watches, which became an important feature of daily life when it

2 Wolfgang Schivelbusch, *Geschichte der Eisenbahnreise.* Eng. trans. *The Railway Journey: The Industrialization of Time and Space in the Nineteenth Century,* Berkeley, Calif.: University of California Press, 1986, p. 103ff.

3 See John F. Stover, *American Railroads,* Chicago: University of Chicago Press, 1961, p. 24.

became important for people to recognize and be able to distinguish time down to the minute or even the half minute.[4]

When it came to the definition of time, however, chaos reigned. Hours then ticked by differently in every city: when the clock struck midday in Chicago, it was 11:27 in Omaha, 11:50 in St. Louis, 12:17 in Toledo, 12:31 in Pittsburgh. According to the *Chicago Tribune,* Illinois then had twenty-seven local times, Wisconsin thirty-eight. The Union Pacific Railroad operated with six different time zones.[5] Yet no one thought it bizarre that each of the railroad companies ran to its own private clock, with its own corporate Standard Time. In a single railway station, time might be different for every single line. The Buffalo, New York station had three separate time zones, Pittsburgh six. Only much later, owing to railroad inefficiency (on account of the difficulty of coordinating timetables), was a *standardization of time* introduced. Not until 1883, in fact, did the railroad companies finally divide the United States into four separate zones – four railroad time zones that were to be commonly recognized but that would not legally be the four current US time zones (Atlantic, Central, Mountain, and Pacific) until 1918, after World War I.[6]

Dwelling in different times depending on which line you happened to be on was actually one of the most innocuous bits of craziness occasioned by the ruthless competition between the railroad companies. Robber barons like Commodore Cornelius Vanderbilt, Jim Fisk and Jay Gould were notorious for their ruthlessness and dishonesty and for the brutal war they waged, marked by a spate of gunfights and fatal shoot-outs between their rival private armies, including the legendary Pinkerton Agency.[7] Their struggle to control the rails triggered one of the most vicious commercial wars of the nineteenth century. The competition was so intense that often a speculator would threaten, or even begin, to construct a second line – a ghost line – along another company's already existing route as a form of blackmail, hence the name *blackmail lines.*

---

4   David S. Landes, *Revolution in Time,* Cambridge, Mass.: Harvard Univ. Press, 1983, pp. 228, 285.
5   J. F. Stover, *American Railroads,* pp. 157–58.
6   W. Schivelbusch, *The Railway Journey,* p. 42 on.
7   Matthiew Josephson, *The Robber Barons: The Great American Capitalists 1861–1901,* New York: Harcourt, 1934; this is a blood-and-thunder–style history whose author was the son of a banker with communist leanings.

Countless were the bridges that collapsed owing to their hasty, slipshod construction or to the cheap, low-grade materials used to cut costs; countless were the accidents caused by errors on the part of railroad workers and staff exhausted by the slave-labor conditions under which they worked. Trains were frequently derailed because of drastic cuts in line and switch maintenance.

Such disasters didn't just happen in the nineteenth century, in fact. As recently as 23 September 1993, a Los Angeles–Miami express plunged from a bridge into an Alabama swamp, killing two hundred passengers. Rumor had it that many of the passengers were devoured by alligators or killed by the water moccasins that lurk in the bayou. In fact, though, the deaths were simply the result of Amtrak's negligence.[8] This was nothing compared to the carnage that took place on the railroads around the turn of the century, however: in the United States, from 1898 to 1900 alone, a staggering 21,847 people died in train-related accidents; in 1903, the death toll was 11,006, a veritable massacre. Of every million US travelers, nineteen died; for the same period in Austria, for example, the figure was 0.99, or twenty times less. Sombart provided these statistics to show how "an *economic rationalism* of a purity unknown in any European country serves this desire for gain. Capitalism presses forward remorselessly, even when its path is strewn with corpses. The data that provide us with information on the extent of railway accidents in the United States are merely symbolic of it."[9] (Nowadays, even after a century of progress, 43,000 people die in US car accidents every year. Given that the US population is nearly four times as high as it was at the beginning of the nineteenth century, the number of deaths remains almost constant, despite the changed means of transportation.)

Surprisingly, the mechanisms designed to assure maximum profit – that is, competition, the unfettered reign of the free market and *deregulation* – often instead led to bankruptcy and wholesale panic; instruments created to make money often ended up wasting it. It was finally the banker of bankers, J. Pierpont Morgan, who in 1885 stepped in and put an end to the price war by regulating competition

---

8 Regarding negligence of America's sagging infrastructure, see Kenneth F. Dunker and Basile G. Rabbat, "Why America's Bridges Are Crumbling," *Scientific American*, March 1993, pp. 66–72. For historical background, see the dossier "America's Infrastructure" in *The Wilson Quarterly*, Winter 1993, pp. 18–49.

9 W. Sombart, *Why Is There No Socialism in the United States?*, pp. 4–5.

through an agreement that placed the US railroads under the protection of his own bank. This agreement between the shareholders of the various lines was concomitant with that between the *times* and the *timetables* of the railroads.[10]

While the railroads made Chicago great, the funding behind this immense fortune came from private investors, particularly from the big East Coast and London bankers. In 1858, two-thirds of the shareholders of Illinois Central lived in England. In 1890, of the stock of Chicago, Burlington and Quincy (founded by the Boston bankers Forbes, now the name behind the famous business magazine), 113,198 shares were held by New Yorkers, 166,198 by Bostonians and only 3,104 by Chicagoans. Of the seventeen members of the board of directors of the Northwestern, nine lived on the Atlantic Coast (all but one in New York).[11]

Such heavy financing is hardly surprising, considering that opening a railroad line in the nineteenth century meant a colossal investment. Each line needed its own bridges, tunnels, stations, rolling stock, water tanks and fuel supplies. Private resources, even those of banks, were rarely sufficient. To encourage private investment, the federal government began giving to the railway companies the land that ran alongside their rights-of-way in the form of so-called land grants. Thanks to the railroads, this land inevitably gained in value, enabling the companies to sell it off to settlers at a high price. The first line to benefit from the land grants policy was the Illinois Central, which started off from Cairo, Illinois. In 1850, under pressure from East Coast bankers, the government granted six alternate lots of land for every mile of track built, on condition that the line go as far as Chicago. At that time, Chicago thus represented the western outpost of the East Coast banks, forming a financial alliance between the Windy City and the Big Apple that endures to this day.

An even more profound reason for Chicago's prodigious rise can be found in the logic of capital itself, the same logic that, some 150 years later, lies behind the current airline crisis: the tyranny of fixed costs. Fixed costs were the railroads' worst nightmare, just as today they are the worst nightmare for flight operators.

---

10 Ron Chernow, *The House of Morgan: An American Banking Dynasty and the Rise of Modern Finance*, New York: Simon and Schuster, 1990. Regarding the Great Railroad Treaty of 1885 (also known as the "Corsair Compact"), see pp. 53–58.
11 William Cronon, *Nature's Metropolis: Chicago and the Great West*, New York: W.W. Norton, 1991, pp. 82–83. Many of the following pages are greatly indebted to this book.

More than one-quarter of a company's expenses were to pay back loans for an initial investment. Regardless of how many or how few trains ran on a line, moreover, bridges collapsed and tracks rusted. A locomotive used one-tenth of its wood fuel just to maintain steam pressure and another third to keep itself chugging along. The number of engineers and mechanics required depended on the number of passengers and the amount of freight the train carried, and the same was true for station personnel. For these reasons, about two-thirds of a railroad line's expenses went to cover fixed costs alone. Once the line had been built, together with its stations and infrastructure, a company had no choice but to fill the cars to capacity, even if that resulted in an overall loss. If a run cost 100, it was better to make 90 and lose 10 than to lose 60 in fixed costs, which had to be paid in any case.

The power of fixed costs was particularly despotic for freight train operations. While railways in Europe are generally used more for passenger travel than for goods transport, the passenger sector in the United States has always been of secondary importance. In 1870, passenger ticket sales represented only one-quarter of railroad company revenues; by 1916, they accounted for only one-fifth of the total.[12]

All of this explains why the railroads (1) offered special prices on the longest no-transfer hauls, (2) cut prices when competition was at its most intense, (3) offered special discounts to their biggest clients,[13] (4) kept prices high on hauls where they had a monopoly and clients had no contractual bargaining power. Combined, these four factors led to an unending chain of embezzlements, abuses, frauds and monopoly agreements, prompting Congress to set up several investigative commissions. Railroad company practices were denounced and law reform bills posted. But while all this was going on, the urban geography of the United States was being completely reshaped.

---

12 J. F. Stover, *America's Railroads*, p. 173.
13 Important clients actually blackmailed the railroads, threatening to leave a company if it let their competitors travel for the same price. Railroad tariffs were therefore one of the most murderous weapons companies had at their disposal in their fight to establish and strengthen monopolies and to put the competition out of business. This happened in the oil industry, where John D. Rockefeller systematically exploited railroad tariffs to gain a dominant market position for his company, Standard Oil.

Chicago was the terminus for the Eastern railroads and the departure point for the Western lines that branched off from its stations; here the various competing lines converged and the railroads found themselves competing with riverboats. And in Chicago, not surprisingly, the price war was at its most bitter.

So it was that it became more profitable for an Iowa farmer to send corn to distant Chicago than to nearby Des Moines, just as it was more convenient for a Nebraska livestock breeder to dispatch cattle to the Windy City than to Omaha. And as the rail network grew, Chicago became the preferred destination even for cattle from Montana or for Texas longhorns. With the gradual increase in traffic, prices fell, and Chicago merchants were able to buy high from Western suppliers and sell low to East Coast buyers; Chicago was thus the most convenient market for both. And as the volume of trade went up, so too did the rail traffic, in ever-accelerating growth.

If Chicago owed its fortune in 1850 to its being the "gateway to the West," by the beginning of the twentieth century, it had established its position as the "center of the United States," a key intersection of communications routes as well as a human center of gravity. On 21 November 1848, the 10-mile-long Galena and Chicago Union – the first Chicago railroad – opened. By 1860, the network spreading out from Chicago covered almost 4,700 miles; by 1871, the year of the Great Fire, that network had extended to around 10,000 miles. Come 1880, it had more than doubled again, reaching 23,125 miles in length. (By comparison, the entire French rail network today covers only 21,250 miles; the Italian railway a mere 12,000.) Some forty lines fanned out from Chicago, and it was calculated that more than half the entire US population in 1914 (then 100 million people) lived within a night's train journey from Chicago.

As a result of fixed costs, Chicago became the "natural gateway" to a market that extended from the Rocky Mountains to the Appalachians, from Canada to the Caribbean. In the history of urban civilization, the railway lines have always enlarged to the point of excess the city's hinterland, but the basin of Chicago became virtually endless. The logic of capital was to transform the whole geography of the Midwest, natural and human. Together with corn, wheat, pigs, lumber and cattle, millions of immigrants would eventually ride the railways across the country, initially Germans and Irish, then Italians and Poles, followed by African Americans,

Mexicans, and Chinese. The trains here no longer carry passengers, but freight trains are still going strong. Although the first cause of Chicago's grandeur may have vanished, the logic of capital remains, its tyrannical grip on this megalopolis of 8 million people continuing to spread on the banks of Lake Michigan.

It's extraordinary the way the logic of capital does not depend on its object but is always identical, whether applied on land, on sea or in the air. Although a locomotive is not a jet and an airport is not a station, the same dynamics repeat themselves with meticulous precision. Again, the tyranny of fixed costs has created the surrealist masterwork we know as air ticket pricing, whereby a cabin is divided into a dozen different price brackets even when the seats are the same, or you might be charged more for a single ticket than for a return ticket. At the end of the day, what was Chicago itself if not a railroad hub? When today's cloud-borne human cattle are redirected from outlying airports to central hubs, what are the companies doing if not bowing to the same laws that forced Texas ranchers to put their longhorns on a Chicago-bound freight? These are the same laws that now have triggered a discount price war between airlines on the most fought-over routes, while shorter or less-frequented routes continue to be extravagantly overpriced.

Buy a New York–London round-trip ticket in Europe in low season and you will pay around $350, less than you would pay for a four-times-shorter Rome–Frankfurt return flight. On the nineteenth-century railroads, transporting a steer on the Buffalo–New York train cost only $1, while a passenger ticket from New York to Chicago in 1881 cost as little as $5. By 1888, rail traffic across the States was so heavy that the ticket from New York to California cost only $29.50.[14]

Just as with the railroad companies of the nineteenth century, today's airlines are governed by the logic of fixed costs. To operate, an airline company must first buy a fleet of planes; furthermore, each airline, at least in the United States, must construct and run its own hangars and repair and maintenance centers. A company may easily incur fixed costs of billions of dollars long before the first passenger even sets foot on a plane; this means taking out loans, accumulating debts that will only be paid off decades hence.

It is the regime of fixed costs that leads to irreversibility, which, as Claus Offe

---

14 J. F. Stover, *America's Railroads*, p. 115.

has observed, is characteristic of modernity. You are free to choose whether or not to build a freeway in a given zone. Once you build it, however, it becomes almost impossible to unbuild it; you cannot go back on your initial decision.[15] All too often, we are not in the least aware of this irreversibility when we make the choices.

---

15 Regarding modernity's "extraordinary resistance to revision," see Claus Offe, "L'Utopia dell'opzione zero," in *Ecologia Politica*, Milan: Feltrinelli, 1987, pp. 41–72.

3

The Mathematics of Pork

In Europe, when TV advertising touches on the delicate matter of the human digestive system, normally the ads pushing laxatives – targeting mainly the elderly – portray first faces soured by the effects of constipation and "intestinal laziness," then relaxed, satisfied smiles, the look of relief after a good healthy bowel workout, thanks to the powers of the magic pill. On American TV, on the other hand, advertisements for antidiarrha products – mainly aimed at the young – predominate. These typically show attractive thirty-something couples caught with their pants up in embarrassing situations: at a concert, a gala lunch, a theater performance. Suddenly struck by painful contractions – signaled by an agonized grimace – one of the pair has to make a headlong dash for the restroom. The next time the character is out, of course, the miraculous capsule will avert this threat that lurks in every intestine.

You might well ask yourself why this is, what it is that makes food so different on different sides of the pond? The ritual of eating in American cities is a source of constant amazement, not only in terms of the culture it expresses or the perversions in flavor it engenders, but also on account of the appalling class-related obesity it produces. (The obesity rate is higher among the poor than among the well-off; among ten-year-old children, Black and Hispanic kids are often more obese than their white counterparts.) In the United States, biting into a McDonald's Big Mac – with its regulation toppings of ketchup, mustard, onion and pickle – is a gesture so thoughtlessly smooth that you hardly notice it; it even seems *natural*. It also seems natural that, whether in Seattle or in New York, you can sit in identically furnished restaurants, staffed by identically uniformed employees, and, always for the same price, bite into the *same* hamburger – available wherever, whenever, as interchangeable as a dollar bill. Americans eat 52 billion hamburgers per year – 11 billion pounds of ground meat!

Limitless availability on this scale goes hand in hand with unrestrained voracity. Food available day and night is designed to be eaten whenever you feel the slightest bit hungry: on the street, sauce drips onto the sidewalk from nibbled-at shish-kebabs; on the seats of subway trains, empty styrofoam chop-suey containers shake, rattle and roll; on a Greyhound bus, a fried chicken wing gives off its inimitable fragrance; at a university meeting, a hot dog pops up; in the car, a bite of donut helps you endure the wait for a light to turn green.

Satisfying this interminable hunger, this endless chompathon, is no easy business. Each year, nine thousand plants throughout the United States butcher and process 7.3 billion chickens and 160 million red-meat animals (41 million cattle, 113 million pigs, 1.5 million calves and 4.2 million sheep[1]) in what is known as the "meat-packing" industry. Meat packing is a huge business that not only has shaped the American continent but that lies at the base of its most popular myth – the cowboy, champion of an industry that Americans become aware of, and alarmed by, only at times of a mass food scare.

Every year in the United States, 4 million cases of meat-related food poisoning occur, not to mention the six thousand registered cases of the killer virus *E. coli* 157:H7. The first food poisoning incident I learned of through the American press was in Tacoma, Washington, in a restaurant belonging to the Jack in the Box chain, which operates in the West, with 1,170 restaurants spread over thirteen states and an annual turnover of $800 million. In January 1993, 450 people who had eaten in that Tacoma burger bar were hospitalized with *E. coli*. Twenty-nine suffered kidney failure; twenty-one were put on dialysis. Three small children,

---

1   1999 figures taken from the National Agriculture Statistical Service (NASS) Website, www.nass.usda.gov, and calculated using tab. 1121 of the US Bureau of the Census, *Statistical Abstract of the United States 1992*, Washington, D.C.: Government Printing Office, 1992; and tab. 1138 and 1140 of the 1999 edition, the latest available.

ages seventeen months, twenty-three months and two years, died. The attributed cause of the incident was failure to observe new regulation temperatures for cooking hamburgers (at least 150° F, or 77° C). In truth, though, the meat had been infected when it arrived at the packing plant. Extracted from Michigan and Colorado cattle, it had been processed by Vons Companies (owners of the largest supermarket chain in California). The sanitary commission was accused of negligence for failing to remove the infected part of the herd.

During the Reagan years, federal budget cuts and deregulation of the meat market had reduced the number of inspector positions from 8,400 in 1978 to 7,200. Of these 7,200 positions, 550 had remained vacant. During 2000, the Clinton administration made further cuts in the number of federal inspections carried out on butchered cattle. The Tacoma poisoning had the positive effect of forcing the commission to take on an additional 160 veterinary inspectors, a very small improvement. Analyzing the carcass of one of every five meat and poultry animals would cost $58 billion per year. The federal government currently spends a mere $1 billion per year on controls, less than 2 percent of the needed sum (which means that only 1 of every 290 carcasses gets analyzed).

Within only a few months, the heated emotions aroused by the children's deaths had cooled. Before being wiped completely from the collective memory, however, these deaths were processed into a fatality statistic, akin to those of car accident victims. It's part of the price of progress, paid so that food can be mass-produced and made reasonably cheaply, available on tap, always the same, wherever you go. It's part of the price, just as is the removal of anything remotely resembling flavor from a piece of steak. The food *looks* succulent and tender, but you may as well eat the styrofoam container. It's part of the cost of living in the modern world, just as is the standardization of most other flavors and smells.

It's not just because of a monstrously inflated sense of pride that Chicago multinational McDonald's boasts of selling the same hamburger all over the world, an achievement the planet's various Burger Kings and Jack in the Boxes have tried in vain to emulate. The Tacoma hamburgers came from animals that once mooed and grazed on the pastures of Michigan, from whence the meat traveled four thousand kilometers southwest to be processed in California before it was finally grilled in Washington, some two thousand kilometers north. A piece of beef today is no different from a piece of technology. It's like a telephone whose copper wiring comes from Chile and whose zinc comes from Canada, with the whole package assembled in Singapore. The English may have launched the Industrial Revolution, but the United States, more specifically Chicago, has witnessed another seismic shift in modernity's fault lines, a shift that has influenced both what we eat and how we eat it, profoundly modifying our senses of taste and smell: the industrialization of breeding.

The factory assembly line that was quickly to establish itself worldwide as the standard method of production began its life in the plant where Henry Ford built the Model T, the world's first mass-produced automobile. On an assembly line, the product moves while the workers remain in place, performing the same action, over and over again, whether fixing a bolt or mounting a component. Less widely known, however, is that the assembly line was first conceived as an imitation of the *disassembly line*, invented around 1830 in the city of Cincinnati, Ohio. Initially, in the system's most rudimentary form, pig carcasses were run along a line suspended from a revolving rail, while workers stood still to fillet their cut (always the same cut) or to strip the flesh from a bone (always the same bone). So proud was Cincinnati of its pork butchery that it gave itself the name Porkopolis.

If the meat-packing industry began with pork rather than with beef, it was because (1) pigs, being short-legged, temperamental beasts, were harder to get to market, whereas cattle were more docile and easier to handle: the heroes of Westerns are *cow*-boys, not *pig*-boys; (2) the ratio of total weight to usable weight was superior for pigs, with hardly anything going to waste; (3) traditional methods of conservation (salting and smoking) worked better with pork than with beef.

A farmer from the Far West, then, found it more convenient to transport a pig fed on his own corn than to send the harvested corn itself. "The hog," wrote one English journalist, "is regarded as the most compact form in which the Indian corn crop in the States can be transported to market. Hence the corn is fed to the hog on the farm, and he is sent to Chicago as a package provided by nature for its utilization." Others defined the pig as "two quintals of corn on four legs."[2]

---

2 Citations taken from W. Cronon, *Nature's Metropolis*, pp. 208–9, 226.

From the outset, then, the pig was ripe for industrialization. Because pigs had to travel, however, the pork industry depended on the availability of transport. As long as water (river and canal) remained the most convenient means of transport, more widely available than railroads, Cincinnati held onto its title as Porkopolis of the nation. With the expansion of the railroads, however, transporting pigs thousands of miles became relatively simple. Chicago quickly began to gain the upper hand, and it wasn't long before the Windy City was able to proudly declare itself the new Porkopolis. In Cincinnati in 1848, 350,000 pigs were butchered, compared to a meager 20,000 in Chicago – but by 1860, Chicago was closing fast on its rival, with a total of 250,000. Finally, during the American Civil War, Cincinnati was overtaken. Because the North could not use the Mississippi basin and its canals as part of its supply network, rapid rail transport (the celebrated Cracker Train) was required to convey the huge quantities of food needed for the troops. In the winter of 1861–62, having dispatched 32,000 more pigs than its arch-rival, Chicago became the official Porkopolis of the United States. "Chicago," exulted the *Tribune* in 1864, "is the greatest Pork Packing Point in the United States and in the world."[3]

After the war ended in 1865, what would eventually become the world's greatest slaughterhouses opened in a zone then known as Packingtown on the south side of Chicago; they were the Chicago Stockyards (Chicago's Pride). By 1868, the yards were already capable of simultaneously packing 21,000 cattle, 75,000 pigs and 22,000 sheep. By 1910, the complex (which included banks, hotels and conservation plants as well as the slaughterhouses themselves) covered some 200 hectares, including 13,000 animal compounds, 300 miles of track, 25 miles of road, a 50-mile sewer network, 95 miles of pipe and 10,000 water hydrants.[4] At their height, after World War I, in 1919, the stockyards packed 19 million animals (more than six per Chicago resident at the time) and employed 30,000 of the 46,000 workers in the Chicago meat-packing industry.[5]

---

3   Cited by Louise Carroll Wade in *Chicago's Pride: The Stockyards, Packingtown and Environs in the Nineteenth Century,* Urbana-Chicago: University of Illinois Press, 1987, pp. 32–33.
4   Robert A. Slayton, *Back of the Yards: The Making of a Local Community,* Chicago: University of Chicago Press, 1986, p. 20.
5   In Irving Cutler, *Chicago, Metropolis of the Mid-Continent,* Chicago: The Geographical Society of Chicago, 1973. Reprinted, Dubuque, Iowa: Kendall/Hunt Co., 1982, pp. 160–61.

With their great disassembly lines, the yards were the acme not only of centralization, but also of capitalist-style rationalization. Keeping the slaughterhouses
running smoothly required larger and larger injections of capital. The typical
up-front investment for a slaughterhouse in the early 1860s was $50,000; by the
end of the decade, it had shot up to $500,000. It was the railroad companies, which
loaded and off-loaded the animals, that wanted and financed Chicago's Union
Stock Yards to rationalize routes, tariffs and costs. Of the $1 million starting capital
for the stockyards in 1865, 92.5 percent came from the nine great railroad companies (Burlington, Illinois Central, Altona, and others), while the Chicago meat-
packers provided 5 percent and the public the remaining 2.5 percent. In turn, East
Coast banks controlled the railroad companies. The yards paid off their initial investment. Even during the depression years of the 1870s, dividends amounted to
10 percent of invested capital, peaking at 15 percent in 1879.

Such enormous profits were possible because of the use of increasingly "scientific" methods. It was "scientific," for example, to make use of every part of the
pig, down to the last bristle on its back (used in the manufacture of brushes). Nothing was wasted, a practice that held not only for pigs, but also for cattle and sheep.
After 1870, a method was found to dry blood and extract albumen, which could
then be sold for a marginal profit to fertilizer manufacturers. The gut was used to
make violin strings. Hooves were ground down for glue; the steer's horns became
combs and buttons. The larger bones were used to make knife and brush handles
and even pipe holders. Ground into powder, the smaller bones went into feed for
the next batch of pigs. By 1920, it was possible to extract forty-one by-products
from a thousand-pound steer, not including the sausage made from the forty-one
meters of entrails. Even nowadays, as Joel Bleifuss has reported, 14 percent of the
beef processed in the United States is recycled to provide feed for other cattle. [6]

Here too, in Chicago, were invented the animal-based flours that now pose
such a terrible threat to human health through the syndrome of bovine spongi-
form encephalitis, the so-called mad cow disease that seems like nature's revenge
for the industrialization of the life-cycle of farm animals. Faced with the wild
tremor of mad cows, it seems somewhat paradoxical that there was an ecological
motive for using the whole animal, a communal injunction to get rid of the moun-

---

6   Reported in the review *In These Times*, 24 January 1994, p. 12.

The Chicago Stockyards circa 1910. Photograph by Barnes-Crosby; courtesy Chicago Historical Society.

tains of refuse being produced. Thus, when mixed with carbon, the gas and fumes produced by the refineries could be used as fuel for lighting.

Two by-products in particular, however, were to open up new commercial vistas to the meat packers. First was oleomargarine, an animal substitute for butter, made from waste fat that was refined and processed after butchering. Margarine was invented in France during the Franco-Prussian War and won the approval of the French health authorities in 1872. It was introduced into the United States the following year and, at only half the price of butter, proved an immediate success there.

The second, and by far the most important by-product, was canned meat. The first attempts to preserve food in cans date back to 1820, but the taste of those early products was revolting. Only with the introduction of steam-pressurized autoclaves – available on the open market around 1872–73 – could the meat be cooked rapidly at a high temperature, producing a much superior flavor. In 1874, Wilson of Chicago patented the first "Original Corned Beef." The company Libby, McNeil and Libby went on to become one of the giants of the canned-food industry.

Meat production was also scientific in the strictest sense, in that chemists were brought in as consultants beginning in 1870. Though initially viewed with suspicion, the chemists proved to be a precious resource, forever coming up with newer processes and by-products.

Even more awe-inspiring was the scientific organization of the disassembly line, a rationalization of production never before seen anywhere in the world. In the yards, the disassembly line attained a level of "geometric" perfection; this was "pork-making by applied mathematics,"[7] as Upton Sinclair called it in his 1906 novel *The Jungle*. A Chicago factory applied gravity to the field of pork packing for the first time in 1863. Rather than placing the compounds outside the plant on the ground floor, the beasts in this particular slaughterhouse were pushed up a ramp onto a terrace overlooking the building's two floors. Here the pigs were permitted a day's rest before they were brought down to the packing compound on the second floor, where they were killed with a hammer blow to the head and then had their throats slit and drained of blood. The novelty in this case was that the blood was run down shutes and collected in special reservoirs; the carcasses, meantime, slid down other shutes to the first floor, where they were processed, boned, quartered and packed. On the ground floor, "acres and acres of hams" hung from hooks. Still remaining were the problems of time lost for the hammer blow and the throat cutting, the need to transport the pigs and the fact that the blood tended to staunch in the horizontally laid bodies.

Windsor Leland came up with the solution to these remaining problems in 1866, when he invented the "slaughtering machine." With this machine, a hook was stuck into the shin of the still-live pig, which was then hauled up by a rack rail worked by a steam elevator. Suspended by its legs from an elevated conveyor belt, the pig was carried to where, still alive, it had its throat cut (skipping the phase of the hammer blow), after which it was shaved, scraped, scalded, gutted, quartered,

---

7   Upton Sinclair, *The Jungle* (1906), New York: Airmont Publishing Co., 1965, p. 40.

sectioned and subdivided into various cuts. With the beast killed in this way, the blood was more easily drained off and the quality of the meat improved.

In addition, a butcher using this method could quarter and section nine pigs in three minutes; it took a mere two minutes to hook up the pig, mount it on the apparatus and kill, scald, scrape and gut it. The Chicago Butchers' Association sponsored a competition in 1869 to find the nation's champion butcher: two of the five contestants, Charles Leyden and Thomas Mulroney, were from Chicago, with the others coming from St. Louis, Buffalo and Toronto. Five hundred spectators paid $1 each to witness the young Leyden as he butchered and prepared his meat in just "4 minutes and 45 seconds" to clinch the title.[8]

Not long afterward, in 1876, the hog-scraping machine was invented. Using a system of spring-mounted rotating blades, that machine could completely strip the hairs from a carcass in less than fifteen seconds.

More machines, more science, more rationalization. Although it now took mere seconds to "pack" a pig, such a speed required the combined efforts of hundreds of trained workers. At peak, 126 men would work on the disassembly line to butcher a single pig: at work were the fragmentation of knowledge and know-how, the constitution of individual disciplines, the social division of labor. Difficult, fundamental questions were at stake – questions unlikely to be posed by any of the 157 individuals involved in butchering a single steer in a medium-sized Chicago slaughterhouse.

Butchering and the packing of meat were thus conducted in scientific fashion, in a way "in keeping with the enlightenment of the present age and the progress of our country." With these words began the 1875 annual report of the Pork Packers' Association of Chicago, repeating almost word for word an article by James Parton (subsequently pillaged by historians)[9] published in an 1867 edition of the *Atlantic Monthly*. Chicago, Parton wrote, "now challenges mankind to admire the exquisite way in which those three hundred thousand cattle per annum, and that million and half of hogs, sheep and calves, are received, lodged, entertained, and dispatched," while the meat industry, "a repulsive and barbarizing business is

---

8   L. C. Wade, *Chicago's Pride*, p. 68.
9   *Atlantic Monthly,* March 1867, no. 19, pp. 332–33.

lifted out of the mire, and rendered clean, easy, respectable, and pleasant."

Scientific butchery had two sensory drawbacks, however. Because the pig's throat was cut while the animal was still alive, suspended from a conveyor belt, the blood pumping from its heart was sprayed in all directions, spurting with violence as the dangling animal struggled to the last. In addition, there was the noise. The old slaughterhouses where pigs were dispatched with a blow to the head had been relatively quiet. Here, in these newer facilities, with the hook stuck through its leg, the pig cried out in a litany of piercing grunts and squeals, a terrible, agonized wail echoed by thousands and thousands of pigs.

"One could not stand and watch very long without becoming philosophical, without beginning to deal in symbols and similes, and to hear the hog-squeal of the universe," wrote Upton Sinclair. "Was it permitted to believe that there was nowhere upon the earth, or above the earth, a heaven for hogs, where they were requited for all this suffering?"[10] In his novel, Sinclair shows how the slaughterhouse system used up to the last layer of dried skin, the last powdered bone and drop of blood, not only of the pigs but also of the meat-packing workers themselves, human beasts who either gained entry to the club of self-satisfied carnivores – and thus became accomplices of the "jungle" – or ended up as fodder for their bosses. In keeping with the demands of "enlightened progress," the process of rationalization drove the workers to increasingly frenzied levels of productivity: "In 1884 five splitters treated 800 steers in 10 hours, 16 each per hour, for 45 cents an hour. By 1894 four splitters were processing 1200 animals in the same time, 30 per worker per hour, showing an increase in productivity of almost 100% in only ten years. Yet at the same time their wages had fallen to a mere 40 cents an hour."[11] Meanwhile, over in the canning department, the women were paid five cents for every hundred tins they painted and labeled. On average, a worker could manage twenty-five hundred tins per day.

Sinclair's book caused scandal when it was published and topped both the US and British best-seller lists for six months. Translated into seventeen languages, the book provoked Congress into setting up a commission of inquiry. Paradoxically, the main concern of the people turned out to be the quality of the meat they

---

10 U. Sinclair, *The Jungle*, p. 40.
11 R. A. Slayton, *Back of the Yards*, p. 88.

ate. Though there were demands for stricter controls on meat packing, nobody seemed in the least concerned about working conditions or about the exploitation of workers, victims of cheap day-labor hire through independent agencies. Or perhaps this was not so paradoxical after all. Maybe it was simply the manifestation of a reflex that would appear in other parts of American life as well, in some aspects punctilious and precise, yet nearly blind to the big picture.

The Illinois Humane Society for the prevention of cruelty to animals could do nothing during the 1870s against the "hog-squeal of the universe," yet Sinclair's book brought about considerable protest, indignant letter writing and drawing up of petitions to Congress to demand that the transport of beasts to the slaughter-house be rendered more humane. Concessions were granted. No longer were animals permitted to travel for more than a day without being unloaded, fed and watered at least once; the use of prods, whips and pitchforks was prohibited; and the floors of the train cars were no longer to be fashioned of loose wood planks. All of these measures were in the interests of the meat-packing industry, ensuring that the meat would not be spoiled and would arrive for the butcher shop window intact, free of unsightly bruises or lumps.

Just as it affected land use, urban geography, human labor and leisure, the tyrannical logic of fixed costs now presided over the life and death of animals, shortening a steer's life expectancy to little more than two years. Up until the age of two, calves were permitted to grow; after that, they would waste valuable pasture through consumption for no discernible weight gain and thus must be packed off on the train.[12]

Yet another area was to fall under the despotic reign of fixed costs: the ambit of the seasons, the yearly cycle of warm- and cold-weather periods. Up to the end of the 1860s, as with most other business activities in Chicago, the pork packer's cleaver swung to the rhythm of the seasons. Pigs were normally butchered at the beginning of winter, when they were at their fattest, when the cold permitted the conservation of carcasses and when labor was cheap because the harvest was over. In Chicago, in the period before the Civil War, the number of pigs butchered in July was ten times less than the number butchered in December. Even as late as

---

12 W. Cronon, *Nature's Metropolis*, pp. 222–24.

1870, the packers treated only 6 percent of the plant's annual volume between the months of March and November. The yards were in full production for only a single season and lay idle, despite the millions of dollars invested, the rest of the year. The cold also made the roads unusable and froze up the canals. Stored in ice-bound cellars, the butchered pork would await the coming of spring.

Consequently, it became necessary to make the slaughterhouses function year-round, which meant reproducing the winter conditions in summer – an objective made possible only by the railroads. Once they could operate year-round, the plants could regulate supply, stabilize prices, reduce fixed costs and sell at lower prices, thus extending their markets.

In 1858, winter ice extracted from the Great Lakes was for the first time used to store the summer pork. So it was that trainloads of ice began to arrive in Chicago, shunted in endless convoys from the great frozen lakes of the north. The ice was stored in thermally isolated underground warehouses so that it could be used the following summer. Entire stretches of railroad and station-cum-warehouses were built to facilitate the process, while armies of immigrant workers were dispatched north to hack the ice from the shores of Lake Wisconsin.

Although it began with the pig, the meatpacking revolution would have been incomplete had it not been extended to beef production, a field in which old prejudices about freshly butchered steak still hung heavy. For this reason, the steer that arrived in Chicago would depart still alive for the eastern seaboard markets of New York and other cities on the Atlantic. Much as Chicago liked to proclaim itself "the bovine city," it was more a cattle market than a beef-packing center. Therefore, to keep costs down, a way had to be found to send beef, no longer live but dressed, so that it could be sold at unbeatable prices and thus widen the market. Dressed beef weighed less than half as much as beef on four legs and did not lose weight during the four-day journey from Chicago to New York as the live animals did or become damaged by the butting of horns and hooves.

In 1866, the magazine *Scientific American* suggested the use of "ice-boxes on wheels" to keep the meat fresh during transportation. But while the idea looked good on paper, it was quite another matter to actually build such a box. The first proposal for a solution came from a Detroit merchant, George H. Hammond, who in 1868 constructed the world's first refrigerated railcar by packing the walls of the compartment with ice. The real revolution, however, occurred in the winter of 1877 when Gustavus F. Swift, a Boston butcher who had come west, sent two Chicago-dressed sides of beef to Boston with the train car doors open so the cold could blow in to keep the meat fresh. The experiment was a success. The next step was to construct a container in which the meat would neither come in contact with the ice nor start to rot, where all the various sections of the carcass could be kept at the same temperature and be held relatively still to keep from disturbing the balance of the car. A ventilator was also needed to allow the air to circulate. After a number of failed attempts, Swift finally resolved the problem by placing bars of ice on the car's roof so that the warm air rising from the floor would be fed into the ventilators. From then on, the use of refrigerated cars spread, and by 1884, trainloads of dressed beef from Chicago exceeded consignments of live cattle.

Again the logic of capital (repaying fixed investments) was reshaping the geography of the American continent. Far West farmers were growing corn and breeding pigs and cattle that would be processed more than a thousand miles away in Chicago and then consumed even farther away, on the Atlantic Coast. For this to happen, an enormous rail network was needed, a network that would stretch across the entire continent, as well as the monstrous slaughterhouses of Chicago's stockyards. In addition, the collection and storage of natural ice was a whole new sector of the industry. Philip Armour, prince of the Chicago wholesalers and perhaps the greatest merchant of all time – a man who said he was "just a butcher trying to go to heaven"[13] – had his men build a storage space in Pewakee, Wisconsin, that was 972 feet long and 162 feet deep and could store 175,000 tons of ice.

Simply refrigerating slaughterhouses and train cars at departure wasn't enough, though: the containers had to be kept constantly refrigerated for the whole length of the journey. This meant building ice stations along the track, each with its own store of ice that needed constant replenishment. Five such stations were needed for the four-day journey from Chicago to New York, with each carload of refrigerated beef requiring 880 pounds of ice and 660 pounds of salt per station. To meet the demand, thousands of ice cutters were packed off to the frozen lakes in the middle of winter, with additional thousands of laborers needed to construct infrastructures (roads, deposits, accommodation huts for themselves) and

---

13 Harper Leech and John Charles Carroll, *Armour and His Times*, New York: Appleton, 1938, p. 236.

still more thousands to maintain them. The enormous mobilization of men led to the creation of whole towns. In just twenty years, though, the advent of artificial refrigeration was to replace these specialist workers and their technical skills. Left behind was a ruinous trail of deserted ice stations and underground deposits. The lakes of Wisconsin were returned to their native inhabitants, the trout and whitefish who, for a brief moment, had been witness to a flurry of activity, the bustle and clamor of workers amid the glow of lakeshore fires.

By 1872, a Scotsman had patented a refrigerator that used compressed ammonia to work. Armour had one installed in his factory in 1883, as did Swift in 1887. In 1889, one Chicago saloon proudly boasted of its "Iceless Refrigerator."[14] The number of cattle packed annually rose from 400,000 in 1880 to well over 2 million in 1890. In addition to the artificial refrigerators, the factories had electric lighting by that time and were connected to the business world via telegraph and to their own city offices by telephone.

Within the space of just thirty years, the meat-packing revolution had attained its objectives. Completely centralized were the means of producing American meat. Animals arrived from the furthest reaches of the continent to be treated industrially in immense slaughterhouses before being redistributed all over America – all thanks to the pressure of fixed costs and the need to pay off an initial investment, just as earlier with railroad tariffs and the cereal-crop market. Philip Armour's motto was "We feed the world," hardly surprising considering that, aside from his pork and beef empire, Armour controlled more than 30 percent of the world's cereal production. And it would be Armour who first used refrigerated cars to transport fruit from California, signaling the beginning of the epoch of fruit packing.

Because it could keep meat "fresh," refrigeration created the need to modify the very concept of beef. Leaving the original steer many hundreds of miles back on the meat-packing trail, well out of sight and mind of the customer, the refrigerated car meant that precise standards of quality were needed to ensure that the transported carcasses were the merchandise the customer desired. Chicago's number 1 quality meat, tailored to the demanding gourmet palate, came from Illinois, Iowa, Kentucky and Indiana; number 2 was from Colorado and Montana,

---

14 L. C. Wade, *Chicago's Pride*, pp. 199–200.

homes of the best-quality Western cattle; and number 3 derived from Texas long-horns. Once the ideal quality of meat had been established, it was possible to buy and sell it in advance, in the abstract, on futures markets, just as cereal crops were bought and sold. Now that it had been industrialized, meat was ready for specula-tion: the revolution was complete.

The "iceless refrigerator" thus signaled the triumph of the meat-packing indus-try and of the Chicago slaughterhouses, so evocatively described by Upton Sinclair, that were to traditional butchering what the industrial factory was to the medieval artisan's workshop. Meat packing was the apotheosis of centralization, the apex of the scale economy and therefore of gigantism, attaining the perfect vertical integration from live animal to tinned animal to the animal on the restau-rant table. Meat packing was, too, the biggest business in Chicago. Yet this same artificial refrigeration was to trigger the city's slow decline as a packing center, as Chicago's favorable position (close to sources of natural ice) became irrelevant. Less important, too, was the Windy City's position as a railroad junction: if animal carcasses could travel a thousand miles from Chicago to New York in a refriger-ated car, they could just as well travel two thousand miles from Kansas City. In-deed, in 1890, Philip Armour's assistant, Michael Cudahy, set up a plant in Omaha, Nebraska, while Armour himself opened a packinghouse in Kansas City.

The Chicago stockyards were to reach their apogee just after World War I, by which time the automobile – and with it, the refrigerated truck – was already lying in ambush. Together with artificial refrigeration, automobile transportation was to liberate the meat trade from its enslavement to fixed costs and from the rigid centralization of the railroads. As a result, economies of scale became decidedly less appetizing. By the 1920s, the decline had begun, with the large centralized slaughterhouses giving way to decentralized plants made possible by trucks that could ferry the merchandise to shop windows. By the arrival of World War II, the yards' fate was already sealed. In 1971, after 106 years, the Chicago slaughter-houses closed their doors, supplanted by "peripheral branches" in Kansas City, Omaha and Peoria. Now, even in those cities, the slaughterhouses have become invisible. In vain, I looked for signs of them on the banks of the Kansas River.

Today the stockyards have become ghostly shrines to emptiness and rust sur-rounded by interminable walls of brown-and-gray stone enshrouding them in a silence as agonizing as the pigs' squeals once were. Yet the millions of immigrants brought to the city in waves by the slaughterhouses have remained here, flotsam left by the receding tide. Meanwhile, in what amounts to a pork-and-beef diaspora, the butchers have moved out of Chicago, even leaving behind the head office of McDonald's, the nerve centers of other multinational food giants such as Quaker Oats, and the Mercantile Exchange with the world's greatest livestock market, where brokers speculate on beef and pork futures.

Chicago's Packingtown has become a ghost town, a fossil of railroad capitalism. But the industry of meat packing to which Chicago gave birth, and which now permits us to sit down to a Sunday lunch of dressed beef, is booming as never before. Sinclair's jungle may have disappeared, but one thing remains as visible today as it was in 1906, and that is the logic of capital (the law of fixed costs, the demand for standardization and the need for conservation) that connects the steer that grazes in Michigan with the hamburger consumed in California – the moo of the universe.

4

Buying the Future

Chicago is the city that not only invented futures trading, but began buying and
selling the future before it existed. That was in 1833, a mere 170 years ago. At the
point where the insignificant Chicago River flowed into Lake Michigan, there was
as yet no metropolis, no great railroad station, not a single slaughterhouse. Only
350 people lived in the settlement that had recently proclaimed itself a town;[1] not
a single paved road ran through it. There was nothing but a few farms and American Indian encampments, outposts of French fur traders, a garrison of American
soldiers – and, of course, speculators.

By 1836, however, when the population of the town had risen to 4,000, parcels
of land that in 1829 had sold for $33 were going for $100,000 apiece ($1.2 million in
current dollars). This was the price for vacant holdings, prairies left fallow by
American Indians evicted after the 1832 Blackhawk War – land described by the
rare traveler to the zone as "wilderness." The price boom resulted from a prediction that values would shoot up following construction of a canal connecting Lake
Michigan to the Illinois River, tributary of the mighty Mississippi. With Lake
Michigan already connected to New York and the Atlantic Coast – initially via
Lake Erie and then by its eponymous canal (opened eight years previously, in

---

1   Figure from I. Cutler, *Chicago, Metropolis of the Mid-Continent*, p. 19.

1825) – the Michigan–Illinois Canal would link New York and the eastern seaboard to the great central plains of the Mississippi-Missouri basin, with Chicago
becoming the *trait d'union* between these two immense regions.

Ironically, Chicagoans at this time had their hopes still tied to the waterways,
unaware that the coming railroads instead would eventually make them rich. Naturally, following the boom in land speculation was the depression of 1837, when
soaring costs interrupted work on the canal and land prices dived. Not for another
ten years would the canal opened, in 1848. When it did, the inauguration was surrounded by considerably more fanfare than was the inauguration of the city's first
railroad line, the Galena and Chicago. Those who had bought land in 1833 did not
want the desolate stretch of waste that appeared before them but the land that it
would become once the canal was opened. In short, the purchaser had bought
into a "future." In this case, however, it was a future that would never arrive.

Instead, the land wager set in motion the wheels of a different destiny. When
the canal finally did open in 1848, Chicagoans no longer speculated solely on the
future of the city's real estate, but rather on the trade of cereal crops. The influx of
corn and wheat from surrounding farms increased tenfold with completion of the
canal; no longer did smallholders need to face an uncomfortable land journey to
market along muddy tracks peppered with puddles and potholes. Significantly,
1848 was also the year when eighty-two merchants banded together to form the
Chicago Board of Trade (CBOT).

Oddly, it was the most basic and most ancient form of trade known to human-
kind, that of agricultural foodstuffs and livestock, that would give birth to the
most sophisticated type of market, the "futures" market. The price of crops depended to a large extent on the weather: good weather meant an abundant harvest, and therefore low prices, whereas adverse weather led to a poor harvest and
thus to a rise in price. Similarly, the price of livestock would go up after an epidemic, whereas a poor harvest would cause cattle prices to fall because breeders
would need to get rid of the livestock they no longer could feed economically.

Here's how the futures market works: Suppose I'm a spaghetti manufacturer
and I need a guaranteed supply of wheat. I need to buy the wheat in advance on
the next harvest. The problem is that next year could see a superabundant harvest,
which would mean that the price of wheat then would be much lower than what I

paid for it today. Or imagine that I'm a wheat grower. I sell next year's harvest today, but then a drought next year pushes wheat prices through the roof, so I lose. It was for these reasons that the fixed-term contract was born. The first forward contract on corn – for 3,000 bushels to be consigned the following June – was signed in Chicago on 13 March 1851.

That 1851 handshake between two smallholders who reeked of hay and manure certainly had nothing in common with the spectacle witnessed today in the ultramodern Mercantile Exchange building on Wacker Drive. From the observatory over the trading room there, you look down on a pit the size of a football field, where 4,000 people jostle and scream, their faces contorting into exulted grins in adoration of the luminous figures that appear on the walls. Their hands move frenetically, fingers speaking an accelerated sign language, while heads nod in prayer to the shares. If you didn't know better, you'd think you were witnessing some antic ritual, a feast in a Tibetan monastery, a perceptual hallucination verging on ecstasy. Not even Wall Street pulses with this kind of alien fervor.

The enervated, feverishly hypnotic, trancelike state of the floor traders recalls the tribal ceremonies of anthropological studies. And like an anthropologist, you realize that this rite is destined to disappear: "these die away under our very eyes."[2] The Chicago Board of Trade and the Chicago Mercantile Exchange (CME) are already planning to replace the concrete *pits* with online trading: all the sleeve rolling, paper fumbling and shouting yourself hoarse will vanish as the click of a mouse strikes deals on a computer hooked up to the Web.[3] What was not even a distant blip on the horizon in 1848 will perhaps already be gone again by 2005. Gone, too, will be the thousands of traders you see – with short jackets that make them look like waiters – munching on hamburgers in the neon-lit cafeteria, disheveled and wasted after their daylong intercourse with the stock market.

Yet back in the 1850s, even if none of this yet existed, the frenzy had undoubtedly already begun, the glint in the eye that dreamed of untold riches, the terror of bankruptcy. Already in place was the idea of pushing forward, an anxiety over the future that tended to oscillate between burnout and fear about what lay ahead: the

---

2 Bronislav Malinowski, *Argonauts of the Western Pacific* (1922), Prospect Heights, Ill: Waveland Press, 1984, p. xv.
3 "An Uncertain Future for Chicago's Pits," *Financial Times*, 24 August 2000.

nightmarish prospect of failure. It was because of this frenzy that the 350 original Chicagoans of 1833 became 30,000 by 1850 and 334,000 by the autumn of 1871, then multiplied fivefold again in the following twenty years to reach 1.698 million by the turn of the century. Nor did the explosion of people end there. By 1930, Chicago's population had again doubled, to 3.3 million inhabitants. The future had become the present, while already seeming today to be part of a past whose likes shall perhaps never again be seen, thanks to the seemingly irreversible tendency the United States has toward urban decline and "disurbanization." Neither has there been an end to the process of virtualization of trade. The idea of trading in futures, which already seems so incorporeal with respect to their beef or soybean prefixes, is itself in the process of being dematerialized, rerouted on integrated circuits, warehoused in chips and managed by microprocessors.

The slaughterhouses have gone from Chicago, as have the convoy trains of lumber and grain. As a center of material, tangible commerce, the city is in decline. If Chicago continues to rank as one of the great cities, therefore, thanks go largely to the endurance of abstract institutions and of the spiritualized quintessence of commerce. In this sense, the situation of Chicago resembles that of London, a city that has long ceased to be the capital of a colonial empire but that remains the capital of the immaterial yet still-concrete empire of finance and merchant banking: the City. In the same way, the meat trade in Chicago has been replaced by trading on beef futures, and you no longer hear talk of bushels of corn but only whispers of soybean futures.

It is thus the trade in agricultural products and their futures that lies at the base of Chicago's greatness: commerce that not only has helped shape the city but also has modified the products themselves, redefining the very terms *cattle, meat,* wheat and *lumber.* This is because one of the problems with forward contracts is the need to have standards for the future goods to be bought and sold: the quality of wheat, the percentage of humidity, the permissible deviation from the norm. Selling such products as though they were currency requires that the goods be interchangeable and equivalent to each other. In the late nineteenth century, a similar problem arose in relation to correspondence and mail-order buying and selling (another Chicago invention), which has resurfaced today in the form of e-commerce. Without uniformity, we cannot be sure of the quality of the goods we are buying. Futures trading is likewise a form of correspondence buying, the only difference being that the distance is across time rather than through space.

Without standardization, the futures market cannot exist; by the same measure, futures can be traded only on standardized goods. In simple terms, the futures market is the financial form that allows the United States to ensure the constant availability of food products in supermarkets everywhere, subject to quality control and with comparable characteristics. You can never tire of reflecting on the tremendous power of standardization or on the mechanisms it has been able to generate, from telephone sockets that work only if all are identical to bolts and screws purchased from a dozen different hardware stores but all standardized, by gauge and caliber, the parts interchangeable. If campers and caravans can draw water from campsites all over the American continent, it is thanks only to uniform unions and intakes. Nathan Rosenberg has shown how standardization during the nineteenth century was the fulcrum of technological innovation that gave birth to the machine-tool industry.[4] Contrariwise, anyone who uses a computer knows the problems of not having a common standard for software.

For a market trading agricultural futures to function, the terms of each contract must be as tightly defined as possible. The time limit for negotiations, the minimum limit of oscillation, the consignment date, the maximum exposure, the unit of exchange: all must be established. For already-immaterial goods, such as currency, determining the game rules is relatively simple: one pound note or dollar bill is as good as another. When it comes to buying beef or pork, however, how can you be sure that the quality and quantity of the goods you have purchased will match the terms of the agreement? The only way is simply by taking the precaution of stipulating uniform criteria – for quality, quantity, weight, volume and so on. Such rigorous standardization might seem more suitable for tools or machine parts, or for currency, artificial instruments originally conceived in terms of standard values and measures. Harder to swallow is the idea of a standardized hen or egg, calf or pig – or of a standardized quality of wheat.

Nothing must be left to chance. To this end, it has been established that live cattle, bought and sold in units of 40,000 pounds, must be composed of medium-sized animals, each weighing 1,050 to 1,200 pounds, with a maximum devia-

---

4 In the volume *Perspectives on Technology*, Cambridge: Cambridge University Press, 1976.

tion of 100 pounds. In lumber futures, the maximum humidity allowed per unit (11,880 ft.) is fixed at 19 percent; furthermore, the wood must be cut in rectangular planks, bound together with steel tape and paper-wrapped in batches of planks of a length no less than eight feet and no more than twenty feet, in accordance with the federal criteria for construction timber, which may come only from the states of California, Idaho, Montana, Nevada, Oregon, Washington or Wyoming or from the Canadian provinces of British Columbia or Alberta. The list of regulations is endless.

But before any of this happens, the first step is to create a discontinuity of measure – that is, to establish a discontinuous criterion of classification and thus limit the number of grades of quality for each product. There are, for example, no more than five grades of carrot to be ordered, from the most economic (grade 1) to the most expensive (grade 5). Establishing such quality levels, separating carrots into these different types, may be first and foremost a commercial operation, but it is also – in all seriousness – an epistemological one.

Mother Nature, in fact, doesn't provide us with identical grade 1 carrots any more than she does with identical grade 2 pears. Instead, humans arbitrarily group under a single label carrots, pears or other fruits and vegetables that may appear similar but that have many different tastes, qualities and sizes. The variation among different types of wheat, for example, is almost continuous, with tiny deviations in the dimensions of the grains, level of humidity, consistency, color and nutritional value of the flour produced. To convert this continuous scale of nature's bounty into goods that can be exchanged in the abstract – on paper or on the screen – the futures trader must substitute it with a discontinuous classification of limited grades of quality: 1, 2, 3 and so on.

Each grade defines a particular zone, an area in which are grouped, for example, different grains of wheat, which are then catalogued under a single name. In this way, two similar grains that happen to be near the threshold between one quality and another may be placed in different grades – much as the situation of contiguous villages on either side of a border between neighboring countries. No longer is it worthwhile to cultivate species of low quality toward the higher end of the scale; it is more profitable to grow species toward the lower end of the higher-quality range. Definition thus intervenes in the selection of species, favoring those situated at the lower end of a high grade over those at the higher end of a low grade. All of this means that entire varieties of wheat at this higher end will simply disappear, thanks to a wholly arbitrary definition.

Without knowing it, the futures market confronts, and in its own way resolves, the debate of the Middle Ages between nominalists and realists. That debate addressed a question of universals, with scholastic philosophers trying to decide whether the names of things resulted purely from convention, whether ideas actually corresponded to the objective reality of their physical examples – or whether ideas possessed a reality independent of who thought them or of the objects that appeared to correspond to them. To buy or sell a cattle future, the market needed first to define "the ideal cow," "the idea of cattle." Once this idea had been defined and a set of standards fixed, the living cows actually had to live up to that reality if they were to find a market. In the same way, defining five and no more than five types of apple ensures that the apples produced shall be of five and no more than five different species. Every year in the United States, thousands of tons of apples are discarded because their dimensions are a millimeter or two inferior to the official standard.

In this sense, although it may originally be the result of purely arbitrary convention, the name of a thing produces the thing itself. Furthermore, the name itself defines the essence – the *quidditas* – of an object and excludes everything that does not fall under its definition. In the beef-futures market, for example, what is not defined is the steak's flavor. The same is true for apple futures, which are based on an apple's variety, size and color but do not take into account its taste. The apple's *quidditas* (its "appleness") is defined by color, consistency, dimensions – in short, by form – but not by flavor. Indeed, a flavor that is too clearly defined veers away from the norm: better that the apple taste of nothing than have too much flavor. This form of definition, which ignores the question of flavor, therefore tends to produce food that has none.

Consequently, you find in supermarkets chickens that are all the same, apples of identical dimensions, oranges of a uniform orangeness – all equally flavorless. The reason? It's all so the items can participate in the futures market, so the barons of Chicago (and New York, and Hong Kong, and London, and Singapore) can lay money on them. Which they do not do in the way of us common mortals in seedy, smoke-filled betting shops, but rather in the money temples or, as Oipaz (protagonist of Edward Thompson's brilliant historical novel, *The Sykaos Papers*) calls them, the "bumples."[5]

The first futures contracts began in 1865, at the end of the American Civil War. Today, less than 140 years later, Chicago has become the global capital of the futures market. Nearly one-third of world trade passes by way of the shores of Lake Michigan even now, when increasingly merciless competition from other stock exchanges is threatening the city's number 1 status and forcing it to establish a network of alliances. The Mercantile Exchange has in fact formed a pact with the exchanges of Paris, Singapore, Toronto, São Paulo and Montréal; the Chicago Board of Trade has allied itself with the Franco-Swiss Eurex system.

Since 1865, the futures market has become a much more sophisticated beast. Futures are now bought and sold on agricultural foodstuffs, livestock (both live and frozen), lumber and fertilizers. If you sign a one-year pig-future contract today, for example, you are buying a contract for the purchase of pigs the following year. This same general concept is valid for any number of other contracts; indeed, any kind of raw material can become a future.

Moreover, if I am a US importer of German cars, I know that I'm going to need German marks in a year's time. It was for this type of situation that the futures market was extended to currency speculation (introduced in 1972, a year after then President Richard Nixon decided to float the US dollar). In fact, because futures make sense for any commodity whose value tends to fluctuate over time, we also have futures on interest rates, on eurodollars, on LIBOR. We even have futures on share indexes themselves: in Chicago, futures are traded on both the Standard and Poor's 500 Index and the Nikkei.[6] In fact, the futures markets could be widened even further: why not trade futures on government bonds, on the indexes of federal and state loans, on mortgage rates?

In 1982, some unsung broker had an ingenious idea. Since futures were themselves variable, why not trade futures on futures: futures squared? And so it was

---

5   Edward Thompson, *The Sykaos Papers*, London: Bloomsbury, 1988.
6   The Standard and Poor's Index is based on 500 companies – 400 industrial, 40 financial, 40 service and 20 transport – that together account for 80 percent of the value of shares quoted on Wall Street.

that "options" on futures made their appearance. In 1999, the volume of contracts between options and futures reached 254 million on the Chicago Board of Trade (which the previous year hit a record total of 281 million) and 201 million on the Mercantile Exchange (whose record of 226 million dates back to 1989). In 1986, the nominal values of contracts at the CME was $19 trillion, a figure that shot to $50 trillion by 1991 and $183 trillion by 1999.[7] Including related sectors, betting on futures provides work for some 200,000 people in Chicago's metropolitan area.[8]

The figures are staggering. The funny part, though, is that the CME, the cathedral of this speculation frenzy, is itself a nonprofit organization – even when becoming a member today means forking out $580,000. In 1989, access to the only international currency market cost $475,000. The CME's members number 2,700, 1,200 of whom rent their seats out to others. The CBOT, on the other hand, has only 1,402 members.

All these figures seem abstract. In material terms, you see only swarms of people in different-colored jackets: pale green, light blue, yellow, red, depending on where these waiterlike traders – breathless busboys to the dollar – fit in the market food chain. The immateriality of it all, though, is what is so striking. Here are traded options on futures on fixed-term contracts: contracts to the power of three. And there is no reason not to have contracts to the fourth power, or the fifth, in a game that feeds on itself: an immaterial spiral guaranteed by a computer network of some 165,000 connections spread over 118 countries.

Armed with such ultramodern technology, what you bet on is, in essence, the bets themselves. The game becomes doubly dangerous. The first warning shot of this was fired on 19 October 1987, when the New York Stock Exchange fell by 21 percent in a single day. Blamed for the disaster was the futures market, which tumbled by a staggering 29 percent – because although futures trading multiplies share speculation profits, it also magnifies losses. You find yourself imagining millions of tons of frozen pork bellies making their immaterial voyage in cyberspace from Hong Kong to London via Chicago. And you ask yourself, What will become of the pigs, the steers and the carloads of corn when one day the whole system short-circuits?

---

7 Data available from the respective Websites, www.cbot.com and www.cme.com.
8 *Financial Times*, 24 August 2000.

Betting on the future is an ambiguous concept. In the livestock market, what you purchase is the *right* to buy a herd in a year's time. But what other *rights* can be bought? A hunter might buy the right to shoot a hundred ducks on a game reserve during the next year's season. A car owner might purchase the right to full coverage for a given number of accidents; this would be a futures market on traffic accidents, with insurance companies offering shares – yet another viable future.

In March 1993, the Chicago Board of Trade actually began to auction futures on the right to pollute – more specifically, on the right to contaminate the air with sulfur dioxide. The Clean Air Act introduced these rights to pollute, or "clean air" rights, to the stock market in 1990. According to this law, a fixed number of pollution permits were assigned to the most polluted US coal-fueled power stations, each allowing for the emission of a ton of sulfur dioxide in a given year. If the plant emits more than this amount, it must purchase additional pollution rights; if it emits less, it may sell the rights it has saved to others or "put them in the bank" for a time in the future when they may come in handy. The idea is to make it convenient for producers to reduce pollution and to encourage them to adopt machinery that emits relatively little CO_2.

After pollution rights and futures on pollution rights, no doubt we will shortly see the arrival of pollution options. From 1997 on, these new environmental futures have been part of international law. With the 1997 Kyoto Treaty – which the United States signed but which has not received Senate ratification – thirty-nine industrialized nations committed themselves to reducing carbon dioxide emissions by 5.2 percent of their 1990 level by the year 2010. Because the United States enjoyed a period of considerable economic growth during the 1990s and therefore accelerated CO_2 emissions, it has continued to demand that each country be allowed to buy pollution rights that other countries have, so to speak, "saved up." Through the mechanism of futures, the most polluting country in the world is doing nothing to reduce its potential for poisoning the planet but instead is continuing its practices, relying instead on the efforts of other countries to clean up the environment.

A case in point was the failed Aja Summit of November 2000. At that summit, the United States was still insisting on the right to buy emissions from Russia, who, having lost the Cold War, had undergone a dramatic process of deindustrialization and thus had found itself with an abundant surplus of pollution "credits." The idea of a defeated Russia having credits that would permit the victorious United States to maintain its emissions introduces a new type of war damages in the form of *environmental reparations*.

In fact, this market-led solution is invalid, because it presupposes the *interchangeability* and convertibility of a standard unit of pollution, in this case a ton of carbon or sulfur dioxide. From the first auction, those selling pollution rights have been companies based in zones where pollution levels are already low, whereas buyers have been industries in highly polluted areas. The results of the initiative have thus been exactly the opposite of what legislators had predicted: the problem has been aggravated where it was already serious and alleviated where it was less so. A leaky old factory obviously will find it more convenient to buy pollution rights than to adopt costly new machinery, and the oldest factories are naturally concentrated in the historical centers of industry, veritable hotbeds of pollution.

Underlying this apparent heterogenesis of ends (the will to do good that produces evil) is the profound conviction that only the market itself can cure the (environmental) ills caused by the mechanisms of the market. The work of repairing the disaster becomes simply another potential source of profit. Here we find a certain symmetry between the way the market works in general and the way futures work in particular. Just as we can envisage the future of a future of a future, so too can a second business be set up to repair the damages caused by the first business, and then a third to patch up the damages caused by the second, and so on, multiplying to infinity the whirling jig of speculation and profit. It is a dance beyond the wildest imaginings of the Native American and French hunters who once dwelt on the banks of the Chicago River some 170 years ago.

5

Sky Grazing

Chicago is the city that invented the skyscraper – and it shows. The forms of these massive buildings leap catlike toward the clouds, curving in the azure dome of sky, bold silhouettes looming bizarrely overhead, possessed of an incomparable lightness, a levity made possible by the concrete infusion of billions of dollars. It's a levity funded by the world's biggest butchers and sausage manufacturers. Once more, you find yourself meditating on the relationship between aesthetics and shopkeeping, and once again, Venice springs to mind, complete with its grocers and spice merchants.

It was only a century ago, during the 1880s, that the Chicago School laid the foundations of modern architecture. Among the school's greatest exponents were Dankmar Adler, Daniel H. Burnham and John W. Root, William Le Baron Jenney and Louis Sullivan, Frank Lloyd Wright, William Holabird and Henry Hobson Richardson. Influenced by the ironwork construction of European railway stations, they conceived of the skyscraper as a structure borne not by supporting walls but by an internal ironwork frame.

If buildings were living beings, the revolution triggered by the Chicago School would be equivalent to the passage in the animal world from the exoskeleton of invertebrates (with the supporting "skeleton" of the traditional house, like that of a snail, provided by external walls) to the endoskeleton of vertebrates (whose external surface of skin and fat constitutes a form of "upholstery"). Yet the comparison with vertebrates doesn't end here: no skyscraper can exist without an elaborate circulation system, a heart (a generator, an installed power source) to pump electricity, water, central heat and human beings (what would a skyscraper be without its elevators?). In this sense, the skyscraper is inconceivable without the technical innovations of the late nineteenth century, which were to transform buildings from mere objects into complex technological mechanisms that *functioned,* with that functioning dependent on a number of factors. To claim in the previous century that a building "functioned" would have been eccentric to say the least. The metaphor of the skyscraper as a living organism recalls the insistence with which machines in the nineteenth century were compared to bodies: even the city itself was looked upon as an organism whose *arteries* were its main thoroughfares.

In 1883, the Home Insurance Company charged William Le Baron Jenney with the task of constructing a ten-story fireproof office building. The Great Fire of 1871 had shaken all of Chicago. To attain greater luminosity, Le Baron Jenney for the first time employed a skeleton of Bessemer steel beams. By 1890, Chicago's buildings had risen to the then-audacious height of sixteen stories. Grocers and wholesalers ordered these imposing structures, which were furnished by their owners with the canvases of impressionist painters snubbed by the French and therefore available for next to nothing. At only sixteen floors, these steel giants – which would hardly qualify for low-rise status today – were then regarded as a challenge to the heavens. Tallest was the 21-story Masonic Temple, designed by Burnham and Root and completed in 1892.[1]

Curiously, the architects of Chicago revolutionized building techniques at both ends of the construction scale: in the skyscraper, with its metallic frame, and in the single-family home, through the invention of the ultralight wooden "balloon frame." In both cases, the building's *structure* became lighter, with a metallic skeleton substituted for heavy external walls in one case and a lightweight reticulated wooden frame for large beams in the other. Louis Sullivan's idea that "form follows function" also indicates the extent to which functionalism in general has

---

1   Charles Singer et al., eds., *A History of Technology,* vol. 5, *The Late Nineteenth Century, 1850–1900,* Oxford: Clarendon Press, 1958, p. 478–79.

become rooted in the American consciousness. In the wake of World War II, this functionalism was to be further molded in Chicago by Ludwig Mies van der Rohe, former director of the German Bauhaus, whose favorite maxims included "Less is more" and "God is in the details." One thing is certain: from the late-nineteenth-century palaces of Le Baron, to the 141-meter-high neogothic skyscraper that houses the offices of the *Chicago Tribune*, built in 1925, to the harsh minimalism of Mies van der Rohe's designs from the 1960s, right up to the innovative postmodern forms of another German architect, Helmut Jahn (who in 1980 introduced the fashion of varicolored reflective glass that has transformed the city's horizon into a technicolor rainbow of office buildings) – the center of this great metropolis is an extraordinary living museum of modern architecture.

Yet skyscrapers are not simply a technical invention: they also represent a revolution in urban planning; they change our very concept of the city. However much it may have become the symbol of the American metropolis, the skyscraper puts the very idea of the city in crisis, to the point of negating it altogether, if by a *city* we mean a place where people mingle, where not only individuals but entire cultures and activities – all the various functions of social life – fuse. The skyscraper above all else introduces and codifies that separation of urban functions considered by the Chicago School of sociology to be the very basis of the city's evolution, as though the city were a living being that evolves and specializes, in the same way the cells and tissues of an organism develop different functions. The city would thus be composed of zones divided according to function: one for business, one for entertainment, another for residences. The skyscraper gives spatial form to this notion of specialization in so exagerated a manner that almost nothing exists in the United States between it and the single-story house, extremes that make you nostalgic for the six- to eight-story buildings of old. The houses where people live are a distant drive from the workplace: none are to be found in the office district. (At night, the downtown area becomes eerily empty, and the skyscrapers loom in the darkness like the fossils of forgotten dinosaurs.) In the rare cases where skyscrapers do serve as residential buildings, they deny the very notion of the city – as a zone of contact – in that they themselves are isolated, self-enclosed cities. Organized like spaceships launched into the cosmos, fully autonomous and self-supporting (with everything from laundry to gym) and kept running smoothly by armies of mechanics, plumbers, police officers and clerks, each of these buildings is a self-governing utopia right in the heart of the city.

Usually, however, skyscrapers are built to house (and by) *corporations*. The skyscraper is, in fact, designed to reproduce the vertical organization of a huge company, as huge as the building itself. The height of the building is a concrete metaphor of the company turnover, with the leadership occupying its uppermost reaches. Doing everything possible to be in God's shoes, the chairperson gazes down from a throne in the heavens, down to where the pedestrians patrolling the sidewalk some hundred floors below appear as anonymous worker ants.

While its costs may be astronomically high, the skyscraper performs well its symbolic duty; only those above you, or your "superiors," count, while your "inferiors" fade quietly into insignificance. From the office window, your gaze may wander down, but your aspirations are upward (on the social ladder). Mirroring the bitter struggle to the top, the skyscrapers themselves often compete with each other in their bid for the sky: even a building thirty stories high looks overpowered when surrounded by others of seventy floors or more. As anyone who has spent time in the office blocks of midtown Manhattan knows, you find yourself in complete darkness even twenty floors up, deprived of sunlight by the surrounding buildings. Heights that a century ago would have seemed airy realms to be frequented only by a hot air balloon are now at the level of basement flats, submerged in the well of shadow created by their taller neighbors. And the higher the skyscrapers soar, the smaller becomes that desirable luminous portion of them, the more floors are relegated to a crepuscular underground existence. Every new skyscraper, therefore, must be not only tall, but *taller,* giving rise to the race to construct "the world's tallest skyscraper."

What we find taking place is a war between skyscrapers for what is, literally, "a place in the sun." "Why are the trees in the forest so high?" asks Richard Dawkins:

> The short answer is that all the other trees are tall, so no one tree can afford not to be. It would be overshadowed if it did. This is essentially the truth, but it offends the economically minded human. It seems so pointless, so wasteful. ... But if only they were *all* shorter, if only there could be some sort of trade-union agreement to lower the recognized height of the canopy in forests, *all* the trees would benefit. They would be competing with each other in the canopy for exactly the same sunlight, but they would have "paid" much smaller growing costs to get into the canopy. The

total economy of the forest would benefit, and so would every individual tree. Unfortunately, natural selection doesn't care about total economies, and it has no room for cartels and agreements. ... It is generally characteristic of arms races, including human ones, that although all would be better off if *none* of them escalated, so long as one of them escalates none can afford not to follow suit.[2]

Like the trees in Dawkins's forest, city skyscrapers are the fruit of extreme competition that diminishes resources: a tremendous amount of energy and work are required for a skyscraper to be constructed at all and to be able to function at such a height. If competition is the engine that powers the market, you begin to understand why the skyscraper was invented in "capitalism's promised land." What is put in question here is not rationalism per se, but a certain species we might call the rationalism of the shopkeeper, whose neglect of the external world and of external costs often leads to bankruptcy. Building a skyscraper may be convenient when land in the city center is so valuable; then it is worthwhile to multiply the ground floor area (the "footprint") by a further hundred floors, regardless of construction and maintenance costs. As soon as that value begins to slide, however, the skyscraper turns into a financial albatross, and it becomes more profitable to build offices in outlying areas, where land is relatively cheap, in the form of lower, flat-plan buildings. Even so, Chicago remains home to some of America's most magnificent skyscrapers, towering columns of mirrored glass, postmodern structures hundreds of floors high, gabled like Greek temples, blinding sun-enflamed obelisks by day, galaxies of harsh neon strip lighting by night.

A kind of curse comes over the companies that build these megalithic monsters. In the fourteenth century, construction work on Siena's new cathedral was interrupted after the Buonsignori bankers went bust; today's corporations often wait until after they have completed their temples to go bankrupt. In New York, for instance, Pan-American Airways, responsible for erecting one of the city's most magnificent buildings, no longer exists. The tower of once-proud IBM is up for grabs. In Chicago, meanwhile, Sears, Roebuck and Company, constructor of the Sears Tower, which at 1,450 feet was the world's tallest building until 1996 (it has since been supplanted by the Petronas Towers in Kuala Lumpur), has been forced to relocate offices, close down its mail-order catalogue and let go of some

---

2   Richard Dawkins, *The Blind Watchmaker*, London: Norton, 1987, p. 184.

50,000 of its 300,000 staff. The immense structures that seem destined to last an eternity reveal themselves to be extremely frail specimens, susceptible to the slightest hint of recessionary chill: the first expenses corporations cut when growth begins to slow are those connected to real estate. The vertiginous buildings begin to empty, as occurred in the recession of 1990–91, when their expensive marble atriums began to fill with "vacancy" signs.

When skyscrapers are left to their own devices, they decline at a meteoric speed, which is perhaps why entire quarters of US cities resemble the aftermath of the Dresden bombing. An exemplary case is Number 40 Wall Street, a New York skyscraper that at 933 feet had for a brief moment in 1929 the honor of being the tallest building in the world. After 1990, it was abandoned: a structure designed to last for eternity, it had by then begun the sorry slide into ruin.[3] Although it was once worth $123 million, restoration and maintenance work proved to be so costly that at that point the bank would have happily sold it for $10 million. This building was finally renovated by Trump in 1996; other, similar buildings of its era in cities like Detroit have not been so favored.

You begin to suspect that skyscrapers are to industrial modernity what the pyramids were to ancient Egypt: costly monuments to the overinflated egos of their proprietors and to the religion of the day, the cult of the dead yesterday, that of the dollar today. Behind their apparent rationality, skyscrapers embody a Promethean folly in challenging the laws of gravity and the violence of the winds – a folly strangely moving at dusk when the clouds' reflections are captured in the mirrored glass, suspended up there in the sky.

---

3   The story is recounted in the *Chicago Tribune*, 24 January 1993.

6

Houses with Wings

In a room cluttered with bric-a-brac, the stocky protagonist's fist connects with the jaw of his corpulent adversary. The blow sends the latter flying into the wall, which promptly collapses, letting him roll out onto the grassy lawn, where he finishes in a dazed heap. How many times has this scene been replayed in American movies, and how many times has it been attributed to the superhuman muscle power of the Hollywood hero? Actually, though, scenes like this are completely realistic. Practically anyone could knock down the walls of an American house, because the walls are, in reality, nothing more than thin layers of wood.

It's amazing how realistic American cinema is: realistic in the sense Erich Auerbach intended, writing about European literature of the Middle Ages – that is to say, realistic in its *figurality*. When traveling around the United States, you have the feeling of being trapped inside a giant screen, a feeling you cannot shake no matter where you go. Every motel sign you pass on the highway, every fire hydrant you see on the sidewalk, every bar counter creates a sensation of *déjà vu*, deceptively familiar from a thousand movie sightings. Deceptively, I say, because there is always a slight, almost imperceptible gap between what you actually see and what you remember from a film sequence, a subtle but radical difference. You attribute a collapsing wall to the hero's Herculean strength because it seems impossible to you that the hypersophisticated technology of the Hollywood movie machine, with its battery of state-of-the-art digital effects, is in fact portraying a rustic, primitive civilization of clapboard houses. The splicing of wood and cellu- loid seems to form an unnatural hybrid: wood represents the authenticity of na- ture; celluloid, on the contrary, the inauthentic, the synthetic. One refers to a land of woodcutters, the other to the world of supermarkets.

And however absurd it may seem, in the most advanced nation on Earth – with its nuclear aircraft carriers, supercomputers and space stations – even now the vast majority of houses are made of wood. Of every one hundred new habitations be- gun in 1999, seventy-nine were single-family houses, most with a wooden frame.[1] What's more, wood-based construction in the United States is on the *increase*: twenty-five years ago (between 1970 and 1973), single-family dwellings made up only 57 percent of the houses built.

Here, human habitation is so tightly bound to wood that an ecological cam- paign to save a Pacific Coast forest is enough to send house prices all over America soaring. When an environmental pressure group demands an end to the destruc- tion of a forest, you can hear the trunk of the wood futures market over on Chi- cago's Mercantile Exchange begin to creak and sway. In the United States, you might say that home is where the wood is, as was the case in Europe a few centu- ries ago. Because of industrialization and the advent of steel, reinforced concrete and perforated brick, the construction industry in Europe no longer uses wood, except as material for staging or for fixtures or parquet flooring. In Europe, when you think "house," you think stone, walls of solid brick. We appear to be witness- ing here a form of temporal inversion: in the Old World, technological progress has brought about a reduction in the use of the archaic material wood, whereas in the New, such progress has increased its use a hundredfold.

However strange it may seem, it is actually progress that has made the use of wood so practical in the United States. It all began in Chicago, in 1833, at a time when the city was still no more than a collection of huts out in the sticks. Up until then, America's wooden houses had been built in the European manner, with the roof and upper floors held up by heavy beams laid on large pillars and morticed or

---

1 Bureau of the Census, *Statistical Abstract of the United States 1999*, tab. 1200. Washington, D.C.: US Government Printing Office 1999.

tenoned together by precision-made joints and the odd bolt. This method was initially used because nails and screws were scarce; at that time, they were handmade
and extremely expensive. Generation after generation of carpenters passed down
the technique, however, until it became virtually an architectural dogma. In the
United States, particularly with the mad rush for the frontier during the nineteenth century, qualified carpenters were few and far between. And in 1830, something else happened: machine-tooled nails – costing seven times less than the
handmade variety – came onto the market.

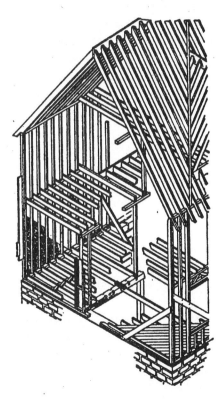

Structure of a balloon-frame house from *A History of Technology,*
vol. 5, *The Late Nineteenth Century, 1850 –1900,* Oxford: Clarendon Press, 1954.

The first indication that the new nails might make up for the dearth of carpenters came with the construction in Chicago of the Catholic Church of Santa Maria, which proved that a structure made of many lighweight wooden planks nailed to transversal floorboards could sustain not only a roof but also a second floor. In terms of construction methods, it was a real conceptual revolution. Slender joists proved capable of doing the work of the old bulky wooden beams, while a compact frame of flexible planks was shown to be even more resistant to the effects of wind and weight than were traditional structures.

The new structure seemed so absurdly light and insubstantial by comparison that its critics ironically dubbed it the "balloon frame."[2] The balloon frame was composed of slim joists of a uniform thickness (two by four inches) placed at a distance of sixteen inches and nailed together. The joists transferred all the weight of the building onto the floor and were extremely stable, both horizontally and vertically. It's interesting to consider how the balloon frame preceded Chicago's other building revolution (with the skyscraper) by fifty years, radically altering the relationship between the building's walls and the supporting armature. In both cases, the modification was in the bone structure, in the building's ribbing, which was made to take the weight formerly sustained by the external walls. On the base of this wooden frame could be laid a slate or tiled roof, along with walls of any number of materials: plaster, brick, plastic or even wood itself. In the United States, whatever type of exterior a house may present, its structure is nearly always of wood.

The advantages of the balloon frame were enormous. In the first place, it allowed constructors to use much thinner logs than in the past: previously, only ultrathick logs with a sufficient minimum diameter along the entire length could be used. Now, svelte pine trees became as desirable to the construction industry as huge oaks. Furthermore, the lightness of the armature made it easier to transport long distances and permitted the mass fabrication of elements in a sawmill, where planks could be cut to measure and numbered according to their position in the frame before being dispatched to their eventual destination. (Several improvements were made to the balloon frame during the twentieth century: it is no lon-

---

2   See S. B. Hamilton, "Building Materials and Techniques," in Singer, *A History of Technology*, vol. 5, p. 467.

ger necessary to use supporting planks two stories high for a two-floor house, for example, so joists the height of a single floor may be placed upon and held up by those below, thus permitting the use of even shorter, flimsier logs.)

Since building one of these houses required only a ladder, some nails, hammers and a few saws, just about any worker could do it, which eliminated the need for costly expert carpenters. Two workers could erect a balloon-frame house in considerably less time than twenty needed to build a house in the traditional manner. In 1855, Solon Robinson remarked, "If it had not been for the knowledge of the balloonframes, Chicago and San Francisco could never have arisen, as they did, from little villages to great cities in a single year."[3]

The ease with which the do-it-yourself home could be constructed was to have a paradoxical effect: around 1900, in many cities (Detroit, in particular), at least as many homeowners were immigrant workers as were well-to-do WASPs. While the latter had elegant and costly homes built the European way, the immigrants constructed their own balloon-frame houses single-handedly.[4]

The balloon frame was also to play a decisive role in colonization of the West. Life in the West would have been much more arduous, the push toward the Pacific considerably slower without these little houses, prefabricated and needing only to be assembled and nailed together, yet able to resist the Montana blizzards and the fierce gusts that swept across the great plains. However much we cling to the myth of the rugged pioneer building a house from tree trunks felled with a trusty axe, in reality, all the farms and ranches across the West were of the balloon-frame variety, with two-by-four-inch planks straight from the big Chicago sawmills hammered together.[5] As early as 1846, you could buy plans for standardized houses, complete with assembly instructions. By 1860, prefabricated boxes were sold complete with doors and windows.

In his celebrated reportage "Chicago," published in an 1867 edition of the *Atlantic Monthly Review,* James Parton wrote: "To economize transportation, they are *now* beginning to dispatch timber in the form of ready-made houses. There is a

---

3 Quoted by Kenneth T. Jackson in his fundamental work *Crabgrass Frontier: The Suburbanization of the United States,* New York: Oxford University Press, 1985, p. 128.

4 Ibid., pp. 118, 126.

5 Other than Kenneth T. Jackson's book, on the role of the balloon frame, see also W. Cronon, *Nature's Metropolis,* pp. 178–80.

firm in Chicago which is happy to furnish cottages, villas, school-houses, stores, taverns, churches, court-houses, or towns, wholesale and retail, and to forward them, securely packed, to any part of the country."[6] Then, as an ironic footnote, he added:

> No doubt we shall soon have the exhilaration of reading advertisements of these town-makers, to the effect, that orders for the smallest villages will be thankfully received; county towns made to order; a metropolis furnished with punctuality and dispatch; any town on our list sent, carriage paid on receipt of price; rows of cottages always on hand; churches in every stile. N. B. Clergymen and others are requested to call before purchasing elsewhere.[7]

Thus it was that an Iowa farmer could select the house of his dreams from a catalogue, send off for the standardized two-by-four-inch planking, doors and windows, and build his farmhouse with his own two hands. In 1895, the *Ladies' Home Journal* began publishing plans for houses along with specifications and assembly instructions for just five dollars. By 1900 the review's circulation had reached 2 million copies (among a total US population of 106 million).

The last major advantage of the balloon frame was that, for at least a century, up until the 1960s, it had managed to drastically reduce the cost of building a house. Together with some other, less politically neutral factors (see Chapter 10, "Faith Can Also Move Banks"), the balloon frame has made the detached home affordable for the majority of American citizens.

But along with its amazing advantages, the balloon frame had several drawbacks. First, between the external and internal walls, the vertical airways that alternated with the joists from floor to ceiling were better than a chimney uptake, better even than a bellows, at fanning flames. This feature made the frame practically a tinderbox, something Chicagoans realized the hard way in 1871 when half of their city was destroyed by the Great Fire. (It was in the wake of this inferno that the Windy City's bourgeoisie began to adopt the steel frameworks of their future skyscrapers.) A partial solution to the problem was found in fire-stop boards, which blocked the flames at various heights in the spaces between the vertical joists.

---

6 James Parton, "Chicago," *Atlantic Monthly Review,* 1867, No. 19, pp. 325–45.
7 Ibid., pp. 334–35.

Then, during the twentieth century, another fire deterrent was introduced in the form of a new, revised version of the balloon frame – called the "Western" – which no longer required vertical support joists to be two floors high. Even so, the danger remains. Although the number of house fires has fallen by 49 percent in the last seventeen years, 303,000 single-family houses burned to the ground in 1997 alone, with 12,300 injuries, 2,700 deaths and damages totaling $3.7 billion.[8] Such fires have proved to be a boon for the antismoking campaign launched in the United States during the 1980s, similar to when tobacco smokers were condemned to death as a fire-prevention measure in Tzarist Russia in 1634.

The second defect of these lighweight structures is the amount of energy they require for heating in winter and air-conditioning in summer. In a country where gasoline still costs only $1.75 per gallon, however, such voracity is viewed as a minor inconvenience. Indeed, there was a huge boom in single-family housing construction in the United States after the Yom Kippur War in October 1973 and the ensuing oil crisis, at a time when the housing industry should have been thinking about saving energy. And in the 1990s, when the Armenian sociologist Georgi Derluguian retraced the immigrant's quest for the American dream (that is, knocked down and rebuilt from scratch a single-family house he had bought in Chicago near Wilmette Avenue), he found stuffed in the air space of the old external walls as a buffer to the biting chill of winter in the Windy City only hundreds of yellowed copies of the *Chicago Tribune*.[9] Here, in substance, was America's energy conservation policy.

Yet another problem has emerged with the balloon frame: technological obsolescence. The balloon frame is a typically American invention, little used in neighboring Canada and practically unknown south of the border in Mexico. Other countries and continents that failed to adopt its revolutionary technology during the nineteenth century have, more recently, developed their own, infinitely cheaper and more resistant methods of prefabricated construction, so that the economic advantages of the balloon frame have nearly disappeared. Here we see the reverse process to that which occurred, for example, in the field of manufac-

---

8 Census Bureau, *Statistical Abstract of the United States 1999*, tab. 391, 392; and *Statistical Abstract of the United States 1992*, tab. 338.
9 Georgi Derluguian, "A Tale of Two Cities," *New Left Review*, May–June 2000, p. 66.

turing machine tools between Britain and the United States at the end of the nineteenth century. The British had developed highly advanced technology in this sector at the beginning of the century and, slaves to past glory, persisted in its use – only to find themselves superseded by new technologies from the States. Toward the close of the century – so Wolfgang Schivelbusch has told me – an English inquiry commission was sent to the United States to analyze technological progress in that country. Eventually the commission concluded that one of the reasons US technology had overtaken Britain was that British factory machinery had lasted *too long*, with the consequence that many years would pass before a machine was replaced by a more advanced generation, while machines in the United States broke down more easily and were thus more frequently replaced by newer models, accelerating the *renewal of technology*. Fragility – the fact that things broke down easily and didn't last – was in this case an ally to progress.

While the balloon-frame house may, in spatial terms, be a solid structure, highly resistant to adverse weather conditions, it is not built to last: with time, it will decay and fall into ruins. To a European, this may seem to be a defect, but Americans view it as quite the opposite. The house's perishability is considered to be an advantage, a crucial factor in the onward march of progress. Indeed, this perishability is the price Americans pay – perhaps the very condition – for their famed residential mobility. The latest figures suggest that US citizens change houses on an average of once every five or six years. Every year between 1992 and 1998, 16.3 percent of Americans (one of every six) moved to a different house, adding up to a yearly exodus of some 40 million people. Of these, 6 percent had moved to another county, while a good 3 percent of the American population uprooted annually and moved to a different state. With a life expectancy of 75.4 years, Americans move to a different house an *average* of more than twelve times (12.2 times) over the course of a life, including 4.5 times to a different county and 2.2 times to a new state.[10]

This results in an extraordinary coming and going of moving vans. With the movers astutely trying to reduce their goods to be moved to a minimum, houses in the United States are often rented already furnished with large wardrobes, fitted

---

10 Census Bureau, *Statistical Abstract of the United States, 1996* and *1998* editions, tab. 33 and 30 respectively.

kitchens with bank-vault refrigerators and washer-dryers in the basement (every new inhabitant would otherwise have to either buy an entirely new set of furnishings again or drag his or her things from one end of the continent to the other). This is also why you can sign a rental contract in the United States for only three or four months. (Another reason is that those who rent – outside of the urban ghettos – are usually fairly well-off.) Again, everything turns on the multifaceted concept of practicality.

Here, geographic and residential mobility is seen as a value and therefore as something for which other comforts may be sacrificed, which is why people are willing to pay so much for it. "Freedom has a price," and mobility is freedom's most immediate and tangible expression. The free man is he who can plant himself anywhere he chooses, changing his house or his job at will. (In terms of American social organization, the "his" is not simply politically incorrect grammar; this kind of freedom is tailored to the measure of man, not woman.)

Yet this change cannot simply remain a remote possibility on the distant horizon. On the contrary, in the United States, you must test out and repeat the process so as to convince yourself that you really are free, especially when, as occasionally happens, you begin to feel fenced in and tied down. While the way to tyranny may begin with roadblocks – restrictions on movement in the form of police permits or internal passports, because without movement there is no real freedom – movement alone is not sufficient to guarantee freedom. Imagine having *only* freedom of movement. Yet in the United States, the freedom of settlement has a much greater emotional value than it has elsewhere, because here is a nation born of movement and migration. It is for this reason that the Exodus, the flight of the Jews from Egypt, resonates so strongly across the Atlantic. Exodus is the founding gesture of the United States, a gesture that retains a stubbornly political valence even in terms of the choices of everyday life.

Speaking of the options each of us has for expressing our dissatisfaction with some particular commodity (such as a car) or with an institution (school) or even with a political movement (a party or union), Albert Hirschman observes that the classical economic reaction, that of the market economy, is of "exit," or defection. If I can't get satisfaction from brand X automobile, I switch brands; if I'm not happy with a school in the education market, I change to a different one; or I might leave party Y or union Z in the politics market, or simply stop voting for them. An extreme case of this is when "investments flee" from a country that turns out to be "hostile" to them. Hirschman goes on to say that you can actually express your malcontent in another effective way, and that is to protest, to raise your "voice." In some cases, indeed, the "exit" option can turn out to be counterproductive, leaving no one to protest against the poor quality of a certain brand or service. This is how private sector competition often leads to a deterioration of public services: being able to take a bus rather than a train, I become less interested in the speed and punctuality of trains *tout court*, with the result that I stop protesting slowness and delays, which means that the trains get later and later. But Hirschman also notes that the choice of "voice" has never really caught on in America, and this is because "the United States owes its very existence and growth to millions of decisions favoring exit over voice. ... With the country having been founded on exit and having thrived on it, the belief in exit as a fundamental and beneficial social mechanism has been unquestioning."[11]

The United States was thus born under the Exit sign. Even the country's most radical protest movements, in denouncing the existing system, have tended to opt for defection and dropout, perhaps by forming an alternative desert community like those of the hippies. Upping sticks, changing houses, moving out are not just ways of exercising constitutional rights: these actions reaffirm the Constitution itself by allowing people to live it in their own lives.

The problem is that this continuous state of being in transit, this restlessness of the soul, with bags perpetually packed and ready, coexists with an all-consuming love of one's own house. Systematic impermanence is forever wedded to adoration of the eternal flame of hearth and home. The same is true of the family, which, although central to the values of American society, in reality is a fleeting, fragmented entity. As soon as the kids are grown, they tend to drift away, scattering across the whole continent in an irreversible diaspora (encouraged and made possible by their mobility).

American law allows you to shoot and kill anyone who enters your house without permission. Kenneth Jackson cites Gaston Bachelard, who saw space as di-

---

11 Albert D. Hirschman, *Exit, Voice and Loyalty*, Cambridge, Mass.: Harvard University Press, 1970, pp. 106, 112.

vided into the two great complexes of Home/Not-Home, just as he saw the world split into I/Not-I. The house, therefore, is a symbol of the Self. And as a symbol of the Self, a shabby, run-down house is indicative of a sloppy, lazy I. It almost goes without saying that only a seedy, dissolute (and poor?) individual would live in a dilapidated dwelling.[12]

The contradiction between this jealous attachment to the house as a value (hominess) – the hearth as heart – and the ease with which you can simply pick up and leave is in reality only a formal one. For the time you live in one place, you manicure your garden down to the last blade of grass, investing body and soul in perfecting the lawn. Then, when it comes time to abandon the space for another identical patch of grass, you do so without regret. The symbolic idolatry manifested toward a house (and its hominess) is equal only to the nonchalance with which the material building is bought, sold and abandoned. The physical construction – the balloon frame – is simply an instrument, a tool of the house-as-value.

Europeans, although less inclined to homemaking, in this sense have a more fetishistic rapport with their family abode: suffice it to recall the rhetoric that surrounds the ancestral home. The physical, material house is viewed as a value in itself. Far from being a mere tool, it represents solidity (while in the United States, it represents "realty"). In continental Europe, not by chance, we talk about investing in *immobile* or *immeuble* (words that relate both to property and to that which is immobile, fixed), in bricks or in stone, whereas Americans speak about *real* estate. The difference is the same as that between an expensive watch given to you as a present when you were a boy (for first communion in Catholic countries), a watch built to last a lifetime, that you fondle with pleasure, like a fine fountain pen, and a Swatch, an economic, precise timepiece of which you have an entire collection, so that you can select the model that best matches the color of your jacket, that you can discard as easily as a ballpoint pen. This comparison with the watch goes back to Alexis de Tocqueville, when he described the nature of products manufactured by "democratic peoples":

---

12 K. T. Jackson, *Crabgrass Frontier*, p. 52.

[The workman] strives to invent methods that may enable him not only to work better, but more quickly and more cheaply; or, if he cannot succeed in that, to diminish the intrinsic quality of the thing he makes, without rendering it wholly unfit for the use for which it is intended. When none but the wealthy had watches, they were almost all very good ones; few are now made that are worth much, but everybody has one in his pocket. Thus the democratic principle not only tends to direct the human mind to the useful arts, but it induces the artisan to produce with great rapidity many imperfect commodities, and the consumer to content himself with these commodities.[13]

This instrumental rapport with the surrounding environment, whereby everything becomes disposable, represented a new and highly different way of relating to the world (and therefore of being ourselves) that began to predominate and spread during the modern age. The causes of this rapport could be attributed not solely to technology or to the laws of the market, nor even to the logic of domination and exploitation: in terms of the balloon-frame house, what would it mean to "exploit a house"? Rather, this rapport proved to be the only possible reconciliation between two opposing myths: that of hearth and home (symbolic of your sense of rootedness, which figured you as an irremovable oak tree) and that of the aspiration to freedom (the pursuit of geographical and physical mobility that would sweep away all roots). To obtain both of these things, to plant the improbable seeds of a "movable oak," it was necessary to dematerialize the roots, to detach them from the physical place where you lived, so that they could now turn up wherever you happened to lay your hat, even in motion itself, literally abstracted from the site where you put down your roots. In the Latin world, the *gens* traditionally resided in the place where stood the altar to the family's tutelary deities, the *Lares;* Americans today do not take their home fires with them, yet standardization of the dwellings and houses guarantees the continuity of hearth and home across space and time. There it is again – that word, *standardization.* The fact that houses are all constructed in exactly the same way, following the same logic, with the same accessories and using the same two-by-four-inch planks means that, no matter where you go, be it Maine or Texas, you will find yourself in the same house. You will *always feel at home.*

---

13 Alexis de Tocqueville, *De la démocratie en Amérique* (1835). Eng. trans. *Democracy in America,* New York: Knopf, 1994, vol. II, p. 50.

The impersonal, anonymous feel of American houses, far from being the result of cut-price construction or a lack of flair on the part of designers, is actually part of the package. As John B. Jackson notes, from its very inception, the balloon-frame house

> was quick and simple to build, it was indifferent to local and folk architectural traditions, and it was seen as temporary; not that it would collapse, but that it would soon be sold and passed on to newcomers. Solon Robinson and other writers on western pioneering thus advised families to build their balloon frame houses as impersonally as possible so that they could be acceptable to any prospective purchaser.[14]

We see here that having houses built "as impersonally as possible" is considered a positive quality, one that facilitates exchange. Standardization, the dwelling as a mass-produced instrument, allows you to find the exact same model of house, with the same lawn, the same driveway, located in a suburb identical to the one you just came from, a thousand miles from "home." Just as you can travel across the world and be sure to find the same Big Mac wherever you go, so too can you move anywhere in America, from the Atlantic to the Pacific coast, and be sure to inhabit the same single-family balloon-frame house as you did before. It doesn't matter if the house is fragile, if it starts to deteriorate within the space of a few years. That house will live again through its myriad copies, its unending replicability.

You could say that it's "the house in the age of mechanical reproduction," to borrow the category Walter Benjamin introduced in the field of art. In this era, Benjamin writes, it is the concept of authenticity that becomes problematic. While we knew the "original" of a work of art to be authentic and its copies to be "fake," still we must ask in what sense a photographic masterpiece is authentic or a reproduction of it fake. The work of art has lost its "aura," where *aura* means the *distance* of its being unrepeatable: by reproducing the work of art, technology *brings it closer* to us. The relationship between technical reproducibility of the balloon frame house across the Atlantic and the aura of the ancestral abode in Europe repeats that of the reproduction to the original artwork. "Uniqueness and perma-

---

14 Cited by Allan D. Wallis, *Wheel Estate: The Rise and Decline of Mobile Homes,* New York: Oxford University Press, 1991, p. 161; on the same page is a schematic diagram of a balloon-frame house specifying the function of every joist, rafter, beam and board.

nence are as closely linked in the latter [the painting] as are transitoriness and re-producibility in the former [the reproduction]." The secular dwelling is as unique and lasting as the balloon frame is labile and repeatable. If through reproduction the work of art is brought closer to all, the balloon frame makes the house afford-able to all.

The difference is not wholly negative. Just as "the work of art becomes a cre-ation with entirely new functions, among which the one we are conscious of, the artistic function, later may be recognized as incidental" and "to an ever greater de-gree the work of art reproduced becomes the work of art designed for reproducibility,"[15] so too may the formerly recognized function become inciden-tal in the formation labeled *house*, while, in the age of mass production, we have a "hearth and home" designed from the outset to be multiplied. A new idea of habi-tation comes into being, a new aesthetic that bears a different relation to the out-side world. What to the foreign eye might seem ugly repetitiveness is, in fact, a creative solution, brought about by industrial standardization, to the problem of how to render compatible two opposing drives, two incompatible sentiments: do-mestic rootedness and existential nomadism.

Only on an American freeway might you expect to be overtaken by a house, cur-tains billowing from behind the windows, complete with chimney stack, sloping roof and occasionally even a front porch. The little house on the freeway is mounted on the enormous trailer of one of those gleaming, chrome-plated trucks with a menacing snout that come roaring up behind you on the Interstate. The standard dimensions of these mobile homes are twelve by thirty-six feet. Accord-ing to the *Statistical Abstract*, of 112.3 million habitation units in the United States, 7.4 percent, or 8.3 million, are either mobile homes or trailers.[16]

Compared to the more refined mass-production methods of the replicant house, the mobile home represents an archaic, primitive means for reconciling perpetual hominess with residential mobility. While moving to a new residence in the previous case entails abandoning your former home for another identical to it,

15 Walter Benjamin, "The Work of Art in the Age of Mechanical Reproduction," in *Illuminations*, London: Fontana Press, 1992, citations from pp. 217–19.
16 Census Bureau, *Statistical Abstract of the United States 1999*, tab. 1212.

in the latter, the house itself is physically transported, functioning in the manner of a snail's shell, a pod you can carry wherever you go, permitting you to keep moving while at the same time allowing you to feel protected. The technological leap is similar to that which took place in the late Middle Ages when, instead of actual money being sent in gold, an order of payment was dispatched (a precursor to the modern-day bank check). In the first case, the gold was moved physically; in the second, the concept was moved, remaining identical even thousands of miles away.

Yet as often happens, the technologically old-fashioned mobile home chronologically postdates the mass-produced balloon-frame house. And because it employs twentieth-century developments in production technology, it presents itself as the more advanced specimen, assimilating the automobile industry into the construction field. Not by chance does the title of the most exhaustive book on the subject – Allan D. Wallis's *Wheel Estate* – allude to real estate; the idea of wheel estate, however, is a contradiction in terms, because it refers to fixed property that is at the same time mobile. Again, two opposing ideas are reconciled, but this time in material terms. And if the mobile home adopts advances from the automobile industry, this is not so much because it is on wheels, as because it is industrially produced on an assembly line.

The hybrid status of the mobile home between the house and the car emerges in the difficulty of defining its essence – that is to say, in defining the nature of its frame. *The Statistical Abstract of the United States* defines a mobile home as "a mobile residence at least 10 ft wide and 35 ft long, designed to be towed on its own chassis and without need of permanent foundations." Whoever heard of a house having a *chassis*?

The problems of definition do not end here: the fact that a mobile home has a chassis gives it the status of a vehicle rather than of a building, impeding its placement in designated residential areas. In addition, a car's chassis is made of metal, while the chassis of a mobile home is wooden, with the result that the US Department of Housing and Urban Development (HUD) has attempted to impose a metal chassis on mobile homes.[17]

---

17 A. D. Wallis, *Wheel Estate*, p. 225.

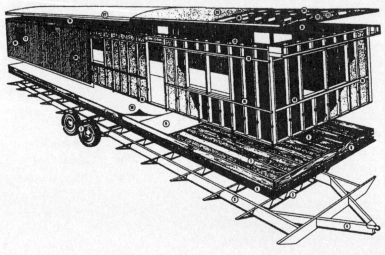

Cross-section diagram of a mobile home, from Allan D. Wallis, Wheel Estate: The Rise and Decline of Mobile Homes. © 1991 by Oxford University Press, Inc. and used by permission of Oxford University Press, Inc.

Halfway between a car and a house, the mobile home has neither the mobility of the former nor the comfort and spaciousness of the latter. Too large to be easily moved, it is at the same time too small to be really lived in. At twenty-seven by twelve feet, it looks enormous on the road, yet it yields a total surface area of less than 330 square feet. And with each mobile home housing on average of 2.4 people, living conditions are, to say the least, cramped. (At 135 square feet per head, you have less *lebensraum* in a mobile home than the standard space per person allowed for [in theory] in the ex–Soviet Union – a roomy 200 square feet.) The most spacious solution, the double wide, is formed by joining two units side by side to double the width of the house, to twenty-four feet, yielding a total surface area of 660 square feet, the size of a small city apartment. And here lies another contradiction: though the mobile home is based on the idea of infinite, wide-open spaces, such as the boundless prairie, people are quite content to live jammed together in poky little rooms in the midst of these prodigious expanses. The thing that imme-

diately strikes you as you drive across the immense spaces of the American countryside is how small the houses are.

As a mass-produced item (their makers now prefer to call their products *manu-factured homes,* because of the negative connotations of the phrase *mobile home*),
the mobile home represents a case of standardization taken to extremes. Not only
are its dimensions standard, its components interchangeable, but it requires a
standardized environment as well. The calibers and gauges of the water inlets, the
unions of the dumpings, the electric sockets must all be the same wherever you
go. To function, the mobile home needs specially equipped identical sites – sites
that recall hospital wards, where the rows of trailers are the bedridden patients
kept alive by a forest of external tubes, drips, and catheters. In this case, though,
we are talking about the form of water and sewage pipes, electric cables and cable
TV sockets.

For the mobile home as well, then, the idea of movement is illusory, because
each time you move, you find yourself at a site identical to the last. Unlike a sta-
tionary house, however, the mobile home's relationship to the external world is
akin to that of a caravan-serraglio – you have the makeshift sense of an oasis of caravans surrounded by desert, of merely a stopping-off point, albeit one where you
may end up "stopping off" for twenty years or more. In this sense, the mobile
home retains the character it had during its golden age, first with the great projects
of Roosevelt's New Deal and then with the war effort, when the government provided accommodation – both transitory and semi-permanent – for hundreds of
thousands of workers: in 1945, 5,000 trailers were added to the already-existing
9,600 prefabricated houses and 16,000 huts at the atomic research center in Oak
Ridge, Tennessee. This model of encampment was highly successful and widely
imitated.

As another example, Exxon constructed a residential village of mobile homes
for 2,000 miners at Battlement Mesa, Colorado, near a deposit of oil shale: when
the mining work was finished, the mobile homes were converted into a residential
village for the retired.[18] Battlement Mesa provides a good example of the extent to
which the so-called mobility of the mobile home is pure myth (the camper is a dif-

---

18 On the use of trailers during the war, see K. T. Jackson, *Crabgrass Frontier,* pp. 261–62; and A. D.
   Wallis, *Wheel Estate,* pp. 83–93. On Battlement Mesa, see Wallis, pp. 192–93.

ferent case, entirely): in reality, 95 percent of mobile homes go straight from the factory to a permanent site and never see another road. Statistically speaking, mobile homes are moved no more than are cottages. In many cases, then, "mobility" has only to do with the structure's greater cheapness, its mass-produced character and the low-rent lifestyle it implies.

The average price of a mobile home in 1998 was $43,800,[19] compared to $185,000 for a new house constructed on site (representing an increase of 58 percent over a period of seventeen years for the mobile home, as opposed to 65 percent for the conventional house). Large mobile homes with three bedrooms and two bathrooms do exist, costing on average of $100,000 apiece, but generally the mobile home is a solution to the problem of "affordable housing," relegated to the poorer classes. To make payments on a $200,000 mortgage requires an income of $70,000 per year (a general rule of thumb in the US housing market is that you will not be granted a mortgage valued at more than three times your annual salary); to purchase a $43,000 mobile home, you need earn only $31,500 per year, a sum hovering on the poverty line.[20] The relationship between house value and annual income is, however, much less favorable in the case of mobile homes, whose mortgages are more expensive because the poor are considered "untrustworthy" and because the homes themselves are harder to keep tabs on, resulting in frequent backsliding or failure to make payments. Once again, the proverb rings true: "Only lend money to those who already have it."

All this explains why mobile homes have become notorious as refuges for society's unfortunates: 37 percent of the families who live in mobile homes have an annual income of less than $20,000 (barely above the poverty line).[21] Populated by the poor, mobile home parks are regarded as closed, alien communities comparable in European terms only to Gypsy encampments. Here, too, as with the Gypsies of the Old World, a campfire community spirit is born in response to discrimination experienced in the external world. Here you have the feeling of being part of an exclusive group, impermeable from the outside: mobile home or

---

19 Census Bureau, *Statistical Abstract of the United States 1999*, tab. 1204.
20 Here I apply to 1998's values the proportions uncovered by a *Chicago Tribune* investigation of 5 May 1993.
21 Data for 1996 taken from the Foremost Insurance Website, www.foremost.com/ market_facts.

camper owners frequently run into each other again on the same campgrounds. It is their mobility (albeit mythical mobility) that separates the internal community from the outside. There arises what sociologists would call a subculture of mobile homes and trailers, a form of *ghettoization*, traces of which appear in American cop movies, where the trailer park is usually the first place the police go in search of the bad guys.

Yet during the Reagan era, and even during the Clinton era, many within the middle classes found themselves in trailer park purgatory. The average constant dollar income of families living in such accommodation actually decreased slightly in the years between 1981 and 1990, from $14,500 to $14,000, dropping even further, to $13,400, by 1996 (even if the nominal value in that year was $24,500). This was the lean, mean decade, when the poor got even poorer.

At the beginning of the 1980s, to boost sales and attract customers of a higher socioeconomic level, the mobile home industry requested that HUD consider the possibility of categorizing mobile homes in different classes, in imitation of the division of habitations into different classes that took place during the 1930s to encourage people to buy private houses. In this discontinuous taxonomy, there must be a luxury A class (double-wide homes mounted on a permanent base with attached side garage), medium-sized B and C classes and finally low-grade D and E classes. Homes built before 1976, when HUD established a national standard, were classified in these groups.

Despite these promotional efforts, the prevailing image of mobile home residents remains one of people who are not only poor, but above all old, usually retired people who have sold off their old permanent house – worth considerably more – to buy a cheap mobile home and live off the difference. The average age of the household head of a mobile home family in 1981 was forty-six; by 1990, it had risen to fifty-one (50.8), and by 1996, it was almost fifty-three (52.8). Even more significantly, in 1980, one out of every four heads of household was under thirty; ten years later, the number of twenty-something parents had fallen to less than one in ten; and by 1996, the figure stood at one in twelve (8 percent), while 27 percent were retired.

More than mobile homes, the elderly tend to buy motor homes, which they use to travel about the continent from coast to coast, giving the impression of being on eternal vacation. It's a vacation that is both cheap and short-lived, lasting only as long as their health holds out. Many use their motor homes to escape the bracing northern winters. Known as snowbirds, they come in convoys in the autumn on the freeways, pursued by icy winds and snowstorms, heading south from Illinois, Michigan, Minnesota and Wisconsin or Ohio toward the warmer climates of Florida, Texas, Arizona or California. Around springtime, the procession of camper vans driven by old-timers – the so-called gray panthers – turns around and heads back north. The rich return to their houses in the north, while the poorer migrate to a campground on the shores of one of the Great Lakes, north of Lake Michigan, beyond Traverse City or at Isle Royale on Lake Superior.

Life in the trailers and motor homes that alight in these camps is even more wretched and cramped than life in a mobile home. While the latter is a house that can more or less be transported on wheels, the motor home is more like a small van pretending to be a house. In the hybrid realm between vehicle and house, it is closer to a vehicle, while the mobile home is more similar to a house. Even the larger motor homes have a living area of only 150 square feet, including driver and passenger seats, kitchen space and bathroom. Imagine living for months in one of these things, elbow-to-elbow with your battle-worn partner. There are, of course, many mongrel forms of habitation: fixed houses with a mobile home attached, mobile homes hooked up to a camper that provides a spare room, two motor homes hooked up to each other.

A final paradox of Americans' fabled mobility lies in the fact that it represents the reverse of two common assumptions about nomadism. First, the elderly reveal themselves to be much more nomadic than the young or middle-aged; and second, those in the low- to medium-income bracket hit the public road more than do their medium- and high-income counterparts. Those well-worn phrases "the restlessness of youth" and "the sedentariness of old age" give way to a *senile restlessness* or, better, *mobile senility*. On the hills of Santa Barbara, California, the world's richest pensioners live in splendid villas. Here, elderly but extremely fit gentlemen pedal energetically to the bakers to buy the morning baguette. Below, meanwhile, on the edge of the Pacific, near the Vons supermarket, the local campground plays host to thousands of middle-class pensioners living jammed together in endless rows of camper vans, along with their menageries of household pets (the number of dogs you can fit into one of those things is incredible!). Like the seabirds who throng the ocean beaches, they seem to have alighted here, ready to migrate in spring, their family heirlooms safely locked in the casket of the motor home.

7

Lumber Mines

"Where have the vast forests of the Great Lakes gone?" The question echoes louder and louder in your head as you slowly make your way through the fields and fruit farms – with their apples, pears and cherries – of Michigan's Lower Peninsula, which stretches from Flint to Charlevoix; or as you head away from Chicago northwest into central Wisconsin; or, again, as you drive through the boundless corn belt that lies to the south of Minnesota. You recall the Hemingway story "Up in Michigan," and images of rugged lumberjacks flash before your eyes. Today, however, nothing remains to distinguish these regions from the great central plains of Iowa, Illinois and Missouri.

You find yourself overcome by a profound sense of delusion, as though someone has robbed you of the woodlands – just as, in Chicago, someone has had the gall to snatch the great slaughterhouses (demolished or fallen into ruin) and Grand Central Station (razed to the ground in 1971) from under your eyes. It hits you once more how the roots of Chicago's greatness have been ripped from the ground, how the city's glory is built on ghosts: the long-abandoned stockyards, the railroads whose tracks lie eaten away by rust, and the boundless woods of the Great Lakes, now deforested.

For decades during the second half of the nineteenth century, Chicago's fast-accumulating wealth grew on trees, as the whole region of the Great Lakes gradually succumbed to deforestation. The world's lumber capital, Chicago is where Puritanism took the shape of a city: the deep, dense forest – wild, pagan and dark as sin, a shadowy realm inhabited by heathen savages – was an obstacle to progress. The forest held back the cultivation of the fields and, at the same time, could provide an ideal means (wood) for colonization. It was civilization's duty to cut it down.

And so, with their typical alacrity, the Americans got down to the task of destroying the biotic canopy of Earth's crust. By the beginning of the twentieth century, according to the most conservative estimates, they had deforested 300 million acres of trees, an area more than four times the size of Italy or two-and-a-half times that of France.[1] While in Europe the increasing scarcity of wood triggered the Industrial Revolution – a shortage that was to determine the triumph of coal and steam – across the Atlantic, the opposite was the case: it was the abundance of wood that accelerated the industrialization of the United States. An example of this may be found in the case of the balloon-frame house: while technological progress in Europe led to a reduction in the use of wood in the construction industry, in the US, advances in architecture (with the balloon-frame house) led to a *boom* in the consumption of wood for housing. America's wood-frame houses, in fact, are responsible for much of the deforestation of the country.

To industrialize the country and colonize the West, wood was needed for everything. Wood fires warmed bodies and cooked food and moved the trains, with wooden cars moving toward stations also made of wood. Farms were surrounded by wood-pole fencing. In 1880, the *Northwestern Lumberman* wrote that:

> Every new settler upon the fertile prairies means one more added to the vast army of lumber consumers, one more new house to be built, one more barn, one more 40 acres of land to be fenced, one more or perhaps a dozen corn cribs needed. ... [I]t means an extension of railroad lines with the vast consumption of lumber consequent thereupon; it means an additional incentive to other projected settlers to take farms near the fast corner; it means churches, school houses and stores, sidewalks, paved streets.[2]

---

1 Michael Williams, *Americans and Their Forests: A Historical Geography*, Cambridge, Mass.: Cambridge University Press, 1989, pp. 489–90.
2 Edition of 22 March 1880, cited by W. Cronon, *Nature's Metropolis*, p. 153. On Chicago as world capital of the lumber trade, see his chapter "The Wealth of Nature," pp. 148–206.

Thus wood fueled the process of industrialization, which in turn devoured wood in an ever-accelerating spiral that from the 1840s on became a veritable whirlwind. The boom was timely, because now, thanks to the opening of the Michigan–Illinois Canal (1848), Chicago could have its slice of the white pine forest. Pride of the Great Lakes, the white pine averaged fifty feet tall and could grow steadily for more than two hundred years until it was fully developed, by which time it might have grown to in excess of two hundred feet (the height of a twenty-story building). The finest examples of the species had trunks up to six feet in diameter. To form a ring around their twenty-foot circumference, four men holding hands were needed. Indeed, until 1880, lumberjacks would not deign to chop down a tree whose trunk had a diameter of less than three feet. The white pine was thus the fruit of a centuries-old accumulation of natural capital, "dead wood" languishing on the earth for countless solar cycles: to Chicago, it was "manna from wood-fuel heaven."

To its great misfortune, the white pine had extraordinary qualities that made it ripe for human exploitation. The fact that the tree shed its lower branches as it grew meant that its trunk was smooth and unknotted for at least thirty feet up. Its extremely strong, highly resilient grain was able to bear enormous loads and tensions, yet it was not coriaceous, so the wood was soft enough to be worked by hand. And as a last decisive advantage, unlike other hardwoods, white pine *floated*, which meant that it could be transported by water. This last characteristic was important: the heavy use of lumber had always been resisted largely because it was so difficult to transport. The woodland areas, notorious for rain, were damp, their slithering muddy paths so waterlogged that negotiation of a horse and cart for any more than the briefest of distances without getting bogged down was impossible. In the regions around the Great Lakes, the terrain was literally a quagmire. (Wisconsin, for example, boasts ten thousand lakes and ponds, a supremacy contested only by Minnesota.) White pine, on the other hand, could be moved by means of mile-long rafts, which required wide waterways but which resolved the transportation problem. Still today on the Hudson and San Lorenzo Rivers you see these endless convoys of logs making their sluggish way down from northern Canada toward the Atlantic. The waterways were crucial for moving wood, which explains why the Great Lakes became so important and why Americans began furiously constructing a vast network of canals during the first half of the nineteenth century. It also explains why Chicagoans were so obstinate in finishing the Michigan–Illinois Canal, which would permit the white pine logs to sail down from the Great Lakes to the Mississippi Valley, then down to New Orleans and, from there, to the West Indies and Europe.

Their obstinacy paid off. While some 32 million board feet of lumber had arrived in Chicago in 1847,[3] by 1851, three years after the opening of the canal, that figure had quadrupled to 125 million; by 1869, 1 billion board feet of wood sailed into Chicago. For the next sixty years, until 1930, the volume of wood unloaded on the city's docks never once dipped below that 1869 figure. At the apex, in 1892, 2.7 billion board feet were docked in the port.

Among Chicago's *arrivals,* lumber was the only sector for which water transportation continued to predominate over shipment by rail, at least until the end of the nineteenth century. (On the other hand, 95 percent of the wood *departing* from Chicago for the big eastern cities or the new western towns went by rail.) Although wood made up three-quarters of the cargos coming into Chicago, the railroads carried less than 10 percent of them up until 1880; until 1898, the railroads' percentage of lumber shipments remained under 40. The epic of lumber is thus very much a waterborne saga.

It was late autumn, after harvest, when the lumbermen came to Chicago to recruit crews of woodcutters. Even though wages in the city were higher than elsewhere (between $100 and $200 per season, along with miserable room and board in a shack), the supply of labor was also greater, and employers could select the best lumberjacks for their crews. In Chicago, the lumbermen could also stock up on equipment (axes, saws, hubs for their carts) and provisions (tons of beans, pork, butter, salt, wheat, fodder, oats for both men and horses). But above all, credit could be gotten in Chicago in exchange for the wood to be peddled the following spring: credit – that is, new money – in a sector that had always suffered from problems with liquidity, dramatic bottlenecks in the flow of cash. What the lum-

---

3   A board foot is the unit of measurement most commonly used in the lumber business: 1 board foot (bf) = 1 foot x 1 foot x 1 inch, whereas 1 cubic foot (cf) = 1 foot x 1 foot x 1 foot; thus, 1 cubic foot = 12 board feet.

bermen shelled out in late autumn they would not get back until six months later, if they were lucky. Credit – that is, the availability of capital – was thus the principal lever that moved the wood that made Chicago great.

When the weather began to worsen, the teams headed north toward the "lumber mines," where trees were ripe for the reaping. For the first few years, they chopped down only those trunks closest to the waterways. It wasn't long, however, before the woodcutters had to move farther and farther away from the banks. In the meantime, the original fifteen-man crews grew to teams of a hundred or more as the woodmen began to penetrate deeper into more icy realms. Ice alone could form a base solid enough that horses could drag the massive trunks along the pathways, whether by sled or cart, up to the edge of the slough. The most famous wood "quarries" of the nineteenth century, in fact, have the names of marshlands: the Beef Slough in Wisconsin or the West Newton Slough in Minnesota.

The enormous woodpiles lay all winter waiting for the thaw. The fate of the harvest depended on how much snow had fallen. If relatively little snow had fallen, the thaw would not produce enough water that the wood would float. A heavy fall of rapidly melting snow was needed, a phenomenon that occurred only once a year and that, for a brief period, allowed the cavalcade of trunks to flow toward the main waterways. From there, these weighty processions set off toward the Great Lakes and the canals.

No historian could restrain from recounting the massive logjams that formed on the rivers when a trunk wedged itself against the bank or on the riverbed, blocking the path of the hundreds of thousands of trunks following it and causing them to pile up into a huge dam. Several of these logjams have attained the status of legend, such as the one that occurred in 1869 at Chippewa Falls in Wisconsin, where the bottleneck of lumber stretched to fifteen miles and at some points the dams formed by the logs were more than thirty feet high. But that was nothing compared to the number of trunks that jammed on the Menominee River in 1889 – totaling almost 80 billion board feet of wood, three times as much as in the Chippewa Falls jam. Unblocking the dam was a dangerous job, the stuff of legends among lumberjacks; the obstructing trunks had to be dislodged with hooks, with the risk of the whole pile of logs crashing down on top of you. Even today, photographs of nineteenth-century woodcutters strolling underneath a huge, chaotic mass of trunks, looking for a way to unblock them, are fascinating.

Yet the song of the lumberjack would never be able to compete with that of the cowboy in terms of legendary resonance. Perhaps the destructive nature of the work prevented the woodcutters from attaining the mythic status of the good hero (although it could be said that cowboys, too, drove their steers to the slaughterhouses, even when they were not responsible for butchering them). Or perhaps the lack of status is because the wood industry became immediately prey to the lumber barons (similar to the railroad barons of nineteenth-century US capitalism). On this account, a Frederick Weyerhauser had nothing to learn from a Daniel Guggenheim, Andrew Carnegie or John D. Rockefeller.

The ruthlessness of the sector was rooted in its material base – in the ability to grab huge expanses of forest at the lowest possible cost. Around 1860, Ezra Cornell bought half a million acres of white pine forest in the Chippewa River valley to exercise what he himself called "a fearful and terrible monopoly"[4]: gazing today at the Arcadian idyll that is Cornell University, you would never imagine it was founded on such monopolistic terror. The power of capital joined forces with the connivance of politicians in selling off state property, with lots of national forest going to "friends" at special bargain prices, just as vast stretches of territory had gone to the railroad companies through land grants. Behind the lumber companies, too, lurked the shadowy hand of the banks, in particular the ubiquitous J. Pierpont Morgan.

When at the beginning of the twentieth century Theodore Roosevelt launched an offensive against the big monopolies, an inquiry was also opened into the concentration of power in the wood industry. Although the inquiry began in 1906, its findings were not made public until 1913 (an indication of the level of resistance the commission encountered). According to the report, in the so-called Lake States of Minnesota, Wisconsin and Michigan, 12 percent of the available lumber was owned by the leading 4 proprietors, 22 percent by the leading 17. The leading 44 proprietors owned 37 percent, while a total of 215 proprietors retained 65 percent.[5] In 1913, this concentration was even greater on the Pacific Coast, where

---

4   M. Williams, *Americans and Their Forests*, p. 217
5   Ibid, p. 218.

Frederick Weyerhaeuser laid claim to 96 billion board feet spread over a surface area of around 2 million acres (a region the size of Rhode Island and Delaware together); the Northern Pacific Railway owned 36.5 billion board feet on about 3 million acres; and the Southern Pacific Railroad owned 106 billion board feet on 4.5 million acres.

These "big three" companies alone controlled 9.5 million acres of woods. But in reality, their monopoly extended even further. While Weyerhaeuser owned 96 billion board feet, he was able to control – through share packets, reciprocal holdings and dummy companies – a staggering 292 billion board feet, or one-quarter of all US commercial lumber.[6] (These billions of board feet of wood were counted while the trees were still planted in the earth, each with its branches, pinecones and green leaves. If measuring living trees in terms of volume was difficult, there was certainly nothing illogical about it; the process was the same as that used today to estimate the capacity of an oil field.)

The concentration process required larger sawmills that had to process even bigger quantities of wood to justify their existence, resulting in the deforestation of increasingly vaster areas of land. Transporting all of this wood required a system of collection basins and booms (hence the term *booming companies*). In 1850, only a few thousand dollars was needed to get started in the lumber business. In 1870, Weyerhaeuser and his partners invested $1 million to start up the Beef Slough booming company.

So that they could work not only in winter but in all seasons, the great lumbermen began building rail lines to penetrate the sylvan solitude, their sole aim being to carry away the felled trunks (building these lines was fairly simple to do, because, thanks to government land grants, much of this territory already belonged to the railroad companies). Traversed by this tight weave of railway lines, certain parts of Wisconsin, when mapped, took on the physiognomy of an embroidered lace doily. Oddly, these lines were to diminish Chicago's importance, because they permitted the lumbermen to dry their wood at the railroad terminal and to dispatch it to customers already cut, thus circumventing the Chicago merchants and wholesalers. The city had built its fortune as a world lumber capital and as Queen of the West on the principle that wood arrived there by river and left by

---

6 Ibid, pp. 426–28.

rail. When lumber began not only to leave but to arrive by rail, it no longer needed to stop in Chicago. It was just passing through.

But the lumber industry was to survive the decline of its most important center by only a few years. It's appalling to think today of the speed with which the lumbermen came, saw, destroyed entire regions and then vanished. The first great area boom was at Muskegon (in the Michigan's Lower Peninsula) in 1864. In 1870, the Beef Slough boom was inaugurated in Wisconsin. Between 1875 and 1883 on the Saginaw River, Michigan, 500 to 600 billion board feet of wood were being processed annually.[7] But in 1890, after little more than a decade, Frederick Weyerhaeuser was to shift the base of his operations to Idaho and Washington state. The wood by the lakes was running out; the lumber mines were close to exhaustion. For millennia, the nomad peoples of the Eurasian steppe would migrate once their flocks had reduced entire plains to desert. In nineteenth-century America, the lumbermen were the nomads of capital who had replaced the shepherds.

Wood production in the Great Lakes region reached a peak of 9.9 billion board feet in 1890, after which it began to decline. It leveled off at around one-tenth of that peak sum in the 1920s and in the years following World War II, when assault on the nation's forests shifted to the West and the South. (The lumbermen's subsequent murderous offensives in various regions have led to a disorienting shift in America's woodland geography: you wouldn't expect that southern regions such as eastern Mississippi, Louisiana, Alabama and Georgia are today among the most densely wooded in the country.)

So it was that vast stretches of Wisconsin, Michigan and Minnesota began around the turn of the century to resemble convulsed deserts dotted with odd stumps of trees, torn-off branches, trunk stubble – deserts that the authorities subsequently tried to recycle into improbable fields for the cultivation of new homesteads. They tried and failed, that is, because deforestation of these northern lands had left nothing but sandy earth and inclement weather. In the meantime, the mountains of sawdust, wood chippings and shavings left by the woodcutters provided fuel for huge, uncontrollable blazes ignited by railroad sparks: the Michigan fire of 1881 and the Hinckley, Minnesota fire of 1894, for example. In 1871, around

---

7   Ibid, pp. 204–5.

fifteen hundred people perished in a fire at Peshtigo, Wisconsin – more than in the Great Fire that destroyed half the city of Chicago in the same year.[8] The region lay scattered with ghost towns, abandoned villages that for a few brief decades had pulsed with the frenetic buzz of sawmills. (Around the same time, the winter gathering of ice for summer refrigeration and the transportation of meat in refrigerated train cars also disappeared, as artificial cold replaced natural, and tens of thousands of ice cutters vacated the region.) By the time of World War I, the great lumber trade and wood industry were just another of Chicago's fading memories. Where once had sprouted boundless forests of towering trees in a human desert whose only inhabitants were Native Americans, there now stood a treeless, cultivated desert. The Native Americans were no more. Instead of trees, there were now skyscrapers; in place of the woods were urban ghettos. Just as American fauna had been stripped of its herds of buffalo, so too, in the space of a few decades, had the white pine forests vanished from the flora – a flora that Henry David Thoreau had described around 1850 as being "like great harps on which the wind makes music," remarking that "nothing stands up more free from blame in this world than a pine tree."[9]

Here is where the theme of nature's innocence takes center stage. It is an innocence of animals and children that erupts into the nineteenth century, the epoch of progress, when Dostoyevsky found the sound of a crying child to be intolerable and Ivan Karamazov wished after a child's death that he could give back his ticket to the universe. Here, too, is the old nag stung by a driver's lash, which Friedrich Nietzsche, on the brink of madness (according to a widespread oral tradition), embraced in a Turin street in January 1889 before bursting into tears.[10] No self-respecting inhabitant of the seventeenth century would ever have claimed trees to be innocent, no more than one would have been moved at the sight of a horse being whipped; the deafening racket of a child's howls would have aroused only a somewhat vexed tolerance; and infant mortality would have been experienced as *destiny*, eliciting an emotional response no different than the response to the death

---

8   W. Cronon, *Nature's Metropolis*, p. 202.
9   Extracts taken from the *Journal,* entries for 16 September 1857 and 20 December 1851, respectively, cited in W. Cronon, pp. 151 and 425 (note 11).
10 This episode is cited in Lesley Chamberlain, *Nietzsche in Turin: The End of the Future,* London: Quartet Books, 1996, pp. 208–10.

of an adult. The horse's suffering became moving and began to arouse empathy when you could no longer hear the poor animal's puffing – but rather the chug of the locomotive – beneath the lash. Whipping had become pointless. The draft horse was about to retire from its historic role and was already plodding down the road to extinction. (It was during the nineteenth century that associations for the prevention of cruelty to animals and for the protection of children and wildlife were born.)

And just as "the savage" suddenly became noble when the West had more or less wiped him out (a tradition running from Bartolomé de las Casas to Jean-Jacques Rousseau, which, up to the twentieth century, propagated the idea – commonly held in the United States – that "negroes are like children"), so too did love of the sylvan realm begin to appear only when destruction of the forests was at its height: Thoreau retired to Walden Pond in 1845. Up until then, the woods had been in such abundance as to appear obvious; their omnipresence made them invisible. During his travels of 1830, a mere twenty years before Thoreau was moved to write of the white pine's innocence, Alexis de Tocqueville had observed:

> In Europe people talk a great deal of the wilds of America, but the Americans themselves never think about them; they are insensible to the wonders of inanimate nature and they may be said not to perceive the mighty forests that surround them till they fall beneath the hatchet. Their eyes are fixed upon another sight: the American people views its own march across these wilds, draining swamps, turning the course of rivers, peopling solitudes, and subduing nature.[11]

In America, the transcendentalist current represented the other face of the capitalist exploitation of wood. While lumbermen looked upon a wood and saw a lumber quarry measurable in board feet, transcendentalists descried a burgeoning spring of spirituality: "in the woods we return to reason and faith," wrote Ralph Waldo Emerson. While the *hommes des lettres* sought in the woods a fountain of spiritual sustenance, the capitalists found in them a fountain of riches of an entirely different color: "Unlike the Puritan pioneers who thought that morality stopped on the edge of the clearing, the transcendentalists thought it began there, for man was inherently good and not evil, and perfection could be maximized on

---

11 A. de Tocqueville, *Democracy in America*, vol. II, p. 74.

entering the forests," comments Michael Williams.[12]

Though they may be two sides of the same coin, these radically different sensibilities have seldom come into conflict. Rarely has one who revered the woods as "nature's cathedral" opposed the carnage wreaked by the buzz saw; nor has a fondness for animals necessarily prevented one from biting into a juicy steak. The same Emerson who had found faith and reason in the woods was to envisage a future in which "these wild prairies should be loaded with wheat; these swamps with rice; the hill tops should pasture sheep and cattle," and above all *"the interminable forests should be graceful parks for use and delight"* (italics mine).

If the United States began to worry about the disappearance of the forests and the consequent erosion of the soil just as it began the process of industrial extermination, then, a compromise was reached between the frenzied use of timber and the passionate love for the woods by rationalizing the use of this raw material and planning its "cultivation." (The first alarm bells sounded in 1847, at the same time as Thoreau was eulogizing the spirit of the woods.)

The intensive use of chipboard and plywood in place of solid hardwood allowed for a certain reduction of waste. (In the cutting phase alone, 10 percent of the wood was lost because of the thickness of the circular saws.) The use of wood pulp and the recycling of paper and cardboard have further reduced consumption. Enormous savings in wood used as a fuel for locomotives, cooking and heating have been made with the substitutions of coal, petroleum, gas and, lately, uranium. In this way, the annual per capita consumption of lumber fell by two-thirds from 157 cubic feet in 1900 to a historic low of 54 cubic feet in 1975. At the same time, cultivation techniques have slowed the process of deforestation and, in some areas, have even permitted regeneration of woodland. Since 1952, the forested area of the United States has increased by 70 million acres (a surface area equivalent to that of Italy), from 664 million acres in 1952 to 737 million in 1992 (according to the latest available figures).

Yet rationalization and planning eventually come up against an insuperable limit. Even as the per capita consumption of wood has fallen by two-thirds, the population itself has tripled. Furthermore, per capita consumption since 1975 has again *increased* by 148 percent, to 134 cubic feet, in 1997. With this surge and the

---

12 M. Williams, *Americans and Their Forests*, p. 17. The citations from Emerson appear on p. 16.

demographic explosion combined, in 1997, with a population of 270 million inhabitants, the United States consumed 36 billion cubic feet of timber, compared to 14 billion in 1900, an increase of 157 percent. From being one of the principal exporters of wood in the nineteenth century, the United States is now one of the world's main importers, particularly from Canada.

The new cultivated woods are to the ancient forests what wheat fields are to the wild prairie lands. Just as scientific breeding methods have fixed a steer's life span at little more than two years (so that it may grow rapidly and die profitably), so too has silviculture selected varieties of pine that grow at lightning speed, with a shorter and more uniform life, to accelerate the production cycle. Seeds are planted, fields sown, plants sprayed in pesticides, the harvest reaped and placed in storage. But of the ancient forest habitat, virtually nothing remains; many species of trees are close to extinction, and indigenous herbs are becoming ever rarer. Meanwhile, the forest area has been cut by more than half, its species impoverished. It is genetically more fragile and requires the use of increasingly potent pesticides, just as the exhausted soil has become dependent on fertilizers. And so the spiral continues. Except for a few natural reserves, where it is a "graceful park for use and delight," the American forest is now basically a "wood cultivating area." Nor could it be otherwise: wood makes up 30 percent of all the raw materials used in the United States. The wood industry employs 1.4 million people (1996) and has an annual turnover of $267 billion (1997), one-quarter of the Italian gross national product.[13] Inevitably, the myth of the pioneers cohabits with the world of tree farming, the love of nature with the wood industry. From his own innocent wooden balloon-frame house, the ecologist indignantly protests against the deforestation of the Amazon basin and the "irresponsible governments who are suffocating the lungs of the earth."

In Yellowstone National Park, Wyoming, campers look to revive the old campfire spirit of the Western pioneers, to sample once more in the glow of the flames a vanished primordial nature. The rangers, meanwhile, are trying to prevent the forest from being pillaged by hunters of firewood. The campers want

---

13 Figures taken from Census Bureau, *Statistical Abstract of the United States 1999*, tab. 1150, 1151 and 1152; *Statistical Abstract of the United States 1992*, tab. 1133 and 1137; and from M. Williams, *Americans and Their Forests*, pp. 8 and 487–88.

wood that is easy to light. A *practical* solution comes in the form of an automatic log distributor. The logs, already cut to size and wrapped in plastic, are sold at two dollars a pack.

8

A Streetcar Named Progress

On the outskirts of Chicago, the suburbs all have Arcadian names. At least fifty of these pertain to trees, woods and gardens. Sixteen are "Parks" (Calumet Park, Oak Park, Elmwood Park, Evergreen Park), while nine are designated as "Woods" (Homewood, Riverwoods). The ten "Groves" include Spring Grove, Prairie Grove, Elk Grove, Fox River Grove and Buffalo Grove, and the various "Forests" include River Forest, Forest View and Forest Lake (as well as Lake Forest). Add to this the various brooks (Willowbrook) and dales (Wooddale), as well as all the combinations and their inversions (Forest Park, Park Forest, Woodlawn, River-dale): the list is endless. The Chicago area clearly follows the rule of American developers who name the little towns they place on sale after the trees that have been felled so that the towns might be built.

Here the names designate not so much reality as the aspiration of commuters to have their own "little house in the woods," their personal "fireside abode." In these sylvan appellations the innocence of the trees that so impressed Thoreau permeates the suburbs and the lives of their inhabitants. The forests of the Great Lakes may have been leveled to procure wood for endless rows of balloon-frame houses, but the trees have not fallen in vain. Thanks to their noble sacrifice, entire human communities have been shaped into bucolic parks and groves, close to a metropolis for workplace, shops and entertainment (malls and commercial centers) but far from the city's ugliness, pollution, traffic and crime.

> In the town poor men demonstrated: beggars held out their hands in the street: disease spread quickly from poor quarters to the residences of the comfortable, via the delivery boy, the washerwoman, the seamstress, or other necessary menials: the eye, if not carefully averted, would, on a five-minute walk in any direction, behold a slum, or at least a slum child, ragged and grimy. ... In the suburb one might live and die without marring the image of an *innocent world,* except when some shadow of its devil fell over a column in the newspaper. Thus the suburb served as an asylum for the preservation of illusion. Here domesticity could flourish, forgetful of the exploitation on which so much of it was based. Here individuality could prosper, oblivious of the pervasive regimentation beyond. This was not merely a child-centered environment: it was based on a childish view of the world, in which reality was sacrificed to the pleasure principle.

So wrote Lewis Mumford in his classic study *The City in History.* The American suburb is twice "innocent" – toward nature and toward people: innocent both of the vanished woods whose glades it apes and of the devastated city from whose violence it takes refuge. Yet even Mumford falls into the trap of considering the metropolis in terms of *before* and *after. Before* is a time when the city was caught up in its own chaotic growth, a growth both violent and possessed of a great vitality, when it was impossible to ignore the surrounding misery and when

> sensitive and intelligent souls could not remain long in such an environment without banding together to do something about it: they would exhort and agitate, hold meetings and form parades, draw up petitions and besiege legislators, extract money from the rich and dispense aid to the poor, founding soup kitchens and model tenements, passing housing legislation and acquiring land for parks, establishing hospital and health centers, libraries and universities, in which the whole community played a part and benefitted.

After was a time when the city spread out and fragmented into suburbs that not only kept "the busier, dirtier, more productive enterprises at a distance"[1] but "likewise pushed away the creative activities of the city. Here life ceased to be a drama, full of unexpected challenges and tensions and dilemmas: it became a bland ritual

---

1 Lewis Mumford, *The City in History: Its Origins, Transformations, and Its Prospects*, New York: Harcourt, Brace, 1961, p. 494.

of competitive spending" (italics mine).

For Chicago, the *before* period would thus correspond to the time during the nineteenth century when the city was becoming a metropolis, innervated by a public transportation network of trams and buses, while the *after* would refer to the twentieth century, when the general flight from the city opened the way to the suburban diaspora and when public transportation was defeated by the private car. To escape from something, it seems logical that it first of all has to exist. Yet as Kenneth Jackson demonstrates in his *Crabgrass Frontier,* the truth is somewhat less reassuring, less easily ordered into a harmonious, logical script that depicts a solid past built on urban, philanthropic moral values and then swept away by the inhumanity of the twentieth century.

In terms of the fate of the city, we see in reality a recurrence of the same mechanism that Michel Foucault described in relation to prisons: there was no *before,* in which prisons became institutions, followed by an *after,* in which penitentiary reform was proposed. Prison reform, as Foucault shows in *Discipline and Punish,* was born alongside the modern penitentiary system. The two events were simultaneous. In the same way, exodus from the metropolis is concurrent with the birth of the metropolis itself, when the city ceases to be peripatetic, the product of an artisanal culture, and instead becomes a technological construction composed of numerous "pieces" – circuits, mechanisms (the sewage system, water and gas mains, transportation systems, electric cabling, networks of streetlights, garbage collection and recycling systems) – with their attendant *pannes* and breakdowns. In this respect, the city is just like any other technological product. A spaceship is composed of millions of pieces and yet is considered a single item that is more or less advanced, functional and comfortable. Likewise, the city is an ensemble that, though its functioning depends on millions of different elements, is rarely thought of as a single technological city-product, about which you might ask: Is it "practical?" "comfortable?" technologically "advanced" or "obsolete?" or even "consumer friendly"? Only when you visit countries culturally far removed from your own do you realize that *you don't know how to use* any city – and that it requires time to learn to use a city. Only with practice can you understand which cities are most "user friendly."

Although the use of the city becomes visible only through disorientation, then, a metropolis of millions of inhabitants would be inconceivable without arteries to allow its people, water, electricity, gas and garbage to circulate freely. Even during the classical period, a city such as Rome was able to house more than a million inhabitants only thanks to its aqueducts, its sewage system, a rudimentary street-lighting system and its several-story buildings.

The modern city is born, therefore, as both a *product* and a *center* of industry. Though it functions as a railroad junction and thus serves the railroads, these railroads at the same time serve it; without them, an agglomeration of millions of people would be unthinkable. "The railroads carried into the hearth of the city not merely noise and soot but the industrial plants and the debased housing that alone could thrive in the environment it produced."[2] As an example, nineteenth-century Manchester was born from what Friedrich Engels called "industry's power to concentrate":

> It was not only industry but population and capital which became centralized. ... Big industrial establishments need many hands massed together in one building. They have to live together and the labour force of even a relatively small factory would populate a village. Others are attracted to the vicinity of the factory to satisfy the need of the operatives and these include such craftsmen as tailors, shoemakers, bakers, builders and joiners. ... In this way a village grows into a little town and a little town in a city. The more the town grows the greater are the advantages which has to offer to industrialists. It has railways, canals and roads and there is an ever-growing variety of skilled labour available. Competition between local builders and engineers reduces the cost of building new factories to a level below what has to be paid when a factory is built in a remote spot. ... The new town has its market and its exchange, which are crowded with buyers. It is in direct contact with manufactured goods can be sold. All this explains the remarkable rapid expansion of the great industrial towns.[3]

What Engels wrote in 1845 about Manchester could equally well serve as a description of Chicago's development between 1850 and 1900: the canals (the Michigan–Illinois); the railroads; the stock exchange (Chicago Board of Trade); the cereal, wood and meat markets; the slaughterhouses and sawmills; the manufac-

---

2   Ibid., p. 461.
3   Friedrich Engels, *The Condition of the Working Class in England* (1844), Chicago: Academy Chicago Publishers, 1993, pp. 28–29.

ture of combine harvesters and Pullman cars and thus the steelworks.

Factories, too, were a product of the railroads. In every city – in Manchester as in Chicago – factories were built close to the station. The workers lived nearby in overpopulated, badly ventilated slums, with neither toilet nor running water, huddled together in the malodorous filth and squalor of poverty. The railroad lines tore through the city center, whose streets became coated in layers of dark, greasy soot from the locomotives and the factory chimneys. Road surfaces were smeared in excrement from the hundreds of thousands of horses used to transport goods, machinery and people over short distances. Canals were choked with sewage and factory waste. A Chicago Board of Health report defined the South Fork, a tributary of the urban river, as "a stagnant pool of abominations," "a dark putrid fluid" that attracted "millions of flies." The phrase is almost identical to the one Engels used to describe Manchester's River Irk: "It is a narrow, coal-black, stinking river full of filth and rubbish … from the depths of which bubbles of miasmatic gases constantly rise and create a stench which is unbearable,"[4] just as, according to nineteenth-century visitors to the Windy City, "Chicago stinks herself to death."[5]

The steam-powered transportation, both land- and waterborne, that converged on the great city encouraged the spread not only of goods and people but also of disease. Historians generally agree that the wildfire spread of cholera during the nineteenth century was attributable to steamboats and trains. (It was cholera to which Hegel, the philosopher who sang hosanna to the triumph of the absolute spirit, was to succumb.) Overcrowding and filth did the rest. In Chicago, there were repeated outbreaks of cholera: after the 1851–52 epidemic, an outbreak in 1854 resulted in the deaths of more than 1,400 people. The disease erupted again at the end of the Civil War, with 990 deaths in 1866,[6] and remained endemic, especially among immigrants, up until the turn of the century. In the summer of 1885, the *Chicago Sun* reported several cases of cholera among Polish infants, although the newspaper "omitted the family names because they were

---

4 Ibid., p. 60.
5 L. C. Wade, *Chicago's Pride*, pp. 131–32.
6 William K. Beatty, "When Cholera Scoured Chicago," *Chicago History*, Spring 1982, vol. XI, no. 1, pp. 1–13.

'unpronouncable.'"[7] In 1882, the infant mortality rate was so high that more than half the children born in Chicago died before reaching the age of five, with a rate three times higher in the poorer areas than in residential districts.[8]

Inevitably, "Coketown" – the name given to the metaphorical metropolis in Dickens's *Hard Times* and a name Mumford would in turn use to describe cities founded on the triad of "railway, factory and slum" – was mainly populated by immigrants attracted by the work opportunities the factories offered. Indeed, Coketown's very identity was inseparable from the poor, unwashed human tides of immigrants who came to inhabit it. Just as many in the twentieth century would attribute the exodus from America's inner cities (commencing in the 1960s with the Black ghetto revolts) to the influx of Blacks, so too was it common in the nineteenth century to attribute rejection of the city to the presence of white ethnics: Irish, Germans, Poles and Italians. Engels had already written about the plight of the Manchester Irish back in 1845, but in the United States, the phenomenon was more serious. In 1890, only one-third of all Americans lived in cities, as opposed to more than two-thirds of the immigrant population. By 1910, the percentage of foreign-born people living in cities had risen to 72. The affluent, meanwhile, got out of the center as soon as they could, fleeing its infernal cocktail of rank miasma, epidemics, pollution and noise.

Even a communist such as Engels was appalled by conditions in London: "The very turmoil of the streets has something repulsive, something against which human nature rebels."[9] Yet the same railroads that made the cities so sprawling and monstrous also provided a means – for those *with* the means – of escaping from them. The transportation revolution that forged the big city at the same time triggered the exodus from it. As early as 1832, New York had a railway line that ran up to 125th Street, where country houses slumbered in idyllic peace. (If you get off the subway there nowadays, you find yourself in the middle of Harlem.) Commuter season tickets were expensive and were therefore available only to a few

---

7   L. C. Wade, *Chicago's Pride*, p. 298. Citation from the *Chicago Sun*, 27 August 1885.
8   Data taken from Bessie Louise Pierce's monumental work *A History of Chicago* (vol. III, p. 154) –
    widely considered the key text on the subject – published in three volumes over twenty years; New
    York: Knopf, vol. I (1937), vol. II (1940), vol. III (1957).
9   F. Engels, *The Condition of the Working Class in England*, p. 31.

wealthy customers, costing between $35 and $150 at a time when a lumberjack was lucky to earn between $100 and $200 a year. Little by little, however, as the transportation network began to diversify and become integrated into the city, larger segments of the population had the chance to flee from urban damnation. After the railroad and ferryboat, the three great phases of urban transportation were to be defined by the horse-drawn bus, the tram and the automobile.

Nonetheless, the old technologies did not give up without a fight. Nathan Rosenberg notes how "builders of sailing ships responded to the competition of iron and steam by a number of imaginative changes in hull design, including the use of iron itself" in the nineteenth century, making the sailing ship of 1870–1880 "faster than its predecessors, with double the space for cargo in proportion to tonnage, and manned and navigated by about one-third the number of men." As a result, sailing ships "continued to be the *more economical carrier*"[10] for coal. In similar fashion, closer to our own era, the advent of the computer led to the birth of a new generation of typewriters considerably more advanced than their predecessors.

Thus, when mechanical traction first appeared on the scene, ways were immediately sought to improve animal traction. Toward 1830, an attempt was made to lay tracks on the roads for horse-drawn carts; rails caused less friction on the wheels, so the horse could pull previously unthinkable loads. The rails protruding from the road surface impeded the progress of other traffic, however. In 1852, a roadside rail was invented, embedded in the soil rather than sprouting from the ground like the ordinary railroad. This rail did not interfere with other forms of transportation.

Thanks to improved brake technology, a pair of horses could now pull a wagon carrying thirty to forty passengers, at greater speed than ever before (six to eight miles per hour). As a result, fares tumbled, and for the first time, it became relatively cheap to get around town. By 1853, New York's horse-drawn tram network was carrying 7 million passengers. In the 1860s, similar trams were introduced to Chicago, Cincinnati, Boston, Philadelphia and Pittsburgh. By the mid-1880s – the tram's golden age – 525 horse-drawn tram companies were operating in 300 US

---

10 Nathan Rosenberg, *Perspectives on Technology*, p. 205.

cities on 6,000 miles of track. More than 100,000 horses were employed to carry 188 million passengers per year, an average of twelve journeys per year per resident (newborns included) for a town of more than 2,500 inhabitants.[11]

The horse-drawn trams thus constituted the first real mass public transportation system. What is more, the drawbacks we normally imagine to be symptomatic of twentieth-century urban ills had already begun to appear by the mid-1800s: "People are packed into them like sardines in a box," ran one newspaper article of the time, "with the perspiration for oil. The seats being more than filled, the passengers are placed in rows down the middle, where they hang by the straps, like smoked hams in a corner grocery." (Note how the metaphors come from the food industry, even if the sardines tend to jar with the hams.)[12]

Nonetheless, the horse-drawn tram allowed the masses for the first time to live far away from the place where they worked, stretching the city's boundaries even further. With the workplace no longer within walking distance, the walking city exploded. The first step had been taken toward democratization of the suburbs, as trams became integrated with railroads. As well as extending the suburbs, the horse-drawn tram expanded the city center to include anywhere within a few horse-car stations. By 1888, the total population of Chicago's suburbs exceeded 300,000, while commuters to the city numbered more than 70,000.[13]

The biggest push toward the suburbs came with the trolley car, however – a form of transportation adopted by the United States with amazing speed. The first prototype was built in 1880, and it was a mere ten years before the trolley car went into widespread service (whereas it took more than twenty-five years for the automobile to catch on). As opposed to its animal counterpart, electric traction did not defecate or get sick, nor did it slip on the ice; it didn't need to be whipped or require supplementary horses to help it surmount steep inclines; it was faster, too, reaching speeds of ten to fifteen miles per hour; and it could carry more passengers (up to a hundred people during rush hour). Fares continued to fall, with the

---

11 Frank Rowsome, *Trolley Car Treasury: A Century of American Streetcars,* New York: McGraw and Hill, 1956, p. 17, and ch. 2, "The Railway." Other sources record 415 companies as opposed to 525.
12 K. T. Jackson, *Crabgrass Frontier,* p. 41.
13 Ibid., p. 93.

average cost of a journey going down from a dime to a nickel by the end of the nineteenth century. By 1890, these "street railways," as they were then called, were carrying 2 billion passengers per year, twice as many in the United States as in the rest of the world put together. In cities of more than 100,000 inhabitants, each person – including babies – averaged 172 journeys per year. By comparison, Berlin, which had the finest tram network in Europe, would have rated only twenty-second on the American list.[14] Thousands of little private companies sprang up, competing for business on the same lines; between 1890 and 1893 alone, there were mergers between some 250 companies.

It was in Chicago that the trolley car's progress was at its most rapid and capitalistic. Such progress had a name: it was Yerkes – Charles Tyson Yerkes. A share speculator, Yerkes had already done time in jail in 1871. Upon his arrival in Chicago in 1881, he immediately plunged into the cereal market, setting himself up as a grain broker. Using some money he had borrowed, he bought an option on the North Chicago Street Railway and gradually acquired shares in other lines. He thought up a technical system that was highly innovative for its time, adding some 500 miles of surface lines, 240 of which were electrified, and building the elevated Chicago Loop that to this day encircles the half-mile square of the center (then known as the Loop). This elevated railway has become so much a part of Chicago's identity that residents these days refer to it simply as "the L." By 1895, Chicago thus boasted more lines, more track and longer trips than any other city on the planet.

Yerkes, "really a gallant though perverted soul,"[15] was the prototype of the money-grabbing tycoon, the man who greased the palms of politicians and didn't care about whatever purgatorial discomforts the tram riders had to put up with. "It's the folks hanging on the handles who pay your dividends," he once told his shareholders. So Theodore Dreiser described him in two novels, *The Financier* and *The Titan*. Despite Yerkes's donation of $250,000 to the University of Chicago for an astronomical observatory – the Yerkes Observatory, which boasted what was

---

14 Much of this data is taken from K. T. Jackson, *Crabgrass Frontier,* pp. 103–15; and from I. Cutler, *Chicago, Metropolis of the Mid-Continent,* pp. 201–31.
15 So Yerkes was reappraised in 1935 by an old enemy, Carter Harrison Jr., cited by David M. Young in *Chicago Transit: An Illustrated History,* DeKalb, Ill.: Northern Illinois Univ. Press, 1998, p. 53.

then the world's most powerful telescope – the man's unpopularity was to be a major factor in the shift toward municipalization of the transportation system (a demand we find in all union manifestos of the period).[16] In 1897, Yerkes attempted to have his contract renewed for another fifty years. "His" aldermen were on the point of giving their consent, when a furious mob surrounded the town hall. The renewal was blocked, and in 1899, Yerkes's aldermen were voted out of office. Yerkes sold his Chicago lines for $5 million and, in 1901, invested that money in electrification of the London Tube. (While the United States was much more advanced in the tram sector, Europe had the edge when it came to subways: the first Underground was built in London in 1866, followed by the Paris Metro in 1898. Across the Atlantic, the first section of the Boston subway was not opened until 1897. New York would have to wait until 1904 for its great subway, and Chicago would not see the dark of day before 1943.)

The trams extended beyond all measure the process of suburbanization that had begun with the horse-drawn omnibus. For the first time it became possible to "explore" the city. Tram companies published guides and timetables, enabling passengers to vary their routes and change lines. At the end of the lines, huge amusement parks were built, with bars (such as New York's Coney Island or Chicago's Riverside). As a result, the number of passengers swelled on Sundays and during the summer as entire families set off to visit quarters of the city, monuments and gardens that had previously been unreachable. What it must have felt like – that sense of anticipation as the tram came into view, the hunger for the unknown and the unexplored, the mixture of apprehension and curiosity that assailed those intrepid tram riders – we can never know.

The tram permitted millions of people to flee the urban chaos, to enter and exit the city on a daily basis. The city, in fact, was extended to a "metropolitan area" defined by the tram itself. In 1910, public transportation carried 1 million commuters into the Chicago Loop, a figure that was to remain surprisingly stable throughout the century; the number of commuters would continue to oscillate

---

16 William T. Stead, *If Christ Comes to Chicago!*, Chicago: Laird and Lee, 1894, p. 110. (In another edition, the title was changed to *If Christ Came to Chicago: What Would He Do?*) The first US edition of Stead's book sold over 100,000 copies. Pages 110–15 provide an emphatic description of the corruption of Chicago's city hall.

State Street looking north from Madison Street circa 1905. Photograph by Barnes-Crosby, courtesy Chicago Historical Society.

LIVERPOOL JOHN MOORES UNIVERSITY
LEARNING SERVICES

between 800,000 and 1 million, with only the means of transportation changing. When you look at photographs from those years, you can easily understand what made people wish to escape. The crush on the streets was unimaginable. In the soot-shrouded atmosphere of Coketown (of a city that used coal for everything: trains, cooking, heating, factories, even to produce electricity), with whistles shrieking, steam locomotives criss-crossed the city streets at some (rarely respected) 2,000 level crossings, provoking countless incidents and monstrous hold-ups. Beneath a web of tightly meshed aerial wires, the jam-packed trams cut a slow swath through torrents of pedestrians and ranks of porters bent double under their heavy sacks, stuttering forward amid columns of fledgling automobiles, seigneurial gigs and horse-cars as well as snarls of overloaded carts piled up with logs or tremulous mountains of barrels, carts whose horses felt the teamster's lash every time they blocked one another's path.

With its retinue of pedestrians, steam trains, electric trams, horse-drawn vehicles and coaches, the early-twentieth-century city was a truly multimedia environment, much more so in fact than is the metropolis of today. The crowd reigned absolute in a way that makes the present-day Western city appear decidedly mute by comparison. There was a real sense of physical and mental pressure: the friction of millions of skins, both animal and human, pressed together; the smells, the filth and sweat, the fug of engines, the noise. The only valid modern-day comparison would be not the Chicago of today, but an Indian city such as Calcutta, with its perpetual cloak of coal dust that turns clothes and bodies black in the space of a morning or its Howrah bridge traversed by millions of rickety trucks, bicycle-, horse- and man-driven rickshaws, sluggish oxen-drawn carts, cars, bicycles and pedestrians who nonchalantly clamber over each other. And then there are the lame, the mutilated and the deformed that the modern-day visitor to Third World cities finds so appalling. "I have never seen so many mutilated fragments of humanity as one finds in Chicago,"[17] wrote William T. Stead, a polemical English journalist who originally came to Chicago in 1893 to witness the august celebrations of Columbus's discovery of America and the neoclassical monuments built for the occasion. Stead then stayed on to describe the city's beggars and brothels, its corrupt

---

17 W. T. Stead, *If Christ Comes to Chicago*, p. 187.

politicians, lady benefactresses and various other hypocrites. (Stead's reportage scandalized the genteel Chicago society of the time. Not until eighteen years later, when Stead went down with the *Titanic* on his way to America to participate in a peace conference, did the *Chicago Tribune* see fit to dedicate two whole pages to the journalist under the title "William Thomas Stead, Scholar, Dreamer, and Humanitarian: Story of a Remarkable Life, with a Still More Remarkable Ending."[18])

In 1894, Stead had been appalled by the paralytics and the deformed individuals who found themselves out on the streets after accidents at work in the slaughterhouses and sawmills, or in the steelworks and the factories of McCormick and Pullman, lame dogs who were further mutilated by the indifferent traffic: in the absence of bridges, the level crossings became deadly traps, causing serious injury to tens of thousands of people each year and accounting for a steadily mounting death toll that ran into the hundreds (294 in 1890; 323 in 1891; 394 in 1892; 431 in 1893).[19]

And bipeds weren't the only victims. Even as late as 1910, horses in the city constituted an equine army, used to pull not only trams but private carriages, cabs and goods carts; there were 68,000 horses in Chicago alone. New York, with 128,000, had almost twice that number. Even a relatively small town like Milwaukee was home to 12,000 horses. By 1920 – when millions of Model T Fords were circulating on the streets – even with their former numbers reduced to half, 56,000 horses remained in New York and 30,000 in Chicago. In addition to urinating and defecating, the horses got sick and attracted swarms of insects. In the turn-of-the-century metropolis, lacerated by the driver's lash and exhausted by the immense loads they had to bear, malnourished, badly treated and housed, draft horses died by the thousand. Around 1880, 15,000 horses were dying in the streets of New York every year. In 1912, the toll in Chicago was still as high as 12,000 – a rate of 32 horses per day.[20] The spectacle of a horse being clubbed to death in broad daylight became so common that it no longer seemed such a strange idea to be moved by the innocence of horses, nor did Nietzsche's mad embrace of the old nag in Turin seem so crazy after all. Less surreal, too, was the passage in

---

18 *Chicago Tribune,* 12 April 1912.
19 W. T. Stead, *If Christ Comes to Chicago,* p. 194.
20 K. T. Jackson, *Crabgrass Frontier,* p. 106.

Dostoyevsky's *Crime and Punishment* in which Raskolnikov dreams of being a child who sees a horse beaten to death by a gang of drunken peasants: "With a howl he forced his way through the crowds towards the little grey mare, flung his arms round her dead, bloodied muzzle and kissed it, kissed her on the eyes, on the lips."[21]

The tram took so little time to gain sway in part, then, because it helped eliminate the use of horses as a means of transportation. Another factor was that it further democratized the road to the suburbs, allowing millions of Chicagoans to live far from the center, thanks to the construction of more affordable (if not exactly cheap) suburban housing. In such a city, those who had the means to get out were envied. Nowadays, urbanists – and humanists along with them – are quick to unite in condemning this general flight toward the suburbs, but at that time, who in their right mind wouldn't have wanted to get out? Not by chance did Stead give his reportage the curious title *If Christ Comes to Chicago,* hinting at the ignominy that Christ would have found in the city. That hint evoked another recurrent motif of the nineteenth century, Christ returning to Earth to see the results of his gospel, as for example in Ivan Karamazov's dream of the "Grand Inquisitor." It was a motif that would penetrate even twentieth-century consciousness through novels such as Carlo Levi's *Christ Stopped at Eboli.* Rudyard Kipling, another famous visitor to the Chicago of those years, wrote: "Having seen it, I earnestly desire never to see it again."[22] If Chicago made Kipling take to his heels after a single visit, imagine the workers and craftspeople who had to live there. As soon as they were able, they invested their meager savings in a house far from that abomination, a quiet place miles away from the hordes, which they could now reach by (albeit crowded) trolley car.

Now that the workers could live far from the factories and from the inner city, however, the factories themselves began to move away from the center and the central stations. Huge plants were uprooted and relocated in the outskirts. In Chicago, the steelworks were originally located to the immediate north of the downtown area, along the Chicago River. But at the end of the nineteenth century, they

---

21 Fyodor Dostoevsky, *Crime and Punishment,* London: Penguin, 1991, p. 94.
22 Cited in K. T. Jackson, *Crabgrass Frontier,* p. 93.

were moved to the Calumet River area, on the Indiana border, from which they would expand even further south beyond the state line. It was here, to the far south of the city, that two of America's biggest steelworks were built at the beginning of the twentieth century: in 1901, the Inland Steelworks in East Chicago, on the east side of Indiana Harbor Canal; and in 1906, the United Steelworks in Gary, Indiana.[23] In Europe, too, there was talk of outlying industrial zones and *banlieues rouges*: a prime example was the new Fiat factory at Lingotto, built in 1915–18 in what was then the outskirts of Turin. The electricity revolution speeded the shift of heavy industry to the outlying areas by replacing steam power with turbine generators. The first book to deal with the deindustrialization of the inner cities ("the shifting of factories, one by one, to the edge of the city"[24]) and the formation of industrial suburbs in the United States, published in 1915, was a study by Graham R. Taylor. The city center was thus no longer the industrial nucleus of the surrounding region, but merely its tertiary pole, the site of service industries and commerce. The smokestacks had been banished from the center, another reason for the popularity of the tram.

Finally, the trams had the effect of modifying the spatial layout of the suburbs. When connections had depended on steam locomotives, which where slow to accelerate and even slower to halt, a distance of at least two to three miles between stations was required. Thus the suburbs lay remote from one another, each clustered around its station, with service personnel, both public and private, living in the same suburb as their employers, servants huddled around the master's abode. Every suburb reproduced in miniature form the structure of the city. Here, too, the poor tended to amass around the railway station.

Trams, by contrast, allowed for more frequent stops, with the result that residential nuclei began to unravel. No longer separated by tracts of country, the suburbs were spread out evenly along the tram lines. Because tram rates were much lower, servants, shopkeepers, clerks and craftspeople of the richer suburbs could more conveniently go to and live in cheaper areas and come to work by tram. Patrons were even willing to pay travel expenses to cleanse their eyes and nostrils of

---

23 I. Cutler, *Chicago, Metropolis of the Mid-Continent*, p. 175.
24 Cited by K. T. Jackson, *Crabgrass Frontier*, p. 183.

the sights and smells of the underclasses. This marked a decisive watershed in modern civilization. It was the moment when patrons lost contact with their servants, when intimate dialogue, such as the one Diderot imagines between Jacques and his master, became impossible. It was at this point that the suburbs became socially segregated, with a different zone for each separate class and underclass. From then on, spatial definition would automatically imply social definition.

One thing the trams did maintain, however, was the radial structure of the metropolis. This was partly because the population density between suburbs was too low for a connecting public transportation system to make sense. Public transportation would be possible only if it connected a periphery to a center along a line laced with suburban areas. Here we see signs of that ambiguous rapport established between suburban innocence and population density, a rapport extant even today. If the tram extended the suburbs, it did so in a way that maintained their tributary, subaltern relationship to the city's downtown area.

In a city like Dallas – which has no center other than the mirage cast by its gleaming new skyscrapers, acres of desolate office space where "the sound of silence" is on 24-hour rotation – the tram is, understandably, seen as an archeological curiosity. Dallas's nineteenth-century tramways are no more than a theme park fun ride, a vehicle for fleecing gullible tourists, much like the pushcarts of New York, Rome or Chicago itself, or the pedal rickshaws that, though fast disappearing from Asian cities, have now resurfaced in Los Angeles and Vancouver, where they are driven by dauntless blond-headed youths.

9

Suburban Paradises

The experience of a tram journey on a Yerkes line in late-nineteenth-century Chicago is, fortunately, something we have been spared. But anyone who has ever dangled from a local bus in Africa or India, however environment-conscious they may be, would become sympathetic toward Americans and their passion for cars, for *individual transportation*. For although the industrial nineteenth century worshiped the individual, it did so only for the upper classes; only among the upper classes was it possible to conceive of an individual who was *free*.

"My freedom ends where yours begins": so ran the liberal dogma of the time. If I were well-to-do, this meant that my freedom ended at the fence surrounding my garden, where your garden began, while your freedom began in your carriage, which was a different and wholly separate carriage from mine. If I were among the underclasses, however, my freedom ended at my stomach, against which you had your elbow jammed, or with my nose, which was buried in your armpit. Where would my freedom begin and yours end in a tiny room that slept five or in a tram into which were crammed a hundred people or more? The individual, the Cartesian "I," was a currency that was legal tender only among the leisured classes or the management elite, where, capitalized, it became the Hegelian "I," the Subject of History, the Bank Account Owner. The nineteenth century reserved the right to privacy – to "private ownership," that is – to this class of subject, just as it imposed forced community (communism?) on the lower classes.

Not by chance did the rationalization of industry and administration consist of rendering the human element interchangeable, ensuring that one worker was exactly the same as another and thus replaceable by another, equally anonymous and massified, like an ordinary foot soldier. From the dawn of the modern age, that which was public (and thus either free or *excessively* cheap) was discredited in favor of that which was private (and therefore costly). Financial success alone would permit you to escape from the malodorous misery and promiscuity of communal living: from this derives the charm, much abused by advertising, of the verb *personalize* and its participle *personalized,* which have been fastened onto a range of anonymous products destined for millions of customers. In this comic guise is cloaked a real, tragic sentiment: the aspiration of the masses no longer to be considered as part of the mass but rather each to be considered as an individual "person."

In 1906, Woodrow Wilson predicted that the automobile would lead to socialism, because it incited envy of the rich. But Wilson failed to take into account the specific form that, according to Pierre Bourdieu, social struggle was to assume in the West – that is, of *leapfrogging* between classes. At first, only the ruling class lived in suburban villas, but after a century, the proletariat also were tending their lawns in the suburbs; initially, you could afford a car only if you were affluent, but within the space of fifty years, a modest income was sufficient to buy one; in the beginning, only the bourgeoisie frequented holiday resorts, but before long, holiday traveling became a mass phenomenon. The temporal distance, or *décalage,* in this game of leapfrog expressed the distance between classes. In this sense, the last century can be seen as a huge leapfrog competition to become individuals.

The automobile of the masses, Henry Ford's Model T, thus represented much more than an industrial revolution, because it permitted even those who weren't particularly well off to become individuals. It didn't matter whether you were a factory worker, a clerk or a street sweeper; with a car, you were somebody. "In a considerable degree the rapid popular acceptance of the new vehicle centered in the fact that it gave to the owner *a control over his movements* that the older agencies denied. Close at hand and ready for instant use, it carried the owner from door to destination by routes he himself selected and on schedules of his own making," according to a report presented to President Herbert Hoover in 1933 (italics mine).[1]

This conceptual revolution took place relatively early on in the United States; indeed, in the first quarter of the century, it enjoyed a progress that has never been repeated. In 1920 in the United States, there was 1 car for every 13 inhabitants, as opposed to 1 for 228 inhabitants in Britain, 1 for 247 in France, 1 for 1,017 in Germany and 1 for 1,206 in Italy. The European ratios of the time are similar to those we see in Asia today, with 1 car for every 436 inhabitants in China, 1 for 238 in India and 1 for 81 in Indonesia (1997 figures). Car density in the United States was thus a hundred times higher than it was in Italy and nineteen times higher than in France. By 1997, the gap between America and Europe had closed, however, with Italy and Germany even superseding the United States in terms of number of cars per person. In that year, there was 1 car for every 2.24 inhabitants in France, 1 for 2.23 in the United Kingdom, 1 for 2.09 in the United States, 1 for 1.98 in Germany and 1 for 1.86 in Italy. If this data is hard to believe, it's because of the taxonomic perversions of the US Census Bureau, which, beginning in 1986, no longer counted pickups, personal passenger vans, passenger minivans and sport utility vehicles as cars, but rather counted them as trucks, which means that US and European data are not comparable. In any case, even the classificatory evils of the US statistics cannot hide the fact that other rich Western countries are now more or less aligned with America in terms of car density.

Yet even if today's Westerners have more cars, they have to spend a much higher portion of their income to buy one. The past eighty years have seen cars become steadily more *accessible* and then, again, less so. In 1909 in the United States, a worker needed twenty-five months' pay to buy a Model T Ford. But by 1925, the cost of cars had fallen drastically, and the same Model T could be acquired for just three months' pay.[2] Today in the United States, as in Europe, three months' pay will buy you only half a car.

When on 5 January 1914 Henry Ford doubled his workers' wages from $2.30 to $5 per day, he wasn't doing it simply to expand his market by paying the men

---

1 President's Commission on Recent Social Trends in the United States, *Recent Social Trends in the United States*, Washington, D.C.: Government Printing Office, 1933, cited in Jackson, *Crabgrass Frontier*, p. 173.

2 Ibid., p. 161.

who built his cars enough salary that they could buy one. The wage rise was at the core of a much broader social vision, one that exhorted employees to make every possible effort to become individuals and to earn this status by their own labors. To this end, Ford offered wages that placed the much-sought-after quality of *individuality* within their reach: one was an individual, not in theory but in practice, because of how one lived and moved about, because of "having control of one's own movements." Placing individuality within the reach of all therefore meant making a personal vehicle that suited all pockets: the automobile was as much a single-family dwelling as was the balloon-frame house. But just as Henry Ford was pushing his workers to win their own individuality, he was also introducing into the factory the assembly line, a process that effectively segmented the men's work personalities to the point of turning them into anonymous, interchangeable components. Nonetheless, the idea of *being a person* remains perhaps the only illusion we cannot do without.

On the subject of the cars and trucks of the United States, too much has been written, said and seen already, so I'll limit myself to a few fairly obvious points. The appearance of cars and trucks was to upset the radial structure of the city, a structure left intact even by the tram, which required a sufficiently high density of users for it to be practical, if not profitable. By contrast, the car required a low enough density of drivers for it to remain mobile. Whereas one moved by tram from periphery to the center or vice versa (with the exception of one or two "circular" lines), it was possible to move by car from one suburban zone to another. For this reason, intrasuburban commuting was already beginning to take root in the United States by the 1930s. Rather than going to work in the center, commuters simply traveled to another suburb.

The population of Chicago city reached its peak of almost 4 million in 1940, then gradually dwindled to 2.784 million by 1990 and rose again slightly, by 15,000 inhabitants, to 2.799 million in 1999. The city's metropolitan area, meanwhile, has continued in its sprawling, metastatic growth. In 1940, its population numbered 4.570 million inhabitants; sixty years later, by 1999, that figure had almost doubled, to 8.9 million. Whereas in 1940 eight of nine Chicagoans lived in the city, two of three live in the 'burbs these days, with two-thirds of these suburbanites working in other suburbs. Also, the number of people who live in the city but go to work in the suburbs has doubled: some 250,000 drivers now migrate daily from the city center to their jobs on the outskirts, compared to 10,000 in 1960. Here is a revolution that has radically altered the lifestyles, as well as the relationships between work, play and family, of tens of millions of people. Today, more than 100 million Americans live in the suburbs, 40 percent of the entire US population. Half of those live in areas not frequented by public transportation.

Because it substitutes horizontal (or transversal) for vertical (or radial) mobility, the automobile modifies the relationship not only of the individual citizen to the city, but also of the city to its surroundings and to itself. Meanwhile, the city must have its parking lots and garages. No words could adequately describe the way these car parks have disfigured America's cities. Next to coquettish boutiques are the ugly, charmless spaces, the inky black chasm of the multistory parking garage, reticulated in cheap cement. In front of the Chicago Hilton (once the world's largest luxury hotel), bespangled doormen parade up and down on red carpet, gesticulating furiously. Immediately behind the hotel, surrounded by wire fencing that moans and creaks in the wind, begins a concrete wasteland, its surfaces culled from the sites of demolished buildings. The parking lot disrupts the urban fabric, creating a *terrain vague* that breaks up the social network. At night, its spaces become dark and cavernous, gaping jaws that hold the promise of a mugging, beating or rape. (The fear of being assaulted in a parking lot is one of the pillars of the metropolitan imaginary.)

Right alongside the Magnificent Mile, the parking lot that sits sandwiched between chic café, fashion boutique and gourmet restaurant provides training in that special art – in which Americans are so expert – of *looking without seeing*, using one's eyes as we have become accustomed to using our ears. After being subjected to millennia of noise, we have learned to listen without hearing, picking out sounds that interest us from the indistinguishable background buzz. So it is that unpleasant particulars in the American metropolis, such as the unspeakable ugliness of the car parks, another "inevitable cost of progress," are regarded as *visual background noise*.

For cars to reach the city, fast roads were required. The first road artery to be constructed specifically for automobiles was William K. Vanderbilt's Long Island Motor Parkway (1906–11). To make commuting easy, freeways had to penetrate as far as possible into the heart of the city. Rather, they had to traverse the city from one part to another, carving "inevitable" scars in the urban fabric. Next to these, the breaches opened in the streets of Paris by Baron Haussmann to make way for the Grands Boulevards looked like the work of an amateur DIY enthusiast. Every twentieth-century American city has had its own Haussmanns: Robert Moses in New York, Mayor Richard J. Daley in Chicago – men who, according to Marshall Berman, saw themselves as the demiurges of a state-funded modernity. Moses, in Berman's description, constructed bridges, coastal roads and freeways and therefore had to demolish houses, streets, entire neighborhoods. Moses, out of reverence for his beloved New York, made the Bronx what it is today, a no-go concrete jungle, when he gutted it to make room for an expressway that forced some 60,000 inhabitants to pack up their belongings, swept away thousands of buildings and rendered thousands more uninhabitable thanks to the smog and noise from passing vehicles. The urban freeways degraded and destroyed the neighborhoods they tore through, just as the railroad had done during the nineteenth century. When asked whether the freeways created human problems different from those in the country, Moses replied, "There's a little discomfort and even that is exaggerated." The only difference here was that "there are more houses in the way … more people in the way – that's all. … When you operate in an *overbuilt* metropolis, you have to hack your way with a meat ax" (italics mine).[3]

With the same meat ax and the same federal funds, Daley cut a swath through Chicago to build the Dan Ryan, Kennedy and Adlai Stevenson Freeways. Even in elegant Boston, a freeway cuts through the center like an unhealed wound, passing near the city's eighteenth-century buildings and blotting out its nineteenth-century rooming houses: it's another eye test for the "non-seeing." Indeed, the freeway has become such a familiar part of the landscape that no one notices it anymore. One of Dallas's finest seafood restaurants sits tucked under an overpass. On your way out, you are met by the roar of passing trucks. Meanwhile, along Lake Shore Drive, Chicago's urban expressway, you see hundreds of joggers padding along the hard shoulder, oblivious to the exhaust fumes.

---

3   Marshall Berman, *All That Is Solid Melts into Air: The Experience of Modernity:* New York: Simon and Schuster, 1982, pp. 293–94. The first part of the last chapter of this book, "In the Forest of Symbols: Notes on New York Modernism," is devoted to Moses.

During the twentieth century, the freeway brought to completion the progressive emptying of the street as a "piece of the public sphere." The previous century had already seen the passage from village road to urban boulevard. "The village road," writes Franco Moretti,

> was certainly a thousand times poorer in stimuli than the city street. On the other hand, however – and this is the point – the near totality of life occurred in the road. The city has certainly given full value to the street as a channel of communication … but it has drastically and irreparably devalued it as a place of social experience. … The great novelty of urban life, in fact, does not consist in having thrown the people into the street, but in having raked them up and shut them into offices and houses. It does not consist in having intensified the public dimension, but in having invented the private one.[4]

The village road was where villagers met and was thus a space of frequentation; the urban boulevard, on the other hand, was merely a scenic backdrop along which strangers passed, giving rise to the category of *passerby* and its accompanying lyricism: the attractive stranger we will never have the chance to love; the eyes that meet ours for one brief moment before disappearing forever out of view; the hand we never brushed; fleeting glimpses of impossible happiness. The street becomes a place of solitude, and of the lone individual who imagines encounters, who *daydreams*.[5]

The urban boulevard thus became the stage for a solitary intimacy, where each person followed the thread of his or her own experience. The street was public only in exceptional cases; assembly there, or in the square, immediately became seen as a form of "demonstration," a subversive act, with a sense of protest derived from its being a public gesture when, in the sphere of daily life, the street had now become a private place. This tendency to consider public spaces only as backdrops for private experience has reached its culmination with the Walkman and the cellular telephone, devices that enable you to move from ignoring background noises to actually erasing them, to filtering them out. The individual, no

---

4 Franco Moretti, "Homo Palpitans: Balzac's Novels and Urban Personality," in *Signs Taken for Wonders* (1983), London: Verso, 3d. edn., 1997, p. 127.
5 While rummaging around a flea market, the French singer Georges Brassens found a poem, "Les Passantes," written in 1913 by an unknown poet called Antoine Pol, which he famously set to music.

longer hearing the street sounds that have become an irritable nuisance to be eliminated, crosses the road immersed in a freely selected sonic ocean, whether a melody booming across a pair of headphones or a distant voice carried on radio waves.

The envelope of metal and plastic that is the car can be seen as a Walkman headset carried to the *n*th power, isolating the driver not merely from sounds but from any form of contact with the outside world. When in your car, the Other (whether another vehicle or a pedestrian) becomes a pure *obstacle* between you and your destination. In this sense, the car is private not simply in terms of being a form of property, but because it transforms into private experience that which for centuries was part of public, communicative time: travel – from the pilgrim's journey in Chaucer's *Canterbury Tales* to Tom Jones's coach to the train on which we encounter Myskin in Dostoyevsky's *The Idiot*.

First in theory, then in practice, the automobile effectively banished the passerby from the street. The person on the street is no longer a passerby, but is rather a *human vehicle*, a self-propelled biped. The car requires road arteries fashioned in its own image, a private place. This is why the streets of every city, except for those in the center (and those only during open hours), have tended to be deserted, the main thoroughfares desolate, with only the odd modest street-corner gathering. To measure the extent of the revolution that has taken place over the last fifty years, it is enough to compare the indescribably mobbed streets of the early twentieth century with the silence and emptiness of streets today. The street has become an *abstraction*.

Without doubt, the car never had it so good as in the abstract floor plan of American cities, where it found a familiar habitat in the gridiron structure of the roads, a grille of perpendicular streets that cut the city into regular blocks (around ten in every square mile). New York adopted the gridiron structure in 1811, and before long, the design had spread across the whole city. Straight lines reduced disputes over borders, simplified zoning problems and facilitated "buying, selling and improving real estate." Daniel Drake, a doctor of the time, remarked, "Curved lines, you know, symbolize the country, straight lines the city." The process of making a gridiron of the United States was to culminate in 1862 with the Homestead Act, which offered land in the West to aspiring farmers at a nominal price.

The land was divided into 64-hectare lots, one-quarter-mile square, each bordered by roads, transforming much of the nation into an immense grid.[6]

By the twentieth century, traffic circulation had replaced the market as the main motive for gridirons. Whereas curves held up the flow of traffic and impeded road vision, creating irrational junctions and crossroads, the gridiron constituted a perfect system of traffic intersections. The advantages for cars didn't end there, though. If the natural preference for cars was the wide-open road, here were thoroughfares as wide as runways. Sloping parking lots? No problem. Anything resembling so much as a hump was leveled to an asphalt pool table.

Cars aren't too keen on trees, either, as can be seen from the fact that tree-lined thoroughfares remain something of a rarity in large US cities, limited to Commonwealth Avenue in Boston, a brief stretch of Broadway above Sixtieth Street in New York and a few others. Then, at night, fatigued after a hard day's drive and seeking repose in a more refined environment, cars migrate back to the suburbs where cozy garages await, even heated for them in winter in the colder regions. Here their biped servants are finally allowed some restorative shut-eye – so as to be up and ready the next morning, engines tanked up with cornflakes, chassis smelling sweetly of aftershave.

Here we are, then, in our sylvan suburb, far from the Loop. Here are possible, indeed actively sought out, all those things that the city denies us. The streets no longer are just numbers on a grid, but have actual – for the most part tree-related – names. (Even in the city, in neighborhoods wishing to set a certain tone, the streets are *named* rather than *numbered*: I lived for a while on Chicago's Near North Side on a street called Oakdale, though the area was obviously devoid of both oak and dale.)

Then there are the curves, which, as we all know, are the height of elegance. When a suburb's streets curve, there is a corresponding rise in house prices; as Drake said, "curved lines symbolise the country" and nature in general. Even more expensive are the areas that have kept their hills and hollows, momentarily hiding the landscape from view, only to reveal its splendid panorama over the

---

6   On the gridiron system, see K. T. Jackson, *Crabgrass Frontier*, pp. 73–76.

next rise. Here, hillocks and bends are considered the height of chic, to be created specially, if need be, by urban landscapers in the service of the real estate brokers. People here will spend a fortune trying to re-create what nature thoughtlessly bestows upon its most humble valley: slopes and curves.

In the suburbs, children, too, are able to do what they cannot do in the city (and this applies not only to American cities): to play in the street. Forty years ago, during my own Roman childhood in a typical middle-class district of the medium-sized capital of a medium-sized European country, between the ages of five and ten, I could still play on the sidewalk with the other neighborhood kids. We ran around in innocuous gangs firing paper pellets at each other through plastic peashooters. By the end of the millennium, however, social interaction on the street between neighborhood kids had been forbidden for middle-class children, who, to play in the open air, must proceed to a designated play area (such as a park or a public garden) and even then must be accompanied by an adult. These children no longer can experience the thrilling rite of passage that is life beyond the watchful eye of adults, the parental or school panopticon, a form of infantile complicity and conspiracy woven through with secrets not for "their" ears.

Nowadays, only the children of the underclasses (once labeled the *dangerous classes*) experience the pleasures and perils of street life in the city, in the poor urban ghettos, where they run in gangs of so-called street kids. Here we see the process of criminalization that leads to the idea that "a good child doesn't play in the street" and to visitors asking hotel managers whether this or that street is "safe." The street becomes criminalized to the point where the only form of social exchange, the only "piece of the public sphere" remaining, is the criminal one, whether it be drug pushing (the exchange of drugs for money) or prostitution (the bodily commerce of so-called streetwalkers).

With the advent of electricity, human civilization finally seemed to have turned off the night. Much more than philosophical enlightenment, actual lighting appeared to have won the age-old battle against the forces of darkness: during the late nineteenth century, visitors to the city were filled with admiration for the nocturnal spectacle of the streets, streets so abrim with life, traffic and bustle that, as Wolfgang Schivelbusch notes, forms of artificial darkness had to be invented (such as the movie theater or the amusement park ghost train). The defeat of night was not to last long, however. Even if real darkness is by now practically unknown (we hardly notice the cosmos above us) and the city horizon is perpetually immersed in a luminous halo, the night has regained it rights and re-imposed its nightmares, those "nocturnal fears" we know so well.[7] In the wee small hours, the city street returns to the way it must have looked at the time of Rembrandt. A new sentiment – that of "odophobia," or fear of the street – becomes mixed in with our more primal fear of the night.

In the suburbs, however, children can play in the street, just as adults can walk or cycle up and down it, because the street is private, and any intruder is immediately noticed and kept under surveillance (however ridiculous it may seem that a street could have *intruders*). Signs placed on the street encourage the citizen to be always on guard, to keep watch and notify the police of any unusual encounter: panels feature the head of a man wearing a menacing-looking broad-brimmed hat traced in black silhouette.

At the same time, the act of speaking to passersby, awkward if not dangerous in the city, here becomes an act of courtesy; the passerby is a *neighbor*. Whereas houses in Europe are usually surrounded by a fence or a wall, with the garden placed at the front, the American single-family house presents a defenseless front, a garden without fence. The family's open-air life takes place out of sight in the back garden, where the barbecue is installed.

Children from Europe often go into raptures over the US pairing of suburb and single-family home, with its corollary of well-manicured lawns and open-air games, where life, as Mumford has observed, is truly innocent, where the individual can flourish in a domestic idyll. Meanwhile, the cities, reduced to violent ghettos gutted by urban freeways and pockmarked with parking lots, are simply the place where one goes to pay the price to become this individual, to be "somebody."

But the story doesn't end there. In addition to its lawn and trees, each suburban house must also have access to the street. For every two single-family houses, therefore, there must be a stretch of road across which they can face each other. If

---

7 Wolfgang Schivelbusch, *Lichtblicke*. Eng. trans. *Disenchanted Night: The Industrialization of Light in the Nineteenth Century*, Berkeley: University of California Press, 1988. See the chapter "The Street," pp. 79ff, and his discussion of darkening the theater, pp. 203ff.

each house is to have its lawn stretching for sixty-seven feet of road, half a mile of two-lane road is needed for every one hundred families, not to mention two sidewalks. That works out to 62.5 miles of road for ten thousand families, not counting crossroads, main thoroughfares, fast roads, service areas and shopping malls. The desire to live close to nature, to trees and lawns, paradoxically produces more asphalt per person than the most artificial concrete-and-steel metropolis. In addition, it leads to multiple sewage and telephone networks, electricity cables and water systems.

As the number of infrastructure systems per inhabitant shoots up, so too does the amount of energy needed to build and run them (to say nothing of the fact that each house has its own heating system, and many have air-conditioning). Just for each house to wash its biped, quadruped, and two- or four-wheeled inhabitants and to sprinkle the lawn requires an obscene amount of water. Nothing brings home the irrationality and destructiveness so much as the houses that lie scattered across the California desert, each with its brilliant emerald lawn surrounded by an endless wasteland of rock and sand: a green shade bought with the thousands of gallons of water it takes to douse the grass equivalent of a postage stamp while the earth all around literally dies of thirst. Behind the apparently innocent facade – the breezy, carefree exterior of the suburb and its balloon-frame houses – lurks an unbounded voracity, an insatiable hunger for wood, asphalt, water and energy.

The suburb also sucks up human resources. Its inhabitants are so thinly spread out that protecting them requires an extremely costly deployment of police. (If people huddled together for centuries in medieval villages and towns, it was to *protect themselves* and to *find safety*.) Even this show of force would not be sufficient to guarantee security were it not for the strict division of territories between the police (who control the suburbs) and the gangs (which rule the inner cities). Each generally avoids the other's turf, except on occasions when one group is compelled to visit the other, in which case they tend to behave like an invading army on enemy-held territory. During the 1992 Los Angeles riot, not a single window in the wealthy suburbs of Beverly Hills received so much as a hairline crack. In return, police let the whole of the Central District be looted as they awaited intervention from the National Guard, which was viewed as an external "expeditionary force" and was thus considered more "neutral" than the Los Angeles Police Department. Many Americans protested, in fact, when the government sent the marines to Somalia instead of dispatching them to South Central. The division of territory into different patches, or turfs, in some ways explains another pillar of contemporary imagination: the fear of the psychopath who has escaped the control of police and gangs alike and who therefore might strike anywhere. Even more than the gangs, it is the psycho-killer who jeopardizes the safety of suburbia. With his dark silhouette and menacing cap, he might lurk behind the easy-going facade of a next-door neighbor. From here arises the petty suspicion, the fear and watchfulness that the suburban layout generates and feeds on: solitude turns out to be much more threatening than the crowd.

Fear is also a powerful incentive toward social conformity. People seek refuge from their fears by having neighbors who are similar to themselves, with similar jobs, cultural backgrounds, skin color and, of course, income, a form of affinity imposed by the property values in a particular suburb. Another incentive is geographical mobility: if I must move to a place thousands of miles away, to avoid nasty surprises I look for a house in a suburb in which I recognize myself, where there is a minimum of social dislocation and where I can be sure that my kids won't fall into "bad company" or my spouse be assailed by "dubious characters." Against dispersion and fragility, the suburb defends itself through uniformity and self-segregation. In a very real sense, the suburb is an urban diaspora, parceling out society into socially distinct, disconnected segments.

If the car has made this form of human habitation possible, the suburb in turn excludes the possibility of any other transportation system. The population density is so low that public transportation of whatever form makes no sense. In effect, the suburbs have been financed and constructed through the systematic dismantling of public transportation. And now that the 'burbs exist, it becomes impossible to reintroduce buses or trams, because they are incompatible with the new system of organization.

As a consequence, children and teenagers not yet able to drive go everywhere with a companion – usually a friend – whether to the swimming pool or to the movies. Their mothers are effectively no more than glorified chauffeurs. The suburbs were initially built around and conceived for the typical housewife and mother, who was supposed to dwell there in domestic bliss, far from the anxieties of work, crowds and *strangers*. For feminists such as Betty Friedan, however, suburbia represented a form of concentration camp in which the average American woman, that particular human species otherwise known as the "suburban (similar to 'subhuman') housewife," had become entrapped. The experience of the camps "seems terribly remote from the easy life of the American suburban housewife. But is her home in reality a comfortable concentration camp? Have not women who live in the image of the feminine mystique trapped themselves within the narrow walls of their houses? They have learned to 'adjust' to their biological role. They have become dependent, passive, childlike, they have given up their adult frame of reference." Certainly the metaphor should not be exaggerated: "The suburban house is not a German concentration camp, nor are American housewives on their way to the gas chamber. But they are in trap, and to escape they must … finally exercise their human freedom, and recapture their sense of self."[8]

Both cars and single-family houses appeared as (and in a way are) a means by which we could conquer our individuality and become a person. The old liberal formula was also applied to this idea of being a person, but in a new version: "My (male) individuality begins where your (female) individuality ends (in the kitchen), just as my personality is built on your anonymity," which is to say, "My freedom is based on your entrapment," or rather on my "keeping you in your place." A common hymn is sung in praise both of the suburban and the feminine mystique. And suburbia was never so praised as in the period when women finally began to flee from this rose-tinted trap. In a classic mechanism, the ideology of self-segregated suburbia trapped within the boundless horizon of its own flower beds celebrated its triumph at the tail end of the 1970s, with the rise of Reaganism, at which point its paradise became endangered by entry into the workplace of tens of millions of married women, mothers of young children and suburban housewives.

In 1970, the American workforce included only 31.5 million women (43.3 percent of the US female population). By 1997, that number had risen to 63 million, or 59.8 percent; in just 26 years, more than 31 million women had entered the job

8 Betty Friedan, *The Feminine Mystique* (1963), New York: Bantam Doubleday, 1983, pp. 307, 309.

market. The figures become even more striking if you compare them with those of 1960, when a mere 28.8 percent of married women between the ages of twenty-five and thirty-four had a job. By 1997, the corresponding figure was 71.9 percent, which means that while two of three young wives had kept the home fires burning before, the same number were now out winning bread. Equally glaring is the increase in the proportion of working mothers, with 63.6 percent of married women with children under the age of six in jobs today, compared to 18.6 percent in 1960, less than one-third the current figure.

This American cultural revolution has passed more or less unnoticed in Europe, though there was for a while the very real possibility that it would lead to the collapse of the whole system of suburban life in America. The first response to the crisis has been to multiply the number of cars in circulation, so that not only the Ulysseses, but also the Penelopes of suburbia can now, when tired of the spinning wheel, set out on their daily four-wheel odysseys: 44 percent of new car buyers are, in fact, women. In addition, a large number of offices have been moved to the suburbs. Housewives are being offered more part-time jobs, given that they continue to do most of the weaving at home. Finally, a massive campaign is being launched in defense of so-called family values, a crusade to bring back the good old days of motherly, home-makery feminine mystique. It is not yet clear, however, whether women will be so easily lured back to the hearth, or whether the suburban idyll will be plunged into crisis and, if so, what the chances of establishing a new balance will be. What is certain is that the gilded cage and its attendant unhappiness even today remain the price that women and American society pay to live in the innocent world of the suburbs.

It's simply another of the many exorbitant costs of the American dream. In effect, this dream consists of nothing more poetic or profound than having "a little suburban house with white picket fence, two cars, and annual vacation."[9] To the eyes of an outsider, the price of such a dream might seem untenable, if not downright ruinous. Yet it is this dream that has moved hundreds of millions of people, convincing them to abandon home and family to head off into the unknown, often in the face of a racist and hostile society. To understand the power of this mi-

---

9 Juliet B. Schor, *The Overspent American* (1998), New York: HarperCollins, 1999, p. 11.

rage, for which people are willing to go through terrible humiliations and hardships, it's enough to look at a nineteenth-century photograph and note the pride with which an immigrant woman "owns" her wooden single-family house. Some 60 million American families have realized this dream, in the form of personal property, in the fact of owning their own homes. Yet even the category of ownership is not without its ambiguities – or, for that matter, its unpredictable, undesired consequences.

10

Faith Can Also Move Banks

It cures you more effectively than a shot of penicillin. It strengthens you more than any sport. It nourishes you more than books and learning. Is it love? Is it Zen Buddhism? No, it's private property: your *own* home.

More than anything else, Walt Whitman wrote, it is owning our own home that makes us really human: "A man is not a whole and complete man, unless he owns a house and the ground it stands on."[1] Possessing a house, Russell H. Conwell affirmed in his celebrated speech *Acres of Diamonds,* is a moral panacea: "A man is not really a true man until he owns his own home, and they that own their homes are made more honorable, and honest and pure and true and economical and careful, by owning the home."[2] The privately owned house is what made America great, said Calvin Coolidge: "No greater contribution could be made to the stability of the Nation and the advancement of its ideals, than to make it a nation of homeowning families." Privately owned homes even rendered their owners more heroic and courageous: "A nation of homeowners, of people who won a real share in their own land, is unconquerable," asserted Franklin D. Roosevelt, while Herbert Hoover declaimed that the privately owned single-family

1 K. T. Jackson, *Crabgrass Frontier,* p. 50.
2 Russell Herman Conwell, *Acres of Diamonds,* New York: Harper and Brothers, 1915, p. 19.

house had generated poetry, lyricism and songs such as could never spring from rented or communal homes: "To possess one's own home is the hope and ambition of almost every individual in our country, whether he lives in a hotel, apartment, or tenement. ... Those immortal ballads, *Home Sweet Home, My Old Kentucky Home,* and *The Little Gray Home in the West* were not written about tenements or apartments ... they never sing about a pile of rent receipts."[3]

What we see here is a real sense of faith. Like a guardian angel, private property can perform miracles. Like the god of the Israelites, it brings about the resurgence of nations. Like divine justice, it tempers the character. It says we are the just. Marx was not the only one to consider private property the fulcrum of our society. United in common prayer to this divinity, we find such diverse figures as Whitman, the poet of *carpe diem* and rugged sensuality, and Russell Conwell, the Baptist preacher (and first dean of Temple University) who struggled to reconcile capitalism and Christianity. Presidents on opposite sides of the political spectrum have come together to extol the virtues of homeownership, for once united in common praise: Hoover, who presided over the 1929 stock market crash, and Franklin D. Roosevelt, architect of the New Deal.

The privately owned home is literally *salvific,* and it has long been the state's task to guide each American along the path of righteousness toward salvation. This means enacting laws that make it more convenient to buy than to rent. For this reason, the American fiscal system constitutes one enormous incentive to purchase a home: rent payments are not tax deductible, whereas mortgage payments are. To pay a monthly rent of $2,000, you need to earn at least $2,500 per month (after taxes have been deducted), whereas if you pay the same $2,000 per month in mortgage installments, all interest payments are deducted from your taxes, making the effective cost less than $1,500 per month. Such fiscal exemptions on mortgage payments cost the federal government each year more than its annual spending on housing subsidies.

The financing of private property sometimes takes a more indirect form. The federal government pays for the freeways that connect the suburbs to the workplace. The state foots the bill for part of the infrastructure as well as almost all

---

3   K. T. Jackson, *Crabgrass Frontier.* The pronouncements of the three presidents are reported on pp. 362 (note 14) , 190 and 173, respectively.

maintenance costs on private properties. City tenants are taxed to favor suburban homeowners. During the 1930s, in fact, Blacks in the inner city of Atlanta, Georgia, paid out of pocket for municipal services, road maintenance, health and sanitary costs, as well as for state schools in the white suburbs of the city.[4]

The private sector had already done its part in enabling citizens to attain the beatitude of homeownership by providing cheap, buildable land and reasonably priced frame houses. A Chicago advertisement of 1875 offered a 25-by-125-foot lot and a small frame house comprising a 10-by-12-foot parlor, two small bedrooms, a kitchen and a pantry, all for the price of $600.[5] To immigrants who built their own houses, developers sold lots of bare land, enabling countless immigrants to realize the American Dream as they purchased their own little house. In 1920, in the zone of the Chicago stockyards, 57 percent of the neighborhood's residents owned the house in which they lived, with 90 percent of those residents foreign born.[6] Meanwhile, in the years following World War II, the dream of every working-class bride was to own a Levitt house, with its 12-by-16-foot living room, two small bedrooms, kitchen and bathroom, all measuring a snug 750 square feet.

However small or inexpensive a house was, however reasonably priced the land on which it was built, too often the homeowner's paradise turned out to be a short-lived mirage. Too often were Americans cast out of their private Garden of Eden for the sin of being unable to pay the mortgage. Families often had to go to loan sharks to come up with a down payment (equivalent to half the value of the house itself) and then, inevitably, piled one mortgage upon another, the second of these always at a steeper interest rate.

The number of mortgages protested for nonpayment rose steadily, and more and more aspiring property owners were forced from their houses. During periods of recession, the number of unpaid mortgages would multiply. In 1932, with the country still reeling from the great crash of '29, 250,000 mortgages were written off every month, to say nothing of farm mortgages: that year, 3 million families lost the homes for which they had already made dozens of payments.

---

4 Ibid., p. 132.
5 L. C. Wade, *Chicago's Pride*, p. 67.
6 R. A. Slayton, *Back of the Yards*, p. 31.

The Roosevelt administration responded by creating two new federal agencies: the Home Owners' Loan Corporation (HOLC), approved by Congress on 13 June 1933, and the Federal Housing Administration (FHA), approved the following year, on 27 June 1934, to which the Veterans Administration would be added ten years later.[7] More than any other measure, these agencies were to contribute to turning America into an unconquerable nation of homeowners.

In terms of how they set about achieving their immediate goal, these agencies were models of simplicity and efficiency. You can't but admire the speed with which they set about making it cheaper and easier to buy a house than to rent one. In 1933, construction began in the United States on a mere 93,000 houses. That number had risen by 1937 to 332,000, and it continued to rise in the following years, to 458,000 in 1939 and 614,000 in 1941. By 1972, in one year alone, the FHA helped 11 million families buy houses and another 22 million carry out home improvements. In the meantime, the percentage of American homeowners had climbed from 44 in 1933 to 63 in 1972. (The figure in 2001 stands at 64 percent.) In 1995, 40.5 million families were paying a mortgage (41 percent of all American families).

The FHA has the additional merit – extraordinary in the eyes of Americans – of not costing the taxpayer a single cent. Yet these agencies are at the same time responsible for leaving in their wake an utterly devastated society. Again we find ourselves faced with a double-edged sword: on one hand, we have the lightness and simplicity of the balloon-frame house, the extraordinary docility of the car, the efficiency of the FHA; on the other, we find their tremendously destructive implications.

The role of the HOLC was to refinance endangered mortages. In the two-year period from 1933 to 1935, it handed out more than $3 billion to cover more than 1 million mortgages, one-tenth of all the mortgages in the United States. The FHA, by contrast – which was to have by far the bigger influence in the long run – neither provided loan money nor built houses, but instead insured mortgages started by banks or construction companies. (For this insurance, it received a commission

---

7   Regarding these two agencies and their policies, data are taken from ch. 11, "Federal Subsidy and the Suburban Dream: How Washington Changed the American Housing Market," in K. T. Jackson, *Crabgrass Frontier,* pp. 190–218.

that was shuffled into a risk fund, so that its balance at the end of the year actually showed a small profit.) In case of a debtor's failure to pay, the FHA reimbursed the creditor.

Together, these two agencies were responsible for fixing and regulating the functioning of mortgages in the United States. First they lengthened the time limit on repayment to the current standard periods of twenty or thirty years. Fixed interest rates became the norm, and variable ones the exception. Moreover, because the FHA guarantees all mortgages, backed by the US Treasury and all its political muscle, the interest rate on a thirty-year mortgage has fallen dramatically (according to the Bureau of Census, it stood in 1997 at 7.2 percent per annum). Unlike its European equivalents, the US mortgage holds such importance that the American statistical abstract reports data on interest rates, bank commission charges, average time length for repayment (26 years) and percentage of protests.

As a final decisive point, the FHA's guarantees allowed people to start up mortgages with a down payment of a mere 7 percent of the value of a house, significantly less than the 50 to 57 percent they had needed under the previous system. The purchase of a house costing $100,000 required a down payment of only $7,000, for example. This fact, together with the extremely low interest rates, brought about a Copernican revolution in the property market, putting a house within reach of (nearly) all Americans. Today the total value of debts on US single-family home mortgages amounts to $4.37 trillion,[8] three times the Italian gross national product.

Because the down payment is so ridiculously low, the ceiling on the price of a house a person with a given income can buy is rigidly fixed. In the United States, banks and financial bodies refuse to grant a mortgage *if the value of the house is more than three times that of the applicant's annual salary*. Each piece of data is a loop in the chain: there would be no sense in granting mortgages with such low down payments were it not for the fact that American houses cost much less than houses in Europe. The average price of a single-family home in the United States in October 2000 was around $208,000. So it was that, thanks to the HOLC and the FHA, the United States gave itself a head start in the race for private homeownership. (In the wake of World War II and the American victory, however, the countries of Eu-

---

8   Census Bureau, *Statistical Abstract of the United States 1999*, tab. 820 (1998 figures).

rope have by other ways and means also become unconquerable nations of home-owners).

But of course the federal agencies couldn't just lend money (or offer guarantees) at random; they couldn't risk financing houses whose values would later fall. They had to follow criteria that would safeguard their interests and adopt the right strategies to protect their investments. The positive side of this was that they fixed construction and habitation standards throughout the nation: no species of shark, in fact, is more vicious than the American real estate agent. But the need for safe-guards had other consequences as well. Because the HOLC and FHA financed and guaranteed mortgages for values as close as possible to the run of the property market, they had to establish criteria for classifying various housing areas. This meant introducing a grading system, a discontinuous taxonomy like the one the Chicago Board of Trade had established for wheat and wood in order to launch the futures market. After all, a mortgage loan is also a wager on the future – on the future value of a property.

We find the same logic at work, with the substitution of a discontinuous taxon-omy for a continuous variety of minimal differences. What should make land and houses worth more in one area than in another? The HOLC divided housing zones into four categories, each marked by a different color: green for zone A, blue for B, yellow for C and red for D. The zones were defined as follows:

> A – green: Green areas were new and homogeneous, always "in demand as residential locations in good times and bad." *Homogeneous* was an epithet for "American business and professional men." Jewish areas, for example, or even those that had seen an "infiltration of Jews" "could not be considered best any more than they could be considered 'American.'"
> B – blue: "Still desirable," these areas "had reached their peak" but were ex-pected to remain stable for many years.
> C – yellow: C neighborhoods were "definitely declining."
> D – red: This category included neighborhoods in which "things taking place in C areas have already happened."[9] Areas inhabited by Blacks were in-

---

9 These classifications are taken almost literally from K. T. Jackson, *Crabgrass Frontier*, pp. 197–98.

variably red zones, whereas those with prices that "might attract undesirable elements" – that is, white ethnics – were marked yellow.

From financing the purchase of a first house, then, the HOLC went on to evaluation of the property; from fluctuations in the property market, it moved to classification of residential areas; from the grading of zones, it shifted to evaluating the racial and ethnic composition of a neighborhood.

The FHA introduced a system that was even more precise, based on eight criteria, each with its relative weight. Here is the list, with its percentage weight in parenthesis:

1. Relative economic stability (40 percent)
2. Protection from adverse influences (20 percent)
3. Freedom from special hazards (5 percent)
4. Adequacy of social, commercial and civil centers (5 percent)
5. Adequacy of transportation (10 percent)
6. Sufficiency of utilities and conveniences (5 percent)
7. Level of taxes and special assessments (5 percent)
8. Appeal (10 percent)

Although the FHA insisted on including and weighting all of these eight criteria, however, its recipe too closely resembled that for the celebrated lark paté, made of equal parts lark and horse: one lark and one horse. In fact, the first two criteria alone had a combined weight of 60 percent: they made up more than half of the total consideration and more than the other six criteria combined.

But what, exactly, were "adverse influences" – and what determined a neighborhood's "stability"? The 1939 *Underwriters' Manual* explains that overcrowding reduces desirability (and that single-family–home neighborhoods are thus more desirable than apartment-block areas); that smoke and smells constitute "adverse influences";[10] and that "if a neighborhood is to retain stability, it is necessary that properties shall continue to be occupied by the same social and racial classes." The FHA was greatly afraid that "*inharmonious* racial and nationality groups" would cause property values to fall, and this fear spurred them to insert restrictive covenants into their contracts, whereby the buyers of a house in a white zone had to

---

10 Ibid., pp. 207–8.

promise not to sell the home to Blacks. Not until 1948 did the Supreme Court rule such covenants to be unconstitutional. The Americans' faith in the virtues of property had somehow become an application form that produced racial segregation.

The FHA was one of the pillars of the New Deal. In Europe, Franklin D. Roosevelt is widely regarded as the most progressive president in US history. In this case, however, his policies not only turned America into a nation of homeowners, but made it one of racially segregated homeowners, of citizens who had an economic interest in maintaining a distance between races. Can such a result be attributed solely to what Albert Hirschman calls "perversion"? Perversion, according to Hirschman, is a classic conservative's argument whereby any "attempt to push society in a certain direction will have the effect of making it go in the opposite direction." This was an argument originally applied to the French Revolution, which sought liberty but produced tyranny. Joseph-Marie de Maistre, whom Hirschman cites, even saw in the Revolution "an affection of Providence: the efforts people make to attain a certain objective are precisely the means employed by Providence to keep it out of reach."[11]

And it isn't merely the right that adheres to the thesis of *perversion:* those on the left also find it highly suggestive, to say nothing of the ecologists. The car designed to facilitate movement ends up producing traffic, paralyzing traffic jams to the extent that the average speed of a car in the city today is lower than that of the horse-drawn tram of old. The perversion argument always ends up defending the existing state of affairs, however, claiming that any change to that state would simply make things worse. It is the modern equivalent of Leibniz's "best of all possible worlds," in which Voltaire's Candide was such a stout believer. If the world that exists is the best of all possible worlds, then any attempt to change it must inevitably result in a turn for the worse.

An alternative to the perversion thesis is the concept of "bad faith." Did legislators and political powers really act in good faith when they translated anxiety over property values into a policy of racial segregation? Here we have the *cynicism* hypothesis, often more attractive, if not downright irresistible. True, presidents and

---

11 Alfred Hirschman, *The Rhetoric of Reaction: Perversity, Futility, Jeopardy,* Cambridge, Mass.: Bellknap Press of Harvard University Press, 1991, p. 18.

poets probably sincerely believed in the thaumaturgic virtues of private home-ownership, but how do you forget the arrogance of the Pennsylvania Railroad in the nineteenth century when it proclaimed that the company had nothing to fear from strikes because its employees "live in Philadelphia and own their homes, and therefore, cannot afford to strike"? How can you *not* feel a mix of admiration and disgust at the sheer effrontery of the first president of Boston's Provident Institute for Savings, who said, "Give [a man] hope, give him the chance of providing for his family, or laying up a store for his old age, of commanding some cheap comfort or luxury, upon which he sets his heart; and he will voluntarily and cheerfully submit to privations and hardship." At the same time, the cynicism hypothesis acts as a buffer, ultimately referring to conspiracy theories, the idea that a design is at work in capital – in short, that a secret history exists in which human destiny is deter-mined by a web of intrigues, congeries and subterranean plots, as occurs, for ex-ample, in Thomas Pynchon's *The Crying of Lot 49* or in the novels of Don DeLillo.

The result is the same in each case. If we naively accept good faith – and its per-verse effects – we are powerless to do anything. If, more shrewdly, we go for the hypothesis of cynical reason, we must be its dupes, never knowing who are the real "puppet masters" and therefore left, once more, impotent. To borrow Adam Smith's notion, we find ourselves manipulated by two "invisible hands": one di-vine (perversion), the other human (cynicism).

More likely is the hypothesis of an inextricable morass of both good and bad faith, cynicism and sincerity, a complex, contradictory web resulting from the am-biguity inherent in the idea of property itself – and in the possibilities of its posses-sion as a mass phenomenon. We are unable to gauge precisely the degree of destructiveness involved, the primordial distinction between the I and the Not-I. Nor do we really know when the rapport between Me and Other-Than-Me be-comes deformed, when it is translated into the opposition between Mine and Yours. In more down-to-earth terms, property speculators who baptize tracts of bulldozer-leveled cement with the names of trees, parks, hills and dales in reality share with the poor dupes who buy the tracts the same arcadian aesthetic. Cer-tainly, the logic of real estate weighs like an albatross on American society – and not only on the marginalized and the segregated, but on that very constituency who should, by all appearances, enjoy its benefits to the full.

Possessing one's own home ought to produce "parsimony," security and stability. Yet precisely because everything in the States is bought on credit, with hardly any deposit – whether a house, holiday, car, schooling or a new refrigerator – people's general attitude is to spend, spend and spend some more (on credit). Everyone is buried in debt. The next several decades of peoples' lives are on the installment plan, as are those of their children. And if everything is on credit, then it can all be taken from you as soon as you start to backslide on the payments. Nothing is more ephemeral than this kind of property. The repo man is always just around the corner. The anxiety to own things soon becomes the fear of losing them.

The nation's unconquerable homeowners consequently live in perpetual terror. In the United States, you can be hired and fired within the space of a day, and your job might depend on the tiniest shift in your boss's mood or on the slightest whiff of recession. In many cases, you can't even get sick if you want to keep your job. Chained one day to a mortgage for the next thirty years, you can equally well find yourself out on the sidewalk tomorrow. In a very real sense, you have mortgaged not only your own life but also the lives of your family. The coveted serenity of your "home sweet home" has you waking up in a cold sweat (not that more affluent families sleep any more soundly). Because you effectively are what you own, it follows that the more you earn, the more you have to have and the more debts you accrue.

Precariousness forces optimism. The American, to borrow Juliet Schor's phrase, is "overspent," while the United States itself is a country that literally lives on credit: credit that allows the purchase not only of houses and cars but also of consumer electronics, the kids' college tuition, holidays in Mexico and dental bridgework. The total debts of US families in 1997 amounted to the staggering sum of $5.5 trillion, with debt service taking 18 percent of Americans' available income.[12] This Kilimanjaro of debt determines all aspects of Americans' behavior, up to and including the curve of their lips and their facial expressions. The deeper in debt you are, the more positive you must be about your future. Try asking a European the ritual courtesy question, "How are things?" and you will no doubt receive one of the muttered responses, "Not too bad," "Could be worse [or better]"

---

12 Juliet B. Schor, *The Overspent American*, p. 72.

or, at most, "Can't complain." Ask the same question of an American, and the response will be an unmistakable toothy grin accompanied by an emphatic, "Great," "Wonderful," "Fine" or, at least, "Good." You begin to suspect that so much stereotyped self-satisfaction and well-being is simply in obedience to Benjamin Franklin's injunction that debtors do their best to tranquilize their creditors, because "the most insignificant actions can have an influence on your credit."[13] But this pumped-up trust in today masks an anxiety about tomorrow. And money alone does not guarantee security, because you need a reasonable amount of money before you can get into debt: the poor can't even ask for a loan.

Property is thus subject to eternal postponement: more than something one has, it is a goal to be pursued. The business of daily life becomes the unending search for this property that eludes your grasp. It is like the mechanical hare on a greyhound track; the dogs will never catch it, no matter how fast they run, because, just when it seems to be within their reach, it accelerates away again. If all goes well, you spend the best part of your life paying off the mortgage. And when the thirty years are up, if you've been lucky enough to make all the payments, you're old and retired, your kids have gone to live in another city, and you are left with a house that's too big and that you'd be better off selling to buy a motor home. Congratulations! You've spent your entire life paying for a house that, in the best of all possible worlds, you'll be able to sell so your progeny can apply for a mortgage of their own.

Leisure World is a private residential complex of some 5,000 inhabitants. Located near Phoenix, Arizona, it's a place with its own institutions and rules. It is by no means the biggest private old folks' community in Arizona, however. Sun City, for example, numbers 46,000 residents and houses ten shopping malls, along with numerous bookshops, parking lots and swimming pools and a museum of fine arts. In addition, Sun City has its own emergency phone line, fire department, symphony orchestra, armed police force and day-care center.

---

13 "The most trifling actions that affect a man's credit are to be regarded. The sound of your hammer at five in the morning or eight at night, heard by a creditor, makes him easy six months longer..." This passage, from *Advice to a Young Tradesman* (1748), was made famous by Max Weber in *Die Protestantische Ethik und der Geist des Kapitalismus* (1920), in ch. 1, par. 2. Eng. trans. *The Protestant Ethic and the Spirit of Capitalism*, New York: Routledge, 1993, ch. 1, par. 2, "The Spirit of Capitalism."

But back in Leisure World, as Joel Garreau recounts,[14] two irksome snags arose. The first was a clandestine immigrant. A 42-year-old doctor, after suffering a nervous breakdown, had become temporarily unable to look after himself, so his parents, who had a house in Leisure World, had decided to put him up for a while. The only problem was that the rules of Leisure World forbid anyone under the age of forty-five to live there. The doctor's parents were informed that they would have to leave if they wanted to continue to offer hospitality to their son. That they did. The second snag was that the local newsletter fell into disfavor with the community's private board of directors, who decided to stop its circulation. The editor protested, only to discover that the First Amendment of the Constitution (protecting freedom of expression) did not apply on private property.

Then there's Evan McKenzie's account of an incident that took place in another community, in Santa Ana, California,[15] when a 51-year-old grandmother received legal notice for having violated the rules of her association. Her crime? She had been seen "kissing and doing bad things" in a parked car. The woman in question admitted having kissed a friend goodnight but filed suit against the association.

In fact, these are all private communities, founded on the idea that the homeowners' association not only owns the houses and the surrounding terrain, but also holds sovereignty over everything that goes on there. The official name given to these private enclaves is common interest developments (CIDs), and more than 150,000 of them exist today in the United States, housing some 30 million Americans. Among the CIDs are the fabled *gated communities,* actual fortified cities that, according to Edward Blakeley and Mary Gayle Snyder, numbered 25,000 in 1997, including some 3 million housing units. Such communities are no longer limited to exclusive holiday clubs or old folks' homes but increasingly take the form of alternative residential areas located at the city limits, particularly in New York, Houston, Phoenix and Los Angeles.[16] Gated communities are these days being built even inside the city itself. Separated from the rest of the city by insurmount-

---

14 In *Edge City: Life on the New Frontier,* New York: Doubleday, 1991, pp. 184–92.
15 In "Trouble in Privatopia," *Progressive,* October 1993, pp. 30, 34.
16 Edward J. Blakeley and Mary Gail Snyder, *Fortress America: Gated Communities in the United States,* Washington, D.C.: Brookings Institution Press, 1997. The map and diagram showing the growth of fortress cities is on pp. 5–6.

able iron grille fencing, one has now sprung up in Chicago on the site of the old Stewart-Warner factory, an enclave of rich citizens barricaded inside a golden cage, where they are defended from the desperation of the nearby Lathrop Projects, inhabited only by Blacks and by what the affluent residents courteously refer to as "white trash."

What we see here is a belief in property taken to extremes, its thaumaturgic virtues transferred or extended from the privately owned house to the *privately owned* city. Just as American construction companies no longer limit themselves to offering houses or skyscrapers, but now put on the market entire towns (complete with their own town hall, police station, church and schools), so too do buyers crave not merely a house (always subject to political power) but their own private enclave, a community with its own laws, its own police, its own taxes – in other words, its own "public thing," the republic itself.

After the house as temple (of the household divinities) came the house as commodity. Now the city, too, has become a commodity: a city-commodity that can be exchanged, bought, sold, even floated on the stock market. What is more, through property, the world of commodities reveals itself to be contiguous with that of politics: in a society based on property, ownership becomes the highest form of sovereignty. And so we see the appearance of private government, which seems a contradiction in terms, because what a government governs, after all, is the *public* thing. But here the public sphere has been subsumed within the private. In these private cities, the homeowner hopes to avoid the ills of the public city, from its delinquency to its uncleanliness to the diseases it harbors – but, at the same time, to conserve all the privileges of citizenry. The private city is the extreme, most realized form of the suburban ideal. Here egotism is codified, segregation endorsed, intruders shot on sight. Here there are no outsiders to fear, only the razor wire that surrounds the compound.

Private cities are where belief in property turns fanatical, in a sort of fundamentalist religion of ownership. Such an experiment is by no means new. In Indian cities, since the days of Empire, there have existed institutions called, aptly enough, colonies. In New Delhi, for example, there was the Defense Colony and the Friends Colony. These residential complexes, normally situated in wood- or grassland, are fenced off from the outside world and patrolled by private armed guards.

Governed by internal rules and furnished with internal services, they represent enclaves of ease and privilege amid a world of chaos. Without knowing it, these were to foreshadow the utopian ideal of privatizing the entire public sphere: the utopia of a fortress under siege.

Metacity

An Imperial Metropolis

American cities demand to be perceived and studied from a certain angle that would be impossible for a European metropolis, unless, like the Greek *polis,* it belongs to the realm of ancient history. You feel constrained to regard cities in the United States as though they were individuals or, rather, individual subjects of history – that is to say, subjects that exist independently of one another, autonomous in the way the communes were during the thirteenth century. It would hardly be feasible to write a history of Paris from 1800 to the present as a subject considered independently of the subject of France. Likewise, one couldn't really speak of the subject of London considered apart from the subjects of Manchester, Edinburgh or Glasgow or removed from the subject of the United Kingdom. Still, it is possible to write a history of Los Angeles, such as Mike Davis's *City of Quartz,* in the same manner that Giovanni Villani used to recount the vicissitudes of Florence in *Cronica.*

American cities, in fact, turn an almost paroxysmal gaze on themselves. It is possible to write a scholarly study like *Chicago and the American Literary Imagination, 1880–1920.*[1] More unlikely would be a book entitled *Frankfurt and the German*

---

1 Carl S. Smith, *Chicago and the American Literary Imagination, 1880–1920,* Chicago: University of Chicago Press, 1984.

Literary Imagination. It's a form of self-regard that verges on, and frequently falls into, provincialism.

American tourist guides have the habit of including information about the celebrity progeny of various cities. In *Frommer's*,[2] for example, we learn that Chicago is the birthplace of Walt Disney, Kim Novak, Johnny Weissmuller, John Dos Passos, Edgar Rice Burroughs and Ernest Hemingway. Kansas City's tally, by contrast, is somewhat more modest: jazzmen Charlie Parker and Ben Webster, film director Robert Altman and actor Ed Asner. Denver has to settle for Douglas Fairbanks and bandleader Paul Whiteman.[3] Even in their production of fame, cities fall into a hierarchy.

Of the architectural geography of the United States, 99 percent is made up of houses of one or, at most, two stories; skyscrapers are the exception rather than the rule. The presence of the skyscraper serves merely to demonstrate the power of the host city, just as elaborate medieval cathedrals were designed to show off the prosperity of the urban bourgeoisie. Chicago's skyscrapers, the tallest in the United States, express the city's bourgeois values in the same way that Milan's duomos represented the opulence of the city's merchants. This is why cities persist in erecting skyscrapers, even when the population density is so low that the price of land could never justify vertical construction, when there is no economic sense in doing so. This is why even in Los Angeles, for example, a clutch of skyscrapers rises on the run-down downtown area over endless tracts of single-story houses. Counting a city's skyscrapers is a way of establishing an urban league table: Denver totals thirty, above Kansas City's twenty-something, followed by the dozen or so in Des Moines. From the freeway, even at a distance of several miles, you can size up a city's importance simply by measuring the height and number of the skyscrapers rising over the flatlands.

Cities are just as proud of the relationship they enjoy with their own university (or universities), where we see the same interweaving of business and doctrine, money and culture that existed in the Middle Ages between Bologna and Pisa and their respective universities – the same interweaving that persists today in certain European provincial cities such as Camerino, Montpellier and Heidelberg, centers

---

2 *Frommer's Guide USA, 1993–94*, New York: Prentice Hall Travel, 1999, p. 510.
3 Ibid., pp. 605, 621, 767.

that owe a considerable portion of their revenues to their seats of higher learning (although Rome and Hamburg cannot be said to be particularly proud of their respective universities). New York, by contrast, nurtures a tacit inferiority complex about its Columbia University, compared to Harvard and MIT, the elite universities of Boston. San Francisco, Chicago and Minneapolis, meanwhile, are somewhat immoderate in their boasts about their own institutions.

Here in the United States, you often hear sentences such as "In terms of its gross product the Los Angeles area constitutes the 12th richest nation in the world." Or, as Irving Cutler writes, "Only eleven foreign nations have a gross national product higher than that of Metropolitan Chicago."[4] It is as though the city had its separate dealings with the outside world, its own balance of trade. Or you might come upon data regarding the "capitalization of the leading hundred companies based in Chicago." The very nature of the American press, with its regime of regional monopolies, ensures that every city reads only its own newspaper, whose circulation mirrors its area of influence. In this way, the ranking of daily newspapers respects that of the cities themselves: first New York (with the *New York Times*), then Los Angeles (with the *Los Angeles Times*), then Chicago (with the *Chicago Tribune*).

This way of perceiving cities as though they were separate states reached its culmination in the nineteenth century, when Washington's grip on the affairs of the nation was much slacker than it is today. There was as yet no FBI (formed in 1924), no Federal Reserve (launched in 1913).[5] There wasn't a single currency; paper money was scarce, with each bank printing its own. Different bank notes were considered legal tender depending on which city you happened to be in, creating exchange problems for visitors and heightening their sense of their own foreignness by giving them the impression that they had somehow wandered into another country. Accounts of the nineteenth-century rivalry between Boston and New York are similar to those of the standoff between the maritime republics of Genoa and Pisa, complete with real trade wars.

---

4 I. Cutler, *Chicago, Metropolis of the Mid-Continent*, p. 279.
5 The Federal Reserve System only managed to get off the ground with the passing of the Federal Reserve Act after the financial panic of 1907. See R. Chernow, *The House of Morgan*, pp. 120, 130, 181–82.

Thus the nature of American cities, their role and the way we perceive them, contributes to that overall sense of anachronism that makes the time lines of European and American history seem so out of joint. Each of the two continents appears in some respects more advanced than the other, in others more barbaric. The United States was light years ahead of Europe during the nineteenth century in terms both of the speed with which industrial capitalism expanded and of its politics in general: it was already a republican, democratic state that spanned an entire continent, while back in mainland Europe – in Italy, for example – Carbonarist rebels continued to confront the Holy Alliance in dukedoms such as those of Parma or Piacenza. In terms of internal dynamics, however, the United States was back in the age of the maritime republics and communes.

A comparison of certain dates will reinforce this time lag, which gives you the impression of living in a sort of *Elsewhen,* to borrow the title of an H. Beam Piper science fiction novel. In Europe, 1848 was the year of revolutions, the year of the Paris communes and the Roman republic. For Chicago, 1848 was equally important, but for wholly different reasons: that was the year the Michigan–Illinois Canal opened; the year the first telegraph connection was installed; the inaugural year of the city's first railroad, the Galena and Chicago, and of its first wood-paved road, an eight-foot-wide thoroughfare that permitted carriages to travel (for a fee) at speeds of up to ten miles per hour. In Europe, Marx and Engels published their *Communist Manifesto* that year; in Chicago, the Chicago Board of Trade was founded, setting in motion the trading of futures, the most lucrative activity available to its citizens outside of bank robbery.

Emblematic at the beginning of the nineteenth century was the competition between various US coastal cities to construct navigable canals and thus to control communications routes with the interior of the continent. While New York was building the gigantic 356-mile Erie Canal to connect the Great Lakes with the Eastern Seaboard, Philadelphia responded with an even more titanic canal venture, the Main Line, which, at 406 miles and with hundreds of locks, ran right up to the Ohio River. Cut off from the canals, Boston tried to launch itself in the railroad business, just as Chicago sought to defeat the St. Louis riverboats with *its* railroads. St. Louis, in turn, was to try all possible means to block construction of railroad bridges over the Mississippi, bridges that would ensure Chicago's eventual victory. Here we have a vision of history in which the subject is no longer the bourgeoisie per se, but the separate city bourgeoisies locked in a fiercely competitive struggle against one another.

It was in Chicago, in fact, that this city-centric vision was to reach its culmination. "In ancient times," one journalist wrote, "all the roads led to Rome; in modern times all the roads lead to Chicago." Here we witness a mode of comparison to recur throughout the nineteenth century in relation to the imperial destinies of American cities. "It is sure to be the seat of empire forever. Chicago, the inevitable metropolis of the vigorous northwestern third of the prairie world." So wrote James Parton in 1867.[6] San Francisco's seven hills were like the seven hills of Rome. Even a contemporary urban historian, Mike Davis, notes in *City of Quartz* how "Los Angeles was just a backcountry town, *tributary to imperial* San Francisco" (italics mine). [7]

In fact, this presumed relationship with antiquity was already present at the inception of the United States. The minutes James Madison kept of the talks at the 1787 Philadelphia Convention are peppered with references to ancient history. At one point, Madison finds himself asking: "Can the orders introduced by the institution of Solon, can they be found in the United States? Can the Military habits & manners of Sparta be resembled to our habits & manners? Are the distinctions of Patrician & Plebeian known among us?"[8]

Implicit in these comparisons with classical antiquity was the idea that imperial cities had gradually moved west from Persia to Greece; then to Rome, Spain and Great Britain; then, finally, on to the New World. In this way, the United States felt itself to be the sole legitimate heir of the imperial heritage. Speaking of New York, an Albany newspaper reporter wrote: "A city sustained by that trade can never languish. ... [it] must be far greater then even Alexandria or Thebes." Nineteenth-century America's obsession with the idea of transposing the age of classical civilization onto its own future, imagining its own ruins to come, is almost incredible. While Goethe wrote, "America, in this you surpass / our old continent

---

6   James Parton, in *Atlantic Monthly,* March 1867, p. 327.
7   Mike Davis, *City of Quartz*, London: Verso 1990, p. 25.
8   James Madison, *Notes on Debates in the Federal Convention of 1787*, Athens, Ohio: Ohio Univ. Press, 1984, p. 185.

/ you have *no ruined castle* / *nor marble monument*" (italics mine), the Americans were busy forging one of the most typical sentiments of modernity: *nostalgia for the future.*[9]

Logan Reavis, who prophesied that St. Louis would outgrow the Atlantic coast cities, foresaw a time when "sentimental pilgrims from the humming cities of the Pacific coast will be seen where Boston, Philadelphia, and New York now stand, viewing in moonlight contemplation, with the melancholy owl, traces of the Athens, the Carthage, and the Babel of the Western hemisphere."[10] In 1857, the *Chicago Magazine* estimated that "700,000 square miles of Western territories" either were or would soon be "partially tributary" to Chicago, with the word "tributary" expressing perfectly the underlying imperial metaphor: the idea that military empire had given way to a commercial dominion. To a Cincinnati contractor writing in 1846, commerce was a "mighty conqueror, more powerful than an army with banners."

When on 8 October 1871 the Great Chicago Fire broke out, killing 250 people and destroying 17,000 buildings, leaving 100,000 of the city's population without a roof over their heads, a New Orleans newspaper reporter wrote with barely concealed schadenfreude: "Chicago will never be like the Carthage of old. Its glory will be of the past, not of the present, while its hopes, once so bright and cloudless will be to the end marred and blackened by the smoke of its fiery fate."[11] But by 1875, the *Chicago Tribune* was able to declare about the Union Stock Yards that "strangers visiting the city would as soon think of quitting it without having seen them as the traveler would of visiting Egypt, and not the pyramids; Rome, and not the Coliseum; Pisa, and not the Leaning-Tower." It would never enter the mind of somebody from Europe to compare a slaughterhouse to the Coliseum. Remarkably, no European city would take pride in carrying the label "Porkopolis," as Cincinnati did, or in being declared the "Bovine City," as Chicago was. Even to-

---

9   "Amerika, du hast es besser/Als unser Kontinent, das alte/*Hast keine verfallene Schlösser/Und Keine Basalte.*" From the poem "Den Vereinigten Staaten," in *Goethes Werke*, band 1, 12 neubarb. Aufl. München: Verlag C. H. Beck, 1981 ("Hamburger Ausgabe").

10 Citations taken from W. Cronon, *Nature's Metropolis*, pp. 42–43. Significantly, Reavis's book was entitled *A Change of National Empire; or Arguments in Favor of the Removal of the National Capital to the Mississippi Valley* (1869).

11 Cited in I. Cutler, *Chicago, Metropolis of the Mid-Continent*, pp. 30–31.

day, Wisconsin proudly defines itself as the "Dairyland of America," a label that appears on its state automobile license plates, yet an accolade that Europeans would probably find less than flattering.

In this we witness a hierarchical difference between the two continents. When we study American history, facts and events that would have no place in European history books – which are filled with international congresses and summits, elections, battles and peace treaties – take on great importance, while a list of characters wholly different from our roster of generals, politicians, artists and thinkers comes to the fore. The dates that mark the passing of epochs stress a side of historical processes that stands in marked contrast with those of Europe. Here in the United States, the milestones are of a different shape and hue: 1842, for example, is noted as the year when Joseph Dart, owner of a Buffalo hardware store, introduced the steam-powered grain elevator; in 1873 in DeKalb, a small town fifty miles west of Chicago, Joseph Glidden invented barbed wire; in 1866 in Chicago, Windsor Leland invented the slaughtering machine. The protagonists of this history are not musicians or poets but more prosaic individuals who have nonetheless contributed to shaping the future. Legends abound about the likes of musket manufacturer Eli Whitney, who first introduced interchangeable weapons parts, while a vast literature exists on Cyrus Hall McCormick, inventor of the combine harvester and founder of the McCormick Harvesting Machine Company, one of the most powerful Chicago dynasties. During the London Exposition of 1851, Queen Victoria wrote in her diary, "Mr McCormick's reaping machine has convinced English farmers that it can be economically deployed. ... In agriculture, it appears that the machine will be as important as the jenny and power loom in manufacture."[12]

One effect of this out-of-jointness can be seen in the toponymy of Chicago's streets and buildings, many of which are named after butchers, brewers, dentists or grain merchants: an entire book is even dedicated to the history of Chicago street names.[13] One avenue bears the name of the grain merchant Elli B. Beach, while brewer Michael Diversey is evoked in the names of three different places: an

---

12 Extract cited by Charles Wilson in *A History of Technology*, vol. 5, p. 817.
13 Don Hayner and Tom McNamee, *Streetwise Chicago: A History of Chicago Street Names*, Chicago: Loyola University Press, 1988.

avenue, a parkway and a square. Halstead Avenue takes its name from a Philadelphia banker, and Palmer Boulevard immortalizes one of Chicago's most important merchants, a partner of Marshall Field's and patron of the Art Institute. Another great avenue recalls Archibald Claybourne, Chicago's first commercial butcher, who arrived in the city in 1823, ten years before it became a commune. In 1832, Oliver Newberry started up a pork- and beef-packing company, and somewhat later, his son Walter opened Chicago's great Newberry Library; today in Chicago there is a Newberry Avenue, just as there is a McCormick Place and a Hutchinson Street, named after the "Hutch" family of meat packers (butcher Charles Hutchinson founded the Art Institute of Chicago). John D. Parker Avenue and Joseph Throop Street are both named after lumber merchants, while another street is dedicated to the city's first dentist, Walter Alport. One of the city's tallest skyscrapers, the Hancock Center, bears the name of the man who, during the nineteenth century, presided over the Chicago Board of Trade. The building is also known as "The Bull" because of its darkly solid mass and the two antennae that sprout from its top, and perhaps also as a way to remember the animal that made the city's fortune and that also gave the local basketball team, the Chicago Bulls, its name. Indeed, several of Chicago's skyscrapers have "horns" in the form of antennae, including the Sears Tower, once the tallest such structure in the world.

There's a kind of justice in this toponymy: it gives to Caesar what is rightly Caesar's and to the grocer what is the grocer's, recognizing the role of commerce and trade in forging the great power of Chicago, a city commonly regarded as a separate, autonomous organism, an economic and cultural force in its own right.

PART TWO

11

The Mayo Curdles in the Melting Pot

As you stand on the metal drawbridge that spans the mouth of the Chicago River, and then as you look up, you are seized by an overwhelming sense of vertigo, a giddy fear of falling, as your eyes trace the vanishing points of skyscrapers plunging upward into the sky, skyscrapers of every shape, hue and material hanging in an inverted abyss. This vertigo derives partly from the feeling of limitless power and world-dominating arrogance conveyed by these buildings. But it also comes partly from your awareness that such a glut of power sits on the subterranean foundations of more than a century of hard labor, the unwritten biographies of untold masses of peasants who made the long journey from the Old Continent.

If Chicago became within the space of a few decades "the inevitable metropolis" of the Northwest, as Parton dubbed it in his reportage of 1867,[1] "sure to be forever the seat of Empire," it was thanks not only to the millions of cattle, or the tons of wood and grain, or even the tangle of railroads that passed through the city, but also to the thousands, eventually millions, of European immigrants off-loaded by those same railroads on the shores of Lake Michigan, together with the corn, wheat, pigs and white pine. The city streets resounded with a myriad of idioms to the point that, in the words of one journalist, Chicago became "more than the

---

1 J. Parton, *Chicago*, p. 327.

Marseille of our Mediterranean,"[2] a chaotic land- and seaport whose babel of languages, customs, tastes, smells and dirt brought together Greeks and Danes, Poles and Irishmen, Scots and Sicilians, Swedes and Serbs, Dutchmen and Ukrainians, Lithuanians, Bulgarians. By the end of the nineteenth century, more than twenty-five different ethnic communities were present in Chicago. In 1910, more than two-thirds of the city's population consisted of immigrants or their progeny: immigrants who had arrived not en masse but in a series of waves.

First came the Irish, forced to flee from their island after repeated potato famines (from 1845 to 1860). By 1860, though, Germans streaming into the States outnumbered the Irish. To begin with, the Germans were mainly political exiles who emigrated after the repression of the great uprisings of 1848 in Prussia, Baden and Württemberg and after the closure of the Frankfurt parliament the following year; these came to be known as the "Forty-Eighters." But the influx didn't end with the unification of the Bismarckian Reich. On the contrary, it turned into a flood, and by 1914, with 800,000 inhabitants either German born or of German descent, Chicago had become the most Germanic of American cities, as well as the fifth largest "German" city *tout court*.

The period from 1860 to 1890 also saw a marked increase in the number of Scandinavian immigrants; after these came the Russian Jews, the Italians and, above all, the Poles (more than 1 million of Chicago's inhabitants these days are of Polish origin). A cousin of Lech Walesa lives in the suburbs of the Windy City. The Italians, too, were relative latecomers. In 1850, only four Italian immigrants lived in Chicago, and just forty-three lived in all of Illinois. Ten years later, that number had barely risen to a hundred. But by 1880, 1,357 Italians lived in Chicago, with the numbers rising to 13,000 by 1890 and more than 124,000 by 1920.

More generally, European emigration to Chicago can be divided into two distinct phases, a pattern that also holds true for emigration to the United States as a whole. The vast majority of the 8 million or so Europeans who emigrated to the States between 1840 and 1880 hailed from northwestern Europe, in particular from Britain, Ireland, Scandinavia and Germany. By contrast, the 24 million immigrants who arrived between 1880 and 1930 came for the most part from eastern or southern Europe – among them Poles, Russian Jews, Italians, Slovaks, Croats,

---

2   Ibid., p. 330.

Serbs, Hungarians, Spaniards and Portuguese. The old migrant nations continued to furnish a sizable contingent, however, with more than 1 million new immigrants arriving from England and Germany between 1891 and 1930.[3]

The Irish exodus reached its peak in the years between 1847 and 1854, when 1.2 million Irish immigrants set foot upon American soil, while the height of German immigration came in the years from 1881 to 1892, when 1.7 million Germans disembarked in the land of the free. Russian Jews had their moment between 1901 and 1914, with more than 2 million entries to the States. In the same period, the flood of immigrants from Poland and Italy reached diluvial levels, with more than 3 million Italians landing on US shores at a rate of 200,000 per year. After the short interval of the Great War, the flux was about to recommence, with 222,000 new arrivals in 1921,[4] when the United States suddenly closed its doors to immigrants.

Each of these groups had its own specific motives for coming to America. While the Irish were spurred by the potato famine, southern Italians began to appear in large numbers only after 1860, when a newly unified Italy had reduced the southern part of that country to misery. The Bohemians, meanwhile, were driven to Illinois by the Habsburgs' repression of the 1848 rebellions. But triggering a human tsunami of 2.5 million people could take as little as the gesture of one anarchist, such as the assassination of Tzar Alexander II. To justify their subversion, the Russian authorities found a scapegoat in the Jews, inciting the population to organize pogroms by digging up old allegations about Jews practicing child sacrifice during Passover. In the end, the Jews fled west to America in a new chapter of their perpetual exodus.

A wave of Polish immigration exploded in the years following 1871, when Chancellor Otto von Bismarck imposed his policy of Germanization on the eastern provinces of the Reich. Millions of lives were overturned by the chance effects of small events occurring hundreds of miles away. According to the dynamics of chaos theory, a slight breeze on one side of the Pacific can modify the course of a hurricane on the other. In this case, a despot's rage was enough to alter the ethnic composition of a city on the other side of the Atlantic.

---

3 Stephen Steinberg, *The Ethnic Myth: Race, Ethnicity and Class in America* (1981), Boston: Beacon Press, 1989, p. 35.
4 Census Bureau, *Historical Statistics of the United States*, series c 89–119, vol. I, pp. 105–6.

So when a Pole got into an argument with an Italian on a Chicago street, if you wished to unravel the chain of causes leading to the event, you would soon become enmeshed in a morass of political vicissitudes, from the decrees of a German chancellor to the desperate act of a Russian nihilist. The same thing occurred to Leibniz as he wondered what had spurred him to write his *Treatise on Monadology*: "There is an infinity of past and present shapes and motions that enter into the efficient cause of my present writing, and there is an infinity of small inclinations and dispositions of my soul, present and past, that enter into its final cause. And since all this detail involves nothing but other prior or more detailed contingents, each of which needs a similar analysis in order to give its reason, we do not make progress in this way" and it is therefore necessary to seek a "sufficient reason."[5]

In our case, we might be tempted to wonder what would constitute "sufficient reason" for these human tidal waves pouring onto the prairies, or crowding onto the marshy banks of a lake that would be frozen in winter and swarming with mosquitoes in summer. One possible cause was medical progress, which led to a drastic reduction in infant mortality and so produced the demographic time bomb we now attribute to the Third World but which, at that time, was happening in Europe. In 1800, the United States and Europe together numbered 185 million inhabitants (180 million in Europe, 5 million in the US). By 1910, those numbers had spiraled to 542 million (450 million in Europe, 92 million in the US), without counting Europeans who had emigrated to Latin America or Australasia. In little more than a century, the population of the Western world had tripled.

Another factor enabling massive immigration was the steam engine. We have already seen the significant role steam power played in forging Chicago. Likewise, the advent of the steamship produced modern mass immigration. For one thing, the steamship was the main cause of this great uprooting: it was so cheap to transport not only American but also Russian, Australian and Indian grain and livestock to Europe by steamboat that the livelihoods of millions of European peasant farmers – whose lands were not sufficiently fertile and who thus could not compete with foreign prices – were effectively ruined. Because of steam power, harvests

---

5   Georg Wilhelm Leibniz, "Monadology," in *Discourses on Metaphysics and Other Essays*, Indianapolis and Cambridge: Hackett., 1991, p. 73.

from the prairies and the cattle herds of the Far West led to millions of European peasants literally becoming superfluous. Steamships were not only the indirect cause of the exodus, however; they were also what made it possible. Before the advent of steam power, crossing the Atlantic had taken several weeks: now it required only ten days. At one time, the cost of crossing was exorbitant, but by the end of the nineteenth century, you could purchase a place on the third-class deck for twenty-five or thirty dollars, a sum that even a lowly farmhand could scrape together (just as today's emigrants from Third World countries can normally afford the price of an air ticket).

Once set off, the mechanism began to feed on itself. The uprooted European peasantry went to work in the stockyards, for example, and thus helped increase productivity in the meat-packing industry. As William T. Stead wrote in 1894,

> indirectly, Mr. Armour and his class have played a very considerable part in the social revolution which is going on in Great Britain ... Armour was rendering it difficult for the small farmers on her Gloucestershire estates to obtain paying prices for their cattle, and there is no doubt that the immense development which Mr. Armour and his allies and rivals have been able to give to the American meat exporting trade has had a very powerful effect upon the British politics. ... [T]he price of Irish cattle is influenced largely by the ruling prices in the Chicago market. ... If many of our aristocrats are little better than splendid paupers ... these results are chiefly due to Mr. Armour and his class.[6]

The influx of immigrants, because it contributed to the impoverishment of those who had stayed behind, thus became the spur for more departures. Yet these explanations alone are not sufficient; they are "causes," not "reasons." Aside from that, they leave one mystery unresolved. How was it – in the words of Stephen Steinberg's seemingly incongruous query – that from 1865 on, after the abolition of slavery, the Northern industries did not draw on the enormous well of labor constituted by the Southern Blacks already in place but summoned instead millions of Europeans from across the ocean?

Simply put, if Black ex-slaves were to be used in the factories of the North, someone would have to replace them as cotton pickers in the South (cotton was

---

6 W. T. Stead, *If Christ Comes to Chicago!*, pp. 84–85.

the raw material for one of America's most important industries and biggest exports). And however poor they may have been, European immigrants were not willing to work in the cotton fields. So the plantation owners considered using the Chinese, who were also used to the gruelling work of the paddy fields. As one owner put it, "We can drive the niggers out and import coolies that will work better at less expense, and relieve us from the cursed nigger impudence." After the arrival of the Chinese, the owners thought, the Blacks would cease to demand their "forty acres and a mule," in the words of one Kentucky journalist: the new law would be "Work nigger … or starve."[7]

The only problem was that most of the Chinese were already employed in the mines or at work constructing the Western railroads, so few could be lured to the South. Those who did go stayed only a short time, leaving soon after experiencing the backbreaking work in the fields, for which they were paid a meager wage, or the cruelty of the white masters. In short, having liberated the Blacks from slavery, the United States felt nonetheless "bound" to keep them in the cotton fields of the South, where their servitude could be reorganized. This situation would change only with the outbreak of World War I, when the influx of immigrants from Europe suddenly dried up.

Here we begin to move closer to Leibniz's notion of "sufficient reason." During a phase of tumultuous industrial development, without a steady flow of immigrant labor, the United States would have suffered a serious shortage of manpower. Labor would have become a precious and expensive commodity, leading to a rise in workers' wages. But with millions of immigrants flooding into the country, the cost of labor fell dramatically, and its availability was such that workers competed to sell their services to the lowest bidder. Although US historical statistics are somewhat vague on this point, per capita gross national product rose by 250 percent during the period from 1870 to 1910, but the increase in average yearly income over an even longer period – 1860 to 1910 – was only 20 percent.[8]

While the wealth produced by each individual was 2.5 times what it had been in the mid-nineteenth century, then, the wages received had grown by only

---

7   Cited in S. Steinberg, *The Ethnic Myth* , p. 184.
8   Census Bureau, *Historical Statistics,* series D 722–727, D 733–773, D 779–793 and F 1–5, p. 164.

one-fifth. In other words, to produce the same degree of wealth as before, a job could be paid for at half the former rate. This was possible not merely because of progress, but because of the millions of immigrants who continued to provide an abundant source of cheap labor and who were easily managed and most importantly *mobile*. If mobility is a sign of freedom, regarded as a positive value, the mobility of labor is a sign of the freedom of capital, the ability to hire, fire, accomplish extraordinary feats or relocate to distant factories and construction sites almost at will. Amazingly, 58 percent of America's industrial workers in 1910 were foreign-born, a percentage that rose to 76 percent in the clothing industry and 67 percent in the iron mines.

Nor was there any subterfuge or hypocrisy in the use of European immigrants. Often the immigrants would depart from their homelands with a job contract already in hand, summoned at the behest of US employment agencies. Even more frequently, they were called in by employers as scabs, just as the employers contracted with convicted prisoners or used women to carry out certain jobs, as in 1864, when the *Chicago Times* took on a number of women to break a printers' strike. Also in 1864, the Illinois Central Railroad Company imported engine drivers from Belgium to defeat strikers,[9] and during the great strike of 1886, Philip Armour, "the butcher who wanted to go to heaven," had thousands of workers brought in from Baltimore, Philadelphia and New York,[10] most of them Poles, Czechs and Germans.

Throughout the nineteenth century, immigrants were the great weapon of the factory owners against workers' unions, a weapon that enabled owners to keep down wages and crush strikes. Because of this, one of the major American unions, the Knights of Labor, campaigned in support of the first anti-immigration law, the Chinese Exclusion Act of 1882, which closed US borders to Chinese immigrants willing to work for excessively poor pay in abominable conditions.

Here we see how mistaken is the common assumption that the reactionary, conservative segments of society are the xenophobes, the ones who want to close the borders to immigrants, while the progressive and antiracist segments wish to keep them open. During the most conservative periods of its history, the United

---

9   B. L. Pierce, *A History of Chicago*, vol. II, pp. 163–64.
10 L. C. Wade, *Chicago's Pride*, p. 252.

States has, in truth, absorbed its biggest waves of immigrants: at the end of the nineteenth century and again during the Reagan years. It is, in fact, those on the right who open the floodgates, while preaching the need to close them, just as it is the most racist traders who take on illegal immigrant workers, using immigrant labor to keep down wages because the immigrants must accept slave pay. This leads to racist feelings among the lower classes, because immigrants fix a price ceiling on the labor market and compete for precious resources: livable housing, overbooked hospital beds, decent schools for their children.

It thus becomes clearer why, in many countries, unions and labor movements are often against immigration, which threatens the hard-won standards of living they defend. The desire to discipline the workforce and to make it as economical as possible therefore has the effect of translating the class struggle into ethnic and racial conflict. Older generations of immigrants oppose subsequent waves for the same reason.

In the United States, as soon as one group had become (relatively) established and integrated and its workers had begun to organize themselves, a new wave would appear to offer its services at even more rock-bottom prices. This sentiment is clear in an editorial that appeared in the German-language newspaper, the *Illinois Staats-Zeitung*, on 11 August 1888. The piece, entitled "Unwanted Guests," concerned the new wave of Italian immigrants:[11]

> The investigations carried on by Congress, in regard to the Italian immigrants, reveal very disagreeable facts. The Italian immigrants possess such a low degree of culture and education, that the American workers, accustomed to a higher standard of living, cannot compete with them. It is impossible for the Americans to stoop to such low levels of existence, as has been discovered by the congressional investigators, as for instance, living on refuse, being crowded together like animals, and knowing nothing about cleanliness.
>
> There can be no advantage to this country in letting these people come here. At best, they may contribute to bring about a condition of barbarism. If, in addition to this,

---

11 There were (and still are) dozens of ethnic newspapers published in Chicago in an exotic range of tongues. Around 1940, the government funded a research group to compile (and translate in English) an anthology of the city's ethnic press from its nineteenth-century beginnings to the present. The fruit of this enormous labor was the *Chicago Foreign Language Press Survey*, preserved on microfilm, from which I have taken all of the following citations from "ethnic" articles.

one takes into consideration that these half-civil people will have the right to vote a few years hence, and thereby help to decide the destiny of this country, one can not help but shudder as to the future entrusted in such hands.

A certain Anglo-American newspaper calls the Italians the "Chinese of the East." A law against immigration from Italy seems justified on the same basis as the one against Chinese. ... We have to admit in justice to the Italian Government that it tries its utmost to keep its dirty sons from our shores. It made immigration laws more severe, in order to remove inducements for emigrants. It is obvious, however, what little effect these measures have, because even during the investigation Italian workers are hired by contract and transported to the United States.

This passage includes all the related issues: unfair competition in the labor market, comparison with the Chinese, the uncleanliness of the "new arrivals," a demand that the Italians be prevented from entering, admission that the Italians have in fact been summoned by American factory owners. Here is a classic example of the mechanism that immediately translates economic conflict into racism, class struggle into a clash between ethnicities. As other examples, a mob of Irishmen in 1864 attacked twelve Blacks working in the lumber docks;[12] and the 8 April 1910 edition of the Greek newspaper *Loxias* reported an assault on a Greek trash collector by a group of Irishmen, who warned the Greek to "Get out of the garbage business or we will kill all of you Greeks!"

But the Irish were not the only persecutors. A certain Italian called Fiepi was accused of employing only Sicilian garbage collectors and of demanding a "commission" of five dollars for each post.[13] A Chicago Lithuanian, Stanley Balzekas Jr., recounts the experience of his father, who arrived in the United States in 1912: "He was a concrete mixer for a company where everyone was Italian, and when they found out he was Lithuanian, they fired him. Then he went to Chicago. ... [H]e worked as a blacksmith in a German place and of course when they found out he wasn't German, they let him go. Then he went to a Swedish blacksmith shop, and it was the same thing all over again."[14]

---

12 B. L. Pierce, *A History of Chicago*, vol. II, p. 26.
13 *L'Italia*, 25 June 1904.
14 Richard C. Lindberg, *Ethnic Chicago*, Lincolnwood, Ill.: Passport Books, 1994, p. 126.

In a celebrated article, Robert E. Park introduces to sociology the notion of marginality. Whereas the migration of old was always a "migration of peoples," with entire nations or tribes uprooted, led by their kings (the *völkerwanderungen* so dear to historians of German Romanticism), modern migration, Park notes, is a migration of individuals – or at most of a family – leaving their homeland.[15] "Migration, which was formerly an invasion, followed by the forcible displacement or subjugation of one people by another, has assumed the character of a peaceful penetration." In the former case, the migrant – the invader – subjugates the invadee (the first European migrants to America were of this type). In the modern case, on the other hand, "migration of peoples has been transmuted into mobility of individuals." Power relations thus become inverted, so that now the migrant is subjugated and brought into submission – "domesticated" – by the invadee.

The truth, however, is more subtle and complicated. With modern migration, it may be the individual who departs, but *the people arrive*. Each person leaves the homeland as an individual but, upon disembarkation in America, is immediately transformed into an Italian or a Pole or a German, becoming part of that particular "community," the people who will defend his or her rights, will find for the individual not only work but also a house, a means of expression and political representation. Ethnically based mutual-aid societies were formed to welcome the new arrivals: the German Relief and Aid Society, the Bohemian Society, United Hebrew Charities, the Scandinavian Relief Society. In Catholic communities, such societies were integrated with or even replaced by the local parish church. In reality, however, the communities built their own churches, just as they would later establish secret societies such as the Irish Clan-na-Gael, founded in 1867 by the Fenian Brotherhood. Every community had its own undertakers and cemeteries as well, as can still be seen today in newspaper death announcements.

So the individual was defined by belonging to a particular "race" (as it was called then) or "ethnicity" (as it is called now) or "community" (to use the official terminology). When two rival produce-grocers disputed control of the market with baseball bats, it was thus a clash between the Greek *people* and the Italian *people* (as the *Greek Star* reported on 18 August 1908). When a street brawl broke out

---

15 Robert E. Park, "Human Migration and the Marginal Man," in *The American Journal of Sociology*, vol. XXXIII (May 1928), no. 6, pp. 881–93.

between Swedes and Italians, the newspaper *Italia* commented, "The two races exchanged blows" (23 June 1904), while a shootout between German and Italian gangs was defined as a "race riot" by the *Chicago Tribune*. In 1874, a German newspaper expressed elation because the Swedish press, "which for a long time was rather hostile to everything German, has changed its attitude and is beginning to realize that salvation for the Swedes does not lie in opposition to but in harmony with the Germans."[16] Meanwhile, the Polish newspaper *Dziennik Zwiazkowy* accused its Ukrainian counterpart *Swoboda* of attacking Poles (on 3 August 1918).

It was obvious that the first immigrants to arrive of a particular group should immediately start up a newspaper in their own language. That newspaper would then become two papers when the ethnic group split into opposing factions. The Germans had four newspapers, whereas both the Swedes and the Czechs had three, and so on. In an uninterrupted outpouring of fiery editorials, in a dozen or more languages, a babel of angry, indignant voices patriotically cursed the chauvinism of others, intolerant themselves yet demanding tolerance from others. It was a case of who could shout loudest to spread their own message, and also an attempt to remember and keep alive the mother tongue, a form of self-defense against the surrounding contempt, a chain of spite from one ethnic group to another, more or less reflecting their order of arrival on the American continent, with the first to land feeling themselves superior to the second, who in turn felt themselves above the third, and so on.

Excluded from this pyramid of castes, however, were the "outcasts," those who really *were* "first" to land in America: the Native Americans and then the Latinos (a cross between Spanish and Indios), followed by the Blacks, who had arrived shortly afterward with the early slave traders. All of these groups were, and still are, excluded from the hierarchy of ethnicities, for the simple reason that, even today, they are regarded not as ethnic groups, nor even as peoples, but simply as "races."

Outcasts aside, the descendants of the English colonizers despised the Irish who came shortly after them to such a degree that vacancy ads published in newspapers such as the *Chicago Tribune* commonly included the addendum: "Irish need

---

16 *Illinois Staats-Zeitung*, 27 November 1874.

not apply." Second in order of arrival – and thus also in the table of contempt – were the Germans, who were regarded as beer-swilling drunkards. In 1849, an antiforeigner party, the Know-Nothings, was formed (as a secret society) and, in a move against the Germans, declared its support for prohibition. (Xenophobia in the United States is often shot through with prohibition of one form or another; in the past, it was against alcohol; today, it's drugs.) Supported by the Know-Nothings, Chicago Mayor Levi D. Boone in 1855 imposed a closing law on bars for Sundays, the only day of repose for workers of the nineteenth century, and raised the cost of the alcoholic beverage license to $300. In response, Chicago witnessed its first-ever "political" uprising, the so-called Lager Beer Riots.

The German press responded to the waves of contempt that assailed the Germans from all sides, boasting of German temperance and accusing the Irish of drunkenness. On 7 March 1873, the *Illinois Staats-Zeitung* referred to a "Fight between German Policemen and *Irish Drunkards*" (italics mine). Only a few months earlier, on 17 August 1872, the same newspaper had published the following account of a labor conflict: "A violent fight took place yesterday … between German and Irish working men. As usual the Irish could not endure the praises the Germans were receiving from their employers for their application and temperance."

At the same time, contempt for those below (meaning those who arrived afterward) was coupled with resentment toward those above. While Protestants despised Catholics, within their own ranks, Catholic Poles resented the Irish. As late as 29 October 1931, one Polish newspaper, the *Przebudzenie,* portrayed the situation as follows:

> Everyone of us Poles understands that in the Irish parochial schools our children are being systematically and purposely deprived of their Polish soul, and finally yield to the process of "Irishization." But this is not all. The Irish in America never were friendly towards us and they never will be. They consider themselves a higher and more privileged group here and look upon us with contempt. We have witnessed many incidents when an Irish priest from the St. Mark's Church, admonishing children who were playing near the church, shouted: "Get away from here, you dirty Polack!" And imagine! To these "friends" of our nation our poor Poles are sending their children for education.

In turn, other groups despised the Poles and Italians, and indeed eastern and southern Europeans in general. In its editorial of 20 October 1912, the *Italia* takes up arms against Woodrow Wilson:

> In his *History of American People*, volume five, page 212, [the Democratic candidate Woodrow Wilson] viciously expresses himself as follows: "Immigration poured steadily in as before, but with an alteration of stock which students of affairs marked with uneasiness. Throughout the centuries men of sturdy stocks of the north of Europe, had made up the main strain of foreign blood, which was every year added to the vital working force of the country, or else men of Latin-Gallic stocks, of France and Northern Italy. But now there came multitudes of men of the lowest class, from the south of Italy, and men of the meaner sort out of Hungary and Poland, men out of the ranks where there was neither skill nor energy, nor any initiative of quick intelligence; and they came in numbers which increased from year to year, as if the countries of the south of Europe were disburdening themselves, of the more sordid and hapless elements of their population. And yet the Chinese were more to be desired as workmen, if not as citizens, than most of the coarse crew that came crowding in at the eastern ports."

Noticeable is the distinction Wilson makes between northern and southern Italians, a distinction that actually had official status; the *Reports of the Immigration Commission* (1911) did not distinguish between Bavarian and Prussian Germans but for statistical reasons did divide northern and southern Italians into two separate categories, indeed almost into two different nations. Among the northerners, the number of qualified workers was rated at 20 percent; among the southerners, it was only 15 percent. For the northerners, the illiteracy rate was 12 percent; among southerners, it was as high as 30 percent. Here, too, regional origin meant a different slot in the labor market.

Just as the structure of ethnic hatred mirrored the social hierarchy, so too did the labor market become an ethnic job market. Irishwomen were to nineteenth-century America what Filipinos are to contemporary Europe: the epitome of the domestic servant. Of the 29,470 domestics recorded in an 1855 New York census, 23,386 were Irish. In 1900, according to the United States Immigration Commission, 71 percent of Irish immigrants were classified as "domestic and personal servants," in contrast to only 9 percent of Italians and 14 percent of Jews. Indeed, during that period, even the most cultivated individuals were asking themselves why Irishwomen seemed to have this natural "vocation." The Jews and Italians maintained that their womenfolk refused to go into service for reasons of chastity, common decency, family pride and other such nonsense. (Back in Italy, Italian girls were going into service like it was going out of style, and Jewish women were frequently arrested in the States for prostitution.) So it was that a discourse of ethnic – one might even say racial – predisposition was constructed, whereby Irishwomen, for example, became innately suited to domestic service.

The real explanation was much simpler. Because of the potato famine, marriages in Ireland had diminished: one-third of men and women between the ages of twenty-five and thirty-five were single, while one-sixth of the population was never to marry. For this reason, the Irish were the only ethnic group in which many women *emigrated alone* – so much so, in fact, that there were 109 women for every 100 men among Irish immigrants, while the corresponding ratio for Italians was 27 women to 100 men (with only one in five Italian immigrants being female), and for Jews, 77 women to 100 men. In 1869, the Irish population of New York numbered 117,000 women and only 87,000 men. Once disembarked, these women immediately went in search of work, and the closest at hand was domestic service. Furthermore, unlike other immigrant groups, the Irish had the advantage of already knowing English. Taking advantage of this spontaneous influx, American employment agencies began importing Irish girls for service, while their English counterparts – such as the London Female Emigration Society, the British Ladies Emigration Society and the Girls' Friendly Society – exported them from the archipelago. All of this explains the so-called Irish "predisposition" for domestic service, a prime example of how a clearly demographic and market-driven logic can become translated into an inherent ethnic or racial character trait.[17]

If the ethnic hierarchy mirrored the social order, and if new arrivals were drawn into unfair competition with those who were already established, inevitably the last off the boat wanted to bolt the door behind and not let anyone else in. It was not just the *Illinois Staats-Zeitung* of 1888 that regarded the Italians as unwanted guests. Chicago's German Jewish newspaper, the *Occident*, in a 19 May 1891 edi-

---

17 On the question of Irish domestic servants, see S. Steinberg, *The Ethnic Myth*, pp. 153–66.

tion expressed the following sentiments about the arrival of Russian Jews:

> The Jews of this city, who always care well for any of their race in distress, object to
> receiving any of the immigrants' fund provided by Baron Hirsch, and object, also, to
> the sending of expelled Russian Jews to this city. This is right and proper. A good
> thing is charity, but charity should be broad and cover all phases of a situation. The
> presence in Chicago of any large number of a poor class, alien in thought and lan-
> guage, would be misfortune from every point of view. This is not the place for the
> unfortunates expelled from Russia. Baron Hirsch's scheme for a colonisation in
> South America is much more reasonable. The Russian Jews already in Chicago,
> some 12,000 in number, form a colony by themselves, and are in many cases a bur-
> den upon the well-to-do of their race and religion. The attitude assumed by those
> prominent in Jewish charitable work here is fully justified. Chicago has enough of
> the unfortunate strangers. In fact, this entire body of immigrants comes within the
> restrictions of our immigrant laws. They are assisted to cross the ocean; but a few
> are self-sustaining. ... [T]hey are poor, many are diseased and many are criminals.
> This is the judgement of the most intelligent American Jews and the Russian *exilés*
> should not be permitted to settle in this country.

This passage is particularly illuminating regarding the rapport between class and
"race" consciousness. It shows Jewish identity to be less consolidated than is commonly believed today, demonstrating the extent to which that identity became reinforced and crystallized by the surrounding anti-Semitism, which had, in fact,
crossed the Atlantic as part of the immigrants' cultural baggage. As the president
of the Polish National Alliance, M. Osuch, put it in 1888: "The Poles are one thing,
and the Polish Jews are another."[18]

Furthermore, the *Occident* provided a new linchpin for the discourse on migration to latch onto, claiming that not only were exiled Russian Jews poor – they
were poor and *criminal*. The mark of innate criminality apparently became a baton
that various immigrant groups passed on to one another in a relay race of contempt. An 1860 edition of *Harper's Magazine* stated that "nearly 75% of our criminals are Irish, fully 75% of the crimes of violence committed among us are the
work of Irishmen," while the debate about the "causes of the alarming rate of

---

18 B. L. Pierce, *A History of Chicago*, vol. III, p. 37.

crime among the Irish centered on ethnic traits, especially the intemperate disposition of the Irish 'race.'"[19] Allegations of criminality soon spread to the Jews. In 1908, Theodore Bingham, chief of the New York Police Department, attributed half the crime in the city to Jews:

> It is not astonishing that with a million Hebrews, mostly Russian, in the city (one quarter of the population) perhaps half of the criminals should be of that race when we consider that ignorance of the language, more particularly among men not physically fit for hard labor, is conductive to crime. … Among the most expert of all the street thieves are Hebrew boys under sixteen who are brought up to lives of crime.[20]

No group of immigrants felt the mark of criminality so hard or so deeply as did the Italians, however. In 1908, Arthur Train, then assistant to the New York district prosecutor, wrote that the Italians of the north were *"molto simpatico* to the American character"; displayed "many national traits … singularly like our own"; and resembled Americans in being "honest, thrifty, industrious, law-abiding, and good-natured."[21] On the other hand, southerners were "apt to be ignorant, lazy, destitute, and superstitious." In addition, "a considerable percentage, especially of those from cities, are criminal."

Not that the Irish and Jews didn't have their own share of delinquents. Among Chicago's famous sons were Irish gangster-politicians such as John Coughlin, elected as an alderman in the city's first district, site of numerous brothels, gaming clubs and speakeasies. Coughlin's partner in crime was "Hinky Dink" Kenna, another gang boss who, like Johnny "de Pow" Powers, owned several saloons and gambling joints and boasted of being able to buy an Italian's vote with a glass of beer. At the turn of the century, the Jewish underworld hit Chicago, led by characters such as Ike Bloom (né Gitelson) and Jack Guzik, who had a sideline in the white slave trade, and gangsters such as Davey Miller and Samuel "Nails" Morton, both regarded as Jewish Robin Hoods.[22] And, of course, Italians included "Diamond Jim" Colosimo, John Torrio and, in the 1920s, Alphonse (Al) Capone, the

---

19 S. Steinberg, *The Ethnic Myth,* p. 116.
20 Ibid., pp. 112–13.
21 Cited in Humbert S. Nelli's well-documented *Italians in Chicago 1880–1930: A Study in Ethnic Mobility,* New York: Oxford University Press, p. 126.
22 R. C. Lindberg, *Ethnic Chicago,* pp. 179–80.

man who was to invent the modern crime syndicate.[23] (The English word *syndi-cate* refers to a "capitalist cartel": we talk about "syndication agreements" in a joint stock company.) In the notorious St. Valentine's Day Massacre, a squad of Capone's button men machine-gunned to death seven members of the Irish North Side gang led by George "Bugs" Moran.

Accusations of criminality were not without substance; the problem was that the statistical frequency of crimes became interpreted in terms of character. Following the usual procedure, a situation was identified and described, then observed in terms of frequency. Afterward, the inevitability of the situation was calculated, with the conclusion that the problem must be in the genes. In this way, a social condition becomes destiny, and destiny becomes character. Separate individuals fall under the aegis of one singular capitalized idea. The Irish all become the Drunken Irishman, the Jews the Eternal Wandering Jew, the Italians the Italian Mafioso.

This tendency to label people according to national categories has always proved an extremely powerful temptation, one that not even poor Engels could avoid: although he admitted that the filthy conditions in slums were a general phenomenon, he felt compelled in the particular case of Dublin to add that "the national character of the Irish is partly responsible for this. The Irish are less bound by social convention than some of their neighbors and on occasion actually seem to be happy in dirty surroundings."[24] At the turn of the century, the genetic theory of "character" had become common in a scientific arena dominated by the figure of Cesare Lombroso.

The relationship between criminality and the nationalities of the immigrants was deemed so essential that the United States Immigration Commission published its own study, *Immigrants and Crime*, in which it outlined a scheme of "races and nationalities ... exhibiting clearly defined criminal characteristics." From this report emerged the idea that each nationality had its own criminal vocation, a *ge-*

---

23 For basic biographical information on John Coughlin, Michael Kenna and Alphonse Capone, see June Skinner Sawyers, *Chicago Portraits*, Chicago: Loyola University Press, 1991, which includes 250 short biographies of famous Chicagoans from Cyrus McCormick to John Belushi (son of Albanian immigrants). The criterion used for defining who is and who isn't a Chicagoan is unusual to say the least. Enrico Fermi, for example, is.

24 F. Engels, *The Condition of the Working Class in England*, p. 40.

netic predisposition to certain types of crime. Among those arrested, the Irish were first for drunkenness and vagrancy, while the French and the Jews took the honors for prostitution. The Jews also ran a close second to Americans in crimes against property, such as robbery or receipt of stolen goods. The Italians, meanwhile, showed a marked predilection for violence and for crimes against the person, including murder. In the commission's words, "certain kinds of criminality are inherent in the Italian race."[25]

To claim that criminal tendencies are inscribed in a people's genetic code was by no means a purely conceptual operation; while such claims may have pertained to the philosophy of the social sciences, they could also have extremely serious practical implications. This happened in Louisiana in 1890, for example, in an episode that Italians, who nowadays protest the criminality of Maghrebian immigrants in their own country, seem to have canceled from memory. On 15 October of that year, David Hennessy, chief superintendent of the New Orleans police, was killed. The city's inhabitants blamed the killing on Sicilians because Hennessy had been involved in a crime-busting operation in the Italian quarter. Amid a climate of hysteria, police arrested hundreds of Italian "suspects, nine of whom were sent up for trial. To the American public's great consternation the jury found six of the nine "not guilty," while a verdict could not be reached on the remaining three. Rumors of corruption and threats to witnesses began to spread in the city; politicians and newspapers demanded that this "failure" of justice be rectified. They didn't have to wait long. A mob attacked the prison, dragging out eleven Italian prisoners, whom they then lynched. At this point the affair assumed the dimensions of an international crisis. As H. S. Nelli comments, "For a short time in 1891, war between Italy and the United States appeared to be a distinct possibility."[26] Finally, in December 1891, in his annual speech to Congress, President Benjamin Harrison condemned what had happened in New Orleans as "a most deplorable and discreditable incident, an offense against law and humanity" and offered compensation to the victims' families. The crisis had been averted.

But the lynch mob's sword of Damocles didn't just hover over the Italians'

---

25 US Immigration Commission, *Immigrants and Crime*, Washington, D.C.: Government Printing Office, 1911, citations from pp. 2, 209.
26 H. S. Nelli, *Italians in Chicago*, p. 130.

heads. The 26 February 1909 edition of Chicago's Greek newspaper, the *Greek Star*, reported the lynching of several Greek men in Omaha, Nebraska, because one of them had killed a policeman. At the same time, the article said, "According to the police records of Chicago, the Greeks have committed numerous crimes in some [types] of which they occupy the first place. ... Only a few years ago the Greeks of Chicago were looked down upon whenever some Greek violated the law, especially when some crime was committed. ... Much intolerance, prejudice and contempt, have been directed against the Greeks of Chicago on the part of the native, older Americans, or other immigrant groups." Faced with allegations of criminality, the community closed ranks, indignantly fending off accusations from the outside, while at the same time trying to clean up its own internal act.

In this regard, the Italian community's reaction was typically pathetic. On one hand, responding to accusations that it was dominated by the Manonera (Blackhand) criminal organization, the community's notables founded the Manobianca (Whitehand), a society as impotent as it was short-lived, as the "good" Italian secret sect that stood against the "bad" Italian gang. Needless to say, the Manobianca was a complete failure from the beginning. (The Manonera itself would shortly disappear, to be replaced by Al Capone's more modern, capitalist crime syndicate.) On the other hand, with almost comic self-righteousness, the Italian community's newspapers continued to deny the evidence, as can be seen from the caustic and brusquely indignant conclusion to an article published in *L'Italia* on 8 October 1892: "This fable of the Mafia is an unreasonable stupidity, an imbecility pure and simple. ... To make a long story short, the Mafia exists neither in Chicago nor in Italy."

What is striking about this proclamation isn't so much the sheer effrontery of the lie as the idea that people would actually believe it, like a toddler whining "It wasn't me" even with fingers covered in jam. This was the same sort of infantilism the *Illinois Staats-Zeitung* had shown in its self-congratulatory praise of German virtues: "The Irish could not endure the praises the Germans are receiving from their employers for their application and temperance." Such rhetoric shows the competition between ethnic groups and the safeguarding of national honor for what they really are: pure chauvinism and provincialism.

Right from its inception, Chicago has been one of the most international cities in the world, a city that is by its very nature cosmopolitan. Yet this doesn't prevent it from being at the same time a provincial town. Here we discover one of the most unfathomable aspects of modernity: whereas cosmopolitanism had the effect in ancient societies of eroding the provincial spirit, a cosmopolitan structure in the modern world does nothing to neutralize such parochial attitudes, but rather coexists with those views and may even reinforce them. This is why we are once more beginning to see signs of provinciality in New York and Paris, while Rome, which has never been as cosmopolitan as it is now – not even in the days of the Empire, some sixteen centuries ago – remains a sprawling country village. If cities tend to become increasingly provincial, it is because their cosmopolitan components have become segregated.

The Chicago city council published in 1976 an extraordinary set of five historical maps, with various colors showing the settlement patterns in different ethnic neighborhoods of diverse immigrant communities at five moments in the city's history (1840, 1860, 1870, 1920 and 1950). In no other city in the world would such a map be possible, first because no other bureaucrats would think to dedicate such an amount of time, energy and city funding to the task of establishing where the frontiers of the Ukrainian or Danish section lie and then to monitoring how these linguistic borders have changed over time; and second, because it would be objectively impossible to delineate the different areas, since immigrants of different nationalities would be living in the same zones, without residential segregation of ethnicities, except in a few specific cases. With the various neighborhoods of the city all more or less "integrated," they couldn't each be assigned a different color. In this sense, too, Chicago is the most "ethnic" city in America. Here ethnic rituals, engagements, weddings and funerals are still observed with the minutest precision. As late as the 1960s (some forty years after the arrival of the last wave of Italians), sociologist Gerald D. Suttles wrote apropos of the Addams neighborhood:

> Actually, many of the Italians are quite "americanized." Frequently, however, these people lead something of a double life. During the daytime they leave the neighborhood and do their work without much thought of their ethnicity. When they come home in the evening, however, they are obliged to reassume their old world identity. This need not to be so much a matter of taste as necessity. Other people are likely to already know their ethnicity, and evasions are apt to be interpreted as acts

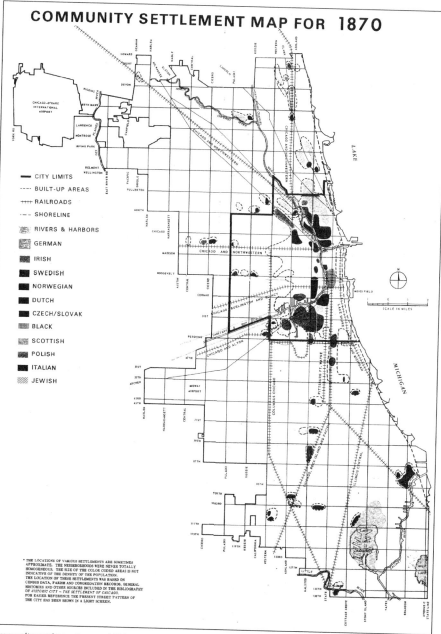

COMMUNITY SETTLEMENT MAP FOR 1870

- ■ CITY LIMITS
- ---- BUILT-UP AREAS
- +++ RAILROADS
- --- SHORELINE
- ▒ RIVERS & HARBORS
- ▒ GERMAN
- ▒ IRISH
- ▒ SWEDISH
- ▒ NORWEGIAN
- ▒ DUTCH
- ▒ CZECH/SLOVAK
- ▒ BLACK
- ▒ SCOTTISH
- ▒ POLISH
- ▒ ITALIAN
- ▒ JEWISH

* THE LOCATIONS OF VARIOUS SETTLEMENTS ARE SOMETIMES
APPROXIMATE. THE NEIGHBORHOODS WERE NEVER TOTALLY
HOMOGENEOUS. THE SIZE OF THE COLOR CODED AREAS IS NOT
INDICATIVE OF THE DENSITY OF THE POPULATION.
THE LOCATION OF THESE SETTLEMENTS WAS BASED ON
CENSUS DATA, PARISH AND CONGREGATION RECORDS, GENERAL
HISTORIES AND OTHER SOURCES INCLUDED IN THE BIBLIOGRAPHY
OF HISTORIC CITY – THE SETTLEMENT OF CHICAGO.
FOR EASIER REFERENCE THE PRESENT STREET PATTERN OF
THE CITY HAS BEEN SHOWN IN A LIGHT SCREEN.

Community settlement map of Chicago for 1870, showing the city's ethnic neighborhoods.

of snobbery or attempts of deception. Moreover, members of the other three groups [Blacks, Puerto Ricans, Mexicans] refuse to accept one's americanization, no matter how much it is stressed. To the others, an attempt to minimize one's ethnicity is only a sly maneuver to escape responsibility for past wrongs or to gain admission in their own confiance. Finally, there are still many "old-timers" in the neighborhood, and it would be very ill-mannered to parade one's americanism before them. Thus, within the bounds of the local neighborhood, an Italian who "plays" at being an American runs the risk of being taken as a snob, phoney, opportunist, coward, or fink.

This is the mechanism of modern migration: the individuals who set out arrive as peoples or ethnicities, forced to assimilate once they get to the host country and at the same time either kept or forced back within the bounds of their own ethnicity. In this so-called melting pot, there is in fact a mayonnaise that has curdled, in which the egg refuses to blend with the oil, which in turn remains separate from the lemon. Society is segmented by bulkheads. This doesn't mean that the people don't consider themselves American. In no country do you see so many houses with the national flag flown proudly from the flagstaff as you do in the United States: a *mille-feuille* of ethnic nationalisms, far from weakening people's sense of American identity, actually serves to reinforce it. Everything is Americanized, but this Americanization coexists with, and lays itself upon, sentiments of ethnic belonging.

One need think only of the myriad cuisines, generally regarded as the bastion of ethnic culture but faithful to tradition only in name here in the United States. The pastrami here is much appreciated, for example, though it has nothing to do with the original. Cooking is one of the main areas in which the "invention of tradition" is practiced, a subject to which we shall return later. Donna Gabaccia recounts the various transformations in taste and consistency that the bagel has undergone throughout American culinary history: bagels, she says, "became firmly identified as 'Jewish' only when the Jews began selling them to their multi-ethnic urban neighbors. When bagels emerged from ghetto stores as a Jewish novelty, bagels with cream cheese quickly became a staple of the cuisine known as 'New York deli,' and were marketed and mass-produced throughout the country under this new regional identity. When international trade brought

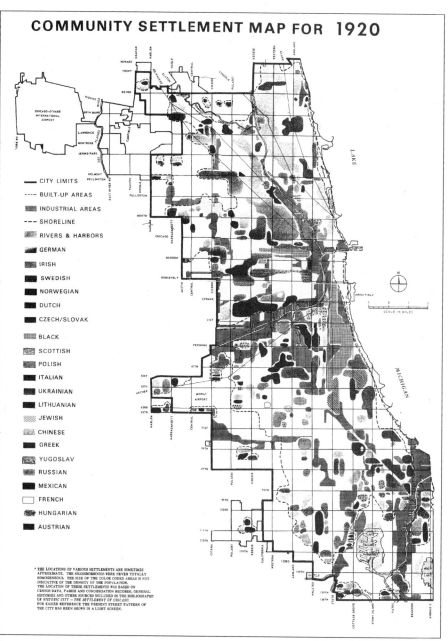

COMMUNITY SETTLEMENT MAP FOR 1920

— CITY LIMITS

---- BUILT-UP AREAS

▨ INDUSTRIAL AREAS

--- SHORELINE

▨ RIVERS & HARBORS

▨ GERMAN

▨ IRISH

■ SWEDISH

■ NORWEGIAN

■ DUTCH

■ CZECH/SLOVAK

▨ BLACK

▨ SCOTTISH

▨ POLISH

■ ITALIAN

■ UKRAINIAN

■ LITHUANIAN

▨ JEWISH

▨ CHINESE

■ GREEK

▨ YUGOSLAV

▨ RUSSIAN

■ MEXICAN

□ FRENCH

▨ HUNGARIAN

■ AUSTRIAN

* THE LOCATIONS OF VARIOUS SETTLEMENTS ARE SOMETIMES
APPROXIMATE. THE NEIGHBORHOODS WERE NEVER TOTALLY
HOMOGENEOUS. THE SIZE OF THE COLOR CODED AREAS IS NOT
INDICATIVE OF THE DENSITY OF THE POPULATION.
THE LOCATION OF THESE SETTLEMENTS WAS BASED ON
CENSUS DATA, PARISH AND CONGREGATION RECORDS, GENERAL
HISTORIES AND OTHER SOURCES INCLUDED IN THE BIBLIOGRAPHY
OF HISTORIC CITY – THE SETTLEMENT OF CHICAGO.
FOR EASIER REFERENCE THE PRESENT STREET PATTERN OF
THE CITY HAS BEEN SHOWN IN A LIGHT SCREEN.

Community settlement map of Chicago for 1920.

bagels to Israel, they acquired a third identity as 'American.'"[27]

And it isn't just the bagel that has become unrecognizable, reinvented by the cement mixer of American society. Bean sprouts may have become the quintessence of Chinese cuisine, but they are never used in China. Likewise, fortune cookies were invented in San Francisco. For local Chinese, the fortune cookie is an object of ridicule, a way of expressing contempt for Americans. While prawns are served whole, complete with heads, in both China and Italy, here they have their heads cleanly lopped off (a nondecapitated prawn would arouse horror) and are peeled long before they reach the table. While dried pasta retains its normal, albeit masculinized, aspect (here you say "a bed of *linguini*," rather than using the normal Italian feminine form *linguine*), it becomes American in the cooking, in the way it becomes a meal in itself or in the various mutations of sauces. The Greek salad contains ingredients that were surely never used by the ancients of Hellas. And no self-respecting Frenchman would eat a Deep French roll. Underlying each ethnicity's form is a genuine American substance, just as in Quebec snails are regarded as a sign of genuine Frenchness, while oysters are eaten with ketchup.

Within the giant container of American society, ethnic groups to a large degree function in isolation. Trying to compact themselves, they compete against one another. Perhaps here lies a partial response to Sombart's question of ninety-odd years ago: "Why is there no socialism in the United States?" What is not clear is whether this age-old translation of social conflict into ethnic confrontation, of the class struggle into a race war, is something that was planned by the ruling classes or is, in fact, a product of the internal logic of American society, irrespective of individual or group will, in a mechanism that has gone out of control and is no longer in the hands of those who initially were simply looking for a way to obtain a cheaper, more docile and mobile, and less rebellious workforce.

Certainly you cannot help but be amazed at the resourcefulness of the American ruling classes, an elite that has been superficially snubbed in Europe but that has shown itself to be capable not only of governing (at least up until now) such an explosive, volatile process, channeling it into more or less controllable forms of rivalry, but also of building within the space of two centuries what is now the

27 Donna R. Gabaccia, *We Are What We Eat: Ethnic Food and the Making of America*, Cambridge, Mass.: Harvard University Press, 1998, pp. 5–6.

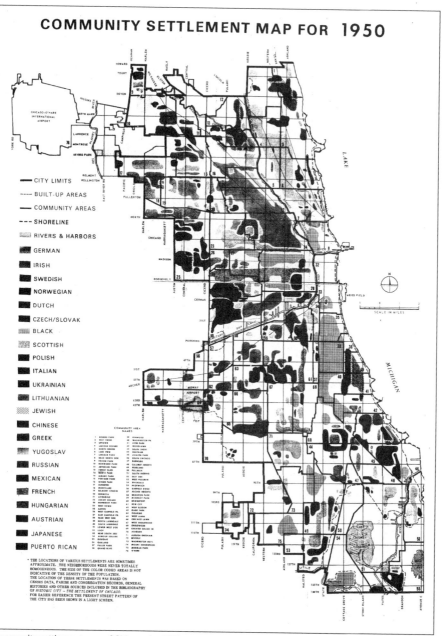

COMMUNITY SETTLEMENT MAP FOR 1950

CITY LIMITS

BUILT-UP AREAS

COMMUNITY AREAS

SHORELINE

RIVERS & HARBORS

GERMAN

IRISH

SWEDISH

NORWEGIAN

DUTCH

CZECH/SLOVAK

BLACK

SCOTTISH

POLISH

ITALIAN

UKRAINIAN

LITHUANIAN

JEWISH

CHINESE

GREEK

YUGOSLAV

RUSSIAN

MEXICAN

FRENCH

HUNGARIAN

AUSTRIAN

JAPANESE

PUERTO RICAN

* THE LOCATIONS OF VARIOUS SETTLEMENTS ARE SOMETIMES
APPROXIMATE. THE NEIGHBORHOODS WERE NEVER TOTALLY
HOMOGENEOUS. THE SIZE OF THE COLOR CODED AREAS IS NOT
INDICATIVE OF THE DENSITY OF THE POPULATION.
THE LOCATION OF THESE SETTLEMENTS WAS BASED ON
CENSUS DATA, PARISH AND CONGREGATION RECORDS, GENERAL
HISTORIES AND OTHER SOURCES INCLUDED IN THE BIBLIOGRAPHY
OF *HISTORIC CITY – THE SETTLEMENT OF CHICAGO*.
FOR EASIER REFERENCE THE PRESENT STREET PATTERN OF
THE CITY HAS BEEN SHOWN IN A LIGHT SCREEN.

Community settlement map of Chicago for 1950.

world's greatest empire from what Woodrow Wilson had charmingly called the "more sordid and hapless elements that Europe was disburdening itself of."

"Give me a yokel, or better, give me a million yokels, and I will move mountains": this was basically the message being sent out by America's nineteenth-century capitalists. The contrast between the separateness of America's various ethnic communities and the sleek compactness of its financial and industrial complex is striking. Yet it isn't simply far-sightedness that has enabled America's ruling class to wipe socialism from the face of the continent. To achieve this end, it has acted somewhat in the manner of the Voltairean hero who boasted of having killed his enemies once and for all with a knowing dosage of prayer, exorcism and arsenic.

12

Black Flags on the Yards

Beneath the concrete abutments, invisible from above, a continuous stream of trucks rumbles along the Dan Ryan Freeway. Back at ground level, where Randolph Street meets Des Plaines (just a stone's throw from the Loop), a broad tract of waste ground lies surrounded by ramshackle buildings that seem to have been sawed through in cross-section, their external walls plastered with billboards. In one corner of this square is the local branch of Caritas. Nothing indicates that the site, Haymarket Square, was once the stage of a drama of unimaginable consequences. Not even a small placard recalls the events of little more than a hundred years ago, in 1886, or the men who for decades would be remembered (and venerated) as martyrs to the workers' movement. Nor does anything reveal that it was here, in what was then an open market, that the first of May was inaugurated as a workers' holiday. (May Day is still celebrated almost everywhere in the world, except in the United States, where it originated.)

Strolling between half-deserted parks and a forlorn Hopperesque gas station, you look in vain for traces of the event that was to destroy the anarchist movement. Chicago, in fact, little more than a century ago was the world capital of anarchism. It was a time that seems a million years away now that anarchy – after decades of oblivion – has once again resurfaced, now in the form of demonstrations against globalization (such as those in Seattle in 1999 and in Prague in 2000).

Through these protests, demonstrators express their anticapitalism without being held down by a communism that resembles the Soviet model; theirs is a form of interiorization of the free market mobilized for subversive aims. In the nineteenth century, anarchists had threatened to defeat capitalism and destroy the very foundations of American society. It was a threat that had to be fought and annihilated.

Chicago went through its most tumultuous period of industrial upheaval (and demographic upheaval, in terms of immigration) during the long years of the worldwide depression, from 1873 to 1896, marked by the most dramatic recessionary lows from 1873 to 1878, from 1882 to 1886, and from 1892 to 1896. In those years, unemployment soared to massive levels, and whole families literally starved to death. In the winter of 1885, one-third of the city's joiners were out of work, and 39 percent of the total workforce was involuntarily inactive.[1]

It was during these three deepest periods of recession that the most violent clashes took place between capitalists and their workers, including the railway strikes of 1877, the eight-hour-week movement of 1886 and the Pullman boycott of 1894. In all three of these cases, the epicenter of the "class war" was Chicago, a city into which – crisis or no crisis – hundreds of thousands of immigrants continued to pour, many of them imported as scab labor to weaken the unions and create ethnic and linguistic division among the workforce. In 1891, Marx's daughter, Eleanor, in a letter to the American union leader Samuel Gompers, wrote, "The most immediate question is that of preventing the introduction from one country to another of unfair labour – i.e., of workers who, not knowing the conditions of the labour struggle in a particular country, are imported into that country by the capitalists, in order to reduce wages, lengthen the hours of labour, or both."[2]

Amid this immense mass of human traffic, however, were also small groups of political exiles. As Theodore Draper put it, "From the very outset the American Socialist movement was peculiarly indebted to the immigrants for both its progress and its problems."[3] On one hand, it was difficult if not impossible for workers

---

1   Bruce C. Nelson, *Beyond the Martyrs: A Social History of Chicago's Anarchists, 1870–1900*, New Brunswick, N.J.: Rutgers University Press, 1988, pp. 11–13.

2   Letter from William Thorne and Eleanor Marx to Samuel Gompers, dated 25 January 1891. Cited in Yvonne Kapp, *Eleanor Marx: The Crowded Years*, vol. 2, London: Virago, 1979, p. 427.

3   Theodore Draper, *The Roots of American Communism*, New York: Viking Press, 1956, p. 31.

of Irish, Italian, Polish and German extraction to form a united front against bosses without the wall of their efforts crumbling into myriad sticks and stones. On the other, these immigrants included among them a number of militants who brought from Europe a sense of "class consciousness."

Xenophobia thus had a new stereotype to sink its teeth into. Not only were the immigrants dirty, lazy and criminal, they were also communist subversives who believed in neither God nor private property. In 1920s America, the word *Italian* evoked images either of the gangster Al Capone or of the anarchists Nicola Sacco and Bartolomeo Vanzetti (both condemned to death in 1921 and executed in 1927). In reality, militant socialists and anarchists represented only a tiny minority of the mass of immigrants, who were for the most part either apolitical or conservative, but it made no difference: in 1915, the American Socialist Party had fourteen affiliated foreign sections, and even in 1917, 40 percent of the party's 80,126 enrollees came from overseas.[4]

Of the million or so Germans who arrived in the United States during the 1850s, several thousand were political émigrés, the so-called Forty-Eighters who had gotten out after the failed revolution of 1848. Most of these were liberal democrats: only a handful were actually socialists, but it was this small group that in 1854 founded in Chicago the newspaper *Der Proletarier*. Socialism may not form an important part of the history of German immigration to the United States, but the Germans were certainly key players in the history of American socialism.[5]

Chicago was a haven for political exiles, much in the manner of Paris or Zurich or Lugano, pullulating with the birth (and death) of socialist, anarchist and revolutionary newsletters written in a babel of tongues: German, Polish, English, Czech and so on. The militants may have numbered only a few thousand – there were 2,500 active members of radical political groups in 1866, along with 2,000 sympathizers – but their influence was enormous, the newspapers they printed infinitely more alive and significant than anything published today. As in corporations where "shares are not counted *but weighed,*" so too the militants and their adher-

---

4 Ibid., p. 32.
5 Albert Fried, ed., *Socialism in America, from the Shakers to the Third International: A Documentary History*, New York: Columbia UP, 1970, p. 181. On the role of Germans in American socialism, see the chapter "The Germans," pp. 181–255.

ents in these political movements had a weight rather than a number. And movements with few affiliates can have enormous weight, whereas others with millions of members may be wholly innocuous and practically irrelevant.

Try to imagine the lives these militants lived in the Chicago of the 1800s, among the slaughterhouses and smokestacks, in this babel of a thousand tongues and nationalities, the stink of butcher meat and train smoke heavy in the air. They stumbled through life in an exuberant fever, from one dead-end job to another, forever without a penny and always in danger from either the police or the American private militias, or from secret agents sent by European governments to spy upon or assassinate them. Naturally they were argumentative, pedantic, typically "German" in their intolerance of doctrinal differences, whether Bakunian, Lassallian (how many people today remember Ferdinand Lassalle?) or just plain Marxist. When they weren't excommunicating each other, they were usually embroiled in irate, polemical exchanges: "They constituted a sect, in the sense of a small, self-contained group that adheres to a narrow and exclusive ideology (or faith). But they were not a sect by choice. ... In fact they were categorically anti-sectarian. Whether they were Marxists, Lassalleans, Anarcho-Communists, the German socialists were uniformly opposed to 'utopianism.'" They wanted to speak to the people, to move the workers to action, even if "they tended to be dogmatic, stiff-necked, and often incomprehensible to the masses they sought to reach."[6] They organized not only demonstrations and strikes but also festivities, dances, recitals and picnics.

Any occasion was a good excuse for a picnic – even the announcement of a newspaper closure, such as that of *The Socialist* in September 1879. And then there were the dances. In Chicago, you could find dances from all over Europe: "Every variety of step might have been witnessed yesterday [night]. The 'Bohemian dip,' the 'German lunge,' the 'Austrian kick,' the 'Polish ramp' [sic] and the 'Scandinavian trot' ... All these countries seemed to be represented, but it is safe to say that the native-born American, the Irishman and the Englishman were conspicuous by their absence."[7] At least eight choirs were affiliated with the workers' movement,

---

6   Ibid., pp. 180–81.
7   Testimony cited by B. C. Nelson, *Beyond the Martyrs*, p. 135. On the social life of the Chicago anarchists, see ch. 6, "Dancing and Picnicking Anarchists," pp. 127–52.

as were several famous revolutionary orchestras.[8]

These revolutionaries had a real passion for organizing parties, as though such festivities were a foretaste of the joyous day of liberation they hoped lay only shortly over the horizon. The most important of these was the *Dawn of Liberty*, celebrated by Chicago's socialists every March for thirty-seven years, from 1872 until 1909, to mark the anniversary of the Paris Commune. Participants numbered more than forty thousand some years, and the festivities included orchestral and choral recitals, *tableaux vivants* of significant political events, and opera and theater performances.

Any occasion was a good excuse for a get-together (and for knocking back a few beers). Whenever a revolutionary stepped off the boat from Europe, it was party time. Such was the case in 1892 when anarchist leader and former Reichstag deputy Johann Most arrived in the United States. Having been imprisoned several times, Most had finally fled Bismarckian Germany in 1878. Punning on the expression "beast of prey," Most called man a "Beast of Property" (also the title of a pamphlet he wrote in 1884);[9] in London, he published the newspaper *Die Freiheit* (Freedom), in which he declared:

> I follow four commandments. Thou shalt deny God and love Truth; therefore I am an atheist. Thou shalt oppose tyranny and seek liberty; therefore I am a republican. Thou shalt repudiate property and champion equality; therefore I am a communist. Thou shalt hate oppression and foment revolution; therefore I am a revolutionary. Long live the social revolution! [July 15, 1882]

The revolutionaries had their own secret societies and armed militias, such as the *Lehr und Wehr Vereine* (Society for Education and Defense), with proper military training. The Chicago *Lehr und Wehr Vereine* also organized picnics, decorated allegorical floats and provided bands for parades and marches.

It's extraordinary to think how the oppressed and subjugated groups of society, in trying to emancipate themselves, seek to copy the instruments of the ruling classes. The passion for secret societies shared by German and Scandinavian anarchists was in imitation of bourgeois models, for example. Similarly, facing violent

---

8 Ibid., p. 129.
9 Reproduced in A. Fried, *Socialism in America*, pp. 213-20.

hostility toward any form of unionization, American workers tried to set up their own Masonic-style organizations. As one example, in 1869, nine garment trade workers from Philadelphia founded the Noble and Holy Order of the Knights of Labor, a society organized into lodges, each with its own leaders and, at the helm, a Grand Master Worker. This profoundly religious order, which opposed the wage-labor system, was to remain secret until 1881. In 1884, the Knights forced railroad magnate (and prototypical robber baron) Jay Gould to negotiate and give striking workers back their jobs. From that moment on, the Knights' number of enrollments grew exponentially: between 1884 and 1886, membership went from 71,000 to 730,000.

With the Knights of Labor ascending, the other major workers' movement of the period, the Federation of Organized Trades and Labor Unions (formed in Pittsburgh in 1881), fell into decline. In December 1884, that organization chose Chicago as the site for its annual convention. The twenty-five delegates present represented barely 50,000 workers among them – yet at the convention, two historic motions were passed. The first, proposed by a Chicago typographer, asked "[t]hat the first Monday in September of each year be set apart as a laborer's national holiday, and that we recommend its observance by all wage workers, irrespective of sex, calling or nationality."[10] The choice of the first Monday in September for Labor Day filled a convenient gap between holidays "at the most pleasant season of the year, nearly midway between the Fourth of July and Thanksgiving."

The second motion, presented by the Federation of Carpenters, concerned a claim that had already taken root in the labor movement: the eight-hour day. Workers from Melbourne, Australia, had in 1856 stated their demand for the "three eights: Eight hours labour, eight hours recreation, eight hours for what we want." During the Civil War years, from 1861 to 1865, leagues supporting the eight-hour day had begun to spring up in America's industrial cities. In 1866, at its Geneva Congress, the First International had taken up the call once again: "The Congress proposes eight hours as the legal limit of the working day. ... As this limitation represents the general demand of the workers of the North American

---

10 Cited in Philip S. Foner, *History of the Labor Movement in the United States* (1947), New York: International Publishers, 1955, 9 vols., vol. II, p. 97.

United States, the Congress transforms this demand into the general platform of the Workers of the World."[11] On 1 May 1867, more than 10,000 demonstrators had taken to the streets of Chicago in what was to be the first great eight-hour strike.

Recalling this historic action, the motion of 1884 declared: "Resolved, By the Federation of Organized Trades and Labor Unions of the United States and Canada, that eight hours shall constitute a legal day's labor from and after May 1, 1886, and that we recommend to labor organizations throughout this district that they so direct their laws as to conform to this resolution by the time named."[12] That first of May was the day the construction business went back into action; the day before, the rent contracts of citizens and farmers customarily ended. The festival became a counter-Easter, a workers' Easter, a proletarian remembrance of the pagan rites of spring.

It took real guts to demand an eight-hour week in the winter of 1884, with the whole country deep in recession, when there was mass unemployment and when entire families were forced out onto the street. The newspapers of the time sounded the alarm: the eight-hour day was "Communism, lurid and rampant" and would only encourage "loafing and gambling, rioting, debauchery, and drunkenness," leading to lower wages, more poverty and social degradation among America's workers.[13]

The climate was even more tense in Chicago at the time than it was elsewhere. In November 1884, a great gathering, "the poor man's march," had passed below the houses of the rich and powerful, of George Mortimer Pullman, Marshall Field, Swift and Armour. At the head of the crowd were the anarchist leader Albert Parsons and his wife Lucy. Born in 1848 to a southern Puritan family, Parsons moved to Chicago in 1873 after running a newspaper in Waco, Texas. An ex-typographer, he went on to become the leader of anarchism in America and founded the newspaper *The Socialist* in Chicago after a spell as editor of *The Alarm*.

The following year, on 4 May 1885, in the suburban district of Lemont, mem-

---

11 Ibid., vol. I, p, 347.
12 Ibid., p. 103.
13 Ibid., p. 103.

bers of the Illinois National Guard opened fire on a crowd of unarmed stone quarriers, killing two. Later, at the end of June, a strike broke out in the Street Car Company: tram personnel demanded shorter hours and equal pay, as well as an end to anti-union repression. In response, the owner, Charles Yerkes, fired sixteen top union leaders. It was then that Captain of Police John Bonfield ordered his men to "shoot to kill," an order whose echo was to resound on the streets of Chicago some eighty years later (see chapter 23, "Prague in Illinois"). Bonfield presented himself as the defender of property owners, setting up a "red squad," whose job was to infiltrate the workers' movement, and training his troops in the latest antiriot tactics.

Also in a state of agitation was another of Chicago's great firms, the McCormick Harvesting Machine Company, handed over in 1884 by the old generation (old Cyrus and his brother Leander) to the much more aggressive Cyrus Jr., who immediately tried to impose a 10 to 15 percent pay cut, even though the business was in relatively good health. Notwithstanding the crisis of the winter of 1884–85, McCormick's had turned a profit of 71 percent on its investment capital. And while the majority of workers with docked salaries were Catholic, the McCormick family donated another $100,000 to Chicago's Presbyterian Seminary.[14] In the wake of this donation, a strike broke out in one of the company's factories in Pilsen. Like Yerkes and many other American bosses, the young McCormick went not only to the police but also to the notorious Pinkerton Agency to protect the scabs he had brought in to ensure that the strike would fail.

A strange and convoluted destiny was to be that of Allan Pinkerton, private investigator, "the eye that never sleeps." Born in Glasgow in 1819 to working-class parents, Pinkerton grew up to become a militant member of the Chartist movement and was forced to emigrate to the States to avoid being sent to a penal colony for political reasons. Newly arrived in Chicago, he was elected sheriff of Kane County in 1840 and the following year opened his Pinkerton National Detective Agency (still active today). Pinkerton's original role was to help escaped slaves from the South flee to safety in Canada, but this noble aim was soon abandoned; before long, the agency had become the armed wing of several powerful industrial groups and was also used in their internecine wars, such as that between

---

14 William J. Adelman, *Haymarket Revisited*, Chicago: Illinois Labor History Society, 1976, p. 11.

Vanderbilt, Fisk and Gould. During the Civil War, Abraham Lincoln appointed Pinkerton as head of the Union Army's Secret Service. After the war, however, the Pinkerton Agency dedicated itself above all to combating workers' strikes, a tradition continued, after Pinkerton's death in 1884, by his two sons, William and Robert. In 1890, the agency had 2,000 agents in active service and 30,000 reserves, more than the federal army; between 1933 and 1935, it had some 1,228 operatives working undercover in every union chapter in the country.[15]

Despite Pinkerton's efforts, the bosses were unable to defeat the strikers. This was in part because of the reluctance of one Captain O'Donnell, the Irish-born head of police in the zone of Pilsen, to take sides against Irish workers (here again, we see the interweaving of class and ethnic struggle). Within only a few months, O'Donnell was reassigned and Bonfield promoted to chief inspector of the Central Division. On 16 February 1886, McCormick locked 1,482 workers (many of whom were enrolled in the K of L) out of his factory. On this occasion, the Chicago police came to the aid of the management, stationing three hundred men outside the factory gates, and on 1 March, the first consignment of scabs entered the factory under their protection. The following day, police charged a peaceful meeting held by the workers who had been locked out and made numerous arrests.

Throughout the rest of the country, meanwhile, campaigns for an eight-hour workday and for a May Day holiday intensified. The majority of the Knights of Labor supported the actions even if their leaders were somewhat guarded, as can be seen from a 13 March 1886 circular from Grand Master Worker Terence Vincent Powderly to his men: "No assembly of the Knights of Labor must strike for the eight-hour system on May first under the impression that they are obeying orders from headquarters, for such an order was not, and will not, be given."[16] In this we see an attitude typical of American unions, that of a fire brigade, a conflict shock absorber or extinguisher of social blazes. After the dissolution of his Holy Order of the Knights of Labor in 1907, Powderly worked as a high-level functionary in the US Immigration Office.

But even as its leaders tried to put out the fire, the movement's base began to mobilize its forces, almost overnight: workers smoked "Eight-Hour tobacco,"

---

15 J. Skinner Sawyers, *Chicago Portraits*, pp. 208–10.
16 P. S. Foner, *History of the Labor Movement in the United States*, vol. II, p. 101.

wore "Eight-Hour shoes" and sang the "Eight-Hour song." The movement started to spread like an oil slick, and bosses' fears grew likewise. Strikes were breaking out everywhere: on 9 April, police in East St. Louis had opened fire on strikers, killing nine. In retaliation, the workers had set fire to more than a hundred railcars. On 1 May 1886, the New York Times reported that members of the local Chamber of Commerce had offered the Illinois National Guard $2,000 for the purchase of a Gatling gun.

The first of May arrived. All over the country on that day, some 350,000 workers went on strike in 11,562 plants. In Chicago alone, strikers numbered 40,000, while around 80,000 people took to the streets. Led by Albert and Lucy Parsons, together with their children (Albert Jr. and Lulu), the people marched arm in arm along Michigan Avenue. In Detroit, there were 11,000 demonstrators; in New York, 25,000. That day in Chicago, a shorter working day was conceded to 45,000 workers, without them even needing to strike. It was reckoned that out of 350,000 strikers in the United States, 180,000 obtained the requested eight-hour day.[17] The day passed without incident; the battle seemed to have been won.

Back at McCormick's, however, it was an altogether different story. May second was a day of calm, with only a few sporadic demonstrations here and there. On 3 May, nonetheless, according to Die Arbeiter Zeitung newspaper director August Spies, 6,000 lumber workers conducted a strike from a freightcar parked near the McCormick factory. Many of the onlookers in the crowd that had gathered were either Bohemians or Poles and couldn't understand a word of what was being said. When the factory siren sounded at 3:30 a.m., however, around 200 of the crowd went to the gates to help the workers tear a strip off the scabs. Bonfield was immediately on the scene with 200 policemen, who charged the mob. More bystanders were drawn into the fray, until Spies himself arrived, followed by a huge crowd. A hail of police bullets met the group, with at least four demonstrators killed and many more injured.

A further demonstration was immediately announced, to take place the next day, on 4 May, at the Haymarket, this time with the authorization of Mayor Harrison. At 8:30 p.m. that day, August Spies (though he had not taken part in organiz-

---

17 Ibid., vol. II, p. 104.

ing the event) stood up on a cart in front of 3,000 people and sent messengers to summon Albert Parsons and Samuel Fielden (who hadn't been told of the rally) to help with the speeches. The mayor was also present. Spies and Parsons had already spoken and had left the gathering when, just before 10:00 p.m., a storm broke and the crowd began to disperse, until only 300 or so drenched listeners remained. At that point, Mayor Harrison himself decided to call it a night and ordered that the 176 police officers present be sent home or reassigned to normal duty. But at 10:30, just after the mayor's departure, when Samuel Fielden was wrapping up his closing speech, Captain Bonfield ordered his men to break up the demonstration by force, deploying the antiguerrilla tactics he had taught them. At that moment, someone threw a bomb from a side street into the midst of the crowd, killing six people and injuring more than fifty. The police responded by opening fire on the crowd. A battle ensued. Nobody knows how many demonstrators lost their lives – only that the wounded numbered around 200.

Nor does anyone know who threw the bomb – or why Captain Bonfield waited until the mayor had retired for the night before ordering his troops to charge the demonstrators. Nor does anyone know why one of the organizers of the Haymarket rally was, from that moment, on the police payroll, turning state's witness against the anarchists. But the fact remains that this was the first dynamite bombing in US history and that it took place just as the battle for the eight-hour day seemed to have been won. News spread throughout the country and was blown out of proportion: Cincinnati resounded with news vendors' cries of "Anarchist bomb-throwers kill one hundred policemen in Haymarket in Chicago."[18]

On the morning of 5 May, the mayor of Chicago declared a "state of war" in the city. Thousands of houses were searched without warrant and hundreds of anarchists arrested. Police claimed to have discovered huge caches of bombs and firearms. Accusing the anarchists of violence was somewhat hypocritical, especially when the police – both public and private – seemed to do nothing but shoot into unarmed crowds. In 1877, when an article published in the *New York Times* had warned that Chicago was in the hands of the communists, the federal government had, to suppress the strike, dispatched an army division from Dakota Territory to

---

18 Jeremy Brecher, quoting Oscar Ameringer in *Strike!*, San Francisco: Straight Arrow Books, 1972, p. 47.

the Windy City, veterans of the war against the American Indians who had killed General Custer: redskins and red workers, enemies both.

Hardly surprising, therefore, is the declamation Albert Parsons made in the anarchists' manifesto, approved at the Pittsburgh convention of October 1883: "By force our ancestors liberated themselves from political oppression, by force their children will have to liberate themselves from economic bondage. 'It is, therefore, your right; it is your duty', says Jefferson; 'to arms!' before concluding: 'Tremble, oppressors of the world! Not far beyond your purblind sight there dawns the scarlet and sable lights of the JUDGMENT DAY.'"[19] Johann Most's pamphlet, "Revolutionäre Kriegswissenschaft" ("The Science of Revolutionary War"), is subtitled "A Manual of Instruction in the Use and Preparation of Nitroglycerine and Dynamite, Gun-Cotton, Fulminating Mercury, Bomb-Fuses, Poisons, etc." The anarchists were far from being lambs to the slaughter, and the press had good sport in its tirade against them. In the wake of the Haymarket incident, the 5 May edition of the *Chicago Tribune* inveighed against the "socialistic, atheistic, alcoholic European classes," while on 15 May 1886, the highly respectable *Albany Law Journal* wrote,

> It is a serious thought that the lives of good and brave men, the safety of innocent women and children, and immunity of property should be, even for one hour, in a great city, at the mercy of a few long-haired, wild-eyed, bad-smelling, atheistic, reckless foreign wretches, who never did an honest hour's work in their lives, but who driven half crazy with years of oppression and mad with the envy of the rich, think to level society and its distinctions with a few bombs. There ought to be some law ... to enable society to crush such snakes when they raise their heads before they have time to bite. ... The state of things almost justifies the resort to the vigilance committee and Lynch law.[20]

Yet the fact remains that the actual weapons found by police after Haymarket were relatively few; years later, the head of the Chicago police department, Captain Frederick Ebersold, would admit that police had deliberately planted weap-

---

19 "Manifesto of the International Working People Association," (1883) in A. Fried, *Socialism in America*, pp. 208–12.
20 Cited by W. J. Adelman, *Haymarket Revisited*, p. 18.

An engaving of the scene in Haymarket Square on the night of 4 May 1886. From *Harper's Weekly,* 1886, courtesy Chicago Historical Society.

ons and bombs in the anarchists' headquarters.[21] Of the hundreds of arrests made, only thirty-one people were charged; of those, a mere eleven were actually convicted, two of whom turned state's witness, while another vanished from sight, never to be found. Thus, in the end, only eight activists actually stood trial: August Spies, Louis Lingg, Samuel Fielden, Adolph Fischer, George Engel, Oscar Neebe, Michael Schwab and Albert Parsons. The list is notable for several reasons: (1) it comprises all of Chicago's main anarchist leaders, men who were not just anybody but who were newspaper editors and famous orators – real commanders of men; (2) of the eight men, seven were foreigners; and (3) at the instant the bomb was thrown, none except Fielden, who was speaking, was anywhere near Haymarket (several hadn't even set foot in the square that day).

The nation was in the grip of hysteria. Churches went on the rampage against

---

21 P. S. Foner, *History of the Labor Movement in the United States,* vol. II, p. 107.

the atheist eight, while bosses demanded that they be made examples as a warning to all subversives. Newspaper cartoonists depicted huge swords smiting down grotesque little monsters. "Liberty or Death,"[22] ran the captions of these truculent drawings: Liberty (to go if you do not like the institutions of our Republic). Or (commit murder and you will punished with Death.l The most lapidary indication of the national mood appeared in the *Chicago Herald* of 22–23 July 1886: "They have tried to destroy society. Society must destroy them."

In his concluding statement, prosecutor Julius Grinnell defined the matter in the most unequivocal terms: "Law is on trial. Anarchy is on trial. These men have been selected, picked out by the grand jury and indicted because they are the leaders. They are no more guilty than thousands who follow them. Gentlemen of the Jury; convict these men, make examples of them, hang them and you save our institutions, our society."

On 20 August, the sentence was handed down: all of the accused were found guilty as charged, and seven of the eight were condemned to death. Oscar Neebe got fifteen years. A worldwide movement sprang up in the group's defense. Demonstrations were held in France, Holland, Russia, Italy and Spain. Oscar Wilde wrote up a petition, which he circulated among London's intellectual community. William Morris and the young George Bernard Shaw both spoke at a rally in defense of the condemned men. In Germany, meanwhile, Chancellor Bismarck prohibited all demonstrations in support of the Haymarket eight. The French parliament took a different view, sending a telegraph to Washington in protest against their imminent execution.

Under these external pressures, both Fielden and Schwab had their sentences reduced to life imprisonment. Louis Lingg, who at the trial had shouted, *"I despise you! I despise your order, your laws, your force-propped authority. HANG ME FOR IT!"*, took his own life in his prison cell, apparently by inserting an explosive capsule in his mouth and blowing his own head off, although the circumstances of the suicide never became fully clear.[23] The remaining four – August Spies, Albert Parsons, George Engel and Adolph Fischer – were all hanged on 11 November 1887. Half a million people attended the funerals, which took place on 13 November on

---

22 *Chicago History*, Summer 1986, pp. 44–45.
23 Ibid., p. 47.

Lithograph showing the alleged conspirators in the Haymarket Riot, 1886. Courtesy Chicago Historical Society.

Milwaukee Avenue, where the houses of Poles, Germans and Bohemians were starred with black flags.

It wasn't just the last farewell to the "Haymarket Martyrs," as the four hanged men were known from then on; it was the funeral of the whole US anarchist movement. From that point on, in America, the word *anarchist* became an unspeakable insult. The bosses took advantage of the witch-hunt atmosphere to fire their unionized workers and to draw up a blacklist of employees who would never work in their town, or any other, again. So it was that the Knights of Labor went into irreversible decline. In their place sprouted the American Federation of Labor (AFL), led by Samuel Gompers, a conservative and moderate.

The battle for the eight-hour day came to a halt, although some of the conquests of 1 May 1886 remained in place. The AFL sent a delegate to the International Labour Congress in Paris, held on 14 July 1889 to celebrate the centennial of the storming of the Bastille, to propose that 1 May be made a worldwide workers' holiday in memory of the Haymarket Martyrs. Since then, countries throughout the world have celebrated May Day as the official workers' festival, except for the United States and, after the Thatcher government, Britain: even Hitler himself, after he came to power, permitted the celebration of May Day in Germany before banning all unions the next day, on 2 May 1933.

In 1889, the *Chicago Times* published the findings of an inquiry into corruption in the city's police department. Through that inquiry, the leaders of the racket were discovered to be none other than Captains Bonfield and Michael J. Schaak (the officer responsible for conducting house-to-house searches at the time of the anarchist terror). These were the men paid protection money by the gambling joints, bars and brothels; the same men paid hefty fees by the industrialists for the services of their "Red Squad," whose job it was to infiltrate the workers' movement. (A century later, in 1975, it would be discovered that Chicago's Red Squad had made use of federal funds to spy on and infiltrate leftist groups.) Bonfield, understandably, tried to have the *Chicago Times* shut down. But in the end, both he and Schaak were forced to resign. Meanwhile, the good bourgeois people of Chicago (led by Field, Armour, Swift and Pullman) donated $100,000 to a fund for the families of the policemen killed in the Haymarket incident and erected a monument to honor the fallen. Defaced several times (especially during the 1960s), the statue of the bewhiskered policeman was eventually moved from the Haymarket to the safety of the nearby Police Academy.

But the Chicago bourgeoisie had more prosaic worries to think about than the glory of their police force. It was Marshall Field who proposed that the Chamber of Commerce, together with the Union League, organize a collection to ensure that the army garrison was stationed closer to Chicago and could promptly intervene at the slightest sign of trouble. His suggestion was warmly welcomed, and the two associations bought a 250-hectare plot of land in Highland, some thirty miles north of Chicago, which they offered to the US government in 1887 to construct a fort. The fort was duly built, and following the death of General Sheridan, a close friend of Field's and Pullman's, its name was changed to Fort Sheridan, under which was inscribed the motto "Essential to Freedom since 1887." The fort was then connected to the city via a military road, Sheridan Avenue, which would allow troops to intervene swiftly in case of civil disorder or demonstrations. From that moment on, peace of mind was assured for the haves, and many well-to-do Chicagoans actually moved to Sheridan Avenue, along the northern shore of lake Michigan, where they no doubt must have felt even safer.

Once again, it was a German who decided to dampen their joy with his moral: a monument for the police, opprobrium for the anarchists. Born in Germany in 1847, John Peter Atgeld was a small child when his parents emigrated to America. He became a lawyer and moved to Chicago, where he set up practice. There he invested his savings in the property market and accumulated a sizable fortune. He began to make a name for himself with the publication of a pamphlet entitled "Our Penal Machine and Its Victims" (1884), in which he demonstrated how the prison system not only failed to reform criminals but actually made them worse: "The great multitudes annually arrested ... are the poor, the unfortunate, the young and the neglected." The victims of law enforcement are recruited "from among those that are fighting an unequal fight in the struggle for existence."[24] In 1892, Atgeld ran for governor of Illinois and won, becoming the first-ever foreign-born governor of the state at what for Chicago was to be a crucial time, with the World's Columbian Exposition of 1893 followed in 1894 by one of the hard-

---

24 Russell Fraser, "John Peter Atgeld, Governor for the People," in *American Radicals*, New York: Monthly Review Press, pp. 127–44. This extract from Atgeld's writings is cited on p. 130.

est-fought social conflicts in US history.

On 26 June 1893, Governor Atgeld signed an official pardon for Samuel Fielden, Michael Schwab, Oscar Neebe and their colleagues who had been hanged, stating that they had had an unfair trial, and that members of the jury had been coerced or selected because they were already convinced of the accused parties' guilt. In his text, Atgeld wrote that the judge, Joseph Gary, had conducted the trial with "malicious ferocity."

It wasn't so much Atgeld's pardon that infuriated public opinion as the motive behind it: to revive the memory of the Haymarket Martyrs. With its customary restraint, the *New York Times* defined Atgeld as "insane," while others went so far as to call him "the Nero of the last decade of the nineteenth century."[25] The *Toledo Blade* was convinced that the governor had encouraged "anarchy, rapine and the overthrow of civilization." The *Chicago Tribune* went even further, saying that "Governor Altgeld has apparently not a drop of pure American blood in his veins." The inhabitants of the town of Naperville marched in protest, burning an effigy of the governor. There was even talk of impeachment.[26]

Even without considering the similarly awkward stance Atgeld was subsequently to take in the 1894 Pullman strike, it's easy to understand why the establishment of Chicago turned so violently against him and did everything in its power to prevent his re-election. Atgeld died of a brain hemorrhage in 1902, at the age of fifty-five. A crowd of some 150,000 people attended his funeral. The same newspapers that had so gleefully participated in his public lynching spoke in solemn, regretful tones about the tragic loss of the forward-looking statesman.

---

25 Ibid., p. 134.
26 J. Skinner Sawyers, *Chicago Portraits*, p. 12.

13

Class Struggle in the Sleeping Car

Deep in Chicago's South Side, the giant metallic skeletons of disused factories rise like rusty phantoms along the elevated freeway, relics of some ancient industrial empire. Here you begin to understand what is meant by the term "the Rust Belt." The smog remains unbearable as clouds of colored smoke continue to drift skyward from the steelworks and from the few refineries and heating plants still in operation. Thick coils of the stuff, ranging from violet to tangerine, seem too heavy for the ether to support. From here you realize why even today Chicago is the biggest industrial center in the United States, the world's greatest industrial power. Between one chimney and the next, the visible horizon is marked by the outlines of vast cylindrical tanks, gigantic silos, metal warehouses the size of football stadiums. You advance along the freeway through this forest of rust, through plumes of smoke that appear to spring from the geysers of a lunar landscape, while down below an elegant white sailboat advances blithely across the mirrored surface of tiny Wolf Lake, as though navigating the waters of Arcadia.

Here, a short distance from Wolf Lake, next to the deserted docks of neighboring Calumet Lake, between South 111th and 113th, at the intersection with Champlain, you come across a cluster of tree-lined streets with brick houses, some decidedly spartan, others more comfortable: in 1975, these buildings were declared a national monument. There's also a little stone church and a dilapidated mansion dating from the late 1800s (when it was the Florence Hotel). This was the town of Pullman, named after that Pullman who in certain parts of Europe has become synonymous with the city bus: in Italy, you take the *Pullman* to go into town.

Normally, if you want to make money, you have to come up with a product that is *cheaper* than its competitors, in the manner of Henry Ford. George Mortimer Pullman, born in New York in 1831, the son of a poor family, was one of those rare capitalists who made their fortune selling a *more costly* product. The first railway sleeping cars had appeared in the United States in 1836, but they were tremendously uncomfortable: in them were three rows of tiny narrow berths, placed one above the other, with neither mattress nor bedding. The candlelight and woodstove heating made breathing difficult, but if you opened a window, you would instantly be covered in soot from the steam engine. In 1859, Pullman built the prototype for his sleeper car. Called the Pioneer, its compartments were copied from riverboat cabins, with the armchair below and a long, comfortable bed above, complete with sheets, blankets and a pillow, which by day could be folded back against the wall. Pullman's sleeper cars cost $18,000, whereas standard couchettes could be built for less than $4,000. The Pioneer was also two-and-a-half feet higher and a foot wider than the sleeper models then in use, which meant that both tunnels and bridges would have to modified before it could go into service.

The Pioneer would no doubt have become a curio from a bygone age were it not for the fact that the Chicago and Alton Railroad decided in 1865 to make the necessary modifications to enable Pullman's sleeper to transport the distinguished person of President Lincoln from Chicago to Springfield. Only a few months later, the Michigan Central Railroad adapted its bridges and tunnels to allow General Ulysses S. Grant the pleasure of traveling on the Pioneer from Detroit to Galena.[1] At this point, the Chicago and Alton put the Pullman car into service on an experimental basis. Everyone thought the venture would be a fiasco, considering the price of tickets (half a dollar more for a chair in a Pullman car). Everyone was wrong, though: the Pullman car turned out to be a great success. Passengers were willing to pay top dollar if doing so meant that they could finally get a night's sleep

---

1   Almont Lindsay, *The Pullman Strike: The Story of a Unique Experiment and of a Great Labor Upheaval*, Chicago: University of Chicago Press, 1942, pp. 21–22.

on the train. Two years later, in 1867, with forty-eight Pullman cars already in active service on the railroads, the Pullman Company was founded in Chicago, with stock of half a million dollars.

Pullman subsequently introduced the first "hotel car," equipped with both beds and a restaurant, followed by the restaurant car and finally, in 1875, the parlor car. By 1894, the Pullman Company was operating on 125,000 miles of railroad (three-quarters of the entire US railroad system), on which it had a monopoly, running its own cars staffed by its own personnel, with guaranteed maintenance and repairs (thanks to an additional two-cent toll on every ticket). That same year, there were 2,573 Pullman cars in service, 1,900 of which were sleepers, 650 buffet cars, and 58 restaurant cars.[2] In 1893, Pullman's factories employed a total of 14,000 workers split into two sections: one to build the cars, the other to assure the maintenance of the Pullman fleet. In 1893, the company built 12,500 freight cars, 650 passenger cars, 939 tram cars, and 319 sleeper cars.

On account of this boom, Pullman decided during the mid-1870s to shift the whole of his operation to Chicago, where he would build a Pullman town inspired by two models: Saltaire, the "owner's town" built in England by the wool tycoon Sir Titus Salt; and Essen, built by the Krupps steel magnates in Germany. Pullman purchased sixteen hundred hectares of land near Lake Calumet, thirteen miles south of the Loop. Work was begun in 1880, and for the first time a landscape artist was hired to advise on a town's construction. Pullman workers made everything, from bricks to fixtures. The town's 1,750 houses could all be constructed in brick, thanks to clay extracted from the surrounding area. The first resident moved in during 1881, and by 1885, 8,500 inhabitants, including 2,700 workers, occupied the buildings. In 1893, when the town was at its height, it housed 12,600 residents, including 5,500 workers (out of a total of 14,000 employees).

All of the houses in Pullman were equipped with water and gas. The workers' dwellings were spartan, those of the company's white-collar employees fairly comfortable. The most luxurious houses were naturally reserved for the management. The roads were of asphalt, and the sewers channeled into a farm, whose soil was thus sufficiently well fertilized to yield an abundant crop of vegetables for the inhabitants and fodder for the cows that supplied the town with milk. Pullman

---

2 W. T. Stead, *If Christ Comes to Chicago!*, p. 86.

town had its own school, its own church, a hotel (the Florence), a supermarket, various shops and even a library with eight thousand volumes selected for "moral uplift."[3] There were also meeting places, a theater (the Arcade, opened in 1883 in the presence of Marshall Field and General Philip Henry Sheridan), parks, gardens, ponds and tree-lined avenues and lawns.

In 1896, Pullman town was awarded a prize by the jury of the second International Exposition of Hygiene and Pharmacy, held in Prague: at a time when Chicago was in the grip of a full-scale epidemic, not a single case of cholera, yellow fever or diphtheria had occurred in Pullman town.[4] In addition, not only the communists had the dream of creating "the new man": in 1893, in a brochure distributed at the World's Columbian Exposition, the Pullman Company announced that the town had witnessed the evolution of a new, superior kind of worker:

> During the eleven years the town has been in existence, the Pullman workingman has developed into a distinctive type – distinct in appearance, in tidiness of dress, in fact in all external indications of self-respect. ... It is within the mark to say that a representative gathering of Pullman workers would be quite forty per cent better in evidence of thrift and refinement and in all the outward indications of a wholesome habit of life, than would be a representative gathering of any correspondent group of working men which would be assembled elsewhere in the country.[5]

Pullman was proud of his town, and naturally he wanted to show it off to the world. During the World's Columbian Exposition of 1893, at least ten thousand foreign visitors would take the guided tour to check out Pullman's "new man" for themselves. There were no hospitals in the town, so the seriously ill were sent to Chicago. There wasn't a prison; wrongdoers were referred to Hyde Park, which lay to the north. The only bar was at the Hotel Florence, specifically for visitors and with astronomical prices to ensure that the inhabitants stayed sober. The rental agreements, like those of today's private gated communities, were meticulous and peppered with pedantic subclauses: enter and exit the buildings in silence; do not enter with wet feet; do not hammer or saw wood either on the floors or in

---

3   Dominic A. Pacyga and Ellen Skerret, *Chicago, City of Neighborhoods*, Chicago: Loyola University Press, 1986, p. 429.
4   A. Lindsay, *The Pullman Strike*, p. 49.
5   Ibid., p. 50.

A view of Pullman in 1881. Print by Western Manufacturers, courtesy Chicago Historical Society.

the cellar; do not smoke in the cellar; refill and clean the gas lamps in the morning; leave some ashes in the stove grating. … But the most significant piece of small print was the "ten-day" clause, which was also valid for shops or public places. The clause stated that contracts could be rescinded with only ten days' notice, even if rent had already been paid for the whole year. This clause allowed Pullman to get rid of any unwanted "guests": union officials and agitators, in particular.

It's strange how every utopia yet realized has had this obsession with controlling even the most minute gestures of its subjects, beginning with the famous egalitarian Jesuit orders in Paraguay, where the road level was raised so that the benevolent padres could peer through the windows during their morning stroll to check up on the morality of the Indios. As one of the residents of Pullman town wrote in a letter to William T. Stead, the inhabitants

> paid rent to the Pullman Company, they bought gas of the Pullman Company, they walked on streets owned in fee simple by the Pullman Company, they paid water tax to the Pullman Company. Indeed, even when they bought gingham for their wives or sugar for their tables at the arcade or the market-house, it seemed they were dealing with the Pullman Company. They sent their children to Pullman's school, attended Pullman's church, looked at but dared not enter Pullman's hotel with its private bar, for that was the limit. Pullman did not sell them their grog. They had to go to the settlement at the railroad crossing south of them.[6]

---

6   W. T. Stead, *If Christ Comes to Chicago!*, pp. 88–89.

(In reality, the people of Pullman town had their grog delivered to them by wagon in secret.)

Pullman town's inhabitants felt constantly controlled and spied upon and did not speak with outsiders for fear that they might be company informers. It was a life of continual oppression, for which all the perfection of their neat little houses and tree-lined roads offered little compensation. "They secretly rebel because the Pullman Company continues in watch and authority over them after working hours. They declare they are bound hand and foot by a *philanthropic monopoly*"[7] (italics mine), wrote the *New York Sun* in 1885. There was no democracy in Pullman town, and as for elections, the very word was an anathema; everything was decided and imposed by the company – that is, by Pullman himself – in what was effectively a regime of feudal capitalism.

But this boss's utopia suffered from two contradictions. Seemingly oblivious to the therapeutic value of home ownership just then being discovered in America, Pullman, to maintain absolute control of "his" town, refused to let his residents buy their houses, preferring to rent them so that tenants could be evicted and sent packing if the need arose. Consequently, residents were unable to develop that quintessentially capitalist feeling of ownership that was supposed to be the mark of *homus novus pullmanianus*.

Nor were they ever able to feel really part of the town. The Green Stone Church, which Pullman built and rented to the Presbyterians, could hold only 650 people (out of a total population of 8,000 to 12,000 inhabitants). In fact, though, the workers were all of different nationalities and religions: in 1892, more than two-thirds (72 percent) were foreign born, and although the majority were Catholic, Lutheran, Episcopalian, Methodist or Presbyterian, fifteen separate faiths were represented in all. Only with great difficulty could Catholics and Lutherans be persuaded to pray under the same roof. Yet it was a Lutheran pastor and a Catholic priest together who were in the end to denounce Pullman's tyranny.

The second contradiction was that, although Pullman saw his town as a utopia, this utopia was an investment and therefore had to turn a profit. The dividend threshold was fixed at 6 percent per annum (whereas the minimum threshold for Pullman Company dividends was 8 percent). The streets were kept scrupulously

---

7   A. Lindsay, *The Pullman Strike*, p. 65.

clean, but the cost of cleaning them was added to the rent, as was the cost of mowing the lawns, pruning the trees and looking after all the other conveniences that were beyond the Pullman worker's means. As a consequence, rents in Pullman town were exorbitant, between 30 and 50 percent higher than in the surrounding area. The gas that Pullman bought at $0.33 per gallon he distributed at $2.25. Every thousand gallons of water bought from the city council for 4 cents cost the user 10. Rent was automatically deducted from the worker's paycheck, and when this practice was declared illegal, workers' wages were paid in two separate checks. One was equal to the sum owed for rent and, when cashed, went straight back into Pullman's pocket. The other was to live on. If the workers tried to go elsewhere to find lodgings, they were fired or, worse, blacklisted.

In 1893, the United States was hit hard by depression. Three million people were out of work, which at that time meant being abject and miserable, losing your home, being forced to beg to avoid starvation or to live in the hope that some charity would provide for you. In Chicago alone, unemployment was as high as 200,000. At the Pullman factory, orders for new cars slumped dramatically (even while the repair and maintenance department kept its habitual rhythm).Of the 5,500 workers employed at the beginning of the year, only 1,100 remained by November. To reduce costs, Pullman cut hourly pay by 25 to 40 percent. Because working hours were also reduced, the cut was in real terms even more drastic – between 30 and 70 percent. By doing these things, Pullman was able to pay his shareholders their 8 percent dividend even the following year and to accumulate for himself nondistributed profits amounting to $2.3 million. Pullman was thus able to rehire many of the workers he had fired. By April 1894, 4,000 men were once again passing through the factory gates.

During this same time, the company refused to reduce rents in Pullman town: like everything else, the town had to earn its keep. With wages so low and rents so high, life in the utopian city became problematic. Because they were working few hours at reduced salary, many workers ended up with only $1.80 in their weekly paychecks, the same amount they would have earned in one day the previous year, and that was all they had to live on for the entire week.[8]

---

8   Ibid., p. 99.

On 7 May 1894, a committee from the factory went to the management to ask for a rent reduction and a pay rise. The company responded with a blunt refusal, followed on 10 May by the firing of three delegates. At this point, a strike became inevitable. As the workers wrote in an appeal to the citizens of Chicago: "The people of Pullman have struck against a slavery worse than that of the negroes of the South. They, at least, were well fed and well cared for, while the white slaves of Pullman, worked they ever so willingly, could not earn enough to clothe and feed themselves decently – hardly enough to keep body and soul together."[9]

To understand the mood that was abroad at the start of the Pullman strike, you need some idea of the violence of what newspapers were calling "the war between capital and labor." Less than two years earlier, a battle had taken place in Homestead, Pennsylvania, on the Ohio River, in front of the Carnegie Steelworks. In 1892, after firing all of its unionized workers, the Carnegie company had ordered a lockout and sent for three hundred Pinkerton agents to guard the works and protect the scabs. Pinkerton's men arrived on two barges, brandishing Winchesters, but were met by a crowd of some ten thousand protesters, themselves armed with rifles, pistols, sticks and shovels. As soon as the agents tried to disembark, the shooting started, resulting in numerous deaths and injuries on both sides. Pinkerton's men tried to withdraw, but the workers attacked their barges, launching sticks of dynamite. By sundown, the agents had surrendered. They were paraded through an irate crowd, jeered at and beaten. The battle had left seven Pinkerton agents dead, twenty with bullet wounds, and many more badly beaten. But the workers' victory was to be short-lived. The Pennsylvania National Guard was summoned to protect the scabs. The Carnegie company brought charges of murder against the union leaders and accused another 150 militants of minor offenses. After four months of strikebreaking and judicial harassment, the strike was defeated.

At the beginning of 1894, the economic crisis spread to the mines. Work became so hard to come by and so badly paid that a strike was the inevitable result, quickly spreading from coast to coast. Bosses began to employ scab labor on such a massive scale that fierce battles broke out all across the country between strikers and scabs. Occasionally, as happened in Du Quoin, Illinois, strikers would hijack

---

9   Ibid., p. 101.

freight trains to sabotage mines reopened by strikebreakers. To prevent the flow of coal, the miners would pile up trunks on the rails and nail down cross ties or fix bolts on them to derail the trains. Often governors would call in the national guard (even Atgeld sent in troops against rioting strikers). But after more than two months of struggle, the strikers were on their last legs. On 30 May, the *New York Times* wrote, "The miners say their wives and children are at the point of starvation. They are subsisting mainly on dandelions, but have no flour, meat or other provisions."[10]

The Pullman strike was now in its nineteenth day. "We struck because we were without hope."[11] Indeed, the Pullman workers' only real hope was the American Railway Union, the ARU. That union had been founded the previous year by Eugene Debs, perhaps the most esteemed leader in the history of the American workers' movement, to overcome divisions and hostilities between the various fraternities of railway workers; it was mainly because of these divisions that the companies so often emerged victorious. After the union wrested a fair contract from the Great Northern Railroad, the number of its enrollments began to grow; by 1894, it had 150,000 members. In an attempt to overcome divisive fragmentation, the ARU accepted everybody: engine drivers, train staff, porters, anyone who worked for a company that had anything to do with the railroads. For this reason, the ARU was able to rope in the Pullman workers, who enrolled en masse (and in secret, because anything that smacked of unions was banned in Pullman) in 1894. By the beginning of May of that year, there were 4,000 ARU members in Pullman's factories, divided into nineteen sections.

Debs and the other ARU leaders were not in favor of direct strike action: on 11 May, they had advised against the strike declared by the Pullman sections. But one month later, as the miners' strike still raged, at the height of the Pullman conflict, 400 delegates met in Chicago for the ARU's first national congress. Every day the delegates went to the gates of the Pullman building, where they spoke with the strikers and witnessed the appalling poverty of the workers, who were slowly being crushed by the power of the company. Debs tried to keep negotiations open, but Pullman refused to budge. It was then that the 4,000 delegates voted unani-

---

10 Details on the miners' strike can be found in J. Brecher, *Strike!*, vol. I, pp. 96–103.
11 A. Lindsay, *The Pullman Strike*, p. 128.

mously for a boycott: the country's railway workers were not to work on any train carrying Pullman cars.

The boycott became operative on 26 June 1894, with participation going beyond all expectations. Within two days, eleven of Chicago's railways were completely paralyzed. The boycott extended all over the country, from the Atlantic to the Pacific. Never in US history, either before or since, has a workers' protest come closer to becoming a nationwide general strike. The *New York Times* of 29 June warned that the strike had "assumed the proportions of the greatest battle between labor and capital that has ever been inaugurated in the United States."[12]

By now, the ARU had to contend not only with Pullman, but with the whole cartel of the big railroad companies united under the General Managers' Association (GMA). Founded in 1886 (in the wake of the Haymarket bombing), the GMA in 1894 included twenty-four railroad companies that represented between them 40,000 miles of track, 221,000 employees and a global share capital of $810 million. The GMA had set up three separate committees: the first to ensure the supply of scab labor in case of strike or conflict with unions; the second to respond to workers' demands and establish uniform salaries (even if it wished to, a company could not concede a pay increase contrary to the GMA's ruling); and the third to respond to crises, sitting in permanent session during periods of industrial action.

It was this crisis committee that on 25 June declared its support for George Pullman: no company would run its trains without Pullman's cars. The following day, the committee decided that it would fire any worker who refused to hook up the Pullman cars. Its coordinator, John M. Egan, took on thirty investigators to discover the union's weak points. But it wasn't simply a question of expressing solidarity with Pullman: as the *New York Times* of 27 June said, it would be a clash between the largest and most powerful railroad workers' organizations and the whole of railroad capital. This was why "[a]ll efforts of the general managers were directed toward one end – the complete annihilation of the American Railway Union."[13]

Yet the strikers were so strong and the strike so well organized that the railroad companies were paralyzed by its calm. With no apparent disorder to quell, they

---

12 Ibid., p. 203.
13 Ibid., p. 139.

could not justify calling in the various national guards; on 2 July, Egan was forced to admit that the railroads had been "fought to a standstill." Meanwhile, the GMA's lawyers were studying a way to get Washington to intervene: "A vital part of the strategy of the association was to draw the United States government into the struggle and then to make it appear that the battle was no longer between the workers and the railroads but between the workers and the government."[14] The companies were assured the support of President Grover Cleveland and even more of his attorney general, Richard Olney, who was given the job of resolving the Pullman conflict. Olney had for years worked as a lawyer for the railroad companies, several of whom had offered him a chair on the board (including the New York Central), and he was himself a former member of the GMA. He was also a shareholder and board member of the Chicago Burlington and Quincy and had interests, along with George Pullman, in the Boston and Maine. This, then, was the man who was supposed to make an impartial decision in the ARU–GMA deadlock. So impartial was he, in fact, that he nominated as his representative in Chicago Edwin Walker, another railroad company lawyer who was then legal adviser to the Chicago, Milwaukee and St. Paul and, of course, to the GMA.

The legal catch that gave the White House the chance to intervene was the interruption of public service: the government could, of course, have sent the mail on Pullman-less trains, but it didn't, and thus the US mail service was interrupted. Some months previously, a judge had invoked the Sherman Act, an antitrust law, to defend a company *against* what he called the strikers' "monopoly": "A strike is essentially a conspiracy to extort by violence. ... I know of no peaceful strike."[15] It was thus on Walker's request that Chicago's judges issued an injunction designed to "protect" twenty-two companies from the "criminal conspiracy" the strikers had formed to obstruct the mail service, forbidding Debs and indeed "all other persons whosoever ... from in any way or manner interfering with, hindering, obstructing, or stopping" any of the business of the railroad that passed through Chicago and "from compelling or inducing or attempting to compel or induce by threats, intimidation, persuasion, force or violence, any of the employees of the

---

14 Ibid., pp. 142, 144.
15 Ibid., p. 157.

railroads to refuse to carry out their duty as employees."[16] As Foner says in his *History of the Labor Movement in the United States*, "Criminal conspiracy to block the mail meant the penitentiary for the strike leaders."

The ARU refused to comply with the terms of the injunction. On 3 July, President Cleveland ordered the commandant of Fort Sheridan to move his troops to Chicago to enforce the federal ruling. But while the president of the United States has the power to send troops into a state to protect it from violence, he may do so only at the request of the state's legislature or, if the legislative body is not in session, of the governor himself. Governor Atgeld not only refused to ask for federal intervention; he even sent a telegram in protest – but to no avail.

On 4 July, Independence Day, federal troops entered Chicago and took control of both the city and its railroads. Soldiers set up camp right in the city center, in parks and on the sidewalks. Only then did the disorder break out, a disorder that the troops were supposed to quell but that, in fact, they had helped to incite. Buildings from the World's Columbian Exposition were set ablaze, as was Illinois Central Station, resulting in the destruction of seven hundred train cars. Soldiers resorted to the use of firearms, killing twenty-five workers and seriously wounding sixty. Troops were brought in from all four corners of the country.

In California, every train was given its own military escort: not since the days of the Civil War had so many soldiers been seen on America's roads.[17] The press launched its own attack on the strikers. "From a Strike to a Revolution" ran the headlines. The bugbear of anarchism was brandished once more: "Anarchists and Socialists Said to Be Planning the Destruction and the Looting of the Treasury"; "Anarchists on the Way to America from Europe." *Harper's Weekly* ran a cover story entitled, "The Vanguard of Anarchy," while the *Chicago Herald* of 3 July featured a dire warning of the dangers of tolerating anarchists such as Debs who would destroy the nation's institutions.

Debs was the main target. As it had done in the case of Atgeld, the *New York Times*, citing eminent figures from the medical profession summoned at the moment of need, sustained that Debs was clinically insane. And while the federal government abolished the freedom to strike and the freedom of speech (that is,

---

16 P. S. Foner, *History of the Labor Movement in the United States*, vol. II, p. 267.
17 A. Lindsay, *The Pullman Strike*, p. 16.

speech in favor of the strike), the big guns of the national press pulled another bogeyman out of the closet, the fear of a workers' dictatorship: "The Dictator's Dream," ran the front-page headline of the *Chicago Herald* of 2 July, while the following day the *Tribune* took up the baton: "Dictator Debs versus Federal Government." From their pulpits, preachers rained fire and brimstone on the heathens. Public opinion was shaped by images of a Chicago in flames, a city ravaged by destruction, so much so that reporters arriving in the city were astonished by the calm they found there. At that point, the GMA had already decided to refuse any offer Debs made to call off the strike. (Debs asked only that striking workers be reinstated.)

On 10 July, Debs and the other leaders of the ARU were arrested and released on bail. Although the strike continued to hold strong across the country, it was now without a leader. The last glimmer of hope was extinguished on 12 July by the AFL union, led by Samuel Gompers, none too cut up about crushing the "competition" from Debs and the ARU. So it was that the AFL decided not to adhere to the general strike in support of the ARU, choosing instead to simply sustain Debs's latest peace offer (which was turned down by the GMA) and then, almost as an insult, to cough up $1,000 for Debs's legal defense out of supposed solidarity. The directors of the AFL were in fact overjoyed; just as the Haymarket bombing had blown away the Knights of Labor, so too had the Pullman defeat wiped out the American Railway Union.

On 17 July, Debs and three other leaders were again placed under arrest (it would be December before they were convicted, receiving sentences of three to six months, with six months for Debs himself). The day following the arrest, officials of the Pullman Company posted a notice that the shops in Pullman would resume operation as soon as a workforce could be employed. Two days later, the army pulled out of Chicago and returned to Fort Sheridan. Though his union lay in ruins, Debs went on to found the American Socialist Party and for decades was a familiar candidate in US presidential elections. Pullman died in 1897, a victorious but lonely and embittered man. In 1907, his town was put up for sale. The last railcar rolled out of the Pullman factory in 1981.

The Pullman strike was not to be the end of the American workers' movement, as demonstrated by the Industrial Workers of the World (IWW), founded in Chicago in 1905, and by the workers' uprisings of 1919 (the so-called "red summer") and 1936–37. It did mark the end of any notion of a general strike, however. For, more than anything else, the Pullman dispute had brutally shown whose side the federal government was on and how much it was prepared to bend and even break every law to ensure that a consolidated workers' movement never got off the ground in the United States.

Comparing the events of the Haymarket and Pullman disputes to the affairs of the Roman or Chinese empires, we would be forced to conclude that the ruling class of the American Empire has deployed the use of force only at certain key historical moments. In those moments, however, it has used that force totally and ruthlessly against strategically chosen targets considered to be its main enemies (first the Knights of Labor, then the American Railway Union). Against such enemies, it has made use of every weapon at its disposal, from the press and public opinion to the legal system and even to the army – and when all else has failed, it has turned to money to defeat and divide these organizations, isolating them from other workers and unions. It is from here that the tacit approval and support of all moderate unions derives. As Werner Sombart wrote in 1906,

> [to the leading trade unionists] a richer reward is held out if they swear loyalty to the ruling party; they will be given a well-paid job, perhaps as a factory inspector or even as an Under-Secretary of State, depending on the significance attached to the person to be provided for. The practice of rendering influential workers' leaders harmless by bestowing on them a lucrative post is a thoroughly established one, and for years it has been used with the greatest success by the ruling parties. ... At the moment the President of the American Federation of Labor ... is said to have been selected ... as Comissioner of the Bureau of Labor, while John Mitchell, the victorious leader of the miners ... is supposed to be receiving a post as Under-Secretary of State in Washington. It has been ascertained that in Massachusetts thirteen workers' leaders have obtained political positions in this way within the space of a few years, while in Chicago thirty have done so.[18]

Sombart's observation has been confirmed time and time again. We have already seen how Terence Powderly was made a high-level functionary of the Im-

---

18 W. Sombart, *Why Is There No Socialism in the United States?*, pp. 36–37.

migration Commission for services rendered. During World War I, Hugh Frayne of the AFL was a member of the War Industries Board, while Samuel Gompers was himself nominated as head of the National Defense Council's Labor Committee.[19] Sombart might have been astonished by it, but this so seemingly American practice has recently spread to Europe. In Italy, for example, a union leader served as Employment Minister under the Christian Democrats, while an ex-union representative was Minister of the Family in the Berlusconi government. Other ex-union members have made similar career moves to become functionaries in various ministries. Several former union managers now work as managers in the private sector. Now that the union movement in Europe appears to be in its death throes, it is perhaps worth reflecting on the historical weakness of American unions, particularly in light of their defeat in what were some of "the greatest battles between labor and capital."

---

19 James Weinstein, *Ambiguous Legacy: The Left in American Politics,* New York: New Viewpoints, Franklin Watts Inc., 1975, p. 58.

14

When the Frankfurters Became Dogmeat

Statistics repeat the facts, but the incredulity remains. No matter how much you travel around and observe, it's impossible to convince yourself that the Germans, rather than the English or even the Irish, constitute the largest ethnic group in the United States. Everywhere you look, you see signs of Blackness, Italian traits, Mexican influences, the stamp of Irishness, the English matrix, even a trace of the French in the Cajuns of Louisiana – but the German influence seems to have vanished into thin air. While the other ingredients of the American melting pot have proudly flaunted their differences, from the "Black Is Beautiful" movement of the 1960s to the emergence of "white ethnic" pride in the 1970s, German identity appears to have been completely assimilated, a strange fade-out when you consider the brutal manner in which the Reich posed the question of "Germanity" to the entire world in the twentieth century.

Yet the figures speak for themselves: the census of 1990 counted 59 million people of German descent, compared to 39 million Irish and 33 million English, which in turn were far ahead of the Italians (14.7 million), Mexicans (11.6), Scots (11), French (10.3) and Poles (9.4).[1] Indeed, the Germans are the most populous ethnic group in all five of the great American regions (Northeast, Midwest, South,

---

1   Census Bureau, *Statistical Abstract of the United States 1993*, tab. 56, 58.

West and Pacific) and in twenty-nine of the fifty states (even in Alaska), including every single state in the Midwest.

The German *absence* is particularly disturbing in Chicago, the most Germanic of America's major cities. While here you can find a Polish, Lithuanian, Ukrainian, Swedish or Mexican museum, there is no such site consecrated to the history of Chicago's German community. You can participate in Tet (the Vietnamese New Year) or in the big St. Patrick's Day parade, but the German element appears only in the persistent Germanic surnames or in the odd street named after Goethe or Schiller. Chicago has had mayors who were Irish or Czech but never one who was German.

This disappearing act seems amazing when viewed against the zeal and vitality of German culture in the United States during the nineteenth century. In the beginning, toward 1830, the early immigrants had tried to transform Texas into a German community, an experiment they repeated in the 1850s in Wisconsin, with the result that "Milwaukee was proclaimed the German Athens of America."[2] "They showed resistance to Americanizing tendencies ... through their pride in their own culture and their own language and this tended to leave German communities as islands in a sea of Americanism."[3] In these islands, they read German newspapers, were treated in German hospitals, studied German at school, listened to sermons given in German in Lutheran churches, sang German songs and played German music. This was German America, the *Deutschtum,* proud of itself but derided by the Anglophone population (who called it the *Dachshund Element,* after the German sausage dog). These islands also harbored socialists and anarchists, though the Germans were for the most part apolitical. Indeed, some Germans went on to become capitalists, notorious for their ruthless attitude toward workers: the fur merchant John Jacob Astor; Frederick Weyerhaeuser, deforester of America; the industrialist George Westinghouse; the sugar king Klaus Spreckles (who later moved to Hawaii); the Anheuser-Busch, St. Louis, brewers who to this day own the Budweiser beer company.

In Chicago during the 1800s, there were more than thirty German-language

---

newspapers. One of the finest hospitals in the city was the German hospital, constructed in 1883. The city orchestra was called the Theodor Thomas Orchestra after the German who founded it in 1890. One of Chicago's most exclusive circles was the Germania Club, created in 1865. The most important choirs were also German. To understand fully the influence German America had on the community, one need only recall that the first Lutheran service held in English (in St. Louis) did not take place until 1890 – or that even Blacks and Native Americans frequently spoke German as late as 1905 in the city of Belleville, Illinois.[4]

But all that was to change with the outbreak of World War I. On 5 August 1914, a crowd of some ten thousand Germans demonstrated in Chicago in support of US neutrality. The war was reflected in the relations between different ethnic groups: Irish Americans were apt to sympathize with the Germans out of anti-English irredentism, whereas Poles were hostile to them (in response to anti-Polish aggression on the part of the Central European empires). In the English camp, meanwhile, there was growing wariness of the Germans. The *Abendpost* of 31 December 1914 issued the following complaint: "We are of German blood and heritage, but we are also citizens of the United States. We call ourselves German-Americans and every day we become more proud of this name. To us, the designation German-American seems proper and fitting. Nothing else would do. But other people do not agree with us. They deny us that right. They scoff at the implication of Germanism contained in the expression and call us 'hyphenated Americans,' which is to say, Americans with a mental reservation, or 'grade B' Americans."[5]

America's WASP heart was beating in hope of the Entente: during those months, the press was waging a violent campaign against "German atrocities in Flanders," reporting that German soldiers were cutting off the hands of children. (These "atrocities" have since disappeared without trace from the history books.)

In German America, meanwhile, many supported the Reich or, as a second option, pushed for absolute neutrality from the United States. Even within Chicago's German community, however, positions were divided right from the moment of

---

4   Ibid., p. 290.
5   Cited in Rudolph A. Hofmeister, *The Germans of Chicago*, Champaign, Ill.: Stipes, 1976, pp. 63–64.

Bismarck's centennial in April 1915. The *Abendpost* of 1 March protested against the celebrations: "Those who have taken the oath of American citizenship should refrain from celebrating in public any birthdays or anniversaries of foreign political leaders, regardless of their prominence." The *Illinois Staats-Zeitung* took an altogether different view and printed entire pages announcing the upcoming festivities in no uncertain terms: "A united Germany is invincible! Dear fatherland, may your righteous cause lead you to victory!" In the end, some four thousand people took part in the centennial, demonstrating in support of US neutrality. Ethnic sensitivity was so finely tuned that when a citizen of German birth, R. Sweizer, stood as a candidate in the 1915 council elections, many Germans refused to vote for him because he had eliminated the *ch* from his original surname, Schweizer.

But as German U-boats continued to sink allied ships in the Atlantic, public opinion began to turn against the Germans. When on 6 April 1917 the United States declared war on the Central Alliance, the Germans of America were labeled deserters from Germany and traitors to the United States, where a witch-hunt began to root out the enemy within. On 7 April, several employees of various industries were arrested on suspicion of sabotage. Even the slaughterhouses, since they constituted a "vital industry," were wrapped in barbed wire for fear of sabotage. In the following days, sixty Germans were to be arrested for taking part in the so-called Hindi Plot (stirring up actions against the English in India).[6]

With war already declared, the influence of the German presence in Chicago was demonstrated in April of 1917 when the city's mayor, William Hale Thompson, refused to receive Marshall Joffre, hero of the Marne and one of the top allied generals: "Here there are only 3,681 French-born inhabitants whereas Chicago is the sixth largest German city in the world, the second largest Bohemian, the second largest Swedish, the second largest Polish and the second largest Norwegian; hence to invite a representative of some nation in the war in the name of all the people of Chicago would be presumptuous."[7]

---

6 Andrew Jack Townsend, *The Germans of Chicago*, 1927 doctoral thesis of the University of Chicago, reprinted in *Jahrbuch der deutschen-amerikanischen historischen Gesellschaft von Illinois*, 1932, pp. 99–100.
7 J. A. Hagwood, *The Tragedy of German America*, p. 297.

But all that was in any way reminiscent of Germany by that time was in the process of being erased. It was then, for example, that wurstel sausages changed their name from frankfurters to hotdogs (the Spanish called them *perros calientes*). Other name changes were less successful: after a fleeting period of being known as the liberty steak, the hamburger went back to Hamburg, while *Sauerkrauten* were no longer known by the somewhat ridiculous moniker liberty cabbage.

Particularly vicious was the campaign against German America's mother-tongue newspapers. On 20 July 1917, in conclusion to an article entitled, "The Disloyalty of the German-American Press," the editors of the *Atlantic Monthly* wrote:

> By temper and tradition, the people of the United states are easy-going and tolerant. We believe in that temper and we respect that tradition. And likewise, we believe in and respect the great body of American citizens of German inheritance. ... But now, these papers, unmindful of their privilege, trade upon our patience. ... [T]he bulk of the German-American press in this country consists frankly of enemy papers. Enemy papers, printed in the enemy language, protected by our laws and admitted to the privileges of the mails! ... The remedy is a sane war-time censorship upon enemy propaganda, and a substantial war-time tax on the printed use of the enemy language ... because here, as in Europe, it is German thinking which is the chief offender...

In a letter to the *Chicago Tribune* published on 8 August 1917, one irate reader finally exploded: "Let us hope that before long our government will stop dilly-dallying with these so-called German-Americans and put them into concentration camps until the end of the war, which end would be materially hastened by such action, especially if coupled with the entire suppression of the German-language press."[8] Although President Wilson had rushed a tough Espionage Act through Congress that June, he had not managed to include a clause on press censorship. His solution was to exclude subversive newspapers from postal discounts and to give "the Postmaster General the right to withhold from the mails any dispatch urging 'treason, insurrection, or forcible resistance to any law of the United States.'"[9]

---

8 Cited in Frederick C. Luebke, *Bonds of Loyalty: German Americans and World War I*, De Kalb, Ill.: Northern Illinois University Press, 1974, p. 237.

Those deemed "enemy aliens" were to present themselves to the authorities (with exemptions made for those who could prove they were from Alsace-Lorraine). In spring 1918, according to the attorney general, there were 14,340 enemy aliens living in Chicago. There were countless roundups, and many Germans ended up in concentration camps. On 12 March 1919, the *Abendpost* estimated that around 5,000 German Americans, many of them Chicagoans, had spent the war interned in one or another of the concentration camps at Fort Oglethorpe (Tennessee), Fort Douglas (Utah) and Hot Springs (North Carolina).[10] Their internment foreshadowed the mass reclusion in 1942 of America's Japanese population, with the difference that the German victims came from one of the largest ethnic groups in the country, a fact that was to have major political and economic consequences.

Among those sent to concentration camps were musicians, bankers – whose properties were seized and never fully restored – and even highly influential and powerful families. Especially damaging were the political implications. In April 1917 in its St. Louis Manifesto, Eugene Debs's Socialist Party declared its opposition to the war: "The working class of the United States has no quarrel with the working class of Germany. ... We brand the declaration of war by our government as a crime against the people of the United States and against the nations of the world ... [therefore] we recommend to the workers ... continuous, active, and public opposition to the war through demonstrations, mass petitions and all other means within our power."[11]

The American Socialist Party had taken a stand against the war. This awkward position naturally triggered a witch-hunt (just as anyone with vaguely leftist leanings during the 1950s was branded a Soviet spy). In the United States, the notion of socialism had always been associated with the Germans, and many members of the Socialist Party were in fact immigrants: in 1915, the party had fourteen "foreign" sections. After the St. Louis Manifesto, many intellectuals (including Upton Sinclair) abandoned the party, accusing it of selling out to the enemy (accusations

---

9   James Weinstein, *The Decline of Socialism in America: 1912–1925*, New York: Monthly Review Press, 1967. Reprinted, New Brunswick, N.J.: Rutgers University Press, 1984, p. 144.

10 R. A. Hofmeister, *The Germans of Chicago*, pp. 70–71.

11 "St. Louis Manifesto of the Socialist Party" (1917), published in A. Fried, *Socialism in America*, pp. 521–26.

to ensure the growing influence of Germans who had taken refuge in the Socialist Party). The government resorted to violently repressive measures. In the last year of the war, of the Socialist Party's 5,000 or more sections, 1,500 were dismantled. In Chicago, the offices of both the *Arbeiter Zeitung* and the *Sozial Demokraten* were searched and then closed down, as was the Radical Book Store.[12] The Industrial Workers of the World (IWW) was even hounded for its neutralism, and, in the mind of the public, its name took on a wholly different meaning: Imperial Wilhelm's Warriors.[13] In Chicago, 166 of the union's leaders were arrested on charges of sabotage and treachery; 99 of these were convicted, as were around a hundred other leaders elsewhere.

At this point, convictions based on the Espionage Act began to rain down, resulting in the imprisonment of some 2,000 people. Among those arrested in March of 1918 were Adolph Gerner, national secretary of the Socialist Party; J. Lewis Egdahl, editor of the *American Socialist;* and Irwin St. John Tucker of the People's Party. The secretary of state for Washington, Emil Herman,[14] was sentenced to ten years' imprisonment, as was Eugene Debs, for "allegedly using 'profane, scandalous and abusive language' in a speech at Canton, Ohio."[15] Debs entered prison a few months after the war ended and remained there until 1921, when he and twenty-three other political prisoners were granted pardons by President Warren Harding. In the presidential elections of 1920, Debs, campaigning from prison, had obtained 920,000 votes. Once again, the real "enemy within" for the United States was the workers and the socialist movement, and the war against Germany served to justify actions against their leaders.

As Hagwood writes in *The Tragedy of German America,*

> Germans in America between 1855 and 1915 lived not in the United States, but in German America. The World War, with its hatreds and its persecutions, its propaganda and its coercion, shook the hyphen loose from its moorings and ended the German-American era which had persisted so long. The Germans in America and Americans of German stock were placed in a dilemma such as so often exists in war-

---

12 A. J. Townsend, *The Germans of Chicago*, p. 105.
13 See Patrick Renchaw, *The Wobblies: The Story of Syndicalism in the United States*, New York: Anchor Books, Doubleday, 1967.
14 Ibid., p. 101; and J. Weinstein, *The Decline of Socialism in America*, p. 161.
15 A. Fried, *Socialism in America*, p. 509.

time for a minority of alien origin which has for a long period resisted assimilation. They had to divide into "Germans" and "Americans" who were by origin of stock German. The "German-American" was an anomaly that could no longer exist.[16]

The first, most immediate form that the erasure of German identity was to assume was in the change of names, a new baptism for anything that hinted even vaguely at the Teutonic. So it was that on 9 May 1918, after fifty-three years, the Germania Club decided to rename itself the Chicago Lincoln Club. Ten days later, the Hotel Bismarck changed its name to the Hotel Randolph, while the Kaiserhof Hotel became the Atlantic. The Kaiser Friedrich Mutual Aid Society was renamed the George Washington Charitable Society;[17] the Bismarck School became the Frederick Funston General School. In the twenty-eighth district, the names of roads such as Berlin Street and Lubeck Street were all changed. The German Hospital became Grant Hospital, while the Theodor Thomas Orchestra was by that time known as the Chicago Symphony Orchestra.

Individuals and families, too, felt obliged to change their names. The *Abendpost* of 20 August 1918 reported that more than fifty citizens had made requests to the court that their names be Anglicized, among them Harry H. Feichenfeld, owner of a poultry shop, who wished to become H. H. Field; Otto W. Mayer, who wished to be known as Mayor; Hans Kaiser, who now saw himself as John Kern; Emma Gutmann, who, after having tried Gutman, eventually settled for Goodman; Bertha Grisheimer, who asked to be called Gresham; and Joseph G. Schumann, who changed his name to Shuman. Here again we see at work the terrible power of naming and renaming.

One by one, the German newspapers began to fold. After seventy years of activity (fifty-five as a daily), the *Illinois Statts-Zeitung* ceased its daily publication in 1918 and was finally closed completely in 1925. Before 1914, there had been fifty German-language periodicals published in Illinois; by 1926, there were only ten, none of which were daily newspapers. The use of the language began to fade. In August of 1918, the state's Grand Masonic Lodge ordered its seven German chapters no longer to hold their meetings in German.[18] Choral groups suspended the

---

16 J. A. Hagwood, *The Tragedy of German America*, p. xviii.
17 R. A. Hofmeister, *The Germans of Chicago*, p. 72.
18 Ibid., p. 74.

traditional singing of *Lieder* on Saturday afternoons. German-language teaching in schools fell into decline. (In Chicago during the 1914–15 school year, 18,160 students in 112 schools had studied German. In 1917, following a council ruling, German-language classes were abolished from primary schools. By 1929, German was no longer taught in any of Chicago's secular schools.) Among the Lutheran churches of St. Louis, around 30 percent used English in 1914, as opposed to 70 percent that used German; by 1929, the Lutheran pastors held only one service a month in German "for the elderly."[19]

The process of Americanization did not begin with World War I, but that was when the real rupture occurred, for the simple reason that the Germans are the only ethnic group in the United States who have been pressed to abjure their original identity. Favoring this break, the influx of German immigrants petered out, thanks to restrictive legislation brought into force in 1921 and again in 1924. The Johnson-Reed Act of 1924 stipulated that each ethnic group had the right to an immigration quota equivalent to 2 percent of the total number from that group already present in the United States in 1890. In this way, (1) immigration was brought to an abrupt halt; and (2) the 1890 deadline had the effect of completely annulling immigrants from southern and eastern Europe, who had come to the United States en masse in the period after 1890. The Johnson-Reed Act was specifically aimed against the Italians, Poles and Russians, but the Germans also resented it as an act directed against their community. As Hagwood comments, "the Germans, as a stock primarily of post-colonial origin, suffered drastic restrictions."

For all the previously mentioned reasons, there would no longer be a German "problem" in the United States from the mid-1920s on, not even during World War II. For as Richard O'Connor writes, "Unlike World War I, pro-Germanism was a dead issue in the United States by the time the country went to war with the Axis. No hysteria this time, except in regard to the innocent Japanese-Americans. How could there have been with an Eisenhower leading the second American expeditionary force against Germany, a Spaatz commanding the bombs which were pulverizing Germany, a Nimitz in command of the Pacific Fleet, an Eichelbecher and a Krueger commanding the two armies under General McArthur?"[20] Since the

---

19 J. A. Hagwood, *The Tragedy of German America*, p. 300.
20 R. O'Connor, *The German-Americans*, p. 452.

Germans constitute the largest ethnic group in the United States, the notion arises that World War II was, in part, a civil war fought between two opposing groups of Germans: Germans from America on one side, Germans from Germany on the other.

As a postscript, however, we must cite at least one precedent to the US generals of German stock mentioned by O'Connor. In Washington, at the northwest corner of the gardens behind the White House, between Connecticut Avenue and H Street, rises a bronze monument erected in 1910, a mere five years before the frankfurters became hotdogs or, worse, dogmeat. The statue portrays one Frederick William Augustus Henry Ferdinand, Baron von Steuben (Prussia 1736 – New York 1794): "in grateful recognition of his services to the American people in their struggle for liberty. … After serving as aide de camp to Frederick the Great of Prussia, he offered his sword to the American colonies. … *He gave military training and discipline* to the citizen soldiers who achieved the independence of the United States." Talk about "Prussian discipline"!

15

In the Capital of Hobohemia

In front of the Social Security building sprouts an obscene erection in the form of a four-story-high wrought-metal baseball bat, the work of Claes Oldenburg, who christened it *Batcolumn*. Nearby, between Halsted and Canal on West Madison Street, stand three fifty-two-floor skyscrapers. These are the Presidential Towers: three floors of offices surmounted by forty-nine of living space, totaling three thousand apartments. The inhabitants are mostly yuppies and dinks who have chosen the towers for their proximity to the center, banks and stock exchange. The construction of these buildings during the 1980s cost US taxpayers more than $100 million in federal subsidies, state incentives, council grants, fiscal exemptions, soft financing, land sale at (politically) favorable prices, demolition work and infrastructure. Judging from its banally corporate aspect and from the infrequency of passersby, no one would ever imagine that a mere twenty years ago this street was the capital of America's Hoboland, complete with dives, used clothes shops, flophouses, barbershops, brothels and pawnshops.[1]

The number of pawnshops in the United States is incredible. In Europe, the sight of a pawn sign is extremely rare. But here you can pawn everything: your

---

1 Charles Hoch and Robert A. Slayton, *New Homeless and Old: Community and the Skid Row Hotel*, Philadelphia: Temple University Press, 1989, pp. 183–85.

watch, your jewelry, your hi-fi system or your 9mm automatic. In Europe, the "pawn stall" seems like a relic left over from the Middle Ages. In the United States, by contrast, once you pass the invisible borderline between neighborhoods (and classes), Pawnshop and Checks Cashed signs begin to multiply before your eyes, flashing on and off in the neon night like the lights of crazed pinball machines. From the things you see in the windows, you know you have left behind the sidewalks of affluence and entered an area inhabited by either the working class or immigrants or the just plain shady.

It takes a while to realize why there should be such a plethora of these shops in the States, but then everything becomes suddenly clear. They are there for those without sufficient guarantees, for those who have bounced too many checks or who are behind on their mortgage payments, for the "illegal aliens" who, unable to open a bank account, have nowhere to cash their paychecks and so are forced to go through one of these artisans of banking who – for a small commission – will transform them into greenbacks.

Not having a bank account here creates more than just economic inconvenience; it's a social black mark that can make life difficult, obstructing you in even the smallest endeavors. In this respect, not having a bank account is like not having a car. (Eighty percent of Americans own a car, and the going can be extremely rough for the 20 percent who do not.) Nowadays, the Pawnshops and Checks Cashed signs have vanished from West Madison Street, once the most famous and densely populated Skid Row in America.

The term *Skid Row* originated in Seattle, where it referred to the street used by Henry Yesler, a local lumberman, to roll or skid logs to his sawmill on the waterfront. Lining the street were cheap hotels, taverns, restaurants, brothels and other services catering to lumberjacks. By the 1920s, however, *Skid Road*, as it was originally called, primarily housed poor, unemployed ex-loggers, as well as short-term workers in the city's service industries. In time, the name of the area was shortened to *Skid Row*, a term used in a pejorative, generic way. Skid Row designated, in any American city, a place where drunks were both concentrated and highly visible.[2] There was also the implication of downward mobility (being "on the

---

2   Ibid., pp. 88–89.

skids"), as well as of a constrained physical, economic and social environment (a "row").

Every city in America has had its Skid Row: the Bowery in New York, South Main Street in Los Angeles, Scollay Square in Boston, Sixth Street in San Francisco. But the most important was Chicago's West Madison Street, the section running from Halsted to the Chicago River. Here crossed the paths of seasonal workers, itinerant laborers, pieceworkers, the jobless, vagabonds of all nations. At that time, America was one uninterrupted coming and going of workers, a frenzy of mobility; in the years between 1880 and 1920, the turnover in Boston was such that nearly the entire population of the city changed every ten years. But it was in Chicago, with its 3,125 miles of railroad, that every day torrents of men celebrated the apotheosis of mobility. Here, in the railway center of America, the trains loaded and unloaded not only corn, pigs and lumber but also human destinies, whole life trajectories.

On the eve of the First World War, according to Hoch and Slayton, authors of *New Homeless and Old*, "as many as 500,000 workers without permanent homes regularly flowed in and out the Windy City. ... As late as 1922 the city still had more than 200 private employment agencies that placed a quarter-million men annually, in addition to the constant hiring going on at factory gates all over town."[3] In the packinghouses, only half the workforce worked the whole year round, while the other half came and went with the changing of the seasons.[4] It was the demand for this mobile, flexible worker – to be dismissed or retained at will – that was to produce that quintessentially modern social figure: the single worker, without family (since other family members were either far away or no longer living) and thus with neither hearth nor homeland, a homeless man who, nonetheless, did have a roof over his head, who lodged in boardinghouses, furnished rooms or inns. It was a phenomenon inscribed in the very fabric of the industrial revolution, first in the exodus from the countryside to the urban factories, then in the form of immigration. Already in 1845, Friedrich Engels had noted the emergence of the "houseless," as these people were known at the time: "Every morning fifty thousand Londoners wake up not knowing where they are going to sleep

---

3 Ibid., pp. 11–12.
4 R. A. Slayton, *Back of the Yards*, pp. 124–25.

at night. The most fortunate are those who have a few pence in their pocket in the evening and can afford to go to one of the many lodging houses which exist in all the big cities. But these establishments only provide the most miserable accommodation."[5]

In Chicago, in the Back of the Yards neighborhood, 27.3 percent of the residents lived in boardinghouses. As soon as the newly arrived immigrants got off the train, they would go to the houses of their co-nationals, who needed to rent out rooms to be able to pay the mortgage. Only rarely did the boarder have the right to a room of his own, however – just as for Maghrebian immigrants in Italy today, the Italians themselves had to sleep ten to a room at that time in Little Italy.

The same logic that allowed workers to be ordered à la carte had its subversive side: it led to the emergence of a new kind of citizen, a citizen who had neither house nor family and who was thus deprived of the two cornerstones of political and social morality. Remember those thaumaturgic powers that had given the people of America over to home ownership, which, in Roosevelt's words, would make the United States an "unconquerable nation." That same capitalism was now creating millions of workers who were inconstant, unstable and therefore potentially immoral and dangerous.

This contradiction was even more apparent in the case of another, newer type of single worker who was "houseless but not homeless." Toward the close of the nineteenth century, a new social figure had appeared: the single female worker (a dressmaker, a factory worker, a secretary or a shop girl). Chicago alone had more than 100,000 female wage earners, and of these, around 21 percent lived in furnished rooms.[6] These female workers preferred a furnished room to a boardinghouse because it offered them greater privacy and freedom. In nearly half of these rooms (49 percent), the tenants were allowed to invite men. This fueled malicious gossip among the self-righteous citizenry. Rumors of immorality began to spread about the furnished-room neighborhoods, owing to a widely held conviction that living without family produced (and was itself caused by) perversion.

There were the disadvantaged "houseless," who could still afford a roof over their head, and then there were the tramps *sans toit ni loi*. At times, a worker

---

5   F. Engels, *The Condition of the Working Class in England*, pp. 37–38.
6   R. A. Slayton, *Back of the Yards*, p. 19.

would end up unemployed; the unemployed worker couldn't find another job; the chronically unemployed became a chronic alcoholic; the alcoholic went a bit off the rails. But that wasn't all: amidst sporadic economic crises, waves of layoffs, tenants late with monthly rent payments and the greed of landlords who spared every expense in maintaining the buildings, the neighborhood went quickly downhill. Facades crumbled, signs drooped, glass fell out of windows. The notoriety of these zones was seemingly confirmed by their ugly, run-down appearance.

So it was that in the Skid Rows of the early 1900s, alongside well-kept boarding-houses there began to appear hovels, flophouses, slum accommodations of every category. The neighborhood became stratified. It was home no longer only to one social group, but to an entire society, with its own hierarchies and even outcasts. Skid Row was in fact ruled by a rigid caste system, at the top of which were the hoboes, seasonal and itinerant workers who could find a variety of jobs as meat-packers, ice cutters, bricklayers or lumberjacks or on the railroads. The hoboes worked hard, even if their jobs were short-lived and they had to travel the length and breadth of the continent to get them, from salmon fishing off the Pacific Coast to fruit gathering in California or oyster fishing on the Atlantic.

Through their migrant labor, the hoboes built America. One writer went so far as to dub them "the storm troops of American expansionism." In his classic study of 1923, Nels Anderson, himself a former hobo, wrote: "Hobos have a romantic place in our history. From the beginning they have been numbered among the pioneers. They have played an important role in reclaiming the desert and in subduing the trackless forests. They have contributed more to the open, frank and adventurous spirit of the Old West than we are always willing to admit. They are, as it were, belated frontiersmen."[7] The hobo was kept apart from the middle classes and the "sedentary" working classes of the factories by his nomadism, which rendered him suspect, though he shared in their common belief in the value of hard work. The bigoted and self-righteous regarded hoboes as drunkards and criminals.[8] The films of Chaplin, however, and the ballads of Woody Guthrie suffuse the hobo with the romantic aura of a carefree vagabond.

---

7   Nels Anderson, *The Hobo: The Sociology of the Homeless Man* (1923), Chicago: University of Chicago Press, 1961, p 92.
8   C. Hoch and R. A. Slayton, *New Homeless and Old,* pp. 36–40.

In the United States, this subterranean nation of tramps, nomads and vagabonds was named Hobohemia, in reference to the bohemians and gypsies of Europe. In the hierarchy of Hobohemia, immediately beneath the hoboes were the
tramps. If hoboes were migrant laborers, tramps were simply unemployed migrants ("the hobo works and wanders, the tramp dreams and wanders")[9] who
lived on odd jobs, petty theft and begging and were proud of their nomadic spirit.
While hoboes were often well dressed, the tramps inclined toward rags and questionable personal hygiene. The hoboes despised the tramps and saddled them
with insulting epithets.

Next in the pecking order, under the hoboes and tramps, were the bums, who,
like every other caste, were subdivided into those who had careers (as dishwash-
ers or hotel porters and those who begged for a living. Under the beggars were
other subcastes, running down to those who didn't even beg, who lived in cardboard boxes and scoured the trash for scraps of food. Thus what appeared to the
outside eye to be a ragged confusion of social outcasts and misfits (of the order
"tramps are all the same") revealed itself on closer inspection to be a rigidly structured universe with its own hierarchies and repressions.

The first Hobohemias were white, male and for the most part American (62
percent American born), composed of singles, the majority of whom were literate
(95 percent could read and/or write; 5 percent were college educated). This was
so much the case, in fact,[10] that Nels Anderson was prompted to write: "The
homeless man is an extensive reader. This is especially true of the transients, the
tramp and the hobo." For this reason, the Skid Rows of America were starred with
bookstores and news agents, as well as with pawnshops. The most frequently
pawned items were clothes, followed by watches and rings.[11] In 1921, there were
some sixty-two pawnshops around West Madison's Skid Row. Chicago's
Hobohemia also had its own restaurant and a school – Hobo College – run by migrants for migrants.

Hobohemia was a segregated world. On the Skid Row of West Madison Street

---

9 N. Anderson, *The Hobo*, p. 87.
10 Ibid., p. 185.
11 W. R. Patterson, "Pawnbroking in Europe and the United States," in *Bulletin of Labor 21* (March
   1899), Washington, D.C.: Government Printing Office, pp. 256–79; also cited in C. Hoch and R. A.
   Slayton, *New Homeless and Old*, pp. 33–34.

there was no room for Blacks; they had their own district further south on State Street, between Twenty-second and Thirtieth. Today the Black Skid Row centers on Martin Luther King Drive. Although there is no justifiable reason for it (why should collar-and-tie racism be any less terrible?), racial segregation is never so bitter as it is in separating white tramps from their Black brethren, or in dividing drunks according to the color of their skin.

In Hobohemia, within the space of the same street, within the same person, even, you can pass smoothly from working class to *Lumpenproletariat*, literally "skid" from "the storm troops of American expansionism" to outcasts and drunken tramps. Here you see how labile is the frontier between unemployment and poverty, between the working poor and the homeless.

Poverty, that uncomfortable word, has finally dared to speak its name, a word that seems so obvious and yet is so embarrassing to define: poverty as a "condition of nature." You are poor in the same way you are old or young. But what is the "poverty threshold," exactly? When do you start being poor? This is like asking, How old do you have to be before you are old? *Poor* is one of those ready-made sociological concepts that Pierre Bourdieu warns us against, a concept whose very spontaneity gives it away, being itself a vehicle for ideology, the unconscious vision of the world that society molds in each and every one of us. *Poor* encompasses a single, indistinct notion of hardship, penury and want, which the sociology textbooks define as follows: "Every type of poverty can be attributed to the fact that a given subject or population lacks in the capacity to cover the basic costs of human production and reproduction."[12] The verb *lack* indicates a deprivation but also a defect in terms of quality. But why is it that so many subjects and populations should be "lacking"?

That poverty was the scourge of Europe was something that Americans understood. In the words of Robert Castel, it "corresponded to the objective characteristics of the Old World: shortage of resources, overpopulation, injustice and irrationality."[13] But why in the United States? Hardly had the rapid industrializa-

---

12 Luciano Gallino, *Dizionario di Sociologia*, Torino, Italy: Utet, 1978, entry for "poverty," p. 536.
13 Robert Castel, "La 'guerre' à la pauvreté aux Etats Unis," *Actes de la recherche en sciences sociales*, January 1978, no. 19; the following citations are from pp. 47–60.

tion of the East Coast states commenced, toward 1820, when the specter of poverty reared its ugly head and the number of reports from poverty commissions (which existed even then) began to multiply. From these reports emerged the idea that "the real scandal is not the number of poor but the fact that they exist." "Pauperism would be foreign to our country," the New York Society for the Prevention of Pauperism wrote in its *Fourth Annual Report* (1821), because "our territory is so expansive, its soil so prolific," because of the excellence of America's institutions and its "ample scope for industry and enterprise, entire freedom from civil and political disabilities, and perfect security of natural and acquired advantages." In their *Annual Report for 1847*, the commissioners for New York's almshouses stated, "In our highly favored country where labor is so much demanded and so liberally rewarded, and the means of subsistence so easily and cheaply obtained, poverty need not and ought not to exist."

If poverty need not and ought not to have existed in the United States, it was because the country was sparsely populated, its lands and resources almost infinite. America was thus the antipode of the situation responsible for poverty described by the Reverend Robert Malthus, whose thesis Engels so vividly summarized: "[Malthus] argues that because the world is always over-populated, it is inevitable that hunger, distress, poverty and immorality will be always with us. He says that an overpopulated world is humanity's eternal destiny from which there is no escape. Consequently men must be divided into different classes. Some of these classes will be more or less wealthy, educated and moral, and others will be more or less poor, miserable, ignorant and immoral."[14]

The Malthusian theory was to be the blueprint for what would later be called Social Darwinism, according to which human beings too were engaged in a struggle for survival. In the view of the English Reverend Joseph Townsend (1739–1816), humans behaved like the bearded goats on Juan Fernández Island. Spaniards had unloaded a pair of the animals on the shores of the island, after which the goats had duly gone forth and multiplied until they had filled the island and begun to go hungry. At that point, Townsend notes, "the weakest first gave way, and plenty was again restored. Thus they fluctuated between happiness and misery, and either suffered want or rejoiced in abundance."

---

14 F. Engels, *The Condition of the Working Class in England*, p. 320.

As was the case for the goats, "It is the quantity of food which regulates the numbers of the human species," and it does so by way of *"afflictions and poverty,"* according to Townsend. "As long as food is plenty they will continue to increase and multiply; and every man will have ability to support his family, or to relieve his friends, in proportion to his activity and strength. The weak must depend upon the precarious bounty of the strong; and sooner or later, the *lazy* will be left to suffer the natural consequence of their *indolence.*"[15] What lay behind this notion of poverty was the idea that humans were by their very nature lazy: "Those crowds of idle and dissolute Indians were the first obstacle" to civilization, wrote Parton.[16] It's strange that this notion of the innate laziness of humans should emerge in the history of ideas at the point when the industrial revolution had begun to regiment labor. The historian Antonello La Vergata traces the course of this "principle of man's innate indolence" through the eighteenth and nineteenth centuries, from the blissful laziness of Rousseau's good savage to the "idle sensuality" into which, according to Dr. Johnson, "if neither disease nor poverty were felt or dreaded, everyone would sink down without any care of others, or of himself."[17] Poverty is thus a spur to overcome our natural indolence: humans act only out of need. The specter of poverty puts them to "a rugged test," as the Scottish Calvinist Thomas Chalmers (who, like Malthus and Townsend, was a preacher) said in 1833. This explains why, following the logic of a tradition of thought that runs from Townsend in the eighteenth century to Robert Nozick in the 1970s, any form of assistance for the poor would be counterproductive.

Here we have yet another variation on what Hirschman calls the "perversion" thesis. (Today we find this thesis repeated verbatim in the debate on Third World overpopulation, with the idea that any form of humanitarian aid would simply lead to a further increase in population and thus aggravate poverty even more: better, surely, to simply leave them to die.) In the view of Nozick, who recently reformulated the theory of the minimum state, the state has no obligation to help

---

15 Joseph Townsend, *A Dissertation on the Poor Laws, by a Well-Wisher to Mankind* (1786), Berkeley: University of California Press, 1971, pp. 37-38.

16 J. Parton, *Chicago*, p. 328.

17 Antonello La Vergata, *Nonostante Malthus: fecondità, popolazioni e armonia nella natura, 1700–1900,* Torino: Bollati Boringhieri, 1990; Samuel Johnson, *The Wisdom of the Rambler, Adventurer and Idler,* London: Longman, 1848, from which these citations are taken.

the poor; indeed, to do so would in principle be immoral, because the state has no right to appropriate the goods of one individual and give them to another: "Taxation of earnings of labor is on a par with forced labor."[18] For the Reverend Townsend, meanwhile, the poor laws merely promoted "the evils they mean to remedy, and aggravate[d] the distress they were intended to relieve" and did "little more than give encouragement to idleness and vice," destroying the "hope and fear" that were "the springs of industry."[19]

Such a thesis has drawn consensus from the most unlikely quarters. In 1833, the English Poor Law Commission found that the poorhouse was ruining the country and was "a check to industry, a reward for improvident marriages, a stimulant to population, and a blind to its effects on wages … a national institution for discountenancing the industrious and honest, and for protecting the *idle*, the *improvident* and the *vicious* … the destroyer of filial, parental and conjugal affection, a system for preventing the accumulation of capital, for destroying that which exists, and for reducing the ratepayer to pauperism" (italics mine). These are the same arguments used today against government welfare programs.[20]

What is curious is that a communist such as Engels should share these views: "[T]he relief encouraged *idleness* and promoted the increase of the superfluous population. Under present social conditions a poor man is obviously forced to be an egoist and if he has the choice between work and unemployment – with the same income – he naturally prefers to live in idleness. All that this proves is that the existing state of society is no good. It does not prove that poverty is an offence meriting severe punishment as a warning to the other potential paupers" (italics mine).[21]

Back in 1795, the writer Marquis de Sade had reached much the same conclusion as Engels and the Reverend Townsend did. Dolmancé, the most Sadean of the characters who appear in *La philosophie dans le boudoir*, has this to say about charity:

---

18 Robert Nozick, *Anarchy, the State and Utopia*, New York: Basic Books, 1974, p. 169.
19 J. Townsend, *A Dissertation on the Poor Laws*, pp. 17, 23.
20 *Extracts from Information Received by the Poor Law Commissioners*, London, 1833, p. xvi; also cited in Engels, *Condition of the Working Class in England*, p. 503.
21 F. Engels, *Condition of the Working Class in England*, pp. 322–23.

It accustoms the poor man to doles which provoke the deterioration of his energy; when able to expect your charities, he ceases to work and becomes, when they fail him, a thief or an assassin. On all sides I hear them ask after the means to suppress mendacity, and meanwhile they do everything possible to encourage it. Would you have no flies in your bed chamber? Don't spread about sugar to attract them into it. You wish have no poor in France? Distribute no alms, and above all shut down your poor-houses. The individual born in misfortune thereupon seeing himself deprived of these dangerous crutches, will fend for himself summoning up all the resources put in him by Nature, to extricate himself from the condition where he started life; and he will importune you no longer. Destroy, with entire unpity, raze to the ground those detestable houses where you billet the progeny of the libertinage of the poor, appalling cloacas, wherefrom there every day spews forth into society a swarm of new-made creatures whose unique hope resides in you purse.[22]

Each had his own ends. Townsend's aim was to instill moral principles, Engels's to subvert social relations, Dolmancé's to reevaluate the practices of "birth control" available in his time – sodomy, masturbation and infanticide. What they shared was the notion that helping the poor was counterproductive, that individuals left to their own devices became lazy, that only necessity spurred them to action. The idea was that poverty was instructive, *orthopaedic* even – a remedy for sloth.

Across the Atlantic, too, providing relief for the poor was considered damaging. In 1821, in his report to the Massachusetts commission on the pauper laws, Josiah Quincy wrote, "The more you help the poor the more you will have to help them. ... [T]he most damaging way to assist paupers, as well the most costly, the most pernicious for their customs and destructive for their work habits, consists in giving them help in the very bosom of their family." So much so in fact that in the view of almost all Americans – then as now – the United States has the finest political regime in history. From this we can only conclude, along with Robert Castel, "Since, despite all those reasons for which poverty in the United States would be impossible, the poor nonetheless do exist there, these poor must carry poverty within themselves." Poverty is a moral evil; the poor man is poor – that is to say he *lacks* money – because he is himself morally *lacking* in the virtues that would en-

---

22 Donatien-Alphonse François de Sade, *La philosophie dans le boudoir* (1795), in *Justine, Philosophy in the Bedroom, and Other Writings*, New York: Grove Weidenfeld, 1990, pp. 215–16.

able him to escape his condition. In its *Eighth Annual Report* (1856), the New York Association for Improving the Condition of the Poor concluded that the official figures demonstrated the extent to which pauperism, in the city as in the country, was a result of *laziness, intemperance* and other such vices.

The nineteenth century saw the beginnings of the intellectual sport (which was to have heavy political repercussions) of separating the "deserving" from the "undeserving" poor. Michael B. Katz, in his book entitled *The Undeserving Poor,* traces the course that the political and sociological debate took from Lyndon B. Johnson's war on poverty in the 1960s to the policies of the Reagan administration in the 1980s. The dichotomy of deserving/undeserving first made its appearance in 1821, when Josiah Quincy distinguished between two types of poor: first, "the impotent poor; in which denomination are included all, who are wholly incapable of work, through old age, infancy, sickness, or corporeal debility," and then "the able poor ... who are capable of work, of some nature, or other; but differing in the degree of their capacity, and in the kind of work, of which they are capable."[23]

According to this logic, one form of poverty was inevitable, another the individual's fault. And since part of poverty was inevitable, and since the resources for alleviating poverty were limited, it became essential to separate the wheat from the chaff, for society to don the mantle of the God of Last Judgement to divide the drowned and the saved. Philanthropists, social workers and governments therefore devoted themselves to the nerve-wracking task of classification in an attempt to decide which of the poor were the deserving and which the undeserving (or the only partly deserving) and thus to define the degree of assistance each had the right to receive, the grades of punishment intrinsic to charity and, finally, the appropriate moral remedies to apply to the moral causes of poverty.

Since the state generally refrains "from plainly condemning a pauper to death by starvation" (Engels),[24] "objective" parameters needed to be established for defining poverty. What can only be described as a perpetual slide or skid from working class to outcast, from unemployment to homelessness (as we saw in the case of

---

23 Citations taken from Michael B. Katz, *The Undeserving Poor: From the War on Poverty to the War on Welfare,* New York: Pantheon, 1989, pp. 12–13.
24 F. Engels, *Condition of the Working Class in England,* p. 323.

Hobohemia) must now be reorganized in terms of a discontinuous taxonomy, classified and sorted, poor from the nonpoor. A poverty threshold must be set, just as the age at which one becomes a pensioner defines the threshold of old age and provides an answer to the question, How old do you have to be to be old? Here the question is, Below what income level do you start to be poor?

To define the poverty threshold, American welfare services used the "Engel coefficient," named after the director of the Prussian Institute of Statistics Ernst Engel. In 1857, this astute functionary had noted that there was an inverse relation between total income and the percentage of income spent on food, with the proportion of income spent on food tending to diminish as income increases. The poorest families eat less well but dedicate a larger part of their money to food, while the more affluent eat well and spend more on food in total but allocate a much smaller portion of their revenue to food buying. It is therefore possible to calculate a coefficient (the aforementioned Engel coefficient) that, when multiplied by the minimal amount spent on food, yields a minimum budget below which you may consider yourself poor. So if M is the minimum amount spent on food and E is the Engel coefficient, the minimum income C required to escape poverty is given by the equation $C = M \times E$.[25]

This definition, based on subsistence-level earnings, explains why people in rich countries may be considered poor even when their annual income would place them in the high earning bracket in the Third World. In the United States, the poverty threshold for a family of four persons was fixed in 1999 at $17,023 per annum, while in India the yearly salary of a senior state functionary would be $4,000 at most. An American family, by contrast, would have to spend $5,000 just to be able to eat.

But what is the minimum expenditure for food? During the 1940s, the Social Security Administration (SSA) made meticulous calculations to determine the average individual's daily calorie requirements and the cost of those calories. Calorie needs vary, however – from 1,200 to 1,800 for a child under the age of ten to 4,500 for a manual worker. In addition, it is nigh impossible to systematically shop for

---

25 Martin Rein, "Problems in the Definition and Measurement of Poverty," in Peter Townsend, ed., *The Concept of Poverty*, London: Heinemann, 1970, p. 50. This volume is a key work on the question of the concept of poverty, even if Rein insists on attributing Engel's coefficient to Engels (with an *s*).

the cheapest food. You never hear people asking a shopkeeper, "Can you give me the cheapest 2,000 calories you have, please?" The minimum cost of the weekly shopping thus turns out to be largely arbitrary.

A second problem lies in the value of the Engel coefficient itself. In 1954, the Agriculture Office estimated it at 0.33 for a family of three or more people. But the Labor Office disagreed, calculating a coefficient of 0.25 for a family of three or more. The difference may seem marginal, but differences like these can alter the destiny of millions of people. The 1999 Census counted the number of poor people at 32.2 million (11.8 percent, or one of eight Americans). However enormous it may seem, though, this figure – the lowest in twenty years – actually *underestimates* the general historical trends of poverty, because it occurred after the longest uninterrupted period of sustained economic growth in US history. Furthermore, were the poverty threshold shifted by as little as 25 percent, the number of poor would suddenly rise to 45 million (or 16.5 percent of the population). This difference decides whether or not 13 million people are eligible for federal and state welfare programs, as well as whether or not they can make use of subsidized school meal programs, free medical assistance and food stamps.

Defining the poverty threshold has become the object of an intense political struggle. Depending on definitions, the number of poor can vary from 32.2 to 53.6 million.[26] And the problem doesn't just concern the 21 million more or fewer poor (a figure equivalent to the combined populations of Holland and Denmark); it concerns the image we have of American society as a whole. In the former case, we see that the richest, most technologically advanced nation on Earth has among its population 32 million poor – but also 241 million *not poor*. In this case, we could take President Hoover at his word when, just before the great crash of 1929, he declared: "Never has humanity been closer to ridding itself of the specter of poverty." According to the latter scenario, however, we would see only 219 million *not poor*, compared to 54 million poor. The difference is that between success and failure. Defining the poverty threshold, as Josiah Quincy well knew, is no mere academic matter; it changes the lives of millions of people, defines the dimensions of the welfare system, fixes the ceiling on state funding, shapes the very idea we have of the society we live in and influences the political choices of the public at large.

---

26 Census Bureau, *Current Population Survey*, March 2000.

But the most glaring example comes with the definition of unemployment. In the United States, flexibility and the mobility of labor, along with effective salaries and the reduction of state contributions, have created millions of jobs, resulting in unemployment rates of between 5 and 6 percent, compared to the rates of 10 percent or more typical in Europe (or so you hear everywhere). To create more jobs, then, Europeans are invited to follow the American model, and the American definition of unemployment has consequently become a political weapon in Europe. The problem, though, is that the United States uses some strange criteria for defining unemployment: "Unemployed persons comprise all civilians who had no employment during the reference week, who made *specific efforts* to find a job within the previous 4 weeks (such as applying directly to an employer, or to a public employment service, or *checking with friends*)"[27] (italics mine). In other words, you are considered in the United States to have a job – to be employed – *if during the whole of the previous week you were paid for even one hour's work*. If unemployment were to be defined by the same criteria in Europe, millions of jobs would miraculously appear out of nowhere here as well.

These criteria are far from innocent. Since Franklin D. Roosevelt passed the Social Security Act in 1935, the United States has provided unemployment insurance, financed through a specific federal tax, that covers 97 percent of salaried workers. If the criteria for unemployment were more realistic (for example, including anyone who had worked less than fifteen hours the previous week), the number of people eligible for the benefit would double. The underlying philosophy would appear to be "If we can't revoke the Social Security Act, what we can do is to restrict its field of application – anything to save a few cents."

What is striking is not so much the avarice as the pedantry with which definitions and subdefinitions are formulated. Looked at from outside, this nit-picking over categories might appear completely absurd, a bit like the war in Lilliput, recounted by Swift, in which Gulliver witnesses the reciprocal slaughter between the big- and little-Endians of those who prefer to break their eggs at the larger end and those who favor the smaller. As is the case with all frontiers, however, while drawing the line may be a wholly arbitrary act, once that line is drawn, it effectively marks the division between an inside and an outside, an "us" and a "them."

---

27 Census Bureau, *Statistical Abstract of the United States 1999*, p. 408.

On one hand, there is nothing "real" about such a dichotomy (that is, the fact that being paid for one hour's work per week is equivalent to having a job). On the other, it creates its own reality, separating those who receive unemployment benefits from those who don't, from those who, working a one-hour week, are not entitled to benefits but are instead considered the working poor and so receive Medicaid and food stamps and qualify for public housing. Were you the ingenuous type, you would no doubt attribute such an ambiguous situation to unemployment (and the criteria defining it). The state, on the other hand, classifies it as indigence. Thus the spotlight shifts from employment policy to charity. Neither the government nor the public is fond of this nebulous gray area, where no clear distinction lies between the poor and the well-off, between the employed and the unemployed – where "fault" cannot be clearly laid at anyone's door.

What emerges is a Hobohemian-type state of hardship and privation, where the boundary between inside and outside is not so visibly marked, where Quincy's distinction between who is able and who is not able to work – and thus between the deserving and the undeserving poor – becomes illusory.

This isn't the only reason that Hobohemia has aroused such hostility, however. Apart from anything else, Hobohemia marked the construction of a community where there was no longer just the solitary outcast, atomized and literally "dispersed," but where there was an entire subculture, an underworld with its own rules, hierarchies and social services, an impoverished yet highly vital economic fabric woven from odd jobs, barter, small trade and favors. The lifestyles of the Hobohemians stood in marked contrast to those of mainstream America: the Hobohemians were single in a world that worshiped the family, and they hated the beloved suburbs, much preferring the city center, where they could meet and make use of services and comforts unavailable to them elsewhere. These were the same motives, paradoxically, as those that attract today's young yuppies to the aseptic Presidential Towers.

Because it was so close to the business district, Hobohemia was also extremely visible – and this visibility proved to be the biggest irritation of all. If only the poor could have the decency to make themselves invisible! This was the reasoning that lay behind the city authorities' decision to bulldoze the flophouses of West Madison – Chicago's Skid Row – and to erect in their place the Presidential Towers.

This same urge to sweep poverty under the carpet was recently witnessed on the other side of the Atlantic. In 1994, Britain's then–prime minister, Conservative John Major, launched an attack on the nation's beggars, whose presence he deemed offensive to the eye as well as damaging to local trade and tourism and who, he thought, should be thrown in prison if the Welfare State wasn't good enough for them. Major's anxiety is one that seems to transcend both history and political differences. A 2000 edition of the *Observer* contained the following story, with the headline "Official: Giving to Beggars Is Wrong."[28] The story reported that Labour Prime Minister Tony Blair had allocated £240,000 to a campaign designed to dissuade people from giving money to the nation's down-and-outs. How can you not think of the astounding letter, cited by Engels, that a distinguished lady wrote in 1845 to the *Manchester Guardian?*[29]

Sir,

For sometime past numerous beggars are to be seen on the streets of our town. They attempt – often in a truly brazen and offensive manner – to arouse the pity of the public by their ragged clothes, their wretched appearance, their disgusting wounds and sores, and by showing the stumps of amputated limbs. I should have thought that those of us who not only pay our poor rates but also subscribe generously to charitable appeals have done enough to claim the right to be shielded from such disgusting and revolting sights. Why do we pay such high rates to support the borough police if they cannot even give us adequate protection so that we can leave our home and walk on the Queen's Highway in peace?

---

28 *Observer,* 8 October 2000.
29 F. Engels, *The Condition of the Working Class in England,* p. 314.

LIVERPOOL JOHN MOORES UNIVERSITY
LEARNING SERVICES

16

At Nature's Feast

It takes a fiery halo to draw our attention to that curious American institution, the single-room occupancy (SRO) hotel. These low-rent, pay-by-the-week hotels are where you go if you can't afford an apartment, if you're one of the working poor, or living on a retirement pension or on unemployment insurance. A typical product of skid row, they even had their own area called the SRO district. Flames come from the fires that periodically break out in these buildings and destroy them. The last to burn down in Chicago was the J. R. Plaza Hotel, more commonly known as the Zanzibar, on 14 February 1999. A hundred guests had to be evacuated, and three were seriously injured. The residents aren't always so lucky, however: Chicago's history is starred with the periodic flicker of blazes that have incinerated so many of the literally poor souls who dwell in them. In Chicago on 12 February 1955, one such fire devoured the Barton Hotel on West Madison, killing twenty-nine people. On 14 March 1981, a short circuit in the laundry room of the Royal Bench Hotel triggered another lethal fire. Amid the ashes and rubble were found the bodies of nineteen people. On 16 March 1993, flames consumed the 130-room Paxton Hotel, just a few blocks from the Magnificent Mile, again resulting in the deaths of nineteen people, with thirty more sustaining serious injuries.

Single-room occupancy hotels have such a high propensity to burn that their flammability has become legendary. One of Chicago's most famous crime writers, Sara Paretsky, based her novel *Burn Marks* on a fire in an SRO.[1] Paretsky's heroine, V. I. Warshawski, is a typical Chicagoan, the daughter of Polish and Italian parents; she is a divorced private eye and a fitness fanatic. In the book, Warshawski finds herself investigating the SRO fire because one of the residents was an aunt of hers, a ruined old lush.

Paretsky's novel takes up the cliché by which SRO equals skid row and skid row equals alcoholism. As far back as 1827, the Guardians of the Poor of Philadelphia sent out a warning to other cities: "From three-fourths to nine-tenths of the paupers in all parts of our country may attribute their degradation to the vice of intemperance."[2] Likewise, SROs carry the stigma of vice and drunkenness; otherwise, they would show up poverty in the form modern people most detest, as a world of slovenliness and petty privations, the quiet desperation of dull, threadbare rooms – in short, a poverty undignified by tragedy.

For poverty can provoke pity and indignation only in its most spectacular forms, those tailored to the needs of TV news bulletins, with images of rag-cloaked derelicts, the frozen body of a tramp lying under a sheaf of newspaper. Extreme homelessness, because it also indicates helplessness, neatly expresses the concept of the "deserving poor." The number of people living under such conditions, however, is really relatively low. "In Chicago there are 40,000 homeless," Charles Hoch notes, "while the number of people who spend the night on the street all year varies between 12 and 15,000. Yet the number of Chicagoans who live under the poverty line is roughly one million." Twelve thousand homeless seems fairly normal for a big city. The idea of a million poor people in Chicago alone, on the other hand, is truly alarming.

Throughout the United States, the ratio remains roughly the same, with 1 homeless person for every 500 inhabitants, or for every 60 poor. The official number of people in America who live below the poverty line is 32.2 million, whereas the number of chronic homeless, while difficult to estimate, stands at around half a million: 200,000 to 300,000, according to the Department of Housing and Urban Development (HUD); 750,000, according to the National Alliance to End Homelessness. More numerous are those who find themselves without a roof over their

---

1 Sara Paretsky, *Burn Marks,* New York: Bantam Doubleday Dell Publishing, 1990.
2 M. B. Katz, *The Undeserving Poor,* p. 13.

head at least once a year: in 1988, the Alliance reckoned that number to be around 1.3 to 2 million.[3]

Only in the last twenty years have the homeless become the public symbol of misery in the West, a further slide down the social scale from those who were houseless during the nineteenth century. Homelessness isn't simply a condition; it's a category. In 1975, not a single study existed on the specific subject of homelessness; by 1984, there were thirty-four such studies; by 1986, forty-eight; and by 1988, the number of titles on the topic would have filled a sixty-page single-spaced bibliography.[4] Equating the category of "deserving poor" to homelessness has shifted the spotlight from the vast majority of the working poor to those experiencing extreme poverty, with the result that those already in dire straits receive all the tea and sympathy, while those teetering on the brink are left conveniently in the shadows. The number of the "deserving" falls, and the gap between benefactor and beneficiary widens. What results is a worst-case scenario concept of welfare, with the homeless offered relief as though they were flood victims – with poverty viewed as a form of *natural* catastrophe.

While the numbers of the homeless have undoubtedly risen since the 1960s, this is in part because of the attention given their plight. In Chicago during the 1990s, 17,000 people lived in SROs. That may seem like a lot, but it's only a small fraction of the 1960s figure, when SRO rooms in Chicago numbered more than 80,000. Through thirty years of successive urban renewal programs since then, more than 80 percent of the SRO hotels have been demolished in a concerted effort to wipe Chicago's various skid rows from the map. The official reason for sending in the bulldozers is to help the residents find more "dignified" affordable housing, according to the welfare bureaucrats' ammoniac notion of dignity, the sweep of insecticide across linoleum. The SRO inhabitants have rejected this notion in numerous surveys, however, declaring themselves to be reasonably content with their lodger lifestyle.

Yet the progressive dismantling of America's skid rows and their human communities is by now a nationwide phenomenon. According to Katz, more than a million rooms (1.116 million) enacted the mystery of the disappearing room in the

---

3   Ibid., p. 187.
4   Ibid..

United States between 1970 and 1982. In the meantime, rents have soared, so that 7 million tenants now spend more than half of their incomes on rent.

The already-ruinous situation of public housing has degenerated into a full-scale catastrophe, considering that only 1 percent of the US property market in 1980 was publicly owned, as opposed to 46 percent in England and Wales (before the onslaught of privatization instigated by the Thatcher government) and 37 percent in France.[5] Only this can explain that absurd aftertaste you get in the SROs: the fact that you end up in a hotel if you don't have enough money to rent an apartment. Here we find echoes of the immortal phrase attributed to Marie Antoinette: "They have no bread? Then let them eat *croissants*."

But although the SROs are relatively cheap, they are no giveaways. At the Zanzibar in 1999, a room cost $125 per week, $540 per month.[6] Six years before that, at the Paxton (burnt to the ground in 1993), rooms were $90 per week, $380 per month. Both prices were only slightly less in their respective times than what it would cost to rent a decent single-room apartment in Chicago. To rent an apartment, though, you first need to come up with a two-month deposit, to be paid either by credit card or by check (once again, we see the barbed-wire frontier marked out by the bank account!), and you need to provide a guarantee of regular income (in the form of a pay stub). The $60 difference between the $540 rent at the Zanzibar and the rent for an apartment in a housing project thus became an unbridgeable gap between the *middle class* and the *poor*.

On the other hand, one might ask what alternative SRO residents have. Perhaps their number might come up in a lottery for public housing, meaning a place in one of the projects. Many people would prefer sleeping on the sidewalk to ending up in a place like Taylor Homes or Cabrini Green, projects that have become bywords for the urban jungle where a child might be killed by a stray bullet while walking to school. And then, of course, there are always the *shelters*.

Every afternoon, a long queue, mostly of Blacks, stretches along the sidewalk of State Street and Balbo, in a neighborhood that is actually in the midst of being "regentrified." Located here is one of the forty-nine temporary shelters listed by

---

5 K. T. Jackson, *Crabgrass Frontier*, p. 224.
6 *Chicago Tribune*, 15 February 1999.

HUD.[7] These shelters – subdivided into shelters for battered wives, transitory shelters (maximum stay 120 days) and overnight shelters (maximum stay 12 hours) – are rigorously single-sex (only the abstemious poor are rewarded). Some shelters cater especially to young people, others to the mentally disabled, others still to homeless veterans. The aspirants form their line quickly, ready for a long wait, because here the rule is "first come, first served"; just as for accommodation in the national parks, you cannot book in advance. For this reason, the ritual repeats itself every sundown, and once you are inside you cannot leave.

The shelters are places devoid of the slightest shred of intimacy, places where, in theory, you are forbidden even to open a can of beer. It is true that the poor cannot be denied assistance, but that assistance must be dealt out with the parsimony that society wishes to instill in these incorrigibly improvident riffraff. Welfare has to be hard, it has to be uncomfortable, it has to punish those who benefit from it; welfare must function as a deterrent and make these people realize the error of their idle ways.

The more talk there was of the homeless during the 1980s, the more numerous became the shelters. This was first of all because those very policies that offered a melodramatic, even operatic image of poverty were at the same time multiplying the number of poor people. In addition, by demolishing the SROs, urban developers were sweeping away the alternative to sheltered accommodation. And because the problem of poverty was equated with the absence of a roof over your head, solutions were conceived in terms of basic refuge, fixing a "ceiling" on poverty. In November 1982, temporary shelters in Chicago held less than seven hundred beds. Four years later, that number had risen to two thousand.[8] The number of shelters boomed during the Reagan era, just as in the 1820s there had been an increase in the number of poorhouses, where the penniless, the blind, the old and the orphaned of that time were all piled together, where the wretched of America found refuge but were also disciplined and punished.

As in the poorhouses of old, the guest of a shelter is deprived of autonomy. While the SRO hotels were grouped in zones – with a lively neighborhood community and a dense weave of social relations – shelters tend to be scattered in dif-

---

7 See the Web site www.hud.gov:80/local/chi/shelter.html.
8 C. Hoch and R. A. Slayton, *New Homeless and Old*, p. 224.

ferent parts of the city, poverty atomized to make it less visible. Residents of SROs are independent individuals, with their own gas stoves, able to do more or less as they please, whether reading, drinking or receiving guests – people, in short, who maintain their own privacy. In the shelter, by contrast, the individual is like a refugee, there to be looked after and checked up on.

The decisive term here is "looked after" – placed under surveillance – a service that can extend even to home help. The problem, as always, is that of "regulating the poor," a problem to which Frances Fox Piven and Richard Cloward devoted a now-classic study. Inspectors would make midnight raids on single mothers, abandoned by their husbands and therefore placed on welfare, to make sure that the abscondee in question hadn't secretly snuck back into his bed. In response to the women's protests, judges would simply recite the litany: "Any recipient has a perfect right to slam the door in the face of the investigator. Of course, he runs the risk then of being cut off the rolls."[9] Mothers whose breath was found to smell of whisky during the inspections, or who were for some other reason deemed undeserving of state assistance, ran the same risk.

If "philanthropy becomes a political strategy," as Castels has written, it must incorporate at least one humiliating element, however small, to function as an ideological signal. No one must take state aid for granted; to do so would be morally harmful and would lead to a collapse of social values. Those who need assistance cannot be allowed to accept it with impunity; the road is otherwise opened to the pernicious "idle sensuality" Dr. Johnson warned of.

Food stamps are the perfect example of the humiliating tightfistedness with which the ever-watchful state counts out the crumbs of its help. Every month in 1996, more than 8 million families (26.8 million people) were issued food stamps equivalent to almost $3,000 on average per year per family. Rather than give this subsidy in cash, however, the government gives out actual stamps, and supermarkets in working class areas accept these stamps in payment for food. This system is in ways similar to wartime rations. You could even say that it *is* rationing, although what is being rationed in this case is not food but trust in the beneficiary's good sense. Handing out bread or meat vouchers instead of money is a sign of dif-

---

9   Frances Fox Piven and Richard A. Cloward, *Regulating the Poor: The Functions of Welfare State,* New York: Vintage, 1971, p. 167.

fidence – the diffidence of anxious parents who prepare a packed lunch for their child rather than give out lunch money, for fear the child will use the money to buy chewing gum or cigarettes. In the state of New York and elsewhere, people applying for food stamps are asked whether they own a burial plot. Nebraska and Nevada want to know whether applicants have sold their blood and for how much. Hawaii demands garage sale receipts. South Dakota wants documentation of any bingo winnings. Most of these application forms are more than ten pages long; in California, the form stretches to twenty-one pages, with 120 questions.[10]

Certification of the criteria for poverty is a meticulous, hair-splitting business that repeats itself in every one of the thousands of welfare programs.[11] For nutrition alone, other than food stamps, there is a program for "women, infants and children" (used by 7.2 million people per month in 1996) and a "nutrition program for the elderly" (3.4 million people). Then there are school meal vouchers for the 14.6 million children of 8.9 million families, split into three separate programs: a school lunch program, a school breakfast program (for 6.2 million pupils) and a child care food program in child care centers (1.3 million). Food stamps are just one piece in the complicated mosaic of welfare.

Contrary to current prejudice, government in the US (both federal and local) spends an enormous amount on its welfare state, an amount that increases every year. In 1995, $1.505 trillion was spent on welfare (including subsidies and social security pensions), nearly 1.5 times the entire Italian gross national product ($1.024 trillion) and more than one-fifth the US gross domestic product. This rise in public spending continued through the Reagan era, increasing 65 percent in constant dollars between the years 1980 and 1994, when the government had to slow the growth of social wounds produced by its own fiscal and spending policies. In constant 1995 dollars, the amount spent on welfare for each individual citizen had increased from $3,788 in 1980 to $5,622 fifteen years later.[12]

---

10 From the *Dallas Morning News*, 13 August 2000, which cites a report of America's Second Harvest, "the nation's largest food-bank network."

11 Census Bureau, *Statistical Abstract of the United States 1999*, tab. 613, 1996 figures. Since 1996, the Clinton administration has introduced public spending cuts that have made access to these programs more difficult by, for example, further complicating questionnaires. In the summer of 2000, it was estimated that only 17.3 million people qualified for the Food Stamp Program, as opposed to 26.8 million in 1996.

12 Ibid., tab. 607, 775.

Yet in the end, all this extravagant expenditure on welfare dissipates into a thousand little rivulets, each designed to plug this or that breach, to alleviate a particular misery through its own particular bureaucratic apparatus, its own criteria, inspections and certificates. In the frantic quest for objective, *scientific* criteria – for measurable thresholds – the American welfare system is guilty of the same sin of which it accuses the poor: improvidence, short-term thinking and sheer waste. Between the entry for "Welfare" in the US budget and a real campaign against poverty lies the same difference as between an expense and an investment: the former is conceived simply as a burden, the latter as a payment for a future improvement.

Not by chance, the verb most frequently used in relation to poverty is *alleviate,* as in "alleviating the sufferings of a patient." Starting from the close of the eighteenth century, from when the modern concept of living matter was first elaborated, everything began to be thought of in terms of a living organism: the city, the nation, society itself. With Auguste Comte and the rise of positivism, the study of society became a physiology of the social body. Like any other organism, society had its pathologies: entire parts could succumb to disease, struck by contagion, gangrene, paralysis or convulsions. If poverty was a social malady, governments and philanthropists could only alleviate its symptoms, because, on the one hand, poverty was incurable, a natural phenomenon whose cause was simple "misfortune," and on the other, it was produced by a disease of morals, by the vices of the individual (the "undeserving" poor) and thus was of no concern to the social sphere. Like the goats on Juan Fernández Island, the weak and indolent of humanity were destined to suffer hunger and other privations. Also in terms of social Darwinism, poverty was incurable, because it was part of one's genetic inheritance. As with delinquency – another social pathology, which Cesare Lombroso believed was inscribed in the somatic traits of the criminal-type individual – poverty was believed to be part of an individual's inheritance. For followers of Darwin, as for Malthusians and for countless social "scientists" who followed, any measure taken against poverty could at best alleviate its symptoms and was therefore no more than a palliative, in social terms: a tranquilizing painkiller.

Compared to theories that attributed poverty to moral causes, social Darwinism no longer blamed the poor for their plight: under social Darwinism, one is predisposed to poverty in the same way as to, say, diabetes. In this way, the Darwinists sought to mitigate the forces of moral and legal condemnation used against the poor, demonstrating that these individuals could not be held responsible for their miserable state. Social Darwinism therefore presented itself as a step forward from the idea of poverty as "a vice." And in some respects, it *was* a step forward; from a premeditated crime, poverty became a form of involuntary felony. But involuntariness had its price: in the absence of a sterilization program to rid humanity of its contaminated elements, the poor were now perceived as utterly incorrigible. With social Darwinism, the individual was no longer guilty of poverty. What had in the past been regarded as a moral vice was now considered a genetic vice that reproduced poverty as its "inexorable curse." Often we see this cycle at work in sociology: with the best of progressive intentions, the social sciences develop a theory to exonerate the poor and to explain why it is so difficult to fight poverty, identifying the obstacles to any real change (in terms of personality, genetic and material inheritance, environment and mentality). But this explanation as to "why the poor are poor" inevitably ends up again laying blame on the victim for being in this unhappy state.

Such a mechanism is particularly evident in the theory of the "culture of poverty," a term coined in 1959 by anthropologist Oscar Lewis, who wrote a series of extraordinary books during the 1960s based on the testimony of Puerto Ricans living in New York. Lewis distinguishes objective poverty (financial penury and indigence) from the culture of poverty, which, he says, "is both an adaptation and a reaction of the poor to their marginal position in a class-stratified, highly individuated, capitalistic society."[13] The pressures and problems of day-to-day survival thus lead the poor to focus attention on the present. Lack of opportunity produces a lack of ambition, while the contempt that comes from all sides induces a sense of inferiority. Male incapacity to provide for the family leads to the formation of mother-centered households. Another feature that marks the culture of poverty is "the absence of childhood as a specially prolonged and protected stage in the life cycle."[14] (Contrariwise, the culture of well-being measures itself by its ability to

---

13 Oscar Lewis, *La Vida: A Puerto Rican Family in the Culture of Poverty, San Juan and New York*, New York: Random House, 1966, p. xlvi.
14 Ibid., p. xlvii.

protract and protect the period of childhood beyond its normal biological con-
fines.)

The culture of poverty is therefore a response to environmental pressures.
Once created, however, it "tends to perpetuate itself from generation to generation because of its effect on the children. By the time slum children are age six or
seven they have usually absorbed the basic values and attitudes of their subculture
and are not psychologically geared to take full advantage of changing conditions
or increased opportunities which may occur in their lifetime."[15] This idea of transmission across generations is crucial to Lewis's argument, because it marks the
passage from a present *reaction* to a past – and therefore indelible – inheritance.

The "leftist" bent of Lewis's theory is evident. To explain why the poor have so
much difficulty rising above their condition, he argues that the cycle of misery
feeds itself. Simple material subsidy is not enough; what is required, to adopt the
current jargon, is a multidimensional program of attack. Such an aim is evident
not only in Lewis's work but also in that of one of the American left's spiritual fathers, Michael Harrington. In *The Other America,* a key text in the 1960s' rediscov-
ery of poverty in America, Harrington defines the poor as "those who, for reasons
beyond their control, cannot help themselves. ... Poverty in the United States is a
culture, an institution, a way of life. ... There is, in short, a language of the poor, a
psychology of the poor, a world view of the poor."[16] Lewis himself writes:

> when the poor become class-conscious or active members of trade-union organiza-
> tions, or when they adopt an internationalist outlook on the world, they are no lon-
> ger part of the culture of poverty, although they may still be desperately poor. Any
> movement, be it religious, pacifist or revolutionary, which organizes and gives hope
> to the poor and effectively promotes solidarity and a sense of identification with
> larger groups, destroys the psychological and social core of the culture of poverty.[17]

Within the space of ten years, the "culture of poverty" had become a potent
weapon in the hands of conservative thinkers. While for Lewis only 20 percent of
poor Americans were afflicted by the culture of poverty (which could not account

---

15 Ibid., p. xlv.
16 Michael Harrington, *The Other America: Poverty in the United States* (1962), New York: Penguin
    Books, 1981, pp. 16, 17, 18.
17 O. Lewis, *The Culture of Poverty,* pp. xlviii.

for the remaining 80 percent), conservatives, together with others who wanted to dismantle what remained of the welfare state, considered the culture of poverty to be the determining factor that *explained* why the poor were poor. Lewis's view was different: "The crucial question from both the scientific and the political point of view is: How much weight is to be given to the internal self-perpetuating factors in the subjective poverty as compared to the external social factors? My own position is that in the long run the self-perpetuating factors are relatively minor and unimportant compared to the basic structures of the larger society."[18]

Nevertheless, the general opinion was that the culture of poverty was itself the mechanism that *produced poverty* "without any help from the outside world," as Daniel Moynihan said. Through the culture of poverty inherited from his parents, once again "the poor man carries his poverty within him." Cultural transmission has become the decisive factor that produces poverty. What is clear here is the way the modern conservative uses the concept of culture. As a mark of identity, culture supplants blood, lineage and race. Modern political discourse shifts from race to ethnicity, to national identity considered as "cultural identity": Serb *culture* versus Croat *culture*. For theorists of social racism such as Thomas Sowell, culture is as immutable as one's genes: "Groups today plagued by absenteeism, tardiness, and a need for constant supervision at work or in school are typically descendants of people with the same habits a century or more ago. *The cultural inheritance can be more important than biological inheritance.*"[19]

Meanwhile, social scientists persist in translating into different versions the same tautological explanation: "Poor people lack because they are lacking." They lacked money first because of a lack of moral qualities, later because of a lack of adequate genes. Now the poor are poor because they lack the culture to escape, because they are improvident and resigned and have no sense of family. For conservatives of every stripe, therefore, the culture of poverty is an excellent tool for restoring intellectual dignity to the notion of the "undeserving poor," for preparing the ground for the latest version of this figure, the most undeserving of all: the underclass.

---

18 Cited by S. Steinberg in *The Ethnic Myth*, pp. 123–24.
19 Ibid., pp. 265–66.

It was a *Time* magazine cover story from 19 August 1977, emblazoned with the title "The American Underclass," that first confirmed the term's national notoriety. At first, *underclass* referred to those poor who languish in misery even during times of economic growth and falling unemployment; later, this perpetual *underclass* became a general byword for "dysfunctional social behavior." Under the guise of the new terminology, the old nineteenth-century idea of poverty as a vice was making a comeback. Or, as *Time* put it, "The underclass produces a highly disproportionate number of the nation's juvenile delinquents, school dropouts, drug addicts and welfare mothers, and much of the adult crime, family disruption, urban decay and demand for social expenditures. ... Rampaging members of the underclass ... are responsible for most of the youth crime that has spread like an epidemic through the nation" (once again, the writer resorts to a medical metaphor).

Back in 1821 the *Fourth Annual Report* of the New York Society for the Prevention of Pauperism had rejoiced before the geometric rigor of the creation: "By a just and unbending law of providence, misery has been consecrated as companion and punishment of vice."[20] A century and a half later, the cover story of *Fortune* took up the baton, describing underclass communities as "urban knots that threaten to become enclaves of permanent poverty and vice."[21] Under the category *underclass* were heaped together vice, culture and race: "Underclass describes a state of mind and a way of life. It is at least as much a cultural as an economic condition."

But the term *underclass* also signals a shift in the subject of the "undeserving poor," turning the spotlight away from Skid Row to the ghettos of the inner city, from the poor white to the poor Black or Hispanic, just as it transfers the nucleus of vice from alcohol to crack, heroin and cocaine, from the drunkard to the drug addict. Hypothetically, the culture of the underclass conspires with racial heredity to reproduce crime and misery among young Blacks or Hispanics incapable of finding (or holding down) a job, because these people are either too incompetent or too lazy or because they lack the right qualifications. (The poor must always be lacking in something other than money.) Studying Chicago's Black ghettos, Wil-

---

20 Cited by R. Castels, "La 'guerre à la pauvreté' aux Etats Unis," p. 49.
21 "America's Underclass: What to Do?," in *Fortune*, 17 March 1986.

liam Julius Wilson has redefined the underclass in terms of unemployment, of people who find themselves permanently excluded from the job market: in fact, the map of Chicago's poor areas nearly matches that of its high unemployment zones.[22]

While Wilson invokes unemployment to counter the racial interpretation of underclass, however, he still ends up falling into the "cultural" trap. In any case, there is definitely a racial element in urban poverty, because the industries and firms supposed to create new jobs have abandoned the inner cities where racially segregated populations live. Most of the jobs created in the United States during the 1980s weren't exactly for highly qualified positions. What's more, something frequently overlooked in today's e-economy is that e-commerce, particularly the mythical B2C (Business to Customer) commerce, implies that every order has to be home delivered, giving rise to an army of messengers and couriers to add to the domestic helpers, store clerks, laundry workers and security guards, none of which requires a degree in nuclear physics. (In fact, to work for Pony Express in the United States, you don't even need a driver's licence; riders here brave the Loop on bicycle, unlike their European counterparts, who use mopeds.) It is Mcjobs like these – to use *Generation X* author Douglas Coupland's term – that make up the most substantial core of new employment created first under Reaganism and then under the Clinton boom.

Finally, there exists a whole current of racist thought that identifies the motives for unemployment in the character and culture of Blacks and Hispanics. Once again, we see how concepts introduced for progressive ends have been put to use use for punitive ones: Wilson's idea of structural unemployment has been recycled as an attack on the presumed indolence, incompetence and indiscipline of Blacks.[23] With all these reasons (ethical, genetic, cultural) invoked to "explain" poverty, it's notable that no one has ever suggested that something may be "lacking" in the economic and social system that must be corrected if not revolutionized. Society always appears to be innocent of the poverty it creates and judges so readily. Indeed, the notion of the underclass serves to confirm this innocence, par-

---

22 William Julius Wilson, *The Truly Disadvantaged: The Inner City, the Underclass and Public Policy*, Chicago: University of Chicago Press, 1987, pp. 51–55.

23 See Michael B. Katz's review of Lawrence Mead's book, *The New Politics of Poverty: The Non-working Poor*, in *Dissent*, October 1992, pp. 548–53.

ticularly when linked to criminality and urban gangs. We move from a social problem to a police problem, as once again the poor person is equated with the delinquent and the criminal. Potentially being revived here is the Malthusian thesis, cited by Engels, for which "poverty is an offence meriting severe punishment as a warning."

While the notion of the underclass has gained currency, America's prison population has quintupled to the incredible figure of 2 million inmates. To obtain a similar percentage, Italy would have to incarcerate 330,000 people, when in fact Italy currently has 50,000 prisoners, some eight times fewer. In the United States, prison has now become an obligatory rite of passage for a growing number of young people. It is in this context that we should read the government's frequent declaration of "war on drugs." In reality, the war is against the addicts, in particular against those who reside in the inner cities and who create the illusion that the problem of drugs (and of the poor who take them) can be solved by resorting to semi-military tactics.

Paradoxically, as Katz says, "for all its menace, the underclass was a comforting discovery"[24] because it renewed the nineteenth-century theory of the "dangerous classes" and offered a repressive alternative to social action for a society that denied its own internal class division, yet still insisted that a group existed beneath all classes. The presence of an underclass reduced the problem of poverty to a modest segment of the population: figures vary enormously from expert to expert, but compared with 32.2 million poor, estimates of the number of people belonging to the underclass range between 500,000 and 8 million (a mere quarter of the total number of poor). A more likely figure is from 1 million to 4 million. With the underclass, poverty becomes a question of skin color. The focus is on Blacks and Hispanics, while America's 20 million poor whites are more-or-less ignored, as are the working poor. Urban deprivation is emphasized at the expense of the terrible rural poverty, a widespread problem in the United States (and not just in the Mississippi Delta, known as the Ethiopia of America).

Thus the homeless and the underclass constitute the two sides – the deserving and the undeserving – of the poverty coin. The complex geography of poverty's jarringly multicolored mosaic is smoothed out and simplified, until what emerges

---

24 M. B. Katz, *The Undeserving Poor*, p. 196. For estimates on the extent of the underclass, see pp. 204–5.

from the silence of the metropolis are two distinct figures. On one hand, you have the homeless person, whether the slightly dotty old bag lady guarding her ballooning *matrioshka* of plastic carrier bags or the scrawny forty-something who looks out timidly from beneath a woollen ski hat as he drags a shopping cart filled with his belongings along the hard shoulder of the freeway. On the other is every American's nightmare: the menacing silhouette of the young Black hoodlum, baseball cap back-to-front, T-shirt drooping to his knees, padding along in his huge Converse sneakers. Each of these figures is extreme, almost a caricature, and both pay a price for the image they project. The homeless person may be an innocent victim deserving state assistance but is for this reason considered helpless, almost a social cripple. The kid from the underclass, meanwhile, is no doubt in full possession of his faculties and a highly capable individual, but because of these very qualities, he becomes dangerous, even potentially criminal, and must be repressed.

It matters little that these figures together constitute only a small percentage (less than one-third) of America's poor and, as such, are just the tip of the poverty iceberg. The fact remains that just two images exhaust the whole discourse on poverty, both in terms of the collective imagination (because of their emotive force and phantasmal power) and in terms of social action (because both categories convey the same fatalist message of innate condemnation). And if poverty is composed of just these two groups – the innocent but innocuous homeless and the culpable but dangerous members of the underclass – then there remains no alternative but to consider the problem in the cruel terms of Malthus. Citing the words of a poet, Malthus says that the poor man comes to nature's mighty feast, but there is no vacant place for him, and then adds, "and she bids him to be gone because he forgot to ask society before he was born whether there was any room for him or not."[25]

---

25 Cited by F. Engels in *The Condition of the Working Class*, p. 321. Actually, the passage from Malthus reads as follows: "A man who is born into a world already possessed, if he cannot get subsistence from his parents on whom he has a just demand, and if the society do not want his labour, has no claim of *right* to the smallest portion of food, and, in fact, has no business to be where he is. At nature's mighty feast there is no vacant cover for him. She tells him to be gone, and will quickly execute her own orders." This passage appeared in the second edition (1803) of *An Essay on the Principle of Population* but was omitted from subsequent editions, from 1807 on.

Metacity

Such Compelling Chaos

What avid curiosity, what indefatigable delving and – why not say it? – what arrogance, what self-conviction! From its inception, Chicago has passed most of its time studying itself, recounting its own story. In its 170-year existence, the city has generated a massive bibliography on its own exploits. What is striking, however, is not so much the quantity of these studies as the way in which Chicago has been contemplated: not as one city among many, with its own dynamism and vitality; nor even as an unrepeatable case, unique or singular in the way the world's great cities – such as New York or Paris – like to think of themselves; but as an *exemplary* case, Chicago as sociology, as a representation of The American City.

Yes, Chicago has always been studied, and has studied itself, as an exemplary case, in the sense philosopher John Dewey intended when, during his years at the University of Chicago (1893–1904), he laid the foundations for that most American of philosophical currents, pragmatism. For Dewey, induction – the process classically defined as the inference of a general idea from *several* particular cases – consisted in identifying *one* particularly representative case: "'induction' is a name for the complex of methods by which a given case is determined to be representative. ... The problem of inductive inquiry ... [has] to do with ascertaining that the given case *is* representative."[1]

---

1 John Dewey, *Logic: The Theory of Inquiry*, New York: Henry Holt, 1948, p.436.

As far as the study of modern society is concerned, Chicago is that case. In effect, what better place than this metropolis – which in a mere sixty years rose from nothing – for studying such matters as the organization of urban life, the origin of social malaise or the phases of immigrant integration? It was in Chicago and at its universities that sociology established itself as an academic discipline, "human ecology," under the name of the Chicago School. And just as sociology began in Chicago, it began by studying Chicago.

For the founders of the Chicago School – William I. Thomas, Robert E. Park and Ernest W. Burgess – this city really was the most representative case, in Dewey's sense of the term. (Park and Thomas encouraged their students to attend courses in philosophical pragmatism.) This, Park wrote, was first of all because "[t]he city, in short, shows the good and the evil in human *nature* in excess," which made of it "a laboratory or *clinic* in which human nature and social processes may be conveniently and profitably studied"[2] (note here the use of the term *nature* as well as the allusion to medicine of *clinic*). A second motive, according to Burgess, was that "[t]he outstanding fact of modern society is the growth of great cities," and in terms of urbanization, in the United States, "the transition from a rural to an urban civilization, though beginning later than in Europe, has taken place ... at any rate more logically in its characteristic forms."[3] Thus the privileged object of study was the city, but in particular the American city, which was held to be more *logical* and rational than its European equivalent.

Undoubtedly, Chicago – with its waves of immigrants, its burgeoning industries, its political machine (whose tentacles were spreading as rapidly as the city itself), its criminal underworld, its unemployed, its disheveled army of outcasts, hoboes, tramps and bums – constituted one huge real-time urban experiment. There was certainly no shortage of material. Here you could study "the forces of the urban community in action." ("The science which seeks to isolate these factors and to describe the typical constellations of persons and institutions which the co-operation of these forces produce, is what we call human, as distinguished

---

2   Robert E. Park, "Suggestions for the Investigation of Human Behavior in the Urban Environment," in Robert E. Park, Ernest W. Burgess and Roderick D. McKenzie, eds., *The City* (1925), Chicago: University of Chicago Press, 1967, p. 46.

3   Ernest W. Burgess, "The Growth of the City," in Park, Burgess and McKenzie, eds., *The City*, p. 47.

from plant and animal, ecology."[4])

A European might be almost envious of the energy and curiosity with which Chicago's researchers set about investigating their city, the dogged determination these academics showed in seeking out and frequenting flophouses, dives, brothels and immigrant ghettos. In their inquiries, they applied the ideas of the pragmatist George H. Mead, for whom an individual's "self" was a social structure, the internalization of the process by which a group of individuals interacted with other groups. The self of each person consisted entirely in this reciprocal interaction. As Alain Coulon says, "Individual action can therefore be regarded as the mutual creation of several 'selves' in interaction with each other. In this way these 'selves' acquire a social significance, they become sociological phenomena."[5]

This would explain why the Chicago School of sociology was so interested in the way social actors saw themselves. Viewed in this light, the lies told by interviewees became as enlightening as the truths, since both equally revealed the "self," or the social process. This was the inauguration of the investigation method that Oscar Lewis would take up again some thirty years later in his research into Puerto Rican families. It also explains why so many studies conducted in Chicago have taken the form of real-life stories, verified autobiographies collected over many years of interviews. Examples of the genre include John Slawson's *The Delinquent Boy* (1926), Clifford Shaw's *The Jack-Roller* (1930) and Edwin Sutherland's *The Professional Thief* (1937). Notably, all of these titles are in the singular and use the definite article. We have already met Nels Anderson's *The Hobo* (and not *The Hoboes* or *A Hobo*), but then there was also *The Unadjusted Girl* (1923), by William I. Thomas, and Everett Stonequist's *The Marginal Man* (1937). In these cases, the use of the singular form refers to an individual person within the indicated category: we thus face an individual self whose experience supposedly encapsulates that of an entire social group, who is deemed to be a "particularly representative case." The risk here is that the individual's situation becomes the group's destiny; a transitory state comes to define a human type. For Park, a sense "of moral dichotomy and conflict is probably characteristic of every immigrant during the period of

---

4 R. E. Park et al., *The Growth of the City*, pp. 1–2.
5 Alain Coulon, *L'Ecole de Chicago* (1987), Paris: Presses Universitaires de France ed. *Que-Sais-je?* This little volume is the best available introduction to the work of the Chicago School.

transition, when old habits are being discarded and new ones are not yet formed." In the case of this marginal man, however, "the period of crisis is relatively permanent. The result is that he tends to become *a personality type*" (italics mine).[6] This is how Italians become *The Italian,* Jews *The Jew.*

The Polish Peasant is the title of a monumental study by William I. Thomas and Florian Znaniecki. Begun in 1908 and completed in 1918, *The Polish Peasant* is considered the cornerstone of the Chicago School's theoretical edifice. The terms *Polish* and *peasant* are here run together: *Polish* because the Poles constituted the largest wave of immigrants around 1908 and were thus the most visible source of growth and change in the city; *peasant* because these immigrants hadn't simply moved from one country to another, but rather had come from being country dwellers to being citizens, shedding their old rural mentality and acquiring a new metropolitan one in its place. If it is true, as Dewey sustains, that "in social inquiry, genuine problems are set only by actual social situations which are themselves conflicting and confused,"[7] then what more genuine problem than that of immigration, which bore within itself every kind of conflict and confusion?

Confusion is synonymous with what the Chicago sociologists called *social disorganization.* In Burgess's view, "the processes of disorganization and organization may be thought of as in reciprocal relationship to each-other, and as co-operating in a moving equilibrium of social order toward an end ... regarded as progressive"; urban growth was therefore viewed as "a resultant of organization and disorganization analogous to the anabollic and katabolic processes of metabolism in the body."[8] Here the nature metaphor is stretched so that the city is considered a living organism with its own metabolism (urban road *arteries*). Disorganization for the Chicago School is thus seen as a transitory condition: "The personal disorganization was thus a result of a grand and too rapid transition from pre-industrial folk society to a highly mechanized urban civilization. Few ethnic populations making the transition were able to escape the severe disorganisation, but in time all showed the ability to recover from it."[9]

---

6   Robert E. Park, "Human Migration and the Marginal Man," p. 893.
7   J. Dewey, *Logic,* p. 498.
8   E. W. Burgess, "The Growth of the City," pp. 54, 53.
9   Robert E. L. Faris, *Chicago Sociology 1920–1932* (1967), Chicago: Univ. of Chicago Press, 1979, p. 63.

Not only was disorganization transitory; it also contributed to establishing a new and more varied order. At the base of this attitude was a kind of evolutionary positivism, for whom society (and urban structures) evolved toward an "end regarded as positive." In Park's view, the final destination of immigration was assimilation and integration. What the Chicago School formulated here was essentially the sociology of the melting pot, where various ethnicities would merge together to form a new union. To describe the relation between the migrant and the host community, Park came up with the theory of a four-stage process: competition, conflict, adaptation and assimilation.

1. *Competition.* Initially, immigrants disembark as a pure workforce, and social relations are reduced to a coexistence based entirely on economic relations. At this point, competition – or "interaction without social contact" – predominates. "Competition is the process through which ... organization of society is created," determining the geographical partitioning of society and the division of labor.

2. *Conflict.* While "competition determines the position of the individual in the community ... *conflict* fixes his place in the society." Competition is impersonal and unconscious, whereas conflict is conscious and personalized, creating a sense of solidarity among the immigrant community.

3. *Accommodation.* As in religious conversion, accommodation may be regarded as a kind of mutation: different groups, while remaining potential rivals, come to accept their differences.

4. *Assimilation.* Through assimilation, "a process of interpenetration and fusion ... persons and groups acquire memories, sentiments, and attitudes of other persons or groups, and by sharing their experience and history, are incorporated with them in a common cultural life."[10] Assimilation, however, is not the same as an amalgam: American Jews, for example, are nowadays integrated without being amalgamated.

---

10 Sentences in quotation marks are taken from Robert E. Park and Ernest W. Burgess, *Introduction to the Science of Sociology* (1921), Chicago: Univ. of Chicago Press, 1969, in the following order: pp. 506, 508, 510, 735. In ordering the sequence, I have followed A. Coulon, *L'École de Chicago*, pp. 35–39.

Belief that assimilation is inevitable in the United States has now for the most part faded. At that time, however, it seemed a permanent part of the general hunger for the future, of that reaching out for tomorrow that pervaded daily life. Within the rapid growth of a city such as Chicago – whose every tomorrow rendered it different, new, wholly unrecognizable from each passing yesterday – experience, from a philosophical perspective, would inevitably assume the forward-looking value of a project; this mental attitude particularly marked philosophical pragmatism. While English empiricism had always referred to historical experience, to be cataloged and classified, pragmatism saw experience as anticipatory, a preparation for the future. Not by chance did pragmatism present itself as the philosophical formulation of *democratic optimism*.

Thanks to this optimistic vision, even the marginal man – the figure who most fascinated the Chicago School – appeared in a more flattering light: "a man on the margin of two cultures and two societies, which never completely interpenetrated and fused." Immigrants were thus the ideal marginal figures. For Park, being on the margins meant having a larger degree of freedom: "When the traditional organization of society breaks down, as a result of contact and collision with an invading culture, the effect is, so to speak, to emancipate the individual man. Energies that were formerly controlled by custom and tradition are released. The individual is free for new adventures, but he is more or less without direction and control."[11] Here, in a nutshell, we find our old friend the "culture of poverty," because it is the clash between two cultures that produces disorganization. Yet between disorganization and poverty is an abyss: the "culture of marginality" has its positive sides. The marginal man is the metropolitan *par excellence*. If man is always partly a stranger in the city, as Simmel said, he is for that reason "the free man, practically and theoretically."

The Chicago sociologists were formulating their theses on immigration at a time when the lynching of Italians and Greeks was still common practice, when future President Woodrow Wilson was speaking of the superiority of northern Europe's "sturdy stocks" compared to the "more sordid and hapless elements" of the south. Their work demolished the racist interpretation of "urban pathologies" (the medical metaphor) by providing an ecological account. Burgess was to go so

---

11 R. E. Park, "Human Migration and the Marginal Man," p. 891.

far as to speak of an "ecology of crime."

Swept away was the common assumption that crime resulted from the incapacity of immigrants to adapt to American life. The Chicago School showed how, on the contrary, criminality was born from the process of adaptation, diffuse only in the second generation, among the youths who were already part of the new culture. It was completely absent from the first generation of immigrants who, upon arrival, were impermeable to the culture of the new country, still tied to their old moral code. Old moralist accounts based on deviance were completely dismantled. In the words of Dewey, "Approach to human problems in terms of moral blame and moral approbation, of wickedness or righteousness, is probably the greatest single obstacle now existing to development of competent methods in the field of social subject-matter."[12] Instead, the Chicago School fought for an ethnological approach to the question:

> Anthropology, the science of man, has been mainly concerned up to the present with the study of primitive peoples. But civilized man is quite as interesting an object of investigation. ... The same patient methods of observation which anthropologists ... have expended on the study of the life and manners of the North American Indian might be even more fruitfully employed in the investigation of the customs, beliefs, social practices, and general conceptions of life prevalent in Little Italy on the Lower North Side of Chicago, or in recording the more sophisticated folkways of the inhabitants of Greenwich Village and the neighborhood of Washington Square, New York.[13]

Yet somehow the moral question that had been hounded out the door managed to sneak back in the window. For the Chicago School, the freedom of the individual was from the outset an ambivalent matter that contravened collective values. For these sociologists, the forces of disorder (mental, social and moral) exerted an irresistible pull. Their studies were always investigations of disorganization, never of organization, because they took the latter, along with the criteria it was founded on, for granted. In this way, their work conveyed an image of organization of the utmost banality and prudishness (along the lines of marriage equals organization, divorce disorganization). Unbiased and unconventional in every

---

12 J. Dewey, *Logic*, p. 495.
13 R. E. Park et al., *The City*, p. 3.

way, the Chicago School drew the line when it came to its own prejudices, as William I. Thomas was to discover in 1918 when, at the age of fifty-five, he was caught in a hotel bedroom with a married woman. Forced to resign from his university position, he was never reinstated. (What is worse, the whole embarrassing episode was canceled from the history of sociology and was only made public in 1966.)[14] It was with an ambivalent tremor of fear and pleasure, adventure and danger, that Park braved the city:

> The process of segregation establishes moral distances which make the city a mosaic of little worlds which touch but do not interpenetrate. This makes it possible for individuals to pass quickly and easily from one moral milieu to another, and encourages the fascinating but dangerous experiment of living at the same time in several different contiguous, but otherwise widely separated, worlds. All this tends to give to city life a superficial and adventitious character; it tends to complicate social relationships and to produce new and divergent individual types. It introduces, at the same time, an element of chance and adventure which adds to the stimulus of city life and gives it, for young and fresh nerves, a peculiar attractiveness.[15]

Closed little worlds ... For Chicago's sociologists, just as living species evolve by dividing their cells, so too did the city, when it grew and complexified, divided itself into "natural areas," "each with its own natural function." Here the metaphor takes on a decidedly Darwinian (even Lamarckian) bent. The different urban zones, wrote Park in 1929, "are the products of forces that are constantly at work to effect an orderly distribution of populations and functions within the urban complex."[16]

If the key factor in the development of industrial cities is the demand for labor – immigration, that is to say – it can be said that different zones of the city correspond to different phases of ethnic relations. The immigrant "invasion" of the city "has the effect of a tidal wave first inundating the immigrant colonies, the ports of first entry, dislodging thousands of inhabitants who overflow into the next zone, and so on until the momentum of the wave has spent its force on the last urban

14 A. Coulon *L'Ecole de Chicago*, p. 26.
15 R. E. Park et al., *The City*, pp. 40–41.
16 R. E. Park, "Sociology," in Wilson Gee, ed., *Research in Social Sciences*, New York: Macmillan, 1929, p. 29.

zone" (here the metaphor becomes hydraulic).[17]

According to urban ecology, the one criterion that assigns single zones to different functions is *competition* for the most advantageous urban space: "The first choice of desirable pieces of land *inevitably* is made by the users who can pay the highest prices" (italics mine).[18] The central business district thus develops in the zone most beneficial to banks, offices, company headquarters and luxury hotels, while outside it are located warehouses and light industries. Somewhat further away are the heavy industries that require acres of space but must be sufficiently close to transportation centers. Because they yield less profit than offices or industries, residential areas are generally located far from the center, occupying land that hasn't been reclaimed by commerce. Land near to industrial areas, polluted by noise, odors and poisonous fumes, is not attractive to residents, which is why low-income families tend to inhabit it; the advantages to this area are that it is close to the workplace and that house prices are cheap.

Such competition has the effect of shaping the city according to what is known as "Burgess's zonal hypothesis": (1) central zone: the business district (the Loop, in Chicago); (2) transitional zone: industrial areas, slums and early immigrant settlements; (3) working-class zone: areas outside the slums; (4) middle-class residential zone; and (5) the commuter zone. The zones are not circular but are deformed because of geography and transportation routes.

According to the urban ecologists, *the city is naturally segregated*. This is one of the cornerstones of the American concept of the city. When I left New York for the first time heading toward the Midwestern states, I decided at nightfall to stop in Youngstown, Ohio, an iron-and-steel town of some 200,000 inhabitants. Like any European, I looked for a hotel and a place to eat in the downtown area. In Youngstown, though, I found the whole place in darkness, the streets disquietingly empty. I asked advice of a police officer in a squad car, who told me to turn back toward the freeway intersection to find the motels and restaurants. This was the first time I encountered head-on the separation of functions that you find even in big cities such as Denver or Minneapolis.

Such separation is all-pervading, to the extent that you sometimes feel a sense

---

17 E. W. Burgess, in *The City*, p. 58.
18 R. E. L. Faris, *Chicago Sociology*, p. 58.

of anxiety in American cities; your mind becomes like a chest of drawers, with handkerchiefs in one drawer, underwear in another, shirts in another still. You begin to wonder if these cities have a future. It's a doubt that comes from this rigid division of the various functions of urban life. Where you live, you don't work. Where you work, there is no entertainment. Everything attractive about urban life – the overlapping of functions, the fact that workplace, house, restaurants, shops, cafés and cinemas are all adjacent to one another – is categorically denied. Here, the separation of these functions dictates the geography of the city: the business district that is deserted at night (and therefore dangerous); endless rows of houses without a single bar or news dealer in sight; malls that spring up like mushrooms in the desert; and, along the freeway, the long single-commerce thoroughfares, one with nothing but used-car showrooms, another packed with motels.

To the eyes of a European, this division of spaces and functions is like a sickness, the sad fate that accompanied the formation of the United States and is now simply a fact of American life to be endured. More optimistically, this separation might be considered the involuntary side effect of other goals: having a big house with a nice lawn, being able to get to work or the shops quickly by car, concentrating industries in one area to narrow the field of pollution, cramming offices together as a way to encourage networking and generate further business.

On closer inspection, however, it becomes evident that the segregation of spaces and functions is anything but involuntary; it's something that has been theorized, that is considered more logical (according to Burgess), because here physical space coincides with social space to such an extent that forces of social, family and mental disorganization are concentrated in urbanistically disorganized spaces. It was at the point where separation of functions established the segregation of social groups that sociologists and urban planners began to think that Park's "closed little worlds" (which "touch but do not interpenetrate") had best stay closed – that they had best not spread out – because the place where they met marked an urban border that was at the same time a social frontier and a festering wound. Here, in the very fracture of the social order, where social disorganization was at its height, according to Frederic M. Thrasher's classic 1927 study *The Gang: A Study of 1,313 Gangs in Chicago*, criminality took root.

Nothing is natural about the idea that social space should coincide with physical space. "Space is one of the locuses of power, where power is affirmed and exercised, undoubtedly in the most subtle of forms, that of symbolic violence, a violence which is imperceptible."[19] It is this power that makes the two spaces coincide. While the sociologist formulates the zonal hypothesis, the politicians decide the actual zoning regulations. As Jackson writes, "In theory zoning was designed to protect the interests of all citizens by limiting land speculation and congestion. … In actuality zoning was a device to keep poor people and obnoxious industries out of affluent areas. … Southern cities even used zoning to enforce racial segregation."[20] In this way, according to Pierre Bourdieu, it has "effected a veritable *political construction of space*," which "favours the *construction of homogenous groups on a spatial basis*."[21] Burgess's zonal hypothesis reveals itself as a classic case of a theory that confirms itself on *natural* grounds.

Perhaps now is the time to question this idea of "nature,"' which we seem to encounter at every turn. Nature as a metaphor for social process was rooted in scientific positivism: for Auguste Comte, the sociologist studied society as the physiologist did the human body, prescribing cures for its ailments exactly as a doctor prescribed cures for patients. Chicago in the 1930s was a positivist stronghold: here publication began in 1938 of the *International Encyclopedia of Unified Science* under the direction of three standard-bearers of positivism, Otto Neurath, Rudolf Carnap and Charles Morris. Nature metaphors (of the telluric, geographic or physical type) were not foreign to Marxism, which spoke of social shocks, earthquakes, the eruption of revolutions – while conservative thinkers tended toward more organic metaphors. The Chicago sociologists made use of both types, speaking in the same breath of "waves of immigration" and "urban pathologies."

But when Thrasher talks about a "natural history of crime," what does he really mean by *natural history,* a term that normally refers to the kind of museums where you go to see dinosaur fossils and butterfly collections? The answer can be found in the *Wall Street Journal* of 15 April 1993: "A generation of scholars are find-

---

19 Pierre Bourdieu, "Site Effects," in Pierre Bourdieu et al., *La misère du monde*, Paris: Editions du Seuil, 1993. Engl. trans. *The Weight of the World: Social Suffering in Contemporary Society*, Cambridge, Mass.: Polity Press, 1999, p. 129.

20 K. T. Jackson, *Crabgrass Frontier*, p. 242.

21 P. Bourdieu, "Site Effects," p. 129.

ing out that the most important law of nature is the law of supply and demand."
How could we have been so stupid? It's all clear now. The tendency toward segregation in US cities is "natural," because the inhabitants naturally resist having the
market value of their property cut by Blacks moving into the neighborhood. Likewise, *competition* is natural, because, as the Chicago sociologists said, it is the "organizing force of society" (Park): competition is in fact merely a shorter way of
saying "free market competition." The market economy must also therefore be
natural, as must the struggle for property ownership. Capitalism, with its laws of
supply and demand more invincible than Newton's law of gravity, is inscribed in
human nature. In the pragmatism of the later Dewey, the act of knowing is defined as a transaction: just as neither buyers nor merchandise can exist in the business world without transaction, so too object and subject exist only in the process
of knowing.

Think of it: business practice as a theoretical model to describe the act of knowing! What we are witnessing here is the production of a "myth," in the sense
Roland Barthes intends in his *Mythologies*, whereby things that are a product of history (the eternal laws of the market) are described as a natural phenomenon.
What is in fact transitory and constructed is regarded as immutable ("natural").[22]
According to such logic, cities generate urban ghettos as a natural part of their
growing pains, in the same way that the faces of adolescents become covered in
pimples.

When they were formulating their hypotheses, the theorists of urban ecology
considered themselves progressive. After all, they had set about demolishing prejudices and common assumptions: if urban ghettos were the product of a city's natural growth, the inhabitants were not themselves to blame. Forces of deviance,
the violence of urban gangs and youth subcultures: the Chicago School removed
all this from any form of genetic explanation. But if these theories of urban ecology were able to send the geneticists packing, it was because they substituted for
heredity another equally inexorable but more important (according to the *Wall
Street Journal*) "law of nature," that of supply and demand.

If truth be known, the Chicago sociologists did believe that nature could be
perfected and the city improved, as their protests against urban reform testify.

---

22 Roland Barthes, *Mythologies*, London: Jonathan Cape, 1972, pp. 109–58.

They were optimistic about the dynamics of society, just as Dewey was optimistic in his pragmatism. In their view, disorganization was simply a transitory moment, a form of purgatory rather than hell itself, and in this sense, the gulf that separates the Chicago sociologists from today's sociologists is as wide as that between a social marginal and an outcast.

If the Chicago School subsequently fell into decline, in fact, it was because it was too optimistic and assimilationist; it lacked positivism. In the academic field, this decline began in 1935 when real-life stories were superseded by the quantitative sociology of Talcott Parsons, Paul Lazarsfelds and Robert Merton. Backed by huge contracts from the US armed forces, these later theories and methods were inscribed within a paradigm of total positivism, for which absolute mathematic impersonality was the only valid scientific criterion.

In terms of social reality, it was the "Negro question" that put the Chicago School in crisis, a crisis to which Park's theory of assimilation failed to provide an adequate response, as did the cultural approach. Already within the Chicago School's ranks, E. Franklin Frazier in his 1932 study *The Negro Family in Chicago* had distinguished between cultural and social assimilation, arguing that assimilation of American culture did not mean that the Blacks were socially integrated. It was really only after World War II, however, when the Black question became *the* social problem for America, that cultural and community-based approaches revealed their impotence and inadequacy.

In 1978, William Julius Wilson, a Black sociologist from Chicago (the most segregated city in the United States), published a much-debated volume suggestively entitled *The Declining Significance of Race*. In it, Wilson supported the idea that the emergence of an African American middle class coupled with further impoverishment of the Black underclass had led to the diversification of living conditions, culture and identity among the various sectors of the Black population, thus reducing the importance of race. Race is an issue even for affluent Blacks, however: "The experience of middle-class status is not uniform across groups. Instead, it is colored by the crosscutting reality of race."[23] And yet there remains an abyss between ethnic and race relations.

---

23 Mary Patillo-McCoy, *Black Picket Fences: Privilege and Peril among the Black Middle Class*, Chicago: University of Chicago Press, 1999, p. 209.

When European immigrants first arrived in the United States, they were discriminated against, lynched and used as scabs, just as the Blacks were. At the same time, the implicit message to these immigrants was this: "You will become like us whether you want to or not." For racial minorities, on the other hand, the unspoken dictum was, and still is: "No matter how much like us you are, you will remain apart." It is this unavoidable color line that we now have to cross.

PART THREE

17

Bronzeville: The End of Hope

On State Street at the intersection with Thirty-Fifth, the austere profile of Mies van der Rohe's polytechnic building looms like a sentinel; beyond that, to the south, lies nothing but miles of desolation. On the right, until 2000, stood the Taylor Homes project, whose apartments, even when inhabited, sported fire-blackened, windowless facades barred and grilled off at every floor. Today the area is in the midst of demolition, some of the buildings already leveled. Their ruins sharpen the sensation of death that floats over the whole neighborhood. To the left runs the overhead railway, while further off in the distance lies a stretch of land strewn with scrap iron, abandoned tires and cardboard boxes, and plastic bags borne on the wind. Since 1950, two-thirds of the area's inhabitants have left; two-thirds of those who remain live below the poverty line.

It seems impossible that this intersection was the vibrant center of Bronzeville, the most swinging Black neighborhood in town, from the First World War right up to the 1960s. By day or by night, the area between Twenty-Fifth and Thirty-Ninth on State Street was aglitter with lights, and music poured from every bar. Dance clubs such as the Palace Garden or the Peking played jazz into the early hours to a mixed-race clientele. The neighborhood's seven cinemas showed a different film every day, accompanied by a live orchestra. In one autumn week of 1916, you could choose among *The Girl of San Francisco*, *A Lesson from Life*, *The*

Shielding Shadow, The Soldier from Company K (with an all-color cast), *Forbidden Fruit* and *The Sins of the City*.[1] Indeed, the stern Black weekly newspaper the *Chicago Defender* – along with various charity organizations – set about trying to warn young Black immigrants away from the temptations of the city, its vice dens, bars and lewd dancing.

At that time, Chicago was the "Land of Hope" for Black country folk in the South about to migrate northward – or even, as in some songs, "The Promised Land." *Land of Hope* is also the title of a well-documented study by James R. Grossman.[2] Between the brio of those years and the dull apathy of today, it is possible to measure the collapse of the Blacks' hopes. Perhaps there was a time when the coexistence of Blacks and whites was seen as a goal to be achieved. Perhaps there was even a time when right-minded Americans thought that Black people, even with their dark skin and curly hair, would someday be amalgamated into society. Maybe somebody once nurtured such thoughts, even if never in American history has the school system launched a campaign against the ideology of discrimination. What is certain is that these hopes have now vanished into a gray fog of fatalism. It seems today as though the nation's racial problem is felt as a burden, an inescapable national misery, a chronic bitterness and hostility that is neither peace nor war.

It was more than sixty years ago that Gunnar Myrdal began writing his seminal study *An American Dilemma* (completed in 1943)[3]. Since then, the situation seems to have deteriorated considerably, despite the Civil Rights Act and the revolts in the Black urban ghettos, despite the efforts of the Black Panthers, the Nation of Islam, and personalities such as Martin Luther King Jr., Malcolm X and Jesse Jackson. In the forties, the Black problem seemed to be the prerogative of the South;[4] today, it is most evident in the northern cities.

---

1   These movies were listed, along with thirty-eight others, in the *Chicago Defender*, 7 October 1916.
2   James R. Grossman, *Land of Hope: Chicago, Black Southerners and the Great Migration*, Chicago: University of Chicago Press, 1989.
3   Gunnar Myrdal, *An American Dilemma: The Negro Problem and Modern Democracy*, New York: Harper, 1944.
4   I have deliberately persisted in using Myrdal's expressions "Black problem" and "Black question," even though they may seem somewhat anachronistic today.

If one thing makes you despair of the United States, it is this hostile relationship between Blacks and whites, the oppressive wall of diffidence and rancor that separates the two races. The first thing you notice is what you don't see: and what you don't see represents a double paradox. On one hand, you don't see many black Blacks, those with the kind of black skin that anyone who has been to Africa knows so well; on the other, you do see many light Blacks. (The Blacks of San Domingo used to say that the American Blacks were slightly tanned whites.)

All of this means two things. First, the "Black race" is defined in America by the white population: "Everybody having a *known* trace of Negro blood in his veins – no matter how far back it was acquired – is classified as a Negro. No amount of white ancestry, except one hundred per cent, will permit entrance to the white race."[5] Such an attitude is the very opposite of that which prevails in Africa or in the Caribbean, where a family will privilege and spoil its lighter-skinned offspring in a sort of inverted racism that, as Malcolm X recounts, was present in the United States during the 1920s: "Most Negro parents in those days would almost instinctively treat any lighter children better than they did the darker ones."[6] Nothing of the kind can be said of the US taxonomy of color.

The censuses of the nineteenth century did distinguish slaves according to whether they were M (Mulatto) or B (Black), however, and surveys from 1890 on subdivided Mulattos into those who had one-quarter – and those who had one-eighth Black blood (not quite the degree to which the Nazis were to distinguish Jews, down to the sixteenth part in blood). But such a classification ran contrary to the spirit of the dominant culture. As James Bryce wrote in 1893, "Whereas in Spanish and Portuguese countries persons who are not evidently black are reckoned as white, in the United States any trace of African blood marks a man as a negro and subjects him to the disabilities attaching to the race. In Latin America whoever is not black is white; in Teutonic America whoever is not white is black."[7] So it was that from 1920, the Bureau of the Census would regard as Black anyone who had even the remotest Black ancestor, in accordance with the

---

5 G. Myrdal, *An American Dilemma*, p. 113.

6 *The Autobiography of Malcolm X* (1965), New York: Random House, 1992, p. 7.

7 James Bryce, *The American Commonwealth* (1893). New York: Macmillan, 1917, vol. II, p. 555.

"one-drop" rule.[8] "Seeking to pin down the essence of race, the one-drop-rule actually made that essence unknowable, indeed invisible. It jettisoned the perceptible reality of skin tone for the dream of racial essence; *it made the physical metaphysical*"[9] (italics mine).

Whereas nature offers a continuous gradation of coloring that runs smoothly from raven black to translucent white, society produces a discontinuous taxonomy (here whites, there Blacks) in the same way that the market substitutes discontinuous definitions of apples or beef for the continuous concrete variety of fruit and livestock, so as to be able to trade in futures. And just as the new name in the market for the thing (apple) has produced the new thing itself (the new variety of standardized apple), so too does labeling as Black a person with light skin (though slightly cappuccino colored) have the effect of confining that person to a new Black race – new because this entity called race is no longer defined according to physical properties such as dark skin color but is, rather, simply defined as "not being white." In the United States, in fact, there are thousands such "unconscious Blacks," people with skin as white as cold cream who "don't know" that they are actually Black on the basis of the one-drop rule and learn so only by chance.

Here we see at work again, this time literally in the flesh, the process by which moderns have resolved the medieval problem of universals: *producing reality simply by nominating it.* The fact that the "Black race" is a purely cultural product takes nothing from its concrete historical reality, as Blacks subjected to its effects know only too well. Many leaders of the Black movement have in fact been partly white: Booker T. Washington and Frederick Douglass (both of whom had white fathers), Martin Luther King Jr. (who had both an Irish grandmother and Native American ancestry), W. E. B. Du Bois and Malcolm X. Even the antiwhite extremist leader of the Black Muslim movement Louis Farrakhan has light skin and "Caucasian" features.

The second thing to be inferred from this varying tonality of complexion is that there must have been a great deal of miscegenation in the past. One survey cited by Myrdal showed that 71.7 percent of Blacks interviewed in 1930 had at least one

---

8   Lawrence Wright, "One Drop of Blood," *The New Yorker,* 25 June 1994, pp. 47–48.
9   Scott L. Malcomson, *One Drop of Blood: The American Misadventure of Race*, New York: Farrar Strauss Giroux, 2000, p. 356.

remote ancestor who was white.[10] Undoubtedly, the races mixed frequently during the period of slavery, usually between a white man and his Black female slave. Note how myth narrates a symmetrically inverted and opposite story: white racism is obsessed with the nightmarish specter of the Black male who rapes white women, when for centuries it was the white male rapist who violated Black women (the same mechanism whereby it is the adulterous member of a couple who is the more jealous, because that person projects his or her own behavior onto the partner).

Sexual discrimination in the United States has always been an asymmetrical affair. While relations between a white man and a Black woman are generally less censured, relations between a white woman and a Black man are still considered taboo. Informal or clandestine affairs, echoes of ancillary adventures, perhaps, are more tolerated than marriage. At the top of the list of taboos, then, is the idea of marriage between a white woman and a Black man, a taboo also found in the Black community, as seen in Malcolm X's criticism of white women whom he called "blue-eyed she-devils."

Here you come up against the second thing you rarely see on the streets in many of the states: mixed couples. In other cities with large Black populations, such as Paris or London, you find such couples every day. But then you have to remember that only thirty-four years have passed since the historic moment in 1967 when the US Supreme Court declared illegal all the laws individual states had imposed against interracial marriages: it had been more than a century after the end of the Civil War and the abolition of slavery before such a ruling occurred.

To put this impression of segregation to the test, you need only look at the statistics. Of just over 55.3 million married couples in the United States in 1999, only 330,000 were mixed Black and white – .59 percent, or one in every 170 couples – despite the fact that Blacks represent 12.7 percent of the population (34.4 million, compared to 223 million whites).[11] The racism in such a tiny percentage becomes even clearer if you compare it with the percentage of mixed marriages between whites and other races (Asians, Polynesians, Native Americans). Although these

---

10 G. Myrdal, *An American Dilemma*, p. 133. The study cited is Melville J. Heskovits, *The Anthropometry of the American Negro*, New York, 1930. Heskovits took a sample of 1,551 Blacks.
11 Census Bureau, *Statistical Abstract of the United States 1999*, tab. 18, 65.

groups have populations about one-third that of the Black population (12.8 million compared to 34.4), they account for 975,000 mixed marriages (compared with the Blacks' 330,000): whites marry Asians 7.9 times more than they do Blacks. The child of a white-Black mixed marriage, in fact, is considered Black: the white man or woman who has a child with a Black woman or man inevitably exposes it to racism and discrimination. Implicit in sexual segregation is the notion that "Blacks cannot be assimilated" even if, like the Anglo-Saxons, they have been present in America for almost four centuries.

It is now nearly 140 years since America's Blacks were released from slavery, yet the scales are still tipped against them in every aspect of life, beginning with *life expectancy*, which is 6.1 years less for Blacks than for whites (71.1 compared to 77.2 years) and infant mortality, which is more than twice as high among Blacks as among whites (14.2 per thousand, compared to 6.0 per thousand). Blacks are also 6.6 times more likely to be murdered than whites,[12] and while Blacks account for only 12.7 percent of the US population, they account for 46.5 percent of its prison inmates.

Income also comes into question. The median income of a Black family in 1997 was $28,602,[13] compared to $46,754 for a white family. In the years that have passed since approval of the Civil Rights Act in 1964, the situation of Black families relative to whites has remained more or less the same. Back in the sixties, the average Black family's median income was 59 percent that of a white family. By 1970, it had inched up to 61.3 percent, which is more or less where it remained up until 1997 (at 61.17 percent). In 1998, 26.1 percent of Blacks lived under the poverty threshold, compared to only 8.2 percent of whites. Racial discrimination exists even in terms of ungainliness, with considerably more obesity among Black youths than among their white counterparts (41 percent as against 28 percent, out

---

12 In 1997, there were more Black homicide victims (7,692) than there were whites (7,492), even with a Black population one-sixth of the white population. For these data and those that follow, see tab. 51, 127, 133, 347 and 750 of the Census Bureau's *Statistical Abstract of the United States*, as well as statistics available from the Department of Justice Web site www.usdoj.gov.

13 To obtain the median income (different than the average income), split the population into two equal parts, with one half above the median value and the other half below.

of a national average of 34 percent).[14]

The climate of hatred, oppression and segregation is so unbearable in the United States that you wonder why the Blacks don't revolt – not with one of the minor uprisings that periodically occur in America's inner cities, but by staging an all-out rebellion. In the 140 years that have passed since their emancipation from slavery, the situation actually seems to have deteriorated; Alexis de Tocqueville's prophecy of 1835 seems to be becoming a reality: "The most formidable of all the ills that threaten the future of the Union arises from the presence of a Black population upon its territory; and in contemplating the cause of the present embarrassments, or the future dangers of the United States, the observer is invariably led to this as a primary fact." For Tocqueville, such a malediction was part of the very nature of modern slavery, which limited bondage to a single race. In ancient times, slaves were generally of the same race as their masters; once enfranchised, they thus became equal and indistinguishable. By restricting slavery to Blacks, however, modern white slave owners ensured that the mark of slavery remained visible even after the slaves were liberated: "The tradition of slavery dishonors the race, and the peculiarity of the race perpetuates the tradition of slavery. No African has ever voluntarily emigrated to the shores of the New World, whence it follows that all the blacks who are now found there are either slaves or freedmen."

It has taken almost 160 years for Tocqueville's affirmation to be refuted. Only in the 1980s, for the first time in history, did a wave of *voluntary* migration from Africa – from Somalia, Ethiopia, Nigeria and Senegal – begin to land on American shores. Tocqueville's judgment on the Europeans, however, remains as valid today as it was more than a century and a half ago: "They first violated every right of humanity by their treatment of the Negro, and they afterwards informed him that those rights were precious and inviolable. They opened their ranks to their slaves, and when the latter tried to come in, they drove them forth in scorn. Desiring slavery, they have allowed themselves unconsciously to be swayed in spite of themselves towards liberty, without having the courage to be either completely

---

14 Survey by Louis Harris from the magazine *Prevention*, September 1992.

iniquitous or completely just."[15] Malcolm X qualified this judgment thus: "The white man has perpetrated upon himself, as well as upon the black man, so gigantic a fraud that he has put himself into a crack."[16]

The nature of this crack was spelled out in the names, discovered by Saul Bellow,[17] of two French slave ships, one called *Jean-Jacques* after the Genevan philosopher Rousseau, prophet of the original equality of all men; the other *Contrat Social*, after Rousseau's most important work. Together, *Jean-Jacques* and *Contrat Social* carried Black slaves across the Atlantic.

This curse, or original sin, is what you see every day on every street, wherever you go in these United States. But then this magnanimous and benevolent country declares that one month of the year shall be Black History Month. In the same way that the United Nations occasionally celebrates Earth Year, here one month of twelve is a Black Month – and this in a country where no president has ever once asked forgiveness of the nation's 30 million Blacks for their long enslavement, where no leader has made a gesture similar to that Willy Brandt made in falling to his knees to apologize to the victims of the Nazi wars.

In Chicago, Black History Month, with its countless events and demonstrations, takes on a particularly emotional tone. This is a town where Blacks account for 39.1 percent of the inhabitants and 59.7 percent of the students, a city that holds the record for segregation in the United States, with more than 75 percent of Black families living in 95 percent Black neighborhoods. Likewise, Illinois beats every record when it comes to segregation in schools: a good 83 percent of Black students attend segregated schools. During Black History Month, Chicago not only rediscovers its own Black history, but also recognizes that Blacks have contributed greatly to the city's history as a whole, beginning from the days of the early settlers on the banks of the Chicago River and Lake Michigan: the first fur-trading station was built by a Black trapper, Jean Baptiste Point Sable.

---

15 A. de Tocqueville, *Democracy in America*, part II, ch. 10, "Situation of the Black Population in the United States and Dangers with Which Its Presence Threatens the Whites"; quotations from vol. I, pp. 356, 358, 381.
16 Malcolm X, *Autobiography*, p. 208.
17 Saul Bellow, "Papuas and Zulus," *New York Times*, 10 March 1994.

At thirty dollars a head, with reduced rates for groups of thirty-five or more, a guided tour promises a pilgrimage to the important Black sites of the city. You can take a walk through the Illinois Central Railroad Station where, in the years between 1910 and 1920, thousands of Blacks poured into the city from Alabama, Mississippi, Louisiana and Georgia, as part of the great migration northward triggered by the First World War – the conflict that interrupted the flow of immigration from Europe. It's not often that one pauses to reflect on the long-distance effects of war: for Europeans, the Great War recalls the beginnings of various fascisms, the Russian Revolution, mustard gas, the appalling death toll of trench warfare. Many people would never think to connect the events of the Marne or Kobarid, or the collapse of the Habsburg Empire, with the wave of human migrants from the American South that so greatly reshaped the country's northern cities: between 1916 and 1919, around half a million Blacks abandoned the rural South (to be followed by another million during the 1920s). In 1910, the Black population of Chicago was 44,000; by 1920, it had more than doubled, to 110,000. (A further 150,000 Blacks from the South were to arrive in Chicago before 1930.) Meanwhile, the number of Blacks in New York rose from 91,000 in 1910 to 152,000 in 1920.[18]

Compared to the millions of Blacks who were to abandon the South between the 1940s and 1960, this migration seems meager. (In the 1940s, again, war was the decisive factor.) Culturally speaking, however, it proved to be highly significant, because it gave rise to the figure of the urban working class or underclass Black, whereas Blacks up to that point had been largely confined to the rural South. Blacks were in fact considered to be yokels, ex-slaves, freed farmhands. White southerners regarded them as children: "Negroes are tired of being treated like children," wrote one migrant. Blacks display "a childlike helplessness in the matter of sanitation and housing," was the response of the *Chicago Tribune*.[19] In 1910, the entry for *Negro* in the renowned *Encyclopaedia Britannica* read:

> The negro would appear to stand on a lower evolutionary plane than the white man. ... Mentally the negro is inferior to the white. ... [This] remark, made after a long study of the negro in America, may be taken as generally true of the whole race:

---

18 J. R. Grossman, *Land of Hope*, p. 4.
19 Ibid., citations from pp. 37, 169.

"the negro children were sharp, intelligent and full of vivacity, but on approaching the adult period a gradual change set in. The intellect seemed to become clouded, animation giving place to a sort of lethargy, briskness yelding to indolence." ... For the rest, the mental condition is very similar to that of a child, normally good-natured and cheerful, but subject to sudden fits of emotion and passion during which he is capable of performing acts of singular atrocity.[20]

It's the same old story: again we find the indolence of the savage that the good Dr. Johnson preached against, the laziness of the Native American mocked by Parton. But it doesn't end here. Indeed, time may seem to be frozen. Consider that some eighty years later, in autumn of 1994, a Harvard academic revived the thesis of the mental inferiority of Blacks. "IQ: Is It Destiny?" roared out in bold type on the cover of the 24 October *Newsweek* (with *IQ* referring to intelligence quotient and the question mark taking the intellectual inferiority of Blacks as a given). White southern newspapers were similarly self-righteous in arguing that, since Blacks were effectively children, something perverse in their nature must have tempted them to migrate and given them illusions: a rumor even circulated that German agents had convinced them to migrate.

The whites could not understand that what really attracted the Blacks to Chicago and New York was hope: the hope of a better-paid job that was proletarian and no longer servile; the hope of bright lights, of pleasures as great as the work was hard; the hope of finding a city where they could sit down on a bus next to a white person without being beaten for it (in the southern states, Blacks had to go to the back of the bus at the time; there was even a saying – "to see the world from the back of the bus," meaning through the eyes of Black). And just as they didn't think they would have to travel separately on the bus any longer, so too did the Black migrants hope that there would be no segregation laws in Chicago, no Jim Crow laws based on the principle of "separate but equal" (Jim Crow being the generic name given to a Black). How this hope died is the great enigma of twentieth-century American history.

---

20 *Encyclopaepedia Britannica* (1911), vol. 19, pp. 344–45, cited by S. Steinberg, *The Ethnic Myth*, p. 30.

At times, police would physically prevent Blacks from boarding the trains north. That many white southerners were hostile to Black emigration is understandable. More curious, though, is the opposition of numerous southern Black churches to the exodus. Here we find the mysterious world of Black conservatism, a world that didn't just pop up with the appearance on the scene of Clarence Thomas (nominated in 1991 by then-President George Bush [the elder] as a US Supreme Court judge for having run the federal equal-opportunities commission as an effectively segregationist body) or of General Colin Powell (chief of staff during the Gulf War, nominated in 2000 by President George W. Bush [the younger] as secretary of state, who has in turn selected another Black conservative, Condoleezza Rice, as his national security adviser).

A part of Black conservativism emerged through negotiations with whites, when declaring faith in their most traditional values could lead to larger concessions. So thought, for example, Booker T. Washington. Other Blacks took a conservative stance in order to become the kind of spokespeople for their race that white people would listen. Then there was the conservative separatism of the weekly *Chicago Defender,* whose premise now forms part of the Black History Month tour. Founded in 1905 by Robert Abbott (whose initial capital amounted to twenty-five cents), the *Defender* became with the arrival of World War I the most widely read Black newspaper in America: two-thirds of its sales were outside Chicago. Abbott abhorred the terms *Negro* and *Black.* For him, Black people were simply "the race," while individual Blacks were "race men" or "race members."

The *Defender* was to play a significant role in the Great Migration, encouraging its vision of a prosperous, nonracist Chicago, attacking southern whites and denouncing lynchings. It helped diffuse the ideology of work and professional achievement – in short, of self-righteousness. On 20 October 1917, *The Defender* published the following list of dos and don'ts for the benefit of migrants from the South:

Don't use vile language in public places.
Don't act discourteously to other people in public places.
Don't allow yourself to be drawn into street brawls.
Don't use liberty as a license to do as you please.

Don't take the part of law breakers, be they men, women, or children.

Don't make yourself a public nuisance.

Don't encourage gamblers, disreputable women or men to ply their business any time or place.

Don't congregate in crowds on the streets to the disadvantage of others passing along.

Don't live in unsanitary houses, or sleep in rooms without proper ventilation.

Don't violate city ordinances, relative to health conditions.

Don't allow children to beg on the streets.

Don't allow boys to steal from or assault peddlers...

Don't be a beer can rusher or permit children to do such service.[21]

Don't abuse or violate the confidence of those who give you employment.

Don't leave your job when you have a few dollars in your pocket...[22]

In their self-righteousness, Black conservatives made the prejudices of whites their own. To the oldest Blacks in Chicago, the so-called old settlers, the new arrivals seemed dirty and uncouth, exactly as each new wave from Europe had horrified established German immigrants, or as Chicago's Jews had wanted to stop the influx of Jews from Russia. At a deeper level, the anti-Black prejudices of many Blacks were related to the images whites had of Blacks, as happened to women who internalized a male image of femininity.

Although the parallel between Blacks and women would not be emphasized until the 1960s, Myrdal had already formulated it with great clarity and farsightedness in 1944:

Negroes and women, both of whom had been under the yoke of the paternalistic system, were strongly and fatefully influenced by the Industrial Revolution. ... As in the Negro problem, most men have accepted as self-evident, until recently, the doctrine that women had inferior endowments in most of those respects which carry

---

21 Robert A. Slayton reports the slaughterhouse workers' habit of taking or being brought a pail of beer into the works for lunch; in just one lunch break, 1,065 such pails were carried to the stockyards from the forty-six bars on Whiskey Row. Cfr. R. A. Slayton, *Back of the Yards*, p. 101.

22 Cited by J. R. Grossman, *Land of Hope*, pp. 145–46.

prestige, power, and advantages in society, but that they were, at the same time, superior in some other respects. The arguments, when arguments were used, have been about the same: smaller brains, scarcity of geniuses and so on. The study of women's intelligence and personality has had broadly the same history as the one we record for Negroes. As in the case of the Negro, women themselves have been brought to believe in their inferiority of endowment. As the Negro was awarded his "place" in society, so there was a "woman's place." In both cases the rationalization was strongly believed that men, in confining them to this place, did not set against the true interest of the subordinate groups.[23]

But another factor reinforces the Black-female parallel: "As an inescapable overtone in social relations, 'race' is probably as strong as sex – even in those most emancipated American environments where apparently sex is relatively released and 'race' is suppressed. The Negro Leader, the Negro social scientist, the Negro man of art and letters is disposed to view all social, economic, political, indeed, even esthetic and philosophical issues from the Negro angle. What is more, he is expected to do so. He would seem entirely out of place if he spoke simply as a member of a community, a citizen of America or as a man of the world."[24] "The Negro genius is imprisoned in the Negro problem. ... The broad masses of Negroes are also enclosed in the prison as effectively by the restrictive expectancy of their friends as by the persecutions of their enemies."[25]

William H. Boone, a professor at Clark Atlanta University in Georgia (a Black university for children of the African American bourgeoisie), in explaining to me why female students at the university considerably outnumbered males and also why the rate of school failure among Black males was so alarmingly high, said, "[Y]oung black males are too aggressive. ... [W]e have to teach them to reduce this aggressivity which has so often proved to be self-destructive." Boone attributes such aggression to historical-cultural factors. Myrdal devoted a paragraph to the stereotype of the aggressive Black man as one of the foremost racial prejudices.

---

23 G. Myrdal, *An American Dilemma*, Appendix 5, p. 1077.
24 Ibid., pp. 27–29.
25 Ibid.

Yet where the sense of one's own identity ends and either self-segregation or a spirit of "ethnic cleansing" begins is anybody's guess. It is this imponderable that provoked the debate on political correctness that raged in the United States during the 1990s. Being politically correct means introducing into the curriculum the cultural heritage of ethnic, racial and gender minorities in place of the usual diet of DEWMs (Dead European White Males).[26] Regarding the relationship between identity and segregation, Boone compared the situation of African Americans with that of Jewish culture, a parallel frequently made by Blacks. As J. R. Grossman writes: "Like German Jews who in the late nineteenth century feared that the influx of their coreligionists from eastern Europe would endanger their marginal but substantial foothold in gentile Chicago, black Old Settlers considered themselves vulnerable to stereotyped images dominated by visibly outlandish newcomers."[27] Describing the way the weight of the Black question oppresses Blacks, Myrdal wrote, "A Jewish economist is not expected to be a specialist on Jewish labor. A Jewish sociologist is not assumed to confine himself to always studying the Ghetto. A Jewish singer is not doomed eternally to perform Jewish folk songs."[28]

Even today, the Jews are cited as an example of legitimate perpetuation of a culture's own ethnic and religious traditions. In this sense, they are used as an ambivalent paragon: while discriminated against by the goyim, they are still preferred to the Blacks because of their skin color. The Nation of Islam's anti-Semitic press coverage often uses the term *holocaust:* "600 million Blacks have died in the black holocaust of the last 6,000 years," declared one exponent of the Black Muslim movement in spring of 1994. Implicit in the comparison is the following claim: if Jews defend their culture and prefer to live among other Jews, why shouldn't we exercise our own right to separatism? The uneasy relationship between Blacks and Jews is a recurring theme in the American press. A cover story of *Time* from 31 January 1969 carries the title, "Blacks vs Jews: A Tragic Confrontation." What isn't clear is whether this theme recurs because of its persistent nature (anyone who

---

26 On the relationship between political correctness and identity politics, see the essay by Barbara Epstein, in *Beyond PC: Towards a Politics of Understanding,* edited and with an introduction by Patricia Aufderheide, Saint Paul, Minn.: Graywold Press, 1992, pp. 148–55.

27 J. R. Grossman, *Land of Hope,* p. 144.

28 G. Myrdal, *An American Dilemma,* p. 28.

has seen Harlem of late would have a hard time believing that, up until 1910, it was a Jewish neighborhood) or because of the intrinsic repetitiveness of the American press, which frequently goes beyond mawkishness.

Black separatism thus forms part of a long-standing conservative tradition. Only with the protest movements of the 1960s did it swing to the left. But the conservative side of the separatist movement is also a matter of social class division. Integration would endanger large groups of the Black bourgeoisie, because it is from the condition of apartness that these groups drew their income, jobs, prestige and power. In integrated hospitals, for example, Black doctors would be forced to bow to white physicians or would in this professional niche come under attack. The same is true for schools, where Black colleges have guaranteed a body of Black teachers and lecturers – and for the Black press, which is guaranteed some degree of editorial control in serving an exclusively Black readership. Myrdal refers to this as "the advantages of disadvantages." To take another example, the gangs who lord it over the Black ghettos of the inner cities are likewise conservative and separatist because they can hope to perpetuate their power only in a segregated city.

But separatism is also linked to a more profound sentiment, a desire to be for once part of the majority rather than of the minority. This I learned at Atlanta's Clark University when I asked what pressed students who had won prestigious scholarships to Ivy League colleges (such as Harvard or Cornell) to enroll at Clark. I was told it was because of "[t]he feeling in class of being part of a majority of black students, of representing the rule rather than the exception, to be the norm rather than deviate from it." And here lies the ambiguity: the positive values of a behavior are inextricably tied to its negative, destructive connotations.

Even more ambiguous, however, are the politics of Black conservatism. One of the things the Blacks who migrated from the southern states dreamed of was having the right to vote. Iin the South, electoral laws introduced at the end of the nineteenth century had restricted the criteria for registering to vote so that Blacks were completely banished from the ballot box and would remain so until the battle for civil rights in the 1960s. Illinois, Chicago's home state, was the birthplace of Abraham Lincoln, the Republican president who had campaigned against a South where the advocates of slavery were mostly Democrats. (It's interesting to note that America's most recent Democratic presidents have both been southerners: Carter from Georgia, Clinton from Arkansas.) For this reason, Black migrants to Chicago became adherents of the Republican Party. Following the line taken by Abbott's *Defender,* they supported the city's Republican mayor, William Hale Thompson, a man known to toss out obscene, racist remarks aimed at Catholics, who accounted for the largest number of the city's white immigrants (Irish, Poles, Slovenes and Italians) and who voted en masse for the Democrats. (Kennedy, in 1961, was the first Catholic to be elected president.[29])

Only with Franklin D. Roosevelt's New Deal – and only then with great pains and the carving out of a new "block of history" – were these political allegiances to change: as late as 1932 the Black vote still went to the Republicans, and the public works of the Tennessee Valley Authority were designed to create jobs exclusively for unemployed whites. But all of that was to change in 1934 when Arthur Mitchell, a Black Democrat from Illinois, beat outgoing Republican Oscar De Priest, who in 1929 had been the first Black from the North to enter Congress. In the 1936 elections, three-quarters of the Black vote went to Roosevelt. Yet it was not until after the events of the 1960s that a sizable body of Black Democrats would be established, from Jesse Jackson to former Mayor of Chicago Harold Washington (elected in 1983 and serving until his death in 1987) to Jesse Jackson Jr., a member of Congress from the Windy City's southern suburbs. (The Jacksons provide an example of a Black political dynasty.) And the Black Democrats would be saddled with a reputation for political corruption, just as Black Republicans had been before them. In Chicago in 1917, the *Tribune* had dubbed Oscar De Priest "the black king of vice" for his part in a gambling scandal, adopting the same tone that seventy years later would be used to describe Democratic Mayor of Washington Marion Barry, who in 1990 was found guilty of using and trafficking cocaine.

Political conservatism finds its counterpart in the divisions opened up by social conflicts. In Europe, it is difficult for us to imagine how crucial the race problem has been to the history of the American labor movement. We have already seen how scores of European immigrants were imported into the United States as

---

29 J. R. Grossman, *Land of Hope,* pp. 176–77.

strikebreakers. American bosses have always stirred up ethnic rivalry and racial hatred as a way to reduce fixed costs, cut wages and beat workers' protests. Once assimilated, however, white immigrant workers enrolled in unions and took part in strikes themselves. Erased from memory was the "original sin" of their days as scabs – both their sin and that of others. For scabs who were Black, however, it was a different story: mixed with their skin color, the mark of scab betrayal became indelible.

Because they were taken on as scab labor, the Blacks were considered a scab race in all senses of the word. So it was that racist feeling began to divide workers: white immigrants, themselves former scabs, would open fire on the Blacks who had replaced them as strikebreakers. As Bruno Cartosio says, in such conditions it became difficult "to make a distinction between the forces of white racism who were against Blacks qua Blacks, and those white forces who were fighting for their own survival against Blacks who took the form of strikebreakers, or cheap labour."[30]

In 1894, when slaughterhouse workers went on mass strike in support of the Pullman boycott, the packers brought in trainloads of Blacks from the South. In 1895, striking Italian miners in Spring Valley killed an unspecified number of Black strikebreakers.[31] In the slaughterhouse strikes of 1904, the packers took on 18,000 Blacks as scab labor (1,400 of whom arrived off a single train):[32] six years later, a mere 365 would still have jobs. In Chicago, Blacks provided the scab labor in the Teamsters strike of 1905, in the news vendors' dispute of 1912, and in the great US steelworkers' strike of 1919, when 360,000 workers downed tools for ten weeks and the bosses took on 30,000 to 40,000 Blacks to replace them.

Thus the Great Black Migration was not simply a result of a dearth of manpower or of the interruption of the influx of immigrants from Europe. Also greatly encouraging was the growth of workers' conflicts: in 1916, seventy-one strikes took place in Chicago, compared with only twenty-five the previous year. When the cleaners of Pullman's train cars went on strike in March 1916, Blacks substi-

---

30 B. Cartosio, *Lavoratori negli Stati Uniti,* p. 46.
31 William M. Tuttle Jr., *Race Riot: Chicago in the Red Summer of 1919,* New York: Atheneum, 1970, p. 113. On the problem of Black strikebreakers, see the chapter "Labor Conflict and Racial Violence," pp. 109–56.
32 Ibid., p. 117.

tuted for them. The same year, all a southern Black had to do to get a job at the International Harvester company (ex-McCormick) was cross the picket line.

In 1916, a Black preacher from the South Side of Chicago recruited three hundred Black women in a single night to break a hotel workers' strike. The big packing firms provided handsome funding for Black politicians and churches. During the 1920s, the bishop of Chicago's African Methodist Episcopal Church, Archibald Carey, declared that "the interest of my people lies with the wealth of the nation and with the class of white people who control it": at the beginning of the century, the Armours and Swifts had saved his chapel. During the last great stockyards strike of 1921, Blacks were again taken on in tens of thousands, only this time they were employed for good: the packers had decided to arm themselves once and for all against strikes and against the white unions.[33]

Another aspect of the vicious cycle that for Myrdal characterized the Black question was thus reintroduced in the ambit of worker relations: "White prejudice and discrimination keep the Negro low in standards of living, health, education, manners and morals. This in its turn, gives support to white prejudice."[34] (Myrdal himself considered this situation a motive for optimism: if vice was circular, so too might be virtue, and the reform of one partial aspect of the problem might have positive repercussions on other aspects; thus, if racial prejudice diminished slightly, the social conditions of Blacks would improve, which in turn, by a reciprocal interaction, would further reduce prejudice.)

In terms of worker relations, the vicious cycle meant that Blacks who allowed themselves to be taken on as scab labor out of economic necessity would reinforce the racial prejudices of the unions, which would give vent to their own segregationist tendencies. That is what happened with the American Federation of Labor, whose president, Samuel Gompers, had during the First World War become (in the minds of Blacks) the symbol of the unions' racism, a man famous for saying in 1901 that the Federation "does not necessarily proclaim that the social barriers

---

33 All these facts are reported in J. R. Grossman, *Land of Hope* , ch. 8, "The White Man's Union," pp. 208–45.
34 G. Myrdal, *An American Dilemma*, p. 75.

which exist between the whites and blacks could or should be obliterated."[35] Out
of 110 unions in Chicago affiliated with the AFL in 1919, thirty-six refused to allow
Blacks to join their sections, while thirteen of the fifteen major unions other than
the AFL discriminated against Blacks. This discrimination led to Black hostility
against unions, with the result that any attempts at racial integration on their part
were doomed to failure. This spiral of "war in the bosom of the people" was to be
interrupted in 1935 with the founding of the Committee for Industrial Organizations (CIO) by John L. Lewis and with the great strikes of 1936, but it left its mark
on the American union movement and has remained one of the causes of its enfee-
blement.

The sheer quantity of intellectual resources America has dedicated to the Black
question is truly staggering. As Myrdal wrote, "The intellectual energy spent on
the Negro problem in America would, if concentrated in a single direction, have
moved mountains."[36] But this mine of intelligence has been in vain, as Americans
continue to obsess over the Black problem; the only hope of solving it "is that
whites get other worries to keep their minds off the Negro,"[37] as one commenta-
tor, Frank Tannenbaum, responded ironically.

America has swept the Black question under the carpet, among other ways, in
its manner of recounting the great race riots that punctuated its twentieth-century
history, mostly during the summers. The first of these bloody riots in the northern
industrial cities occurred in 1917, in East St. Louis. As myth has it, the riot was the
inevitable result of suppressed rage that exploded after a petty insult – the same
type of insult that supposedly ignited a similar, though equally mysterious, incident in Santa Barbara. The rage of the Black ghettos is compared to lava from a
volcano, always on the point of erupting, endangering the safety and well-being of
whites. This is what happened in the case of the Los Angeles riots of April 1992, at-

---

35 Letter from Samuel Gompers to the press, 19 April 1901, AFL correspondence file, Washington,
    D.C., cited in Marc Karson and Ronald Radosh, "The American Federation of Labor and the Negro
    Worker" (1894–1949), in Julius Jacobson, ed., *The Negro and the American Labor Movement*, New
    York: Doubleday Anchor, 1968, p. 158.
36 Gunnar Myrdal, *Value in Social Theory*, New York: Harpers, 1958, p. 90.
37 Ibid., p. 96.

tributed solely to the fact that several white policemen had been absolved of savagely beating a Black man.

Today, unused factory buildings and abandoned kiosks mark the area of the Chicago beach that on 27 July 1919 saw the outbreak of one of the first Black uprisings to occur in America's industrial centers. The popular version of this uprising runs as follows: It was a sweltering hot day, and the heat had sent Chicagoans pouring onto the shores of Lake Michigan. In the South Side, a seventeen-year-old Black named Edward Williams was stoned to death on the beach near Twenty-Seventh Street for having passed the invisible waterline there to keep Black bathers away from white girls. Subsequent clashes broke out between Blacks and whites all over the South Side of Chicago. The fighting lasted four days, with things only really cooling down on 8 August thanks to the combined intervention of a torrential downpour and the forces of the National Guard: in all, thirty-eight people were killed (twenty-three Blacks, fifteen whites) and 537 injured. There were scores of arrests, and more than a thousand lost their homes.

To put it mildly, "the situation was a little more complex than that."[38] In the period leading up to that time, between 1917 and 1919, Chicago's white gangs had firebombed twenty-four houses owned by Blacks who had dared to move into white neighborhoods. The end of hostilities in Europe in 1919 aggravated the problem. Four million soldiers were demobilized, while 9 million workers who had been employed in the war effort needed to be returned to their old jobs. As a result, the packers, who had prospered during the war years, with tinned meat and food rations, fired 10,000 Black stockyard workers. Added to them were 200,000 Black war veterans, who were a burden both on the property market (given the lack of housing) and on the labor market. In April 1919, the Chicago Association of Commerce sent the following telegram to southern chambers of commerce: "Are you in need of Negro Labor? Large surplus here, both returned soldiers and civilian Negroes, ready to go work."[39] When speaking about the Chicago uprising, historians neglect to mention that twenty-five additional Black uprisings broke out in cities throughout America in that same summer. Adding another explosive element to the powder keg in Chicago was the re-election, thanks to overwhelming

---

38 For a detailed description of the riot, see W. M. Tuttle Jr., *Race Riot,* in particular pp. 3–66.
39 Ibid., p. 131.

Black support, of Republican Mayor William Hale Thompson, a figure hated by white Catholics of European origin.

A publication of the time ran an article entitled, "An Epidemic of Strikes in Chicago," which stated that "[m]ore strikes and lockouts accompany the mid-summer heat than were ever known before at any one time."[40] For all of June and July 1919, a series of wildcat strikes paralyzed the slaughterhouses. In the first days of July, the Contractors Association locked workers out of 100,000 building sites. Moreover, it was in Chicago on 20 July that the national union committee authorized the vote that gave the go-ahead for the great national steelworkers' strike to commence on 22 September, a strike that was to last ten weeks, until 8 January 1920. For the weekend of the Chicago uprising, strikes involving some 36,000 workers had been scheduled, including all the city's public transportation employees. By the end of July, some 250,000 workers were either on strike or locked out in Chicago.

When the initial clashes broke out, the governor of Illinois delayed sending in the National Guard (as had happened in St. Louis in 1917). During the riot, the big packers, to beat white strikers and stir up disorder, sent truckloads of meat and other foodstuffs to feed the Blacks. Of all the clashes, 41 percent took place in the Back of the Yards neighborhood, which the Blacks normally crossed only to go to work. By 7 August, they were being escorted through the gates by the police.[41]

Perhaps the accusation made by the union newspaper *New Majority* – that the actions of the packing companies had been the cause of the race riots – was in fact false. Perhaps there never has been a capitalist plan to derail the class struggle by turning it into a race war. But certainly it was the logic of capital itself, the logic of keeping wages as low as possible, of suppressing protests and strikes and reducing human costs, that provoked and indeed exploited the cycle of white racism and Black scab labor, race riots and segregation. It is no mere coincidence that that summer, the so-called Red Summer of 1919, which marked a heavy defeat for the US labor movement, also saw the hopes of countless southern Blacks who had migrated north go up in smoke, in a spiral of racial hatred that was to lead to Chicago

---

40 Graham Taylor, "An Epidemic of Strikes in Chicago," *The Survey*, 2 August 1919, vol. 42, pp. 645–46, cited in Brecher, *Strike!*, p 117.
41 W. M. Tuttle Jr., *Race Riot*, pp. 140–41.

becoming the most segregated city in the country. Who would call Chicago a land of hope nowadays?

The events that occurred in Chicago in the summer of 1919 triggered a process now at work in other parts of the world where class conflict is again being derailed, channeled, translated into racial or ethnic tensions – tensions through which race or ethnicity has been rediscovered or imagined *after* the industrial revolution, after modernization and capitalist transformation. Far from being a quaintly Yankee summer pastime, race riots of the Chicago type are what await us in Europe's own future.

18

Allah on Lake Michigan

What Geneva is to Calvinists, Chicago is to America's Black Muslims. Deep in Chicago's South Side, on Seventy-Ninth and South Cottage Grove Avenue, like a sign for gas, the insignia of a sickle moon curled around a five-point star rises from the roof of the mosque built in 1934 by the sect's founder and new prophet, Elijah Muhammad. The mosque has its own Salaam restaurant, bakery and parking lot. It is here in Chicago that the Nation of Islam (NOI) holds its annual convention, which, according to its organizers, brings together some 12,000 of the faithful, who pay thirty to fifty dollars each to hear the pronouncements of their leader, Louis Farrakhan.

No one knows for sure just how many Black Muslims there are in the United States – only that the figure of 100,000 paraded by the movement's adepts is grossly exaggerated. The political muscle of the Nation of Islam, however, is considerable. On 5 August 1995, the Million Man March in Washington, D.C., made world news headlines. Though less controversial, the Million Family March on 16 October attracted an equally impressive crowd. No Black politician will be taken seriously by his own constituency without the approval of the Black Muslims, as Jesse Jackson knows only too well. In 1984, Jackson had to secure the movement's support before he could run in the US presidential primaries. He paid dearly for that support by arousing Jewish hostility because of the NOI's ferocious anti-Semitism, laid out in a pamphlet, *The Secret Relationship between Blacks and Jews,* published in 1991 by its Department of Historical Studies.

The Black Muslims derive their political weight from the fact that they are an organized and highly disciplined force with an iron-solid ideology and their own business interests. The movement publishes a fortnightly newspaper, *Final Call* (circulation 400,000), and also runs a school for nurses, its own chain of hospitals, a university (the University of Islam) and a military training course for its (not exactly) small army of bodyguards, the Fruit of Islam. In all this, the Nation of Islam resembles other American religious movements that are at once a faith, a business, a political lobby and, at times, even a gang: religions that hold not synods or councils but conventions, like those for dentists or commercial salespeople. In the same way, the Nation of Islam is willing to hire out its paramilitary wing as private security and has in the last few years obtained several public building security contracts. The sect has set up four separate security companies, including the NOI Security Agency, that have won contracts to guard housing projects in the District of Columbia, Pittsburgh, Philadelphia, LA, Brooklyn and Chicago, guaranteeing itself within the space of only a few years a turnover of $20 million, but also getting into financial and judicial trouble because of the excessive passion of Black Muslim agents for luxury cars and for the projects' young female inhabitants.[1]

While the Nation of Islam proselytizes in the most impoverished Black ghettos and among the prison population in the name of the "race war," its leader, Farrakhan, lives in an integrated middle-class residential zone, goes everywhere surrounded by gorilla henchmen and loves to show off by giving violin concerts. A single episode suffices to delineate this character: Louis Farrakhan (real name Louis Wolcott), after first defining Judaism as "a gutter religion," gave (in response to accusations of anti-Semitism) a public recital of pieces by the (Jewish) composer Mendelssohn.

For more than thirty years, Farrakhan has been suspected of having ordered the 1965 assassination of Malcolm X, an accusation he has never really denied and has even reinforced through pronouncements such as, "It was Malcolm's work that made each of us a potential killer. When Malcolm stepped over that line, his

---

1   From a series published in the *New York Times* in March 1994 and on 13 September 1996. See also *Washington Post*, 2 September 1996.

death was inescapable." Moreover, when one of the killers condemned for Malcolm X's murder – a certain Muhammad Abdul Aziz (who in the sixties called himself 3X Butler) – was released from prison in 1988, Farrakhan immediately made him chief of security for NOI's Harlem mosque, once headed by the Civil Rights leader himself.[2] Two Black youths who frequented this mosque during the 1980s, Richard (Terminator) X and Chuck D, would go on to form the world-famous rap group Public Enemy.[3] Farrakhan, who has for years been battling cancer, behaves like the televangelists of the Moral Majority who supported Reagan during the 1980s, while his Nation of Islam continues to call for repression, law and order.

The Nation of Islam could therefore well be just another of those numerous cocktails of low cunning and gullibility, roguery and small-time delinquency, profiteering and desire for mutual aid that make up modernity's exasperated attempt to assuage individual desperation. The enigma remains, however. How is it that Black folk from the South, urbanized in this city of railroads, slaughterhouses and disassembly lines, came to seek new hope, a new meaning for their lives and a means of enfranchisement, by converting to Islam (and a decidedly curious form of Islam at that)? How is it that Chicago has come from being the land of hope to instead being the North American Mecca for the country's Blacks? What is Allah doing on the frozen shores of Lake Michigan? And why, in the urban ghettos of Philadelphia and Detroit during the 1950s and 1960s, did kneeling in prayer to Allah seem to many Blacks to be a vital weapon in the struggle for liberation? How did that austere, pedantic Black Muslim leader Malcolm X (who didn't smoke, drink, gamble or eat pork and who disapproved of mixed sexual relations between Blacks and whites – or indeed of any sexual relations outside of wedlock) become one of the spiritual guides of the transgressive, immoralist European student movement of the 1960s? Why have so many inhabitants of the *inner cities* given their support to the NOI's plan to transform the urban gangs into armies of Allah? What on earth was one American ex-boxing champion (Muhammad Ali, born

---

2 *New York Times*, 31 March 1998.
3 Gilles Kepel, *À l'ouest d'Allah*, Paris: Seuil, 1994. Eng. trans. *Allah in the West: Islamic Movements in America and in Europe*, Stanford, Calif.: Stanford University Press, 1997, ch. 2, "Islam to the Sound of Rap."

Cassius Clay) doing in Iran kneeling at the tomb of the Ayatollah Khomeni – or another (Mike Tyson) doing hastening to the mosque immediately after being discharged from prison?

Legend would have it that the Nation of Islam was founded in 1931 in Detroit by one Wallace T. Fard, who had arrived in the United States direct from Mecca the previous year. For Black Muslims, Fard was an incarnation of Allah: "Posing as seller of silks," he "was half black and half white ... to enable him to be accepted by the black people in America, and to lead them, while at the same time he was enabled to move undiscovered among the white people, so that he could understand and judge the enemy of the blacks."[4] Fard's birthday is to this day celebrated by the faithful as a day of salvation. He founded Mosque Number 1 in Detroit, where he taught the word to Elijah Muhammad (1897–1975), the son of ex-slaves from Georgia, whose original name was Elijah Poole. Fard mysteriously disappeared shortly afterward (the history of the Nation of Islam is riddled with such disappearances), and Elijah Muhammad moved to Chicago, where in 1932 he built Mosque Number 2, from then on the sect's spiritual center.

The sect more or less survived until the 1950s when, according to Malcolm X, it had fewer than one thousand members. Then, thanks to the efforts of Malcolm X, the Nation of Islam's mosques began to multiply as the number of its followers grew, attracting national attention. In 1960, Eric Lincoln published his study *The Black Muslims in America,* in which the term *Black Muslim* appeared for the first time. Then Malcolm X broke with his mentor, Elijah Muhammad, distanced himself from the movement and was assassinated. Years later, in 1975, after the death of Elijah Muhammad, the sect became split down the middle: Elijah's son, the Imam W. Deen Muhammad, led the moderate wing, preaching a return to the doctrine of orthodox Islam; Farrakhan headed another, more extremist wing, which was to become predominant. Not until 2000 did W. Deen Muhammad and Farrakhan publicly reconcile.[5]

The power of the Nation of Islam comes in fact from the radicalism of the race war that it promotes and sustains, at least in its rhetoric. The movement's doctrine is

---

4   Malcolm X, *Autobiography*, p. 193.
5   *New York Times*, 2 February 2000.

simple and in a way represents an experiential truth: Christian religion is false; hell is right here on Earth, as far as Blacks are concerned – not in some afterlife of the soul. Hell is here in our society, and white people are its demons. And who would deny that white people have turned the Black person's life into a hell on Earth, first through slavery, then through lynchings and Jim Crow laws and through the misery and abjection imposed on Blacks? To the ears of a Black inmate in Angola penitentiary in Louisiana – one of the toughest, most violent prisons on the planet – or to an inhabitant of East St. Louis or north Philadelphia, the phrase "hell is here on earth for the black man and the white men are its demons" is a revelation that contains a blinding, unassailable truth. In the way that many of us use language, the idea that "hell is here on earth" would be taken as a metaphor, just as for a racist, "L'enfer, c'est les autres," in Sartre's words. For the Nation of Islam and its cosmogony, this phrase is literal.

Here, then, is the Black Muslims' cosmogony, as summarized by Malcolm X. After the moon broke away from the Earth, the first human beings on the planet, who were people of color, founded the holy city of Mecca. Among this Negro people were twenty-four sages. One of these sages, in conflict with the others, founded the Negro tribe of Shabaz, a particularly powerful group from whom descended the so-called American Negro. "About sixty-six hundred years ago, when seventy percent of the people were satisfied, and thirty percent were dissatisfied, among the dissatisfied was born a Mr. Yacub." Yacub became a scientist and a preacher of heretical doctrines in Mecca, and eventually he and his 59,999 followers were exiled to the island of Patmos (where St. John the apostle was to write his Book of Revelation thousands of years later). Outraged by his exile, Yacub decided to create a race of white people by cunning genetic selection: "The humans resulting, he knew, would be, as they became lighter, and weaker, progressively also more susceptible to wickedness and evil. And in this way finally he would achieve the intended bleached-out white race of devils."

The selection of a white race from the original Black matrix was a process that required centuries, at the end of which, "On the island of Patmos was nothing but these blond, pale-skinned, cold-blue-eyed devils – savages, nude and shameless; hairy, like animals, they walked on all fours and they lived in trees." After a further period of six hundred years, this race returned among the original Blacks, and within the space of six months, "through telling lies that set the black men fighting among each other, this devil race had turned what had been a peaceful heaven on earth into a hell torn by quarreling and fighting."[6] But after six thousand years, during which time Yakub's white race would have come to dominate the world, according to the prophecy, the original Black race would have given birth to a man of infinite wisdom, knowledge and power. This would naturally have been Elijah Muhammad.

It would be a mistake to simply smile knowingly at the enormities with which this saga is woven – and not only because there are tens of thousands of people who believe in it, though that alone would be sufficient reason. After all, who are we to feel superior to such beliefs when every year thousands of paralytic Catholics hoping for a miracle make the pilgrimage to Lourdes to duck themselves in a French bathtub?

From its ghetto origins, this sect has honed to perfection one of modern ideology's most subtle objectives: to rewrite history as a weapon for creating it. In this sense, it has put into practice Dewey's thesis: "The writing of history is itself an historical event. It is something which happens and which in its occurrence has existential consequences. ... The Marxian conception of the part played in the past by forces of production in determining property relations and of the role of class struggle in social life has itself ... increased the significance of class struggle."[7] In its own way, this saga has effected a Copernican revolution. As Alessandro Portelli writes, "By claiming that whites are in fact the creatures of Blacks, the story of Yacub undeniably has the result of placing Blacks at the centre of history." It was in precisely this way that Malcolm X, by spreading the word of an implausible fairytale, was able to obtain a very real effect, "contributing more than anyone else to transforming the way history is studied. If nowadays one can no longer maintain that Blacks have no history, no past,"[8] it is thanks to Malcolm X and, paradoxically, to the myth of Yacub.

---

6 Quotations taken from Malcolm X, *Autobiography*, pp. 190–92.
7 J. Dewey, *Logic*, pp. 297–98.
8 Alessandro Portelli, *La linea del colore: Saggi sulla cultura afroamericana*, Rome: Manifestolibri, 1994, ch. "Malcolm X e l'uso della storia" (pp. 121–31).

The story of Yacub contains another highly modern element: in it, the rewriting of history takes the form of religious revelation, in many ways similar to the revelations of America's modern Christian sects. The thesis that the Blacks "constitute the lost and recovered nation of Islam here in the desert of North America" is almost identical to the revelation of the prophet Mormon, conveyed to Joseph Smith in the nineteenth century by the angel Moroni. After abandoning the fallen tower of Babel, the Lamanites, a tribe of Israel that had been "lost and then recovered," would have crossed the Atlantic to become the progenitors of the American Indians. The reincarnation of Allah in the United States is in line with the Mormon tradition, for whom Christ will appear in America after the resurrection. And nobody in the United States dares mock a church that controls the entire state of Utah and constitutes a formidable business and financial empire in its own right. Deeply American is the idea that identity has been "lost and then recovered," the almost pathetic claim to a supposedly forgotten continuity that is sunk in the seas of oblivion before being miraculously saved by the tide of memory. This sense of continuity, however imaginary it may be, is what saves you; it allows you to go from being an isolated individual arbitrarily plopped down on this vast continent to being part of a human, social and religious community ignored not because it didn't exist, but because its existence has been concealed.

The second, less than Islamic, theme of the Nation of Islam's credo is the advent. According to the Yacub story, the white domination of the past six thousand years has finally reached its end, and the arrival of Elijah Muhammad marks the advent of the reign of the Blacks. The advent is a theme common to many Christian sects. The Mormons themselves see their community as the city of Zion, supposedly ordered by Christ to be founded in the New World during "the last days of creation"; the Mormons go so far as to call themselves the Church of Jesus Christ of Latter Day Saints. In fact, many Adventist churches in the United States forecast the imminent end of the world and the ensuing advent of God's kingdom on earth. The first of the Adventist leaders, William Miller, announced that the world would end on 21 March 1844. When that day arrived, the sun came up and the world continued to turn – but the Adventists didn't lose faith. They shifted the big day to 22 October, followed by further postponements. Not all Adventists are extremists such as David Koresh, who believed he was the reincarnation of the

Lamb of God and who perished, together with around a hundred followers, after setting fire to the farmhouse they occupied in Waco, Texas, in April 1993. Nor are they all as ingenuous as the thousands of Chicago Koreans who barricaded themselves inside their church in October 1992 and waited a whole day and night for the world to end, only to burst into collective tears when they realized they would have to go on living another day. In the United States, the Seventh Day Adventist Church alone controls 44 publishing houses, 14 colleges, 437 secondary schools and 4,411 primary schools and funds 437 hospitals and 2,435 radio stations.[9] Fanatics they may be, but they have a head for business and organization.

Belief in the advent is thus deeply personal and goes beyond the normal bounds of religion – whether Christian or Islamic – attaching itself to that notion of positive thinking, whereby every thesis must be instantly demonstrable; assigning to every act of sacrifice a tangible, material redress. The advent in fact terrestrializes, or grounds, the kingdom of heaven, shifting the whole realm of the beyond to the here-and-now. Through it, paradise and God's kingdom are brought down to Earth, just as the Nation of Islam places hell on Earth. Adventism transfers the question of the sense and meaning of our lives from sacred to profane history, from the realm of immaterial souls to the world of individual bodies, from beyond the end of time to the present moment. From this derives the Adventist faith – continually reiterated, despite all proofs to the contrary – in the rapture: the idea that on a given date in the not-too-distant future, at hour X on day Y of year Z, the world will come to an end. Adventism radicalizes to the extreme the Calvinist notion of predestination, since those who placidly await the end of the world are the Lord's elect, with a guaranteed place in his heavenly kingdom. Those who believe in the advent effectively nail themselves to the cross, and they demand as they do so that Augustine's "City of God" be built today, this minute and, if possible, apart from the "city of man."

Here we enter into one of the most intricate meanders of the American labyrinth, the indissoluble bond between religious fanaticism and mental positivism. According to current opinion, a positivist mentality denotes atheism and skepticism:

---

9 Frank S. Mead, *Handbook of Denominations in the United States* (1961), Nashville: Abingdon Press, 1990, pp. 19–20.

a positivist is a materialist who believes only in facts, whereas a religious person – at the opposite end – is spiritualist and fideistic. In reality, however, positivism and fideism have been bedfellows since the beginnings of the modern age, since the time of Auguste Comte, in fact: Someone who reasons in a "positive way" might well also be a religious fundamentalist. To make this leap from positive fact to faith, it is enough to consider the truth of revelation a *fact* and to follow the "instructions" contained in the holy book, just as you would follow the manual for operating a VCR. This is where the *literal* (no longer metaphorical) interpretation of religious affirmations comes into play: this is how "hell on earth" or the "white devil" are taken at face value by the Nation of Islam, for example, or how Protestant sects interpret certain biblical passages to the letter. According to a 1983 Gallup poll, 62 percent of Americans had "no doubts" that Jesus would return to Earth, while a 1980 survey found that 40 percent of the American population considered the Bible to be the "actual word of God ... to be taken literally word for word." A 1988 survey, with questions formulated somewhat differently, placed the number of true believers at a more modest 31 percent – 61 million Americans over the age of nineteen – who believe word for word what the Bible says, up to the terrifying, baroque imagery of the Apocalypse in St. John's Book of Revelation.[10]

Another bond between positivist thinking and religious fundamentalism comes from the immense rhetorical power of numbers in the United States. The mass media exploit the appeal of a diverse array of numeric rhetorical figures, from *repetition* ("In just twelve days with only twelve applications you can take twelve years off your face") to *enumeration* ("One exceptional offer, two lifestyles, three advantages") to *double meaning* ("$99 for ninety-nine days' travel," "620 tons at 620 miles per hour"). A number is never just a number, but is always a linguistic tool that conceals hidden connotations.[11]

---

10 Paul Boyer, *When Time Shall Be No More: Prophecy Belief in Modern American Culture,* Cambridge, Mass.: Harvard University Press, 1992, p. 2. Boyer's book is useful for understanding the modernity of apocalyptic thought in the United States today.

11 Examples taken from an article by Jacques Durand, "Rhétorique du nombre," in the monographic issue *Recherches Rhetoriques* of the review *Communications*, directed by Roland Barthes, 1970, no. 16, pp. 125–32.

In the United States, in fact, a number is something more still. Werner Sombart was quick to notice the all-American admiration "for every large quantity that is measurable or weighable, whether it be the number of inhabitants of a city, the number of parcels transported, the speed of railway trains, the height of a monument, the width of a river, the frequency of suicides." The reason, he reckoned, was that "[t]he estimation of size in terms of numbers has been able to take root in man's heart only through the medium of money as employed by capitalism ... The huge dimensions of the American continent have certainly encouraged this characteristic, but *the feeling for numbers had first of all to be awakened.*"[12] Even now, more than ninety years on, anyone who has lived in the United States for any length of time will recognize the extraordinary power of numbers that pervades its written, oral and visual communications. The number gives a thesis the stamp of truth: reduced to a numerical value, the point becomes positive, verifiable: *a number is a fact*. Only this numeric truth can be used with absolute nonchalance, because its function is not to indicate *which number* it is, but simply *to be* a number.

At this stage, the number's function is no longer arithmetical but *cabalistic* and religious: For Christian sects, 666 is the Number of the Beast. In the minds of Black Muslims, Yacub had 59,999 followers; 6,600 years ago (and not 7,400 or 5,200), a nice round 70 percent (not a messy 68 percent) of the original humans, the Blacks, were satisfied; 30 percent (not a prosaic 34 percent) were not. Malcolm X brought the same rhetorical function into play when he said, "The devil has only thirty-six degrees of knowledge – known as Masonry," whereas Allah "has 360 degrees of knowledge," "the sum total of knowledge."[13] After *literal interpretation,* the number is the second bridge between positivism and fundamentalism. What connects these two aspects is that the number also expects to be taken literally: it is the literal become sign.

Yacub, let's not forget, was also a scientist – a "mad scientist," in fact. So it is that positive thinking and superstition become even more profoundly intertwined. In Elijah Muhammad's original story, it was more than six-and-a-half thousand years ago that Yakub "learned of his future from playing with steel. ... In this he saw an

12 W. Sombart, *Why Is There No Socialism in the United States?*, p. 14.
13 Malcolm X, *Autobiography*, p. 183.

unlikely human being, made to attract others, who could with the knowledge of tricks and lies, rule the original black man."[14] The origins of hell are science and technology, the same science and technology that created the *white devil*.

This contamination of science and demonology is not exclusive to the Nation of Islam nor to Chicago. As Mike Davis notes: "In fact, the fate of science in Los Angeles exemplifies the role reversal between practical reason and what Disneyites call 'imagineering.' Where one might have expected the presence of the world's largest scientific and engineering community to cultivate a regional enlightenment, science has consorted instead with pulp fiction, vulgar psychology, and even satanism to create yet another layer of California cultdom."[15] The relationship between science, religion and magic turns out be more enigmatic than we thought.

While science exerts an undisputed hegemony over modern societies, those societies remain completely ignorant of scientific procedure. Furthermore, the growth of scientific knowledge and the ongoing industrialization of life are bound to lead only to more ignorance. In the gestures of everyday life, not only do we fail to proceed scientifically, but we increasingly ignore how the objects we use – objects considered indispensable – actually function. How is it that what appears to be a plastic bone perforated with holes can transmit sounds over long distances? How is it that total darkness can replace light at the flick of a switch? "I don't know," most of us reply, "and I'm not interested in knowing, either. It's enough that somebody knows." The more sophisticated technological products become, the more our ignorance grows: calculators, for example, have made knowing how to calculate a thing of the past, resulting in a return to arithmetic innumeracy.

For the overwhelming majority of people, science and the products of technology work like *magic*. This kind of *magic* nowadays generally refers to any process in which the effort required to make a gesture is massively disproportional to the gesture's result: it doesn't take much effort to pronounce two words, for example, but if these words happen to be "open sesame," they're enough to move the huge boulder from the entrance of Ali Baba's cave. The same is true of intoning magic

---

14 Elijah Muhammad, *Message to the Blackman in America*, Chicago: Mosque of Islam Number 2, ch. 55, pars. 67, 68.

15 M. Davis, *City of Quartz*, p. 23.

formulas to turn base metals into gold. It is in this sense that society regards science as a kind of magic – whether white magic, of great benefit to humanity; or black magic, a form of wizardry capable of summoning ecological catastrophe or war. In the latter case, scientists are the wicked wizards, or are simply madmen like Yacub.[16]

What is more, if scientific truth represents society's official truth even when society itself ignores the rational procedures of science, then society must simply *believe* that science speaks the truth. The point is that *science is a form of belief;* or rather that modern society's faith is in science. It follows, therefore, that the determinism of scientific prediction is no longer distinguished from religious prophecy. This is why social prophecy in the United States often appears under the guise of scientific prediction, whereas *utopia* becomes science fiction, as in Edward Bellamy's classic *Looking Backward* (1897), which became the gospel of the so-called New Apostles of American socialism.

In the overlapping of prediction and prophecy, the iron determination of mechanical laws increasingly comes to resemble the fatal predetermination of astrology, whereas predestination mapped out in the stars increasingly begins to stand for social destiny. In 1952–53, in fact, Theodor Adorno, cofounder of the Frankfurt School, devoted his time to studying the *Los Angeles Times* astrology column:

> In as much as the social system is the "fate" of most individuals independent of their will and interest, it is projected upon the stars in order thus to obtain a higher degree of dignity and justification in which the individuals hope to participate themselves. At the same time, the idea that the stars, if one reads them correctly, offer some advice mitigates the very same fear of the inexorability of social processes the stargazer himself creates. This phase of astrology's own ambivalence is exploited by the "rational" side of the column. The aid and comfort given by the merciless stars is tantamount to the idea that only he who behaves rationally ... has any chance of doing justice to the irrational contradictory requirements of the existent by adjustment. Thus, the discrepancy between the rational and the irrational aspects of the column is expressive of a tension inherent in social reality itself. "To be rational" means not

---

16 I take up this argument from my essay "L'Abysso non sbadiglia più," published in the collective volume *Gli ordini del caos*, Rome: Manifestolibri, 1991, pp. 22–24.

questioning irrational conditions, but to make the best of them from the viewpoint of one's private interests.[17]

When scientific prediction no longer distinguishes itself from religious prophecy, when racial determinism becomes mixed with astrological destiny and the inexorability of divine providence, then the religious word acquires that force of undeniable, positive certitude that for positivists characterizes scientific discourse. One believes in the second coming of Christ in the same way one believes in Maxwell's equations; one believes in the number of the beast (666) as in Avogadro's number (6.023×10^{23}). This explains the creationists' power in the United States, as well as their recurrent attempts to prohibit the teaching of Darwinian theory in schools, since the biblical episode and evolutionism are viewed as two competing *scientific theories,* one of which must be false (with the biblical episode recounting how God created the Earth some 5,000 years ago and evolutionism arguing that the species evolved over millions of years).

This is why many Christian fundamentalists remove their children from schools: to keep them from learning about Darwinism. In this light, and in a context where Texans boast of being so undisciplined "that they don't even obey the laws of universal gravity" (to allow ourselves a smile for a moment) – the story of the mad scientist Yacub and his 6,600 years no longer appears so ridiculous.

Okay, you might say, but no one could seriously believe that there was steel six thousand years ago, that the Blacks built Mecca and so on. Everything has a limit, even credulity.

What difference lies between being ready to believe the incredible and simply being open-minded? Being "open-minded," in fact, is a fundamental part of "positive thinking": it means being able to accept the new, to seize money-making opportunities, not to exclude any hypothesis, however far-fetched. Thirty years ago, would it have been possible to imagine seeing pedestrians shouting and muttering to themselves, inveighing against the wind, barking into their coat collar as they

---

17 Theodor W. Adorno, *The Stars Down to Earth and Other Essays on the Irrational in Culture,* London: Routledge, 1994.

ambled along the street – without thinking they were escaped lunatics? Nowadays, we know these people are simply talking on cell phones.

The line between credulity and open-mindedness is in fact very thin: reality subjects our powers of reason to a grueling course of assault every day. I listened at dinner one evening as a white liberal thirty-something friend, a good father and scrupulous payer of his mortgage installments, told me in all seriousness that AIDS was in fact a white conspiracy to destroy the Black race (as was crack), driving young Blacks to poverty and petty crime; it was all a way of keeping Blacks under the thumb of white domination. In expressing these sentiments, my friend was in fact endorsing a thesis fairly widespread among Blacks, not just in the Nation of Islam but throughout America's inner cities, where it was more commonly known as The Plan. As Rickey, a Black Chicago youth, told sociologist Loïc Wacquant:

> An' I feel like from 1980 before the drugs scene really, really *hit* – don't git me wrong! Drugs were out there, but there was *nothing near* like it was now. An' I feel man … it was like a *master plan*, ya know. We as people – ya know, black people – we couldn't do nothin' but excel and continue to move forward, ya know what I'm sayin', but when this drug hit us, man! It was like "BOOM": tha' set us back 50 years.[18]

Indeed, *The Conspiracy: Youth Gangs, Violence and Drugs* was the title of a Farrakhan speech sold on cassette. And my friend, seeing my incredulity, resorted to the rationalist "black box" argument: you don't know what happens in the box, but by looking at what goes in and what comes out, you try to find the simplest mechanism to explain how the input is transformed into the output. He reminded me that the gap between Black and white incomes had been diminishing up until 1978, before the spread of AIDS and crack, but from that point on, the gap had begun to widen again. He even cited statistics in support of his argument. Although it still seemed somewhat harebrained, slowly this "urban legend," which had at first made me laugh, began to acquire a degree of plausibility.

But the real doubts concerning this matter – and indeed concerning the question of credulity in general – began to arise when the American press revealed in

---

18 Loïc Wacquant, "Inside 'The Zone,'" in P. Bourdieu et al., *The Weight of the World*, p. 165.

1993 that for decades the army had been carrying out experiments on hundreds of thousands of unknowing human guinea pigs, allegations that were repeated (to no greater effect) in the summer of 1997.[19] During the 1950s and 1960s, the Joint Chiefs of Staff had dispatched entire divisions of conscripts into nuclear test zones to see "what the effects would be" of radiation. The Nazis had of course already carried out experiments on human beings, both on foreigners and on their own prisoners, particularly Jews and gypsies. But that was a dictatorship in which barbarism ruled. Here the situation was altogether different; here a government democratically elected by its own citizens was performing experiments on its electorate. Army laboratories had even let chemical agents and bacteriological germs loose in the New York subway just to see "what the effects would be" on hundreds or thousands of unwitting civilians.

Something blackly humorous lies in the fact that, while deadly radiation was secretly being leaked around,

> In schools they held practice drills for nuclear attack, teaching the students to duck and cover, to lie down on the floor with their heads under their desks in case of a nuclear explosion. Meanwhile their parents were buying nuclear shelters to install in the yard. Cities began to fill up with yellow and black signposts indicating the presence of shelters in public buildings. Manuals were published on how to survive an atomic attack.[20]

When one considers that period, with people completely unaware of the tumors being cultivated in their bodies, the way the authorities led the public down the garden path seems almost diabolical; and the blind trust of the people in their government seems pathetic. It was a trust whereby, as Bruno Cartesio writes, even

> the image of the mushroom became increasingly popular. From the Southwestern states tourists, together with pictures showing the area's great natural beauty, sent their relatives postcards immortalizing the nuclear test shots that had been carried

---

19 For example, in the *New York Times* of 6, 17 and 25 December 1993, or 29 July and 2 August 1997, as well as in the *Boston Globe,* 2 August and 9 November 1997.

20 Bruno Cartosio, *Anni inquieti: Società media ideologie negli Stati Uniti da Truman a Kennedy,* Rome: Editori Riuniti, 1992, p. 153.

out in the Nevada desert. The adjective "atomic" itself became a widespread syn-onym for "exceptional" or "fantastic" ... : there was the atomic café, the atomic laundry, atomic love, atomic kisses and atomic cocktails, atomic carwashes and even atomic pest control. Hollywood actresses too were transformed into "bombs" and "bombshells."[21]

In terms of the current mood, the most disturbing thing about these revela-tions is how little an impression they have made on this country. Here we have cit-izens who hounded one president, Richard Nixon, out of office for recording a couple of conversations and who recently threatened to do the same with an-other, Bill Clinton, for a stain on his suit and an ancillary affair. Yet these same citi-zens don't so much as bat an eye when faced with an exposure of this magnitude – almost as if, deep down, they already suspected as much, as if here we were get-ting dangerously close to that borderline beyond which the hypocrisy of so-called democratic government would become untenable: better to simply keep quiet about it. And if this is the case, why shouldn't we believe that this isn't all the gov-ernment has been lying about, that AIDS *is* actually the fruit of biological warfare research or the result of a conspiracy against Blacks? Or that crack has been delib-erately introduced into the inner cities?

But if the government has been lying to us and continues to do so, if the lie is so enormous, then we might as well think it has lied about everything, particularly about what we can't verify: the past. What reason would whites have *not* to lie to their Black slaves about their history if they happily do so about the present to their own white citizens, such that the future of these citizens is at risk?

It is on the horizon of this immense deception, this cosmic untruth, that the question of the evil demon comes into play. Referring to *white devils* implies that the demon is everywhere, as pervasive as whites themselves, invading your cities, your streets, your whole life: the demon is ubiquitous, omnipresent, assailing you, tempting you at every turn. And in this case as well, the Nation of Islam is far from alone. Satanism – fear of, or belief in the devil – is in fact rooted in the blind faith Americans place in the US Constitution. If the Constitution is perfect, and if men

---

21 Ibid., p. 155.

are fundamentally good, then how can it be that evil, injustice, fury and malice are so rife in this country?

> When the American system fails, as it does, of course, from time to time, Americans don't look for system failures. They look for *human devils* who have mucked up a perfect system. ... The view that the American system is perfect and cannot be made better comes from America's peculiar history. America's Founding Fathers (Thomas Jefferson, George Washington, Benjamin Franklin) were gods or, if not gods, at least individuals more perfect than anyone now alive. They designed a unique system that could last forever without improvements. It was, and it is, perfect. No other country has founding fathers in the sense that the United States has founding fathers. The only other country that did, the USSR with Marx and Lenin, has just officially rejected its founding fathers, by returning Leningrad to its original name of St Petersburg.[22] [italics mine]

Even a layperson such as Lester Thurow uses the term *human devils*: here, as in the debate on poverty and the underclass, the reaction is of astonishment: how is it possible that in the American system, which guarantees everyone the right to happiness, there nonetheless exist widespread misery and injustice? The answer: It's because of the devil. When the Nation of Islam identifies the demon as the white man, it demonstrates its complete adherence to the American system. It shows how the spread of demons is inevitable in any social system whose citizens regard it as impossible to improve (as Americans do their Constitution). Unable to inculpate the system, or class injustice or the one-sidedness of the law, they need to find somebody else to blame for their suffering, for their unhappy lot. That somebody is a demon – millions of demons, tens of millions of demons.

Yet don't forget: these *white devils* were "savages, nude and shameless; hairy, like animals, they walked on all fours and they lived in trees." I recall when I was in Senegal in the early 1970s, a French site manager told me over evening cocktails in a cozy bar in Dakar that his Black workers were good, "but you know, they've only just come down from the trees, *ils sont à peine descendus des branches.*" This is

---

22 Lester Thurow, *Head to Head: The Coming Economic Battle Among Japan, Europe and America*, New York: William Morrow, 1992, p. 261.

what a Black man is for a racist white: a primate just come down from the trees. So is the white man, for the Nation of Islam, a hairy animal climbing down from the trees.

Truly distressing about the Black Muslims is the way the Nation of Islam, in displaying its Black pride – in the very gesture of this counterthrust – reveals the underlying subalternity to which Myrdal refers, a subalternity in terms of the theme of the advent (of the reign of the Blacks against that of the white, blond-haired Jesus): in its choice of chronology (Yakub's 6,600 years versus the Bible's 5,000), in the role of the sciences (the Black scientist who created the white man, as opposed to the white technology that enabled the colonization and enslavement of Blacks) and in the color of its demons (in white European mythology, the devil's color is black). In all this, the Nation of Islam returns to sender the white man's contumely, but it does so from below, in an impoverished, almost parodic form. Its Islamism, invoked as the antithesis of white Christianity, is itself heavily Christianized – almost as though it were the poor Black man's version of the Protestant sects – and reveals much about the movement's religiosity. Yet the Nation of Islam also delineates the fundamentalism of our time: a new, modern fundamentalism based on contact with the Other. The Black descendants of slaves who lived on the shores of Lake Michigan were by now the members of an urban working class or underclass colonized by white Christian denominations, a number of whom had found salvation in an improbable version of Islam.

Because it was removed from traditional Islam, however, this sect "invented methods of action and mobilization that spread to numerous Islamic groups in Western Europe during the 1990s; the war against drug-pushers and addiction, along with the rehabilitation of gangs through the conversion of their members."[23] Moreover, the Nation of Islam has since 1986 been active in Britain, where it claims to have recruited some two thousand believers and where it opened a school, which the government forced to shut down in 1998.[24] But the Black Muslims' influence in the Old World goes beyond direct proselytism. The "Chicago Black way to Islam" has become a model for Maghrebian and Egyptian fundamentalists in both England and France, as well as for Turkish groups in Germany.

---

23 G. Kepel, *Allah in the West*, Introduction.
24 *Christian Science Monitor*, 18 September 1998.

These groups, in turn, have reimported this revised, "reformed" version of Islam into North Africa, Anatolia and Asia, the Koran's original homelands. By a circuitous route, then, the outlandish cult of Yacub has reshaped orthodox fundamentalism in the Arab world – just as if the American reformist Christian sects were to sail back across the Atlantic to evangelize the people of the Old Continent.

Consider this: in the Nation of Islam, every mosque has a *pastor*. The concept of *pastor* is about as close to the Koran as a hot dog. Evoking the idea of a flock of souls, the word *pastor* refers to a Western tradition whose secular application would be the modern welfare state, which gathers in and offers assistance to lost or abandoned sheep, giving rise to a "policing" of happiness.[24] What's more, in the United States, the pastor is the figure *par excellence* of the reformist Christian churches. Talking about the pastor of a mosque is like talking about the rabbi of a pagoda, further demonstrating how arbitrary the Islamism of the Nation of Islam really is, the extent to which the sect is in fact a purely imagined religion related to the notion of inventing one's own past.

This sense of arbitrariness is manifest in the problem of naming. In his postface to *The Autobiography of Malcolm X*, the book's editor, Alex Haley (who went on to write the best-seller *Roots*), concludes: "The Night fell over the earthly remains of El-Haji Malik El-Shabazz, who had been called Malcolm X; who had been called Malcolm Little; who had been called 'Big Red' and 'Satan' and 'Homeboy' and other names … "[25] The surname of Malcolm X's father was Little; when the tall, red-haired Malcolm ran with gangs, he was known as Big Red; later he rejected his surname as a descendant of the slaves belonging to a Mr. Little, calling himself X like other members of the Nation of Islam. Then, in the wake of his pilgrimage to Mecca, when he began to distance himself from the sect, he became El Hadij of the tribe of Shabaz. This casual donning and shedding of names, as though a name were a pair of socks, touches on a central nerve and at the same time describes a whole attitude. The nerve in question is the role the name plays in the transmission of ideology. When Louis Althusser says that "ideology interpellates individu-

---

24 This notion was introduced by Michel Foucault during two conferences held at Stanford University on 10 and 16 October 1978; see "Omnes et Singulatim; verso una critica della ragion politica," in *Millepiani*, 1994, no. 3, pp. 33. Foucault also speaks about "Plato's Flocks."

25 Malcolm X, *Autobiography*, p. 522.

als as subjects,"[27] he means that the individual becomes embroiled in ideology the minute he is interpellated ("Hey, you!"), the minute his name is "called" or he is "named." A name is thus a vehicle of the ideology to which we are subjected. Changing one's name is a significant move.

In this sense, however, Malcolm X's gesture is symbolic of a mentality in which one believes it really is possible to change one's name and, therefore, one's ideology. It was a mentality in which he considered himself free to give his own names. This was the same constitutive element as in European colonialism, as seen in the magnificent pages Tzvetan Todorov wrote in his shipboard diary on what he called "the naming frenzy" of Christopher Columbus:

> Columbus is profoundly concerned with the choice of names for the virgin world before his eyes; and, as in his own case, these names must be motivated ... "To the first [island] I came upon, I gave the name of *San Salvador*, in homage to His Heavenly Majesty who has wondrously given us all this. I named the second island *Santa Maria de Concepción*, the third *Ferdinandina*, the fourth *Isabella*, the fifth *Juana*, and so to each of them I gave a new name."

> Hence Columbus knows perfectly well that these islands already have names, natural ones in a sense (but in another acceptation of the term), others' words interest him very little, however, and he seeks to rename places in terms of the rank they occupy in his discovery, to give them the *right* names; moreover nomination is equivalent of taking possession. ...

> Things must have the names that correspond to them. On certain days this obligation plunges Columbus into a veritable naming frenzy. ... His pleasure seems to be such that on certain days he gives two successive names to the same places (thus on December 6, 1492, a harborage named Maria at dawn becomes Saint Nicholas at vespers); if on the other hand, someone else seeks to imitate him in his name-giving action, he cancels that decision in order to impose his own names; in the course of his escapade Pinzón had named a river after himself (which the Admiral never does), but Columbus is quick to rebaptize it "River of Grace."[28]

---

27 Louis Althusser, "Ideology and Ideological State Apparatuses," in Slavoj Zizek, ed., *Mapping Ideology*, London: Verso, 1994, pp. 130–31.

28 Tzvetan Todorov, *La conquête de l'Amérique: La question de l'autre*, Paris: Éd. du Seuil, 1982. Eng. trans. *The Conquest of America: The Question of the Other*, New York: Harper and Row, 1985, pp. 26–28.

In no place on Earth has this naming frenzy pervaded, and continued to pervade, people's thinking as in the United States. Take any zone at random: New York state, for example, home of Cornell University in the town of Ithaca (an island in the Aegean Sea, home to Ulysses), some forty-four miles from Syracuse (a town in Sicily), which in turn is sixty-three miles from Manchester (an industrial city in northern England), which is seventy-three miles from Palmyra (a town in the Syrian desert), which is another seventy-three miles from Warsaw (the Polish capital). Moving further west to Ohio, we find Canton (in China) seventeen miles from Dover (England), which is just two miles from Strasburg (France) and thirty-eight from Ravenna (Italy). Going even further west, in Indiana, just a short distance from one another on the freeway you find the exits for Angola, Syracuse, Warsaw, La Paz and Bremen.

Again, the question has to do with the relation between names and things, but here the naming frenzy amply shows the form the presumption of liberty has taken for US citizens who, like latter-day Columbuses, postulate their freedom to inhabit and possess a place in the act of naming it. In exercising this freedom through naming, they empty out the place and render it abstract, creating a virtual geography whereby Antiochia is next to Valparaiso, which in turn is near Warsaw. Such freedom, moreover, would have us believe that the concept of "Antiochia" is equivalent to four farms in the Midwest or that Paris, the sophisticated *ville lumière,* is in fact a charming little village of 800 inhabitants in Idaho.

What is more, in exercising this freedom, Americans fall prey to a compulsion to repeat the past. An emigrant from Italy travels six thousand miles, braving the ocean waves and half a continent, only to find himself back in (or to re-create for himself) the Ravenna from whence he departed. The freedom to name thus has the effect of generating a plethora of "lost and recovered tribes" – not only those of Israel or Shabaz, but also the vanished and refound tribes of Berlin, Genoa or Munich. And so this apparent freedom reveals its true face: it is the fruit of being forced to search for your roots, to re-create your own "lost and recovered" tribe, even if this means – as it did for Malcolm Little, trying to free himself from the shackles of white slave trader Christianity – that in the end you saddle yourself with a name that might have belonged to any one of a dozen Arab slave merchants.

19

Cabrini-Green, Where Paradise Once Stood

They show you the bullet holes that riddle the walls, point out the spent cartridges. Not relics from the Second World War, these are the signs of the long-running gang war whose theater is the Cabrini-Green housing project, a war that in one year alone took the lives of three small children.

Mother Frances Cabrini was a nun,[1] the first saint to be born in America. William Green was a union leader. Seen from the outside, this housing complex looks no worse than Sarcelles near Paris or Tor Bella Monaca in Rome. Its bleak 1950s/1960s–style twenty-story buildings are surrounded by bare lawns, where tree saplings planted by progressive architects have long become fatigued and given up growing. The facade of the central sector provides the only point of contrast, with its outdoor balconies sealed in a net of iron grillwork that stretches from top to bottom. On the various floors you see people walking, conversing or sitting behind grillwork, going about their daily business in a cage. Windows are bombed out or fire-blackened. Inside, the walls are covered in a labyrinthine web of graffiti and disconnected fixtures, the floors strewn with trash; on the sidewalk, teenagers bound around in enormous Nikes and Reeboks, wearing long, hooded sweatshirts

---

1 I. Cutler names Mother Cabrini (1850–1917) as one of Chicago's two Italian immigrants who went on to world renown, the other being the physicist Enrico Fermi. I. Cutler, *Chicago,* p. 99.

and reversed baseball caps that in 1992 sported the insignia X (from the Spike Lee film *Malcolm X*) and in 1994 OJ (from the OJ Simpson trial).

The complex is situated just a few hundred yards from the Magnificent Mile, Chicago's most affluent thoroughfare, with its shining new skyscrapers and its doormen in livery patroling the velvet-carpeted marquees. But here at Cabrini-Green, there are 4 to 7 homicides among its 6,000–odd residents in an average year, 20 or 30 sexual assaults, 300 muggings and around 100 burglaries. According to the most recent estimate, Cabrini-Green housed slightly more than 6,000 people in 2000, in contrast to the 20,000 of its heyday, 98 percent of whom were Black.[2] All of those residents lived below the poverty line: 56 percent were under 20 years old, and in most cases, the head of the family was a woman, with the man of the house either dead, in prison, absconded from his paternal duties or kicked out for being an albatross around the family's neck.

Thanks to percentages like these, the project has become the most notorious urban ghetto in the United States, a national disgrace that has spurred Chicago city authorities to vote for its demolition. Another, no less significant reason for this concern, of course, is that the land the projects are built on, so close to the luxurious area of the Gold Coast, is extremely enticing to realtors. The Chicago Housing Authority (CHA) has encouraged people to leave Cabrini-Green so that at least the high-rises can be taken down: three have already been demolished, without so much as a murmur of protest, and the authorities are waiting for residents to move out of the others. These crumbling structures are all that remain of a piece of history scheduled for erasure, the image of a declining arc that has marked the American twentieth century.

The story of Cabrini-Green is a long one. It begins during the Second World War, when the Chicago Housing Authority constructed the first Cabrini complex of 583 apartments in buildings of two or three stories each. Edward J. Kelly (one of many Chicago mayors of Irish origin) opened the complex in 1942. In 1943, when the first families went to live there, 75 percent were white and 25 percent Black, in what was then thought to be the optimal ratio to obtain a successfully integrated mixed community.

---

2   David T. Whitaker, *Cabrini-Green in Words and Pictures*, Chicago: W3 Chicago, 2000, p. 5.

Cabrini-Green housing project around 1940. Photograph by Gordon Coster, courtesy Chicago Historical Society.

But the racial panorama of Chicago was already changing. Up until the 1940s, the southern Blacks who had arrived on the crest of the Great Migration had been concentrated in the South Side, in Bronzeville, near the slaughterhouses and steel-works. With the Second World War, the dearth of manpower and the boom in wartime production (in the steel and canned-meat industries, for example) re-sulted in a much larger second wave of Black migrants pouring in from the South, with 3 million Blacks coming to northern cities between 1940 and 1960.[3] In that period, the number of Blacks in Chicago rose from 277,000 to 812,000. This influx was to completely alter race relations in the city: whereas Blacks had represented

3   Census Bureau, *Historical Statistics of the United States, Colonial Times to 1970,* Washington, D.C., 1975, part 1, p. 95.

only 1.7 percent of the total population in 1900, they accounted for 14.2 percent by 1950, 32.7 percent in 1970. The present figure stands at 42.2 percent.

For this reason, the goal of the city authorities during the 1950s was no longer "integration" but "resegregation." To this end, Mayor Richard J. Daley (another Irishman and the now-deceased father of Chicago's current mayor) launched a project to construct several twenty-story apartment blocks at the Cabrini site (the "Green" part of the complex), where the entire Black population of the city center could be concentrated.

Daley's initiative wasn't exactly disinterested. As a youth in the 1920s, he had been a member of one of the white gangs that went around firebombing the houses of Blacks who dared move into white neighborhoods. Chicago's Irish community has a long history of anti-Black feeling, as do various other white ethnic groups. During the 1960s, Martin Luther King Jr. considered Cicero, a Chicago Italian-Polish suburb, the symbol of apartheid in the northern United States. In the Chicago Irish stronghold of Bridgeport, riots broke out because of plans to build a Black high school.

Between 1958 and 1962, twenty-three buildings were thus erected, ranging from seven to nineteen floors high and comprising a total of 2,992 apartments; in 1962, another eight blocks were constructed, this time of fifteen or sixteen floors each, adding a further 1,096 apartments to the complex. From the moment these buildings were opened, Blacks accounted for almost 100 percent of the tenants. A new resident remarked at the time that "this is paradise" compared to previous living conditions.[4] Forty years later, another resident, Viola Holmes, reaffirmed this sentiment: "I thought I was livin' in heaven. It was beautiful. I'm not kidding," Rochelle Satchell insisted. "[T]hey were perfect."[5]

It was also in 1962 that the operation of "concentrating" poor Blacks was to take another step forward, this time in the South of the city with the even larger, even bleaker (if possible) Robert Taylor Homes project along State Street from Thirty-Fifth to Forty-Ninth. The biggest public housing complex in the entire United States, it had twenty-eight sixteen-floor tower blocks containing a total of 4,312 apartments. The excessive height of the buildings, no doubt due to econo-

---

4   From the front page of the *Chicago Tribune*, 15 October 1962.
5   D. Whitaker, *Cabrini-Green in Words and Pictures*, pp. 32, 36.

mies-of-scale planning, turned out to be socially disastrous, making maintenance difficult and contact between residents almost impossible. During the 1980s, 72 percent of the residents of the Taylor Homes were minors, 90 percent of the families were headed by a female single parent and unemployment stood at 47 percent. Although Taylor Homes accounted for less than 0.5 percent of Chicago's population, 11 percent of the murders that took place in the city were committed there, 9 percent of the sexual assaults and 10 percent of aggravated assaults.[6]

By autumn of 2000, demolition crews had also moved in on the Taylor Homes.[7] Simply taking down the buildings isn't going to solve the problems of the people who live in them, however; it will take more than dynamite or bulldozers to make their poverty go away. The tragedy of these projects is such that the inhabitants actually tried to stop them from being demolished. You feel a lump in your throat when you talk to one of the residents who complains that they don't want to move out, that they refuse to be chased away from this hellhole.[8]

But if the Taylor Homes projects were such a hellhole, why did the residents want to stay there? Perhaps it's because even in the most infernal conditions, traces of community life persist; perhaps because this at least was a familiar bedlam, one they knew how to cope with; perhaps because a roofed-in hell sounded better than a cold, hard sidewalk. Now, as ongoing regentrification of Chicago's Near South Side pushes further south, the poor Black population is being forced down toward Gary, Indiana, or moved to the west. The ghetto may be moving to a new location, the inner city losing its prefix, but as it does so, it is becoming increasingly desolate and segregated. These days, the Far West Side neighborhood has an even meaner reputation than the old South Side did.

In its attempts to resolve the problem of the high-rise projects, the Chicago Housing Authority seems once again to have adopted the Marie Antoinette approach ("If they have no bread, then let them eat cake"). Instead of bulldozing away the conditions of misery and poverty in which Blacks live, it simply bull-

---

6 Gregory D. Squires, Larry Bennett, Kathleen McCourt and Philip Nyden, *Chicago: Race, Class, and the Response to the Urban Decline*, Philadelphia: Temple University Press, 1987, pp. 113–14.
7 Information on this demolition and on various housing projects can be found on the Web site www.thecha.org.
8 I had such an encounter in August 2000 in Philadelphia, during the Republican convention, against which numerous American homeless associations had gone to demonstrate.

dozes the cement walls, the existential envelope of this ignominy. In any case, living in the condemned property of the housing projects is a form of condemnation in itself, like the idea of having to use public transportation, to which the following maxim could be applied: "Anyone who still takes the bus [that is, doesn't go to work by car] by the time he reaches thirty is a failure."

Rather than mitigate segregation, the Chicago Housing Authority simply sweeps it "out of sight and out of mind." The problem here isn't the housing or the high-rises; the problem is America's apartheid.

Residential segregation doesn't affect just the unemployed in the inner cities, but also the Black middle class. In the area where Mary Patillo-McCoy went to study Chicago's Black middle class, she found that 98 percent of the inhabitants were Black.[9] Like their white counterparts, these Blacks aspire to the "American dream" of having their own single-family balloon-frame house, with a little front lawn, situated in a leafy suburb. The only problem is that Black mortgage applicants are turned down more often than white ones.

To guarantee mortgage values, remember, the Federal Housing Administration included segregationist clauses in its contracts, justified (supposedly) by the need to assure the market value of the house. Remember, too, that home ownership is one of the fundamental values of the American Dream. Everyone in this country is either paying off a mortgage or struggling to obtain one. If a poor white factory worker is suddenly fired after bleeding himself dry to make monthly payments and has to sell his dream house, he isn't going to want the value of it to have tumbled because a Black family arrived in the neighborhood. Racial segregation and racism thus become functions of primary economic need, an affair of the pocket much more than of the heart.

Being refused a mortgage is an aspect of residential segregation that concerns only a minority of Blacks, however – the relatively affluent. For the rest, the mechanisms of segregation are even more oppressive, as Douglas S. Massey of the University of Chicago and Nancy A. Denton show in their emblematically entitled book, *American Apartheid*. In 1976, the words of Parliament's song "Chocolate

---

9   M. Patillo-McCoy, *Black Picket Fences*, app. B, p. 226.

City" already labeled the "Chocolate city, vanilla suburbs." The song referred to the intense suburbanization of the United States that had begun with the Roosevelt administration and accelerated during the 1940s and 1950s, with waves of southern migrants gradually turning the chocolate city even darker. Car culture joined forces with apartheid-style urban planning.

The segregation was, in fact, double: Blacks were first concentrated in the city, then pushed into a single zone. Of the 11.5 million people who live in the state of Illinois, 1.7 million are Black; 1.5 million of these live in Cook County, which contains the city of Chicago. Of these, 1.4 million live in the city of Chicago itself. Blacks thus account for 12.7 percent of America's population, 16 percent of the state's, 29 percent of the county's and 40 percent of the city's. In the case of Detroit, such concentration has escalated to apocalyptic levels. Blacks number 14 percent in Michigan, 20.8 percent in the Detroit metropolitan area and 76 percent in the city. So you understand why downtown Detroit looks like a city in the aftermath of a war. The passage from nation to state to metropolitan area to city resembles the process of progressive concentration that takes place in each sucessive link of the food chain. Indeed, Chicago's smart set even boast about how the Windy City has managed to contain such racial concentration – and attribute the city's recent prosperity to this fact. If Chicago has avoided Detroit's fate, they say, it is because it has managed to keep at least 50 percent of the population white by confining the Blacks to a separate zone.

The process of segregation is repeated within the city itself, above all at the zonal level. Not even affluent Blacks are spared: "In the 1990s version of Chicago South Side Black Belt, there is a band of contiguous community areas with a total population of more than a quarter million. ... [O]ver 95 percent of the residents of this stretch of neighborhoods are black," even though "over 69 percent work in white collar jobs and the median family income is above the Chicago median."[10] This segregation is replicated even further in a fractal process from ward to block. Massey and Denton's book contains some truly alarming statistics on the rate of "hypersegregation" in US cities – not merely of segregation itself, but also of isolation, concentration, clustering and all the other indicators sociologists use to mea-

---

10 M. Patillo-McCoy, *Black Picket Fences*, p. 28.

sure racial separation. In Chicago, segregation of Blacks currently stands at 90.6 percent, isolation at 82 percent and concentration as high as 88.7 percent. In fact, this level of segregation is high wherever you go in the United States: 83 percent in LA, 83.5 percent in Philadelphia, 83.7 percent in St. Louis.[11]

This kind of segregation has devastating effects on fiscal and social policy. Fiscal localism is the rule in the United States, with local taxes helping to finance social services such as schools, hospitals and public transportation (at the school district, city and county level). This means that funds are not available to provide services in the urban areas that most need them. The opposite is true in terms of federal and state funding for welfare, however. Segregation has the effect of spatially dividing well-off taxpayers from the poor, who ultimately benefit from government funding, so that people who live in tax-paying zones of the city are convinced that they get nothing in return for the money they dole out to the state, thus reinforcing the antigovernment ideology of "We have to pay while they scrounge a living." In this sense, segregation provides the most fertile soil for the growth of ideologies that call for tax cuts and reduced public spending. The celebrated Proposition 13 to "reduce our taxes" launched in California during the 1970s was the springboard for Reagan's victorious electoral program. Today, supporters of the Lega Nord have taken it up in Italy. Huge, bleak housing projects such as Taylor Homes and Cabrini-Green are only the extreme practical consequences of racial and class segregation, the edifying lesson of the ghetto.

Though segregation in the United States seems to invite comparison with South African–style apartheid, a more appropriate parallel – one obvious to anyone who has visited India – would be the caste system. The first scholar to use the concept of "caste" to analyze the social position of Blacks in the United States was Gunnar Myrdal. Being white or Black or Asian or Native American or Polynesian meant being part of a multiple social order like that of the Indian caste system. Not by chance was the term *caste* actually imported into India by Europeans. (The Portuguese originally coined the word from the Latin *castus,* meaning "pure," which they used to describe the Brahmins and thus by extension the whole caste hierarchy.) To ask someone which caste they belonged to, it was enough to ask their

---

11 D. Massey and N. Denton, see tab. on pp. 71, 77.

name. Once again, we encounter the problem of the name, both in terms of the act of naming and of the state of being named.

Traditionally in India, a person's caste is designated by reference to a color, with as many castes as there are colors in the rainbow. In the United States, the color bar is of a different order. Caste, like race, overlaps with social class. In India, you find members of the "backward" castes and even the untouchables of the scheduled castes who are nonetheless rich, while a Brahmin might equally well be poor. Likewise, a tiny minority of Blacks in the United States are wealthy, while the vast majority are poor. A person's caste is imposed in a previous life – thus it cannot be avoided, just as one cannot escape one's racial origins. "Harvard University professor Cornel West was reminded that neither money, nor education, nor prestige negated the fact that he was black. One empty cab after the next passed him."[12] The only hope of escaping one's destiny lies in the life to come, which in India means one's next reincarnation (hence the mass conversion of the Indian scheduled classes to Buddhism and Christianity to escape the destiny of being a pariah) and in America the spiritual beyond (Black religious fundamentalism, the Black Muslims' "hell on Earth").

Caste was a product of an agrarian economy – like slavery in the United States – but immediately underwent a mutation, adapting itself to the urban life of modern India. Like racism in the United States, the Indian culture of caste is pervasive and contagious: religions who knew nothing of caste, such as Christianity and Islam, were "castefied" soon after they penetrated the Indian subcontinent and came into contact with its cultural universe. The caste system was based on a hierarchy of taboos (alimentary, sexual and behavioral) and prejudices. A similar scale of taboos in United States racist ideology culminates in "the untouchability of the white woman." Yet here the real *untouchables,* in the Indian sense of the word, are the Blacks, who, in a more subtle though nonetheless dramatic way, supposedly contaminate everything they touch: they are financially untouchable, for example, because they devalue whatever they come into contact with, causing the price of land to plummet. They therefore embody a new category of pariah – the *economic pariah.*

---

12 M. Patillo-McCoy, *Black Picket Fences,* p. 210.

The official way of dealing with problems in these two countries has been identical: in both cases, the law officially, formally resolves them. The caste system in India has been legally abolished, just as Blacks in the United States enjoy equal rights guaranteed by a Supreme Court ruling. Unmasking the hypocrisy of this formalism, though, is the fact that the need is felt – in both India and the United States – for *affirmative action*, for the continual proposal of new forms of "positive discrimination," such as the allotment of a certain number of positions (at school or in an office) to a given minority group. The Mandal Commission requested the same criteria adopted to establish Black quotas in US government offices for dealing with the lower castes and untouchables in India.

In real terms, though, affirmative action has had little concrete effect, has been unable to overturn the prejudices of the general public. Since the time of India's independence, Ghandi's efforts have ensured that there have always been ministers in the cabinet to represent the untouchables and the backward castes. Today there are pariah poets, lower-caste musicians and bankers, yet the poverty and marginality among these groups has remained the same. In the same way, the United States has its Black generals, senators, mayors, Supreme Court judges, congressional representatives, pop and film stars and fabulously wealthy sportsmen and women. Yet none of this alters the fact that, after a slight decrease between 1945 and 1950, the gap between the average incomes of white and Black families has once again begun to widen, so that the distance between the two groups today is as great as it was in 1957, more than forty years ago.

The similarities don't end there. In the United States, it has always been and still is impossible to form a Black political party, just as in India every attempt to form a party representing all the scheduled castes has ended in failure: the very principle of caste, like that of race, is divisive, separating out and even generating undercastes. The power elite, meanwhile, do their best to stir up intercaste hatred, the same as the interracial hatred in the United States. Like every multicaste society, the multiracial society of the United States is also multiracist, creating its own system of hierarchies. The white caste is divided along Protestant/Catholic lines (to which orthodox groups are considered inferior). In turn, Catholic whites are divided into Nordic (German and Irish), Latin and eastern European (Polish and Croatian) constituencies. Among America's Asians, the caste system is organized with Koreans at the bottom, which may be one reason for the intense hatred between Blacks and Koreans. Among Blacks themselves, Haitians – who are even denied entrance to the country, suspected of carrying AIDS – have replaced Puerto Ricans as pariahs.

The same prejudices have a tendency to multiply: just as racist Asians believe whites stink, so too do whites think Blacks stink. The Blacks, meanwhile, are not to be outdone. Speaking of white women, Malcolm X once said, "Like a black brother recently observed to me: 'Look, you ever smell one of them *wet?*'"[13] In the United States, the principle of ethnic belonging has thus been replaced by that of castes, which have multiplied as a result (just as they did in India, where some three thousand castes now exist, derived from fragmentation of the original five groups: brahmins, warriors, artisans, peasants and untouchables).

In the unending debate on the root of the problems of Blacks in the United States – whether of "race" or of "class" – American scholars are reluctant to apply the concept of "caste," because that term strikes at the heart of one of the country's most deeply rooted founding myths: social mobility, the absence of a rigid class structure. Americans have always bragged how theirs is a "classless" nation. This idea of social mobility, however, runs up against the barrier of an ethnically (or racially) derived "caste" system from which there is no escape.

The issue becomes even more paradoxical if we consider that the caste system is a holistic system, which, as Louis Dumont has shown,[14] leaves no room for Western individualism. Dumont recounts the various stages and ways by which post–medieval Europe arrived at the notion of the individual as an independent subject of history. Flesh-and-blood individuals have existed wherever the human race has set foot; for many civilizations, however, it is not the individual who constitutes the principal agent of history. In India, for example, the subject of history is the caste; for many other peoples, it is the tribe. For the ancient Romans, the *gens* gave you your name (once again the name makes its appearance). Only the modern West has produced a vision of society for whom the ultimate subject of history is the individual. Moreover, Dumont demonstrates, the opposition be-

---

13 Malcolm X, *Autobiography,* p. 314.
14 Louis Dumont, *Homo Aequalis: Genèse et épanouissement de l'idéologie economique,* Paris, Gallimard, 1977.

tween the aspiration to equality and the defense of individual freedom – between egalitarianism and individualism – is in fact false. For two reasons, these two currents cannot be antithetical: first, the problem of inequality was never raised in traditional societies, since such societies were based on the principle of social hierarchy; and second, *equality* can only exist among *individuals*. The notions of equality and the individual arise with the growth of capitalism and its apotheosis: the individual boss, entrepreneur or capitalist who needs to have at his disposal individuals who are in all respects equal, whether as workers, consumers or citizens.

America, "capitalism's promised land" (to use Sombart's definition), has taken formal equality and individualism to their ultimate limits. Yet the same needs of capital have led to the development and reproduction of a caste system, the fragmentation of the socius into countless holistic subsystems, such that an individual in America is never just an individual; the person is first of all "Black" and then has a "name." This racial caste system was first reproduced with slavery; then by the use of immigrants as a mobile, compliant, strikebreaking workforce; then finally by the property market, which produced further segregation since the dollar value of houses was determined by, and itself reinforced, racial prejudices. In this sense, the logic of capital appears to be cannibalistic. Needing to develop internally, it has broken with and even destroyed several of the cardinal values of the ideology that originally constituted what Max Weber called "the spirit of capitalism."

20

The Color of Cats

It was still dark on Chicago's West Side the night of 4 December 1969 when, at 4:30 a.m., shots rang out on the first floor of 2337 West Monroe Street, followed by more gunfire. The minute the guns fell silent, the street was awash with police. Two corpses were taken away from the scene by ambulance, along with five people who had been wounded. The dead men were 21-year-old Fred Hampton, president of the Illinois Black Panther Party, and 23-year-old Mark Clark, leader of the Peoria Black Panthers. Three youths were arrested, while four suffered gunshot wounds – two males (Ronald Satchel, nineteen, and Blair Anderson, eighteen) and two females (Brenda Harris, eighteen, and Vernlin Brewer, seventeen). Of the fourteen police officers who took part in the raid, one had cut his hand on a broken window, while another had been wounded in the leg. In all, more than a hundred spent cartridges were found.

According to the official version, an informer had on 2 December tipped off the FBI about an illegal cache of arms supposedly hidden in the house, headquarters of the Chicago Black Panthers. For his information, the informer was paid $300. When police broke into the apartment, according to TV news bulletins, the occupants had responded by firing at the door, and the officers had returned their fire. Police agents had ordered the Panthers several times to throw down their weapons, but the firing from inside the apartment continued. Hampton was found in bed, shot in the head twice. The prosecutor announced that the seven surviving Panthers were to be charged with attempted murder.

On 5 December, police searched the house of Bobby Lee Rush, the Panthers' vice-minister of defense, then the highest-level representative of the group still living in Illinois. They found several weapons, and a warrant was issued for Rush's arrest. The following day, Rush gave himself up in front of a crowd of five thousand people, as he read the results of an independent autopsy report stating that Hampton had been killed while asleep. Rush was handcuffed by three Black police officers, among whom was the president of the Afro-American Patrolmen's League. (The front-page headline of the *Chicago Tribune* of 7 December read "Black Policemen Arrest Rush/Panther Leader Before 5,000," while the inside story stated, "Rush surrenders to black cops").

On 8 December, the United Auto Workers union (UAW), along with the National Association for the Advancement of Colored People (NAACP) and another dozen organizations, requested an inquiry into the deaths of the two Panthers. Every day, hundreds of people queued up to see the West Monroe Apartment. "There are youths, workmen in paint-stained clothes, middle-aged women in flowered hats, neatly dressed office workers, elderly people and postal workers in their gray uniforms. ... The crowd is greatest in the late afternoon when lines of school children in brightly colored jackets line up on the sidewalk."[1] Young Panthers showed no trace of bullets around the apartment's entranceway. All of the bullet holes were concentrated above the beds where the dead and wounded had been found.

On 11 December, under a bold-type headline "EXCLUSIVE" covering the entire front page, the *Chicago Tribune* reported the prosecutor's version of events, accompanied by many photos with circles marking the bullet holes in the door. These photos were later withdrawn because the marks indicated were not in fact bullet holes. The question as to whether the police had carried out a political assassination grew into an elaborate Perry Mason–style controversy focusing on the significance of certain doors, walls and angles of entry. On 19 December, the Justice Department convened a sitting of the Grand Jury. Nixon's Republican admin-

---

1 *New York Times,* 10 December 1969.

istration leaped at the chance to embarrass Chicago's Democratic Mayor, Richard J. Daley.

On 15 May 1970, the Grand Jury issued its verdict: police had fired more than ninety shots, while not one had come from inside the apartment. The prosecutor had lied, as had the Chicago police department and its forensic experts.[2] The Black Panthers filed suit against the government, state and city. Years went by before the suit was rejected in 1977. More years passed. Eventually, in 1982, Cook County awarded $1.85 million in damages – to be paid one-third each by the federal government, the county itself and the city of Chicago – for having conspired to destroy the Black Panther Party and violated the civil rights of its members. It had taken thirteen years for the Justice Department to officially acknowledge that both Hampton and Clark had been killed while they slept, and by that time, the world no longer cared. The Panthers were ancient history. After 1971, they had no longer posed a threat to American society. Times had changed. In 1983, Bobby Rush was elected as an alderman in Chicago.

But back in 1969, as far as the US government was concerned, the Panthers were Public Enemy Number 1. Director of the FBI J. Edgar Hoover had stated in March 1968 that "they constitute the single greatest threat to the internal security of the United States." This perceived threat was so great, in fact, that every single national leader of the movement was either dead or in prison by the time of the Fred Hampton killing. The last to be apprehended was 27-year-old David Hilliard, the Panthers' chief of staff, who had been arrested in San Francisco the day before the West Monroe raid. In prison were Bobby Seale and Huey Newton, the two men who had founded the Black Panther Party only three years previously, in 1966, for self-defense. They had borrowed the symbol of the black cat from an Alabama civil rights group, the Lowndes County Freedom Organization. Meanwhile, the group's ideologue, Eldridge Cleaver, had gone into exile abroad.

To deal with this menace, the FBI spared neither money, nor snitches, nor bullets. On 6 April 1968, seven Panthers, including Cleaver and Hilliard, had found themselves surrounded by forty-eight police officers. Cleaver had surrendered by completely undressing in front of them. But 17-year-old Bobby Hutton, who was

---

2 Mike Royko, *Boss: Richard J. Daley of Chicago* (1971), New York: Penguin, 1976, p. 212.

with Cleaver, still had his Panther uniform on when he came out, unarmed, with his hands up; Hutton was riddled with police bullets. On 5 August, three more Panthers were killed in Los Angeles. That September, Newton was convicted of unintentional homicide. In 1969, two Panthers were jailed in Denver, twenty-one in New York, dozens more in New Haven and almost three hundred in Los Angeles. Police helicopters and armored cars swept down on Panther headquarters throughout the country, from Boston to Indianapolis and Denver. In September 1969, Bobby Seale, together with seven other members of the new American Left, was convicted on a conspiracy charge after a riot during the 1968 Democratic convention in Chicago. In the same month, Larry Robinson died in prison from gunshot wounds received forty days earlier. On 13 November, the Black Panther Spurgeon Jake Winters died in a shoot-out with the Chicago police, which also cost the lives of two police officers.

A *New York Times* headline of 7 December read, "The toll for the Panthers is now 28," this being the number of militants killed since 1 January 1968. (On 20 December, a San Francisco lawyer released the names of nineteen of the dead.[3]) On 10 December, next to a report on Chicago Blacks mourning the death of Fred Hampton, a Los Angeles correspondent recounted a police raid on the Panthers' LA headquarters, where shooting had lasted four hours. In the meantime, the *Chicago Tribune* ran an interview with a judge who had convicted Fred Hampton in August for robbing an ice cream shop.[4]

Nearly thirty Panthers have been killed since the party was founded; in the first year of the Nixon administration over 400 were arrested on various charges; Panther offices in Los Angeles, Oakland, Chicago, Des Moines and other fifteen cities have been attacked by the police. Nearly all members of their original Central Committee have been suppressed: killed, jailed or forced to exile. The Justice Department has a special task force on the Panthers; the FBI considers them the greatest single threat to our national security; at least two congressional committees and several grand juries are investigating them.[5]

---

3 *New York Times*, 21 December 1969.
4 *Chicago Tribune*, 12 December 1969.
5 Tom Hayden, *Trial*, New York: Holt and Winston, 1970, pp. 117–18.

Not that the Panthers were exactly shrinking violets. They had been struck by the ongoing spectacularization of the political struggle, which they thought they could manipulate in their favor through their distinctive uniforms, combat boots, black leather jackets and Guevara-style berets. The very name *Panther* sounded more like the title of a film than the name of a political party, and it soon worked its way into the collective imaginary, producing panthers of all colors. In the 1960s, a group of white hippies called themselves the White Panthers, while a re-tired people's association of the 1970s took the name Gray Panthers. In Europe, an Italian student movement of the 1990s dubbed itself *La Pantera*.

In 1966, at the time of the group's founding, guerrilla warfare tactics exerted a peculiar fascination on radical movements. If such tactics had been capable of stopping the powerful American war machine in Vietnam, it was thought, they would prove equally effective on the home front. After the group's founding, its first concern was acquiring firearms and training its members to use them, as the 1970 film *Seize the Time* shows. The Black Panthers made a spectacular entrance onto the political scene on 2 May 1967 when thirty armed and uniformed Panthers burst into the California State Capitol building in Sacramento, forcing Governor Ronald Reagan to run for cover. Fred Hampton may have died in his sleep, but many other Panthers were to be killed in shoot-outs with police.

Somewhat fatuously, the party's Minister for Education George Murray boasted how in 1968 "in the first two weeks of August thirty-eight pigs were killed, many in the area where the party members are at their most organized; in Cleveland Ohio an ambush was laid leaving three pigs dead and wounding twenty-seven more. We also have the great pleasure to announce that the brothers who led the ambush are ex-negro soldiers who served US imperialism in Vietnam but who on their return to the United States, after political re-education, embraced the guerilla struggle."[6] The reference to guerrilla warfare was no accident. Following the line taken by Paul Sweezy, Leo Huberman and later Malcolm X, the Panthers regarded America's Black ghettos as an "internal colony" that would have to fight its own war of liberation in the heart of the urban jungle, like the Vietcong in the Mekong jungle. Ghetto segregation had made the Panthers

6   Cited by Valerio Evangelisti, *Sinistre eretiche: Dalla banda Bonnot al sandinismo,* Milan: Sugarco Ed., 1985, pp. 85–86.

think of themselves as isolated subjects trapped in a colony or, in the language of South African apartheid, in a Bantustan. Certainly the relationship they had with the forces of law and order had much in common with colonialism: the police would enter the inner city as though advancing into occupied territory (as they still do). From here stems the Panthers' Third World-ism, their links with Frantz Fanon and Che Guevara (and not just because of the beret).

For all these reasons, the Panthers considered themselves a "party," along the lines of a paramilitary organization, rather than a sect or a religious movement. This was the origin of their Marxism, a Marxism of a decidedly peculiar brand – full of citations not only from Mao but also from the North Korean dictator Kim Il Sung – through which they were aiming to become the party that, in a bizarre analogy with the working classes, would organize the Black Lumpenproletariat. As Bobby Seale remarked, "Marx and Lenin would probably turn over in their graves if they could see lumpen proletarian Afro-Americans putting together the ideology of the Black Panther Party."[7] Yet the Panthers' Marxism was in the end no more extravagant than the Islamism of Malcolm X, and their Third Worldism brought them worldwide popularity. In July 1968, demonstrators in Dar es Salaam demanded the release of Huey Newton. The Vietcong even offered to release American prisoners of war in exchange for the liberation of Seale, Newton and other imprisoned Panthers.

The fact of the Cold War, together with the ongoing conflict in Vietnam and the tense climate of international relations in general explain in some ways why the FBI considered the Panthers such a major threat. Just as the Germans had been a threat during World War I, and the Soviets during the period of McCarthyism, any source of internal disorder in the United States had always been regarded as the fifth column of a foreign menace. J. Edgar Hoover, it was said, literally "saw red" whenever he heard the word "communist." Yet amid this outspoken fear and paranoia remained something obscure and opaque.

This could be seen, first of all, from the Panthers' internal setup. Seale was the president, Newton the secretary for defense, Cleaver the information secretary,

---

7   Bobby Seale, *Seize the Time*, New York: Random House, 1970, p. ix.

Hilliard the chief of staff, Ray "Masai" Hewitt and then George Murray the secretary for education. For a while, Stokely Carmichael served as secretary for *Colonized Afro-America*. While these titles may perhaps be taken seriously, doubts begin to creep in regarding "Deputy Secretary for the Defense of Illinois" Bobby Rush or "Field Marshal" Dan Cox. Then there is the fact that Chief of Staff Hilliard was only twenty-six. The "president" of the Illinois party, Fred Hampton, was killed at the age of twenty-one, while his "deputy secretary for health," Ronald Satchel, wounded in the same raid, was a mere nineteen. These titles might raise a smile were it not for the fact that many people were willing to kill – and if necessary, to die – for those who held them.

It might seem, in fact, that the mobilization of state forces against the Panthers was somewhat exaggerated. The sprawling, technologically cutting-edge organization of the FBI was brought to bear on what looked from the outside to be little more than a gang of kids, with active members reckoned at its height to be between 2,000 and 5,000 (including hundreds of police infiltrators). By comparison, the Blackstone Rangers gang in Chicago alone had 2,000 members, and thousands of young Blacks today flock to join one of the two major Los Angeles gangs, the Crips and the Bloods. These gangs are even better armed than the Panthers – considering that their arsenals contain not only machine guns but bazookas.

Neither proselytism nor military might explains why the Panthers were so feared. One of two possibilities remains. It is possible that J. Edgar Hoover's paranoia was simply a cunning maneuver, a deliberate exaggeration of the Panther menace as a vehicle for striking out at other enemies, similar to the situation in 1886 when the authorities' real prey behind the soft target of the anarchists had been the Knights of Labor, or in 1917 when anti-German xenophobia had been used to weaken the Industrial Workers of the World, the so-called Wobblies. It is also possible that Hoover really did believe the Panthers were a threat, in which case we need to try to understand the deeper motives that lay behind this fear, a sense of anxiety never produced by gangs like the Blackstone Rangers.

One source of this fear was the movement's politics. The traditional gang *stays on its own turf,* while the Panthers did anything but stay put. So it was that in its usual smug tones, the *Chicago Tribune* announced, "Street gangs, including the Black P Stone Nation and the Vice Lords, have openly been at odds with the Panthers. The street gangs wanted nothing to do with the Maoist teaching, pro-communist philosophy or restrictive discipline of the Panthers. This often led to open hostility."[8] Compared to a communist, this implied, a drug pusher was an angel.

The essential difference, though, was that other gangs live in and off the culture of poverty, but the Panthers belonged to the category, as Oscar Lewis described it, of "the religious, pacifist or revolutionary movement who organizes and gives hope to the poor" and which thus "destroys the psychological and social nucleus of the culture of poverty." In this sense, the Panthers were similar to figures such as Martin Luther King Jr. or Malcolm X, not only because they were destined to be physically eliminated but because they "organized and *gave hope*." If the loss of such hope is the thing that strikes us most about the predicament of Blacks in the United States today, it is not only by chance that this hope has been swept away: in part, at least, it has literally been murdered.

If the Panthers inspired fear as a gang because they were political, they intimidated people as politicians because they were a gang. To Cleaver, the civil rights militants and members of the Student Nonviolent Coordinating Committee (SNCC), along with various exponents of Black Power (Stokely Carmichael, H. Rap Brown), were all "negro hippies, college students who have turned their backs on the black middle class" and for this reason "cannot form an effective political alliance with the Black brothers."[9] If the Panthers scared people, it was because their founders were ghetto kids who would probably be leading gangs of their own if they hadn't created a party. Newton had in fact been part of a gang in the Oakland ghetto, while Seale had been kicked out of the air force for misconduct. Cleaver had spent his youth in and out of reform school and prison, as he recounts in his autobiography, *Soul on Ice*. Newton's aim was in fact to organize "brothers of the block – brothers who ... ain't gonna take no shit, brothers who had been fighting pigs ... the brothers he ran with, he fought with, he fought against, who he fought harder than they fought him."[10] "There was a potent moment in this period, around 1968–9, when the Panthers ... looked as if they might

---

8   *Chicago Tribune*, 14 December 1969.
9   Cited by V. Evangelisti, *Sinistre eretiche*, p. 79.
10 B. Seale, *Seize the Time*, pp. 64–65.

become the ultimate revolutionary gang."[11] As a gang, the Panthers spoke the language of the ghetto; as a party, they translated their demands into a more generalized rhetoric. According to them, the marginalized subproletariat of the inner cities expressed itself as a *general class*. The career of Cleaver closely follows that of Malcolm X, down to the work they both did as waiters on the trains and the time they both spent in prison.

Loss of the party meant a loss of hope, and with that came a return to normality. The Panthers' action politics were abandoned in favor of the old political machine, as several ex-members of the group became city aldermen. Others went back to the gangs. The disappearance of the Panthers was to lead to a general resurgence of gangs during the early 1970s, but the crushing of hopes also meant that, in a way, the Panthers themselves went back to being simply another gang. H. Rap Brown converted to Islam and changed his name to Jamil Abdullah Amin. For a while, he ran a grocery store, but he went back to prison in 2000 after firing at two policemen.[12] After having joined the Moonies, Eldridge Cleaver was, beginning in the late 1980s, in and out of prison for using and supplying crack.

But nothing sums up the Panthers' downhill slide more than the case of Huey Newton, who insisted in his last years on being called Stagolee after the mythical Black outlaw, bad to the bone, preying on everyone:

> Huey Newton may once have incorporated all three men, Malcolm [X], Nkrumah [the African revolutionary] and Stagolee. For most of his last fifteen years or so he was only Stagolee, an addict raging through the streets of West Oakland in the small hours screaming "I am Huey P. Newton!" He ran those streets. ... [H]e ran around begging to be killed, writing a very long suicide note over the name Stagolee. And finally, quite early on a summer morning in 1989, at the corner of Ninth and Center Streets among the West Oakland Victorians, Huey got his three bullets in the head from two other nighttime ragers.[13]

Contrary to what most people believe, gangs are actually one of the pillars of social order.

---

11 M. Davis, *City of Quartz*, p. 298.
12 *Washington Post*, 16 April 2000.
13 S. Malcolmson, *One Drop of Blood*, p. 464.

21

Greek Heroes and
Lumpen Capitalists

You are in the middle of Gangland. The walls are an explosion of graphic fury. Overlapping loops of ungovernable graffiti mesh with jagged scribbles, blown-up numbers, huge cartoon hands, sprays of blood red, electric blue lines that shoot off in all directions like tracer bullets, hieroglyphics of a lost tongue. These chaotic murals are the visual map of what the Chicago sociologists once referred to as social disorganization, the image of *disorder,* in those urban interstices where the forces of social reason seem to have ceded to the complete unpredictability of civilization's wrath, where men are beasts and beasts are wild animals. At least that's how these places commonly get described in articles, TV series and Hollywood blockbusters. They are where hate knows no reason, violence knows no limits, and the present knows no future.

To the uninitiated, these overlapping quiddities may appear to be no more than demented tangles of squiggles. Yet to the trained, streetwise eye, they actually *speak* – they indicate where a gang's turf begins and ends, announce declarations of war or truce. (Canceling another's graffiti is considered an act of aggression.) They tell a story: of a comrade's death, of the overthrow of a leader or a young kid's imprisonment. Or they simply communicate. According to some, you can read in these runes warnings, postings to gang members of upcoming murder contracts. What was noise becomes sound; scribbles become language.

Under the apparent disorder, you glimpse the vague contours of an underlying order, beneath the disorganization the filigree of a structure.

There is no word more mystifying than *gang*. Say the word *gang* and what comes to mind is a band of young hoodlums, the vaguely sadistic violence of adolescence, how cruel kids can be; or you might think of a romantically born-to-be-wild bunch of modern-day brigands and bandits astride their Harley-Davidsons. (These days, the only kids you really see on these motorcycles in the United States are the fifty-something variety: balding, potbellied, sixties acid casualties, gray beard castaways of the *Easy Rider* generation whose bikes even have ridiculous little trailers in tow to carry their luggage.) What you are doing in both cases is projecting the myth of the gang as you experienced it in the movies – from *West Side Story* in the 1950s to Walter Hill's *The Warriors* in the 1970s to Dennis Hopper's *Colors* in the 1980s, along with dozens more (*Fort Apache the Bronx*, *Assault on Precinct 13*) – that is to say, as something halfway between latter-day cowboys and *Clockwork Orange*–style psychopaths.

Some gangs have a membership running into the thousands, like the famous Crips and Bloods of Los Angeles. In Chicago, the two rival gangs are the Vice Lords, whose membership reputedly runs into the thousands, and the Gangster Disciples, which has a membership (according to the press) of between 30,000 and 50,000 spread over thirty-five states.[1] The GD's leader is allegedly Larry Hoover, a middle-aged gentleman who for twenty years has been taking care of business from inside a prison cell. Even Hoover's right-hand man, Jeffrey Hatcher, is in his forties. In 1992, on his release from prison, the Vice Lords' chief was greeted by a coterie of beminked, bejeweled young women and dapper men in designer leather suits and lizard shoes waiting to usher him inside one of a fleet of stretch limos.[2] Gustavo "Gano" Colon, boss of the Latin Kings, another of Chicago's leading gangs, is forty-three; the leader of the Chicago Two Sisters is thirty-six.[3] When you look at all of this, the young-blood romanticism of the myth begins to crumble – even more so when you consider that some gangs, among them the Vice

---

1 *Time*, 19 May 1997, p. 42; *Newsweek*, 1 November 1999, p. 46.
2 *Chicago Tribune*, 20 December 1992.
3 *Chicago Tribune*, 10 January 2000; *St.Louis Post-Dispatch*, 19 September 1997.

Lords, have been on the go now for several generations. Others have changed their names: in Chicago, the Blackstone Rangers (who in the 1960s already had 2,000 adherents) are now called the El Rukns. In Los Angeles, many parents used to be in the same gangs that their kids are in now,[4] and many fathers encourage their sons to join up.

In the early 1980s, moreover, the Vice Lords and the Gangster Disciples arrived in Minneapolis, where both opened branches (or chapters). The LA Crips and Bloods followed suit: it was as though a London or a Paris gang had decided to set up shop in Stockholm.[5] Meanwhile, in Kansas City in 1993, 120 gang leaders from America's major cities united for a grand convention in a luxury hotel to negotiate a nationwide truce, with the blessing of an esteemed organization like the NAACP and with major national network TV coverage.[6] And in 1997, *Time* reported that the Gangster Disciples had set up a nonprofit organization called Growth and Development, through which "the gang organized neighborhood cleanups, midnight basketball games, and local drives in which hundred of bags of Cornish hens, macaroni and cheese dinners and boxes of Stove Top stuffing were given to the poor." Moreover, a certain Wallace "Gator" Bradley, the GD's former war counselor, has twice stood for election as an alderman and was even received at the White House by President Bill Clinton.[7]

All this bears the corporate stamp of high-profile media campaigns that seem incompatible with the spontaneous notion of a bunch of kids running riot. The word *gang* thus covers an unexpectedly vast semantic (and historical) field. Initially, it meant "team," as in the work gangs who laid the railroad track and built bridges in the West, whose members were *gangers* rather than *gangsters*. The whole vocabulary of labor, in fact, carries the mark of scorn. What was a work team is now a *gang*, whereas the *crew* has become the small, improvised unit teamed up to carry out a robbery or a drive-by. The concept of gang thus runs from the small group of teenagers who disband after a few years to veritable armed forces including in their ranks both kids and adults, equipped with whole

---

4   Martin Sánchez Jankowski, *Islands in the Street: Gangs and American Urban Society*, Berkeley: University of California Press, 1991, pp. 180–81.
5   *Wall St. Journal*, 29 April 1993.
6   *Chicago Tribune*, 30 April and 2 May 1993; *The New York Times*, 2 May 1993.
7   *Time*, cit.

arsenals and with networks of branch offices, built to go on for decades.

Equally vast is the temporal horizon of modern American gangs, now covering more than a century and a half of the country's history. Gangs first appeared in the United States together with the phenomena of urbanization and immigration from Europe. Bands of young Irish delinquents such as the Bowery Boys and the Dead Rabbits (who, if stories are to be believed, were striking terror into the middle classes as early as the 1840s) can be credited with having invented the idea of the modern street gang in the slums of the Bowery, Five Points and Paradise Alley. From the start, the gangs were baptized with a certain black humor (Dead Rabbits, Ghost Shadows) or were named after animals: the Egyptian Vipers or the Falcons (of the Addams neighborhood studied by Suttles) or the White Tigers and Flying Dragons (among the Chinese gangs of New York). This is much the same as sports teams today: consider the Chicago Bulls, the Atlanta Falcons or the San Jose Sharks. What we see here is the idea of the gang as a team and of gang life as a sport: while Dallas has its Cowboys football team, Chicago boasts a gang called the Rangers. (It's curious that in a society as violent as America, sports stadium violence is much less widespread and brutal than it is in Europe.)

Thus the term *gang* evokes such a wide-ranging concept semantically as to seem completely meaningless, other than as one of the main ingredients of metropolitan legend, a phantasm built from our social terrors. Yet the myth of the gang as pure distillate of the underclass has an inestimable value on the market of the imaginary. Getting back to reality, though, American gangs have a number of things in common, the first of which is that each has its own territorial base, usually in one of the city's poorest neighborhoods.

In his classic study *The Gang* (1927), a census of the 1,313 gangs then operating in Chicago, Frederick Thrasher located the gangs' turf in the interstices of the city ("the intramural border of gangland"), in zones of social breakdown. Social disorganization today, though, is no longer limited to the city's between zones, those neighborhoods where a fracture opens up in the social order; it now spreads throughout the entire urban fabric. In Chicago, as in other cities, a vast number of inner-city inhabitants now live in slums or ghettos ("chocolate city and its vanilla suburbs"), where the situation isn't so much one of social order with the occasional island of chaos as it is an ocean of chaos in which floats the odd islet of order.

The "ghetto" has become a boundless urban expanse whose hundreds of thousands of residents "do not suffer from 'social disorganization,' but constitute a universe of dependency that is precisely differentiated and hierarchized and organized according to specific principles."[8] Here, as Thrasher wrote, is where "the normally directing institutions of family, school, church, and recreation break down on the intramural frontier of gangland and the gang arises as a sort of substitute organization."[9] The gang is thus a form of institution and as such reflects the principles of hierarchy applied to the lives of the masses of people who live in the inner cities.

This is where the first surprise comes in: these principles are no different from those that govern society in general. The only variation is that they function here in conditions of extreme poverty. If society at large operates according to Malthusian doctrine, the inhabitants of the ghetto find the very world they live in to be Malthusian, not because it is overpopulated, but because resources are scarce, private investment has cleared out and whatever public funding is made available arrives in dribs and drabs: here there are no banks, only *Checks Cashed* and *Pawnshops*.

Like society at large, the ghetto is organized along competitive lines. Because the goal in this case is to appropriate already scant resources, however, the competition becomes extreme, an all-out war, with every person for himself. Normal conditions in the inner city correspond to those described by Thomas Hobbes, where "every man is enemy to every man. ... [M]en live without other security than their own strength and their own invention ... and, which is worst of all, continual fear and danger of violent death; and the life of man is solitary, poor, nasty, brutish and short."[10] In this struggle, people can count only on their own resources, leading to the development of what Martin Sánchez-Jankowski calls *defiant individualism*, a defiance that is also a form of diffidence. Nothing expresses this sense of diffidence so well as the amazing number of bars and padlocks that you see in the poorer zones of the city, where the liquor sections of supermarkets are protected by metal grilles worthy of Fort Knox, as are drugstores. The doors of

8   L. Wacquant, "Inside 'The Zone,'" p. 152.
9   Cited in R. E. L Faris, *Chicago Sociology*, p. 74.
10 Thomas Hobbes, *Leviathan* (1651), New York: Liberal Art Press, 1958, p. 107.

residential buildings weigh heavy with chains. Many people who remain trapped in house fires do so because they are so well bolted into their apartments. Here diffidence takes the shape of a padlock.

The fact that competition is the order of the day in ghetto society means that, in the inner city, too, *social Darwinism* prevails: here, too, is the idea that only the fittest will survive in the selection of the human species. At the two extremes of the social scale, in rich white suburbs as in colored slums, we find the same Hobbesian vision of society as the battleground of a perpetual struggle for survival. Here only the toughest and the best will triumph, while the weakest "are the first to cede," as was the case with the goats on Juan Fernández island, according to the Reverend Joseph Townsend.

But how is it possible that the defeated can believe in social Darwinism, in which the winner is not only dominant but also the best, meaning that those who are defeated are not only losers but also at the bottom of the evolutionary pile? People do not voluntarily regard themselves in this light. (In Christian belief, at least, the last of today will be the first tomorrow, even if tomorrow means in the afterlife.) So the only way to work through this defeat and to find a reason for it, while still believing in the principles of social Darwinism, is to conclude that the game is rigged (hence the popularity of the idea of a "master plan," the notion that a white conspiracy exists to destroy the Black slum populations through drugs). The ghetto team is always bound to lose, because the scales are weighted against it, because cheats abound, because some "players" are more equal than others. As one Los Angeles Chicano youth put it: "The rich Anglos ... they are all organized. So they take all the good stuff and let us and the Asians and Blacks fight it out for the rest." Or, as a Black kid from New York says, "[M]ost of the big things in the life they keep for themselves and then the scraps they let us niggers and spics fight with the spaghetti and potato heads [Italians and Irish] for." A nineteen-year-old Irish kid from Boston comments, "Hell, everybody knows that those Brahmin assholes try to squeeze every penny from you ... that those rich bastards and the pointy heads are just letting us and the niggers and spics fight over shit jobs."[11] Gangs are therefore organizations ("substitutive institutions") that spring up in

---

11 M. Sánchez Jankowski, *Islands in the Street*, pp. 85–86.

the inner cities to procure for their members benefits denied the ghetto as a whole. Many kids join gangs to escape the cycle of poverty and despair that has withered their parents and friends. In the ghetto, paradoxically, it is the gang members themselves who have the greatest faith in the American Dream, who most firmly believe in the individual's own initiative and in the myth of the private entrepreneur who, by taking risks, goes from abject poverty to riches. But what has our hypothetical inner-city entrepreneur actually got to gamble with?

Certainly not financial capital or hard cash; this Hobbesian universe is a realm of "moneyless capitalism." In poor neighborhoods, jobs are scarce, badly paid and extremely unstable. Alongside a few paltry pockets of legal activity, the hub of the economy is a many-faceted underworld of get-rich-quick schemes that run from the quasi-legal to the openly criminal, from benefit fraud (husbands who pretend to have left their wives to receive single-parent benefits) to trafficking food stamps and donating blood for money to loan sharking, drug pushing and contract killing.

Neither could our hypothetical young businessperson make use of professional competence or cultural acumen; in the ghetto, school denotes the first circle of the social inferno. If the purpose of school is to provide training for life, inner-city schools are a lesson in defeat: school failure is the first in a long line of delusions that will scar the ghetto kid's adult life. Marginality begins with the interruption of study through dropout or expulsion from a fourth-rate school. Not one of the last five mayors of Chicago (not even Black Mayor Harold Washington) has sent his kids to a government-run school. And if ghetto schools are fourth rate, it is because local taxes (based on neighborhood property values) finance education in the US. Where houses are expensive, taxes yield a lot of money and the schools benefit from a handsome budget; they are well equipped and their teachers well paid. By contrast, where rock-bottom property values lead to low tax revenues, the teachers are badly paid and the facilities appalling. The poorer the ghetto, the worse the school, the more impoverished the ghetto becomes. One teenager from the South Side of Chicago expresses the sense of despondency felt by ghetto kids well: "It ain't gonna be long before you need a degree in aeronautical engineering to fry hamburgers in McDonalds."

Why should we be surprised, therefore, if our budding entrepreneurs, for want of anything else, lay down the only thing they have to gamble with: themselves, their own freedom? Brute force, knowledge of weapons and training in hand-to-hand combat are the only cards these seekers of the American Dream have to play with. Here "violence is the currency of life and becomes the currency of the economy of the gang."[12] Violence reveals itself to be not a sadistic and senseless way of blowing off steam, as the gang myth would have it, but the rational tool of a Hobbesian universe: "[W]e find three principal causes of quarrel: first, competition; secondly, diffidence; thirdly, glory. The first makes men invade for gain; the second for safety; and the third for reputation."[13] Competition makes use of violence to gain control of goods, while diffidence uses it in self-defense. (We'll leave reputation for later.)

If the car has for decades been the motor of the world economy, the drug trade drives the economy of the urban ghetto. Through terms such as "drug economy" or "crack economy," the present-day international drug trade is compared to the spice trade (pepper, cardamom, cinnamon – but also opium) of Venice and of the Dutch and English merchants. Eric Hobsbawm even went so far as to compare the Medellín cartel to the East India Company.[14] If in Los Angeles the "estimate of 10,000 gang members making their livelihood from the drug trade is anywhere near correct, then crack really is the employer of last resort in the ghetto's devastated Eastside – the equivalent of several large auto plants or several hundred McDonalds."[15] For at least fifteen years, the drug industry has been "the only employer that is in expansion and that without discrimination offers everyone an equal opportunity to earn a living in the heart of America's cities." So writes the sociologist Philippe Bourgeois in the conclusion to his remarkable account of a night he spent in a New York crack house:

> The kids in the apartment block where I live are neither apathetic nor disorganized. In fact, if anything, they're too well organized ... the most determined, fortunate and ruthless among them control sales networks with a daily turnover of thousands of dollars. And most of them aren't yet eighteen. ... Why even bother to ask what makes them turn down low-esteem private sector jobs when they can set up their

---

12 M. Sánchez-Jankowski, *Islands in the Street*, p. 139.
13 T. Hobbes, *Leviathan*, p. 106.
14 Eric Hobsbawm, in *New York Review of Books*, 20 November 1987, p. 35.
15 M. Davis, *City of Quartz*, p. 314.

own cocaine or crack business, a business for which their identity ... no longer constitutes a handicap but actually becomes a trump card? Like all good Americans the pushers nurture an iron-strong belief in the "American Dream": thanks to private enterprise they can go from rags to million-dollar riches. Obviously most of them will never make it. Despite their best efforts they will crumble and most probably fall prey either to addiction or depression. But the one who does manage will get to drive his Mercedes or Jaguar or Porsche up to the fire hydrant where the most far-gone crack-heads will wash and shine it up for him while he stands a few feet away, proudly watching the neighborhood kids gazing in awe at the "cash box."[16]

The key phrase here is "cocaine business," much as one would speak of a business that produces diapers or biscuits. Setting up one's own cocaine business can open up extremely bright commercial prospects. In this sense, we could invert the Marxist expression *Lumpenproletariat*, as Mike Davis does, noting how "the Crips have become as much lumpen capitalists as outlaw proletarians."[17]

Seen in this light, the gang becomes a kind of tertiary industry trading in goods and supplying services that are for the most part clandestine, only because street culture in general constitutes an obstacle to legal activity but is a veritable trump card for illegal businesses. The many attempts gangs have made to set themselves up in legal business, such as buying and selling real estate, have generally ended badly. What flourishes instead are illegal distilleries and rackets such as underground lotteries or cockfights. Another good source of income is the protection and demolition business: protection (or blackmail) of traders and shop owners; demolition (usually by fire) of properties and consignments of goods, perhaps for speculators trying to throw recalcitrant tenants out of a building, or for business operators looking to clear a piece of land, or for loan sharks putting the screws on defaulting debtors. Through services like these, gangs interact with the legal economy of suit-and-tie capitalism.

---

16 Philippe Bourgeois, "Une nuit dans une 'shooting gallery': Enquête sur le commerce de la drogue à East Harlem," in *Actes de la recherche en sciences sociales*, September 1992, no. 94, p. 78.
17 M. Davis, *City of Quartz*, p. 310.

Of course, in the running of their lumpen capitalist enterprises, members of a gang may be arrested and have to do some time in jail. But if the schools provide a lesson in failure, prison is a school for social success; this is because of the classic mechanism, described by Michel Foucault, through which one enters prison as someone who has committed an infraction against the law but comes out a fully fledged criminal. "The other character, whom the penitentiary apparatus substitutes for the convicted offender, is the *delinquent*."[18] What was simply an unfortunate episode in a person's life thus becomes a destiny and a vocation.

The US Prison Boom

Year	Number of Federal and State Prisoners (Thousands)	Number of Prisoners per 100,000 Inhabitants
1930	127	103.3
1940	174	131.8
1950	166	109.9
1960	213	118.9
1970	196	96.5
1980	316	139.8
1990	774	310.8
1999	1,366	500.0

Data elaborated from the Census Bureau, *Historical Statistics of the United states: Colonial Times to 1970*, tab. II 1135–1143, p. 420; and from U.S. Department of Justice Bureau of Justice Statistics, *Summary Finding* and *Correctional Populations 1990–1999*, available from the Web site www.ojp.usdoj.gov/bjs.prisons.htm.

In the last twenty years or so, prison has become so widespread a phenomenon as to have lost part of its dissuasive power. In these twenty years, since the beginnings of Reaganism, the United States has undertaken a program of incarceration that is without precedent, with the result that the number of detainees has more

---

18 Michel Foucault, *Surveiller et punir: Naissance de la prison*, Paris: Gallimard, 1975. Engl. trans. *Discipline and Punish*, New York: Vintage Books, 1979, p. 251.

than quadrupled. The US prison population can be divided into three categories: (1) inmates of federal or state penitentiaries (or "the pen," for short); (2) those imprisoned in local jails for periods of up to one year, amounting to an average of about half of those in federal or state prisons; and (3) minors in juvenile prisons. To determine the total number of people kept under the judicial system's watchful eye, however, you would have to add a fourth category: those on probation or parole. And that total is alarming: in 2000, there were more than 2 million Americans behind bars, while the correctional population of the United States numbered 6.5 million people.

For forty years (1930–1970), the number of inmates in federal or state prison continued to oscillate around an average of 100 per every 100,000 inhabitants (see table). But by 1990, that number had risen threefold, to 311 for every 100,000 inhabitants; in 1999, the figure (for state and federal prisons) stood at 500. The total figures are even more disturbing: less than 200,000 prisoners in 1970 compared to 1.366 million in 1999. Add to this the number of people serving time in jail (606,000 in 1999), along with minors in reclusion (106,000), and the total US prison population in 1999 was 2.078 million, or 764 prisoners per 100,000 inhabitants. (By comparison, the number for the same population sample in Austria is 84, in Italy 86, in Holland 87, and in France and Germany 90 – eight times fewer.[19] Only Russia comes close to the US numbers, with 650 prisoners per 100,000 inhabitants.) If we add to this the 3.8 million people on probation and the 700,000 on parole, the total figure of those under judicial surveillance in 1999 leaps to 6.6 million, compared to 4.3 million in 1990. All of this means that 3 out of every 100 Americans are under surveillance for having fallen foul of the law at any one moment.

This astronomical rise in the prison population is concurrent with the growing number of poor and working poor – with increasing layoffs and with cuts in public spending and welfare – and is coupled with harsher sentences and easier recourse to imprisonment as a solution to society's ills. Faced with the failure of such policies, the public continues to demand, and the authorities to sanction, even more prisons, even tougher sentences. The system is seen as a fundamentalist solution: if it doesn't work, it's not because there's something wrong with it, but because it

---

19 Loïc Wacquant, *Les prisons de la misère*, Paris: Éd. Raisons d'agir, 1999, ch. 2.

hasn't been applied thoroughly enough. This is the idea of people who think that terror is ineffective because it isn't sufficiently terrorizing. As a result, the most powerful and opulent society in history also has the most prisoners.

Considering the number of convictions, the number of prisoners is, paradoxically, much lower than it should be. In an attempt to unclog America's jails, judges have been known to come up with highly inventive sentences, such as making the convicted individual walk around with a sign around his neck indicating the crime committed, a sort of modern-day version of the stocks. None of this takes away from the fact that the penitentiaries are brimming over with prisoners. The Chicago county jail, built in 1928 to house 1,200 inmates, now contains more than 8,000: in 1988, 25,000 of Chicago's prison population were released because of overcrowding. Many convicts never see the inside of a prison because of overcrowding, while others have their sentences reduced to make way for more dangerous guests. Even for prison, there is a waiting, a standby system. Nevertheless, one in four Black youths between the ages of eighteen and twenty-five ends up in jail, while half the population of an entire neighborhood may be subject to some form of judicial surveillance.[20]

Thus prison becomes a familiar part of everyday life, assuming the form of a rite of passage, the gangs' equivalent of an officer training course. Gangs have various levels of social status, and the highest of these go to those who have spent the most time in jail, those who have had the longest sentences or who have been the most active in organizing gang activities from behind bars. Younger members listen in awe to veterans' tales of their prison experiences, of their years in the pen (or, as the Latinos call it, the *pinta*).

Of course, it's best to avoid prison, if possible. One-third of the gangs studied by Martín Sánchez have their own lawyers. Many use minors for certain jobs because the sentences are more lenient: more than a sign of barbarism, child criminality becomes for the lumpen capitalist enterprise a calculated means of minimizing an employee's risk of imprisonment. The gangs use children as pushers for exactly the same reasons that nineteenth-century bosses favored child labor: to reduce costs.

---

20 L. Wacquant, "Le gang comme prédateur collectif," in *Actes de la recherche en sciences sociales*, March 1994, no. 101–102 (pp. 88–100), p. 97n.

A gang's field of activity is not limited to its lumpen capitalist business, however, or to its contribution to the underground economy. This is where the second characteristic of gangs comes into play: the fact that they are all ethno-racially based. American history is marked by a passage of gangs of every hue: Irish, Italian, Jewish, Greek, Chinese, Korean, Vietnamese, Black, Puerto Rican and Dominican. Inconceivable, however, is an Irish-Italian or Chinese-Mexican gang, one that is ethnically mixed. Just as the population in general is ethnically segregated, so too do patterns of intergang violence run along ethnic lines.

The gang's territorial base is a particular neighborhood, its social base a specific ethnic or racial group. In the United States, the combination of these two factors is called a community. A community is defined as a precise ethnic group living in a precise zone. Not only is the gang born from a community, but it cannot survive and prosper without the community's support, without its information network, its code of silence. And these things – support, information, silence – it will obtain only if it in turn proves to be of use to the community. This reciprocal exchange is in fact asymmetrical; the gang needs the community more than the community needs the gang. If the gang disappeared, the community would go on, whereas no gang could survive in a hostile community. For this reason, part of the gang's role is often to protect the members of the community by defending them from unscrupulous speculators, thwarting the plans of outside commercial interests, keeping loan sharks in check and fending off gangs from other neighborhoods.

Jorge, a 59-year-old Los Angeles bricklayer, has this to say on the matter: "People from outside the community are always down to the gangs, but they don't see the good they can do for us in the community. ... For one they give us good protection from people outside our community who would rob and hurt our kids. ... [W]e feel more safe with them than the police." And Raquel, a 47-year-old mother of five, says: "I know that a lot of people think the gangs are bad, but they don't see some of the good things they do for the community either."[21]

In a society that has such enthusiasm for private vigilante armies, the gang stands halfway between the official neighborhood police force and a pressure group. The gang takes on a political role, such that even its criminal acts provoke

---

21 M. Sánchez-Jankowski, *Islands in the Street*, pp. 183–84, 190.

state and federal government into providing more financial aid to help the neighborhood. As Jim, a 52-year-old father of two from New York, says:

> Let me tell you that if it weren't for the gangs, this community wouldn't see any social program and especially any job-type programs. You see, we got a high unemployment rate among people in this area and especially young people. But none of government leaders cares about that. If nothing happened, they'd continue to let 'em be unemployed. They only care when the gangs get active in illegal stuff, then they start a job program. So you see, we need the gangs to help us out. It's their behavior that the policy-makers are concerned about, not some regular kid who's unemployed.[22]

What we have, therefore, is a complex structure composed of elements deriving from the neighborhood, the gang, the repressive and welfare state apparatus (so-called street-level bureaucracy), as well as from politicians and the media, in which every pole interacts with another and in which every rapport reflects retroactively on other rapports, producing various levels of relation. The first and most evident level is the war between the gang and the repressive state apparatus. On one hand, the police are viewed as an invasion force, the "Anglo gang," much like any other gang from outside. Here we have, in effect, the concrete version of the Black Panthers' "internal colony" theory. As one forty-year-old police officer from the LAPD comments:

> The gangs are like animals and nobody in the community knows anything. Something happens right in broad daylight and nobody seen anything. ... So we go and pick up a number of gang members for questioning. Then I go and ask questions in the community and still nobody knows anything. It's a weird feeling when you ask questions in these areas, there is a look on the residents' faces that is pure contempt toward us. I haven't seen anything like it; well, not since Vietnam anyway.[23]

In this backyard Vietnam, the community provides the gang with sanctuaries to hole up in when the heat rises, just like the jungle was to the Vietcong. More-

---

22 Ibid., p. 239.
23 Ibid., p. 257.

over, when social workers and judges try to introduce rehabilitation programs in an attempt to convince gang members that their behavior is antisocial, that they must learn a trade and become productive members of society, such initiatives are viewed as a form of brainwashing, an act of totalitarianism comparable to efforts by sects like the Moonies or to Vietnamese re-education camps.[24]

But this war has been going on unabated in America's cities for 150 years now, during which time it has produced no apparent winners or losers. In the interim, in the conflict's substrata, other types of relations have taken root – relations of symbiosis, of reciprocal dependence, of mutual and mutually diffident parasitism. The police need the gangs to increase their slice of the city budget. The politicians need the gangs both to show how they are waging war on crime and to obtain votes in communities where the gangs operate. The gangs need the politicians to moderate police pressure and social workers to ensure that cash is injected into the community. In turn, the local political leaders of gangland consolidate their positions by acting as mediators between gangs and authorities. For the media, the gangs are a product to sell, as well as a way to sell product; for the movie industry, gangs are a crucial ingredient in the cocktail of designer violence they pump out to provide high-body-count thrills and spills for the public.

Here we see how a radical inversion of perspective has taken place: while gangs initially appeared to constitute a menace to society, they now show themselves to be an integral part of the urban fabric of the United States. If the gang's boisterous instincts at first seemed to dictate its behavior, these same instincts now appear to be the most rational response possible within the bounds of a *Malthusian* universe, in a *Hobbesian* climate subjected to the laws of *social Darwinism* – that is, within the three cornerstones of social doctrine that govern society's policy toward the poor.

If the violence of these human UFOs might have initially shocked us, what strikes us now is the gang's extraordinary conformism, which gives us pause for thought. The modus operandi of gangs at the end of the 1960s was protest, whereas it had turned by the 1980s to conservatism. In the 1960s, CRIPS stood for Continuous Revolution in Progress, and its members invoked theories of Black Power; since then, like the Blackstone Rangers, the Crips seem to have undergone

---

24 Ibid., pp. 274, 355 (note 23).

a veritable "management revolution,"[25] the gangland equivalent of a Western firm adopting the Japanese model of corporate organization. In the 1990s, the Gangster Disciples even set up a political body, Twenty-first Century Vote, as a lobbying force to consolidate its ties with the communities of the inner city. Gangs have therefore tended to follow the same patterns of orientation we see in society as a whole: Guevarist in the 1960s, Reaganite in the 1980s, Clintonite in the 1990s.

Even within its own internal structure, gang politics conforms to canonical models: the more organized gangs have a president, a vice-president, a minister of war (a warlord) and a treasurer. The conquest of power within a gang takes place exactly as it does within a party or a union, with the exchange of votes for favors, whereas holding onto power implies a policy of caution in the face of internal rumblings of dissent.[26] As both an economic and a political subject, the gang behaves in the manner of a large-scale institution.

What is amazing is that poor young teenagers who have been kicked out of school and are headed for jail are able to formulate such rational strategies, or at least strategies strikingly similar to those pursued by politicians and the ruling classes, as though the underlying logic behind the formation of social groups were deeper and more impelling than any form of marginalization or ignorance. (In this we see the inadequacy both of the miserabilist position, which regards ghetto society in terms of pure *hunger,* and of the populist idea, which finds in it an indomitable, primal *creativity.*)

Such conformism is evident even in the smallest of details. A gang's members refer to it as a club: a club to which you are invited or from which you are excluded, a club whose members are all brothers, a poor cousin to the fraternities and sororities of American universities that plant the roots of a future solidarity, that will have a determining role in shaping their members' subsequent social careers.

And in a certain sense, the gangs really are like clubs or elite enclaves. Not withstanding the exaggerated figures trumpeted by the press, the numbers of gang members in Chicago would appear to be around 37,000, while the corresponding figure in Los Angeles could be anything from 10,000 to 100,000, depending on the

25 M. Davis, *City of Quartz*, pp. 299–300.
26 M. Sánchez-Jankowski, *Islands in the Street*, pp. 24, 92–94.

level of fear the newspapers wish to strike into the hearts of their readers.[27] In any case, we're talking about mere tens of thousands in urban sprawls numbering millions of inhabitants, at least 1 or 2 million of whom live in slum areas. However well armed and well organized they may be, the gangs thus in reality represent no more than a tiny minority. It's not surprising, therefore – especially in the case of the largest and most famous gangs – that their members are so proud to belong, as though they were part of a privileged elite. Indeed, one of the strongest motives for joining a gang is to gain others' respect, because in the most despised areas of the city, respect becomes the most important commodity, acquiring a value equivalent to that of life itself. In these neighborhoods, let's not forget, life is generally "poor, nasty, brutish and short," and death is always close at hand. Belonging to a gang therefore means ascending to a kind of substitute immortality, a form of *glory*. "[They] believe in their immortality, an idea that … is nurtured by all gang members [who] constantly talk about their loyal, honorable members who have fallen in the name of the gang. No one forgets who was killed where and for what purpose."[28]

Indeed, these kids in their sneakers, baseball caps and baggy blue jeans apparently adopt the same gestures in honoring their fallen comrades as Homer's warriors did in offering sacrifice to their heroes, if what Lincoln Keiser says about the Chicago Vice Lords is true: before taking a swig from the communal bottle, they pour a drop of whisky on the ground in memory of their dead companions.[29]

---

27 *Chicago Tribune*, 5 May 1993; M. Davis, *City of Quartz*, p. 270.
28 M. Sánchez-Jankowski, *Islands in the Street*, p. 140.
29 Lincoln R. Keiser, *The Vice Lords: Warriors of the Streets*, New York: Holt, Rinehart and Winston 1979, p. 54. Cited by M. Sánchez-Jankowski, *Islands in the Street*, p. 342.

22

In the Cogs of the Machine

You elect the water board, the county sheriff and the town clerk. On the ballot, you indicate your choices for city councillors and school administrators. You go to the ballot box to decide who the next prosecutors and judges will be. By suffrage, you choose the state governor, the lieutenant governor, the secretary of the treasury, state representatives and senators and judges of the state's supreme court. Here in the United States, voting takes place at all levels: federal, state, county, city, town. There are even special government districts designated for mosquito abatement, with their own elected officials.

If democracy is simply a question of the ballot, and if it is measured by the number of publicly elected offices, then the United States is without doubt the most democratic country in our planet's history. Just as medicine has its therapeutic obstinacy, US politics has its electoral obstinacy: in the primaries, you vote to decide whom to vote for. As you observe this celebration of the ballot, verging on the obsessive, you again encounter the absolute faith Americans have in the benevolence of their own way of life. The extremism that we have so often come up against appears once more, this time in the form of ballot box extremism.

In 1906, Werner Sombart calculated the number of times an American citizen was called on to vote, for example, in the state of Ohio, which turned out to be twenty-two times per year. This did not mean that Joe Citizen had to go to the polling station that often, because many of the elections were grouped together. But every year, he had to vote to decide twenty-two public offices. Looking at the same calculation in 2000, a citizen of Chicago votes more than a hundred times in the space of four years, including primaries but excluding referendums. An Italian, by comparison, votes only seven times in five years: even taking early elections into account, he votes on average less than two times per year, or less than one-tenth the US figure.

Electoral indigestion of this magnitude has enormous consequences. Much more than in Europe, the lives of millions of people in America depend on the popular vote: many public offices considered in the Old Continent to be administrative (and thus filled through exams and applications) are in the New World subject to election. Contrary to the common assumption, politics exerts a much greater influence on daily life in the United States than it does in Europe. Whether for water provision or for the nomination and salary level of professors (decided by an elected board), all of those decisions considered in Europe to be bureaucratic are considered in America to be political. What determines the incomes, careers and social prestige of millions of Americans is therefore the conquest of consensus.

The night of the 2000 presidential elections, Democrats in Chicago awaited the results at a huge reception, an enormous buffet of hot dogs held in the Grant Park Hilton. On every floor was a different party. In one room, people waited with baited breath for the announcement of the new president; in another, the waves of expectation regarded a place in the Senate; still elsewhere, guests crossed their fingers for a local government post. Even more instructive was the night of the 1992 US presidential elections, when I was in a Holiday Inn on the outskirts of St. Louis, Missouri, following the results as they came in with a crowd of militant Democrats and union officials, who together made up what was once known as the (political) "Machine." Between the hissing of cans of Budweiser and the munching of hot dogs was a succession of rounds of applause, ovations, presentations of winners, arms raised in triumph as though they had just clinched the world heavyweight title. On the charts affixed to the walls, the flow of results for the offices of attorney, sheriff, clerk of this and clerk of that upstaged the presidential race. The onlookers were trembling to see who got the minor offices, those that would have an immediate impact on their own lives.

In the United States, suffrage pervades the whole of existence: election training begins in school. In high schools, teenagers learn to become candidates for class offices and to orchestrate election campaigns; in college, leaflets tacked on walls and notice boards spread the word of an unending electoral broadcast. Students organize rallies and parades, arming their candidates with squadrons of majorettes, selling T-shirts to finance their campaigns and distributing leaflets, flyers and lapel badges.

Strangely, this absolute faith in the benevolence of the method for assigning executive offices coexists with an equally absolute contempt for politics. Whereas the election itself often seems to be an object of veneration, those elected are routinely reviled. For an American politician, Rule Number 1 is to appear apolitical. And in no other city is politics considered such a dirty business as it is in Chicago. To label someone as corrupt, you can do no better than to compare that person with a Cook County politician.

In the period from the 1970s to the 1990s, more than twenty of Chicago's fifty aldermen were found guilty of corruption. Here the aldermen are known as "gray wolves" because of their legendary greed. One said in 2000 that he had served for twenty-three years, "enough time ... to have seen two dozen of his colleagues go to jail."[1] And what would Gogol have said, you wonder, if he had heard that in 1933 Walter Kozubowski (of Polish origin) was forced to resign from his position as Chicago's town clerk (another elected office) when it was discovered that he had invented a series of phantom employees – dead souls of bureaucracy – as a way of pocketing several salaries for himself? Offices that are obtained in Europe by competitive exam, or administrative selection (such as court or police offices), are in the United States elective, and thus political. What would be bureaucratic malversation for a European, then, is regarded as political corruption in the United States. In 1983, fifteen judges were indicted for corruption, for example. Ten years later, a county judge was found guilty of having sold homicide trials, taking money to guarantee the acquittal of gangsters who had killed their rivals.

---

1 *International Herald Tribune*, 12 May 2000.

This in itself is nothing new: way back in the 1930s, Pat Nash (of Irish origin), then president of the Democratic Party, invited his cousin Tom Nash – Al Capone's lawyer – to become Cook County treasurer. It was the same old story. The problem, though, is in the numbers. An entire volume, with the irreverent title *To Serve and Collect*, is dedicated to corruption scandals in the Chicago police. Corruption has been rife among the city's law officers since the days of the 1886 Haymarket bombing, when several officers were arraigned on corruption charges. Hardly a year goes by without some new case coming to the fore. On one occasion in 1996, seven agents were found guilty of extortion; in 1997, it was discovered that undercover cops who had infiltrated gangs had switched sides and were now working as the gangs' inside men in the CPD. In 1999, it came to light that a several-times decorated veteran officer had been protecting a Miami–Chicago drug route; in 2000, that one of Chicago's most legendary detectives was involved in trafficking stolen gemstones. Also exposed in 2000 were four agents accused of extortion from Polish immigrants.[2] With all these things going on, you realize why there's a joke about the city's law enforcement officers: "One good apple is enough to ruin the whole basket."

Corruption is generally held to be a sign of political underdevelopment, the mark of an imperfect modernity. As a governmental practice and instrument of consensus, it normally gets attributed only to South American dictatorships, to African despots or to feudal systems that function under the guise of capitalism, such as those of Japan or southern Italy. But this isn't some banana republic; this is Chicago, the most industrialized city in the most powerful nation in the world, the city that in just 170 years has sprung from nothing, developing and growing in complete accordance with the logic and needs of capital. It is here in the New World – in "capital's promised land," to borrow Sombart's phrase once again – that we encounter the phenomenon of *structural* corruption.

Like poverty, the spread of corruption in the United States is a *mystery*: Americans realized that the growth of misery and poverty in Europe was part of the leg-

---

2 The 1996 and 1999 cases, plus one of those in 2000, are reported in the *Chicago Sun-Times*, 20 October 2000, in a feature article on the relationship between "cops and mobs"; for the others, see *Associated Press News Service*, 10 February 1997; *Chicago Tribune*, 22 November 2000.

acy of feudalism, the consequence of scarce resources. But how could it happen here, in a continent whose resources were virtually inexhaustible, whose political system was free and democratic? The same goes for corruption, which might prevail elsewhere, in the Old World, in the *ancièn regime*, perhaps, but not in the United States. As Walter Lippmann wrote: "The assumption, inculcated through patriotic text books, is that in the year 1789 a body of wise men founded a new government in a new world," and that corruption "is a kind of *disease*" and so, consequently, "We feel that *it is not supposed to be there*, and that if only we had a little more courage or sense or something we could cut away the diseased tissue and live happily ever after"[3] (italics mine). Here we see how cancer, the *corruption of bodies*, becomes a metaphor squared in standing for the already metaphorical idea of political corruption. This widespread image presupposes a certain idea of a "healthy body politic," a condition in which society would be organized in perfect *transparency*: "We often think of corruption as a disease spreading relentlessly through a body politic, undercutting its strength and integrity and robbing its citizens in the process."[4]

The reality is somewhat less ingenuous. Remember that here we are talking about a society that doesn't ask *how* you made your money but simply *if* you have made money and, if so, *how much*. "In a polity where the key maxim is that money talks, it is not easy to say just where the talkers and what they say have crossed the line of corruption."[5] Nor can we ignore the hard facts of life: good police officers who behave like good citizens could never (honestly) earn enough money to send their children to a good college.

But the contradictions go even deeper. George Cass, president of the Northern Pacific Railway in 1873, famously said that "Wise and good men get corrupt in Congress,"[6] and one could hardly imagine one of the robber barons, notorious for their greed and ruthlessness, presuming to give lessons in morality to a politician.

---

3 Walter Lippmann, "A Theory about Corruption," in *Vanity Fair*, November 1930, no. 35, 3, pp. 61–90. Reprinted in *Political Corruption, a Handbook*, New Brunswick: Transaction, 1989, p. 569.
4 Michael Johnston, *Political Corruption in and Public Money in America*, Monterey, Calif.: Brooks / Cole, 1982, p. 172.
5 Abraham S. Eisenstadt, "Political Corruption in American History" (1978), in *Political Corruption, a Handbook*, p. 547.
6 Cited in Jacob van Klaveren, "Corruption: The Special Case of the United States," in *Political Corruption, a Handbook*, p. 563.

The very public that expects disinterestedness and dedication to the public good from its politicians is at the same time, in fact, ready to swear on the gospel of Adam Smith that society is founded on *private* enterprise, that the general prosperity and wealth of a nation derives from the aggregate of individual self-interests: "It is not from the benevolence of the butcher, the brewer, or the baker, that we expect our dinner, but from their regard to their own interest. We address ourselves, not to their humanity, but to their self-love, and never talk to them of our own necessities but of their advantages."[7]

Yet if the market is the natural "mechanism" that organizes society, then politics too must be organized along market lines and governed by the laws of supply and demand, profit and loss. The struggle for political power thus assumes the form of competition, and the clash of opposing ideas is transformed from propaganda into pure publicity. Competition appears under the guise of an electoral contest in which votes are at once commodities to be bought and resources to be sold. In this market, the trader is the party, and the party behaves like a trader, its function no longer "to compete democratically in order to determine the shape of national politics"[8] but to guarantee the election of the greatest number of candidates to the greatest number of offices.

In the politics market, the result of this competition is an oligopoly that bars entrance to any new, smaller competitors. Just as it is impossible for a small business to break the duopoly of Unilever and Procter and Gamble in the detergent market, so too has the Republican-Democratic duopoly in the US politics market prevented any third party from entering the political arena. Back in 1906, Sombart noted how the "old major parties of America" were compared "with the giant trusts that control such vast capital and dominate so exclusively all areas of supply and sale that any competition against them by third parties is out of question. If a competitor comes on the scene, the old parties summon every thing to devour

---

7   Adam Smith, *An Inquiry into the Nature and Causes of the Wealth of the Nations* (1776), Oxford: Clarendon Press, pp. 26–27.

8   Article 49 of the Italian constitution. In the US, moreover, political parties have no constitutional existence: the US Constitution makes no mention of them. By contrast, article 4 of the French constitution says that "Political parties and organizations compete through the expression of suffrage. They are formed and conduct their activity freely. They must respect the principles of national sovereignty and of democracy." Article 21 of the German constitution of 1949 notes, "The parties cooperate in forming the political will of the people."

him. If need be, they unite for a short time."⁹ American political history is peppered with third-party meteorites, vanished almost as soon as they were formed, from the Anti-Masonic Party of 1830 to the Know-Nothings in the 1850s up to Ross Perot in the 1992 presidential elections and, most recently, Ralph Nader with the Green Party in 2000.

If politics were a market and the parties its traders, then "[f]rom the perspective of the party *entrepreneurs*, votes were resources for gaining control of government offices"¹⁰ (italics mine). The classic form assumed by such a trader in the United States is the "political Machine." Back in 1920, Robert E. Park was already talking about success in politics in terms of football metaphors: "The political machine and the political boss have come into existence in the interest of the party politics. The parties were necessarily organized to capture elections. The political machine is merely a technical device invented for the purpose of achieving this end. The boss is the expert who runs the machine. He is as necessary to the winning of an election as a professional coach is necessary to success at football."¹¹

Park's definition went somewhat against the American grain. The American public, in fact, tends to reserve its purest distillate of antipolitical contempt for the Machine, which it considers a "machine-as-octopus, putting a tentacle into every pocket in a never-ending process of graft, extortion, and outright theft. This machine monster rules by fear and views the legitimate needs and wishes of residents and business with contempt."¹² This revulsion for the Machine is reflected in the way its management class is defined. A respected politician is a *leader,* whereas a politician under attack becomes a *boss,* the head of a gang. From eminent *statesperson,* one goes to being a *slimy politico.* Referring to the former mayor of Chicago, Mike Royko wrote, "The editorial writers decided that Daley wasn't a new-breed, progressive political leader after all. They changed ribbons and wrote him back into 'boss' status, a tool of the Machine."¹³

Like other machines, the political one is a nineteenth-century invention. It first

---

9   W. Sombart, *Why Is There No Socialism in the United States?,* p. 41.
10 Frances Fox Piven and Richard A. Cloward, *Why Americans Don't Vote,* New York: Pantheon, 1988, p. 36.
11 R. E. Park et al. , *The City,* p. 36.
12 M. Johnston, *Political Corruption and Public Policy,* p. 37 and the chapter "The Political Machine."
13 M. Royko, *Boss,* p. 88.

appeared in New York around 1830, when the Tammany Society took over the political organization of the Democratic Party: since then, Tammany Hall (the society's headquarters) has become synonymous with the political Machine as a whole. Such machines, in fact, soon began to spring up everywhere, each readily equipped with its own boss: George Cox (Republican) in Cincinnati, Abe Ruef (Republican) in San Francisco, Thomas J. Pendergast (Democrat) in Kansas City, James Michael Curley (Democrat) in Boston, Edward Hull Crump (Democrat) in Memphis. The Chicago Machines, though, proved to be the most long lasting and powerful, from the Republican Machine of William Hale Thompson to Anton Cermak's Democratic Machine, which has gone on to govern the city for more than sixty years under a succession of mayors: first Kelly, then Nash, then – from 1955 to 1976 – Daley.

As we enter the new millennium, it's no coincidence that another Richard Daley – the boss's son – now governs the Windy City. In fifty years, a lot of Chicago River water has passed under the bridge: the city has lived through Reaganism, waves of privatization and deindustrialization (resulting in the loss of more than 400,000 manufacturing jobs,[14] almost two-thirds of the region's total). Like everything else, the Machine of old was never going to be the same; it had to change. In 2000, however, Daley the younger apparently decided to adhere to the nineteenth-century precept formulated in Sicily by the prince Fabrizio di Salina, protagonist of the novel (and film) *The Leopard*: "You have to change everything so that nothing changes." "Chicago's current governing arrangements are less a return to the old regime than a partially successful attempt to reconstruct the old regime under the new political and economic conditions."[15] In this way, we see what Joel Rast calls the extraordinary "resilience of Chicago's machine,"[16] an institution that is now a century old. Born into a city of horse-drawn trams, the Machine continues to reign sovereign even now that jetliners and computer technology dominate the metropolis.

The Machine is built on three pillars. First is clientelism, often wrongly consid-

14 From 1954 to 1996, cf. David Moberg, "Chicago, to Be or Not to Be a Global City," in *World Policy Journal*, vol. XIV, spring 1997, no. 1, pp. 75.

15 Joel Rast, *Remaking Chicago: The Political Origins of Urban Industrial Change*, DeKalb, Ill.: Northern Illinois University Press, 1999, p. 157.

16 Ibid., p. 167.

ered a residual of *patricianship,* according to the word's Latin origin. As Fox Piven and Cloward remark, in the political struggle, "The very introduction of clientelist arrangements signals that clients have political resources that patrons need to suppress or circumvent." There is no need of clientelism without a democracy in which the patrons are able to apply pressure. Patronage "can thus be regarded as a concession to the working class extracted from the middle and upper classes, and the machine can be seen as embodying a class compromise." In short, patronage is not practicable unless there are goods to be distributed; it depends on conditions of economic development, which "provide the resources that can be used to establish a clientelist basis for assimilating new groups into the polity."[17]

If the Machine is a political entrepreneur and votes are the currency used to acquire public offices, then it follows that these votes must be bought:

> To one person a dollar is loaned; another receives a free railway ticket; in one place coal is distributed on cold days; elsewhere a chicken is given for Christmas; medicine is bought for the sick; where a death has occurred, a coffin is provided at half-price. Along with all this solicitude there is generous treating in the saloons, where perhaps the most important part of the entire election business is transacted. ... One man wants police permission to carry on his street-vending business or to open a saloon; another has contravened the building code or has some such transgression on his conscience. The Machine puts all this right.

The American political Machine acted in the nineteenth century much as Christian Democrats did in Italy after 1947 when the party gave out packets of pasta to the voters or – even better – a new pair of shoes, one for the right foot before the vote, the other for the left after. But it was in August 2000 – not in 1890 – when I saw stalls set up during the Republican Party convention to distribute free bread to the citizens of Philadelphia, the poorest of whom were filling up their sports bags and knapsacks with giant loaves. As in the case of the Christian Democrats, however, the real currency used by the political Machine to buy consensus has been public service jobs.

A hardened preconception has helped propagate the impression that public ad-

---

17 F. Fox Piven and R. A. Cloward, *Why Americans Don't Vote,* p. 36n.

ministration in the United States is svelte and streamlined, that the number of public employees is relatively low compared to in Europe. This impression, like other such common assumptions, is totally false. The United States, regarded as the model of private enterprise, has in proportion to its number of inhabitants as many public employees today as a supposedly bureaucratic country such as Italy. In the United States in 1997, 21.8 million out of a total of 267 million inhabitants were full-time public employees (16.7 million in local and state entities and 5.5 in federal government, including 3.1 million employed by the military). Italy's 1995 figure was 4.2 million state employees out of 57 million inhabitants, or 8 public employees per 100 inhabitants. Reaganism, far from reducing the number of government employees, actually increased those numbers, from 18.1 million in 1980 to 20.4 million in 1990. The real effect of Reagan's policies was to reverse the ratio of federal to local government workers. Whereas more than half of public employees were federal in 1950 (57 percent), federal employees today represent less than one-quarter of the total (23.4 percent, including the military). The Reagan revolution thus represented not so much the victory of private enterprise as of local bureaucracy, moving staff and resources from central government to local government. Reaganism – a movement seemingly typical of anti-Machine politics – simply served to revitalize local Machines that had been starved of resources.

It wasn't until the end of the nineteenth century that the United States introduced competitive exams for the assignment of civil service jobs (under the Civil Service Commission in 1883 and the Civil Service Rules in 1903). And such regulations did not become widespread until the time of Roosevelt's New Deal (through various laws enacted between 1936 and 1940). One can imagine how formidable a weapon public patronage then was to the big parties.

Another gravy train to entice patronage took the form of war pensions. During the nineteenth century, the Republican Machine consolidated its support in the rural areas of the North by showering war veterans with annuities. In 1870, in the wake of the Civil War, 20,000 returning veterans received a pension, and from then on, the number of pensions continued to grow, even if in the late nineteenth century only 40,000 soldiers were in active service. In 1893, the government issued 760,000 pensions to veterans and 216,000 to widows and orphans. Military disability pensions amounted to fifteen times the number of soldiers in service.[18]

The Machine was to discover the real bottomless well of public prebend in local authority and civil service jobs, however, from the police to the fire brigade, trash collectors to ushers. In its new version, the Machine's main political pressure tool is no longer the "patronage army of city employees," but the outsourcing of public service contracts to private enterprise: "privatization lets the mayor hand out contracts to grateful businesses owned by longtime friends who can be counted on to support him politically."[19]

And here we come to the second pillar of the Machine, its local base. We're always hearing how America is a big country. Yet perhaps it is actually too big to be thought of in political terms. For me, as a citizen, there is an abyss between America's destiny as a nation and the destiny of the sewers in my neighborhood, between the country's foreign policy and the efficiency of the local fire department – in short, between the United States as a democratic country and the modestly personal democratic field in which I as an individual can have an influence on that limited part of the world that surrounds and concerns me. It's often said that America is decentralized because of its federal political system, whereas such decentralization is, in the first place, because of the political experience of its citizens. A separation opens up with decisions regarding which roads to asphalt and with the larger political choices of left versus right. And from this gap originates the *depoliticization* of American political organizations, the fact that they are *apparatuses* (with all the ideological opacity this term implies) or, better, Machines. So much for political demand. But localism is also fertile ground for the Machines in terms of supply: "The strength of the city machines was made possible by the high degree of decentralization embedded in the structure of the federal system." The powers invested in state, county, town and individual community are such that the struggle between political parties inevitably comes to focus on local issues, even down to the neighbourhood level, and ignores the great national divides.

The Machine's local roots depend even more on the way society is structured in terms of primary groups or communities – on what Park referred to as a "we"

18 Census Bureau, *Historical Statistics*, vol. 2, series 7, 904–916, and 998–1009.
19 David Moberg, "How Does Richie Rate?" *The Reader: Chicago's Free Weekly*, 19 February 1999, vol. 28, n, 20, p. 28.

group (identifying "us" in relation to "them"). Among organizations "which have grown up for the purpose of controlling the popular vote,"

> the political machine is based, on the whole, on local, personal, that is to say, primary relationships. ... The political machine is, in fact, an attempt to maintain, inside the formal administrative organization of the city, the control of a primary group. The organizations thus built up, of which Tammany Hall is the classic illustration, appear to be thoroughly feudal in their character. The relations between the boss and his ward captain seem to be precisely that, of personal loyalty on one side and personal protection on the other, which the feudal relation implies. The virtues which such an organization calls out are the old tribal ones of fidelity, loyalty, and devotion to the interests of the chief and the clan. The people within the organization, their friends and supporters, constitute a "we" group, where the rest of the city is merely the outer world, which is not quite alive and not quite human in the sense in which the members of the "we" group are.[20]

Finally we come across the word *feudal*. Park was not alone in comparing the Machine to a feud. Long before him, Lord Bryce had written:

> As a tenant had in the days of feudalism to make occasional money payments to his lord in addition to the military service he rendered, so now the American vassal must render his aids in money as well as give knightly service at the primaries, in the canvass, at the polls. His liabilities are indeed heavier than those of the feudal tenant, for the latter could relieve himself from duty in the field by the payment of scutage, while under the Machine a money payment never discharges from obligation to serve in the army of "workers."[21]

But how can the Machine be both a technical device, invented to respond to a wholly modern situation (that of electoral democracy), and at the same time a remnant from feudal days? On one hand, "the ideal machine is an efficient organization. It is in effect a business organization, run for the profit of its members, that must win elections from time to time. In return for divisible material incentives, it gets enough votes to win control of public authority. The astute use of public au-

---

20 R. E. Park et al., *The City*, pp. 35–36.
21 J. Bryce, *The American Commonwealth*, vol. II, p. 122.

thority, in turn, yields more incentives for use in strengthening the machine."[22] On the other, "The machine welds its link with ordinary men and women by elaborate networks of personal relations. Politics is transformed into personal ties. The precinct captain is forever a friend in need. In our prevailingly impersonal society, the machine, through its local agents, fulfils the important social function of *humanizing and personalizing* all manner of assistance to those in need."[23]

Here we have what appears to be an oxymoron: how can an instrument of anonymous mass democracy at the same time be a *personalized* family? The solution we are offered is that of the persistence of the ancient in the modern, the idea that past and present coexist. In this way, the Machine, which is an innovation, an instrument of modernity, is presented as a *remnant* of feudalism. The picture we get presupposes a contradiction between blood ties and modernity, between the logic of lineage and that of money, between primary, premodern relations with a personal clientele and relations mediated by advertising and publicity, which are secondary, impersonal and modern. It is as though Japan, a model of technological hypermodernity and capitalist power, did not at the same time function through a system of patronage complete with its own Machine and Zen ideology. It is as though, on the threshold of the new millennium, the ultracapitalism of the Chicago boys hadn't blended perfectly with obsessive calls for a return to family values in preparing the cocktail of Reaganomics.

Here we come to a crucial point, a decisive question of perspective: modernity creates an electoral system; the electoral system requires a political Machine; the Machine, to carry out its task, has to shape itself into the form of a big family, a clan, a "we" group. The whole of this procedure is seen not as a product of modernity, however, but as a rehash of premodern systems, the resurgence of feudalism. Here is not a question of true or false, of deciding whether or not the Machine displays feudal traits. The question is whether these feudal traits are viewed as remnants of the past or as intrinsic characteristics of the way modernity functions. Between these two perspectives is a crucial difference.

To explain what I mean, let's take the example of German sociologists of the

---

22 M. Johnston, *Political Corruption*, p. 41.
23 Robert K. Merton, *Social Theory and Social Structure*, Glencoe, Ill.: Free Press of Glencoe, 1957, p. 74; cited by M. Johnston, *Political Corruption*.

early 1900s, who would often go on about how the big corporations resembled religious orders: against the desolate cityscape of Detroit, for example, the outline of the General Motors headquarters building irresistibly brings to mind that of a medieval abbey. Yet it would never occur to anyone to say that a corporation is a remnant from the past, an heirloom of feudalism. And here we find ourselves in the unavoidable preliminary battleground of any political struggle, the struggle to define the political itself. Because being able to consign this, as opposed to that, part of the present to the garbage can of history constitutes an immensely powerful weapon. In the eighteenth century, when Voltaire succeeded in defining his adversaries as relics of the (obscurantist) dark ages but himself as a prophet of the light (the enlightenment), the game was over for his adversaries.

To say that the Machine has feudal components is to affirm that – just like corruption – the Machine reflects an incomplete modernity, a dark and obstinate lump of "tribalism," a relic of precapitalist and preurban life. To defeat the corruption and feudalism of the Machine, this implies, the market must be pushed toward ultimate transparency. The political use of such a residue of the past is most evident in the Machine's third pillar, its *ethnic* base. Once again, these millions of dirty and famished derelicts become the great protagonists of American history, whether the whites who crossed the Atlantic from Europe or the Blacks who migrated from the South. Not only do the big trusts and corporations owe their incredible financial power to these boorish hordes, but so do the two great parties and the electoral entrepreneurs, with all their political might. Apart from constituting a new marginal, scab-labor wing of the workforce, these millions of poor, uneducated souls also represented new votes to be courted. They "amounted to a bonanza for political entrepreneurs. … [T]hey were a potential army of voters the size of which had never before been seen."[24] It was thus the Machine's business to welcome them, protect them, threaten and cajole them and, if necessary, to lead them by the hand to the polling station.

Used as polling cattle, these "barbarian immigrants" were soon to be accused of "barbarizing" politics. And contempt for the immigrants bled into discredit for

---

24 M. Johnston, *Political Corruption*, p. 45.

the Machine, which Bailey Aldrich defined as "a despotism of the alien, by the alien, for the alien, tempered by occasional insurrections of decent folk."[25] The movements that mobilized themselves against the corruption of the Machine were thus also anti-immigration movements. Here we see the emergence of that political hodgepodge so typical of the modern world, movements whose politics are based on a mix of flag-waving, border-closing and moralist tub-thumping rhetoric. And here the circle closes: to adopt the medical metaphor, the Machine is a relic of feudalism because it is contaminated by the tribal hordes of immigrants who brought the virus of their precapitalist past with them to the United States. Thus we have a circular thesis that is irrefutable (though also undemonstrable): corruption is an intrinsic feature of feudal regimes, and the Machine is corrupt because it is characterized by European immigrants who hail from feudal societies. This reasoning was all the more pertinent in the case of Black politicians, because Blacks had come from a regime where slavery, rather than feudalism, ruled.

But this is only the first half of the story. To capture the votes and faith of the immigrant electorate, American politics restructured itself along ethnic (and racial) lines, thereby causing the divisions between different ethnicities (and races) to become stable and permanent. Not surprisingly, the early Machines appeared to be appanages for the Irish, who had been the first wave of immigrants to the States, prompting one Harvard professor to write an article entitled "American Cities in Irish Captivity."[26] In Chicago, the job of captain of the city police department would for a hundred years, up until 1960, go to a succession of Irishmen. From the late 1800s, however, it was up to the Germans to decide who would be vice-captain.

Here we rediscover a method deriving from the principle of caste: just as certain government jobs in India are parcelled out based on caste, so a similar carve-up occurs in the United States, only here on the basis of ethnicity. Chicago's mayor has almost always been Irish, but for forty years, up to the arrest of Walter Kozubowski, its city clerk was Polish. As in Italy, where the Cencelli manual distributed portfolios among the various factions of Christian Democracy, here, too, an unwritten manual prescribes the correct dose of each ethnicity for each govern-

25 Cited by Richard C. Wade in "The Enduring Chicago Machine," *Chicago History*, Spring 1986, p. 5.
26 Ibid.

ment office, from the city ward right up to the White House, where it would be impossible to imagine a staff that didn't include at least one Black, one Italian American, one Latino and so on. This is because the Machine in the big city cannot base itself on one ethnicity alone but must stand on an ethnic coalition. Republican "Big" Bill Hale Thompson was elected as mayor of Chicago in 1915 and then re-elected four years later, thanks to a Black-German coalition. In New York, Fiorello La Guardia was able to subsume the ethnic coalition in his own person because his father was Italian and his mother Jewish. In 1930, the Czech property developer and building speculator Anton Cermak, also an antiprohibitionist, remolded Chicago's Democratic Machine by bringing in an array of Poles, Czechs, Slovaks, Germans from the south and Blacks to counterbalance the Irish influence. The Irish later took back the reins, but the coalition was there to stay.

All of this explains why American politics at the dawn of the new millennium is based firmly on ethnic lines. In 1987, Chicago's Black mayor of the time, Harold Washington, ran for re-election against a large part of the Democratic Machine, white ethnics led by alderman Edward Vrdoliak. To measure the various ethnicities involved in this revolt against the mayor, it's enough to look at the names of the aldermen: Slavic names like Aloysiouks, Majerczyk, John Madrzyk, William Krystyniak, Roman Puchinsky; Italian names such as Vito Marzullo, Anthony Lauino, Michael Nardulli, Frank Damato; the lilting Irish cadences of Michael Shenan, Patrick O'Connor, Gerald McLaughlin, Frank Brady; even echoes of German (Bernard Hansen and Jerome Orbach).[27] A few months later, when on 25 November 1987 the successfully re-elected Mayor Washington suddenly died, four Hispanic aldermen – Jesus García, Juan Soliz, Luis Gutiérrez and Raymond Figueroa – seized their opportunity to nominate his successor, not in terms of single votes, but through a "Hispanic block vote,"[28] a current that is becoming increasingly predominant. According to David Moberg, in fact, even now, at the dawn of the twenty-first century, the ethnic factor continues to play a determining role in city politics.

Such a political setup may seem to us excessively archaic and tribal. But this is

27 David K. Fremon, *Chicago Politics Ward by Ward*, Bloomington, Ind.: Indiana University Press, 1987,
   p. 3.
28 Ibid., p. 345.

simply an error of perspective. After all, we are speaking of the youngest political system in history (aside from various communist regimes). In none of the old European systems do we find a similar division of the spoils. The Paris city council is not composed of a number of aldermen from Auvergne who live in the first *arondissement,* others from Bourgognon in the eighth, and a few *pieds noirs* from the nineteenth. Likewise, council jobs in Rome are not assigned according to the candidates' Calabrian, Sardinian or Abruzzian origins. This would not be possible because (1) there is no such thing as a Sardinian or Abruzzian (or, for that matter, Bourgognonian) neighbourhood and (2) councillors are not selected according to such criteria.

Reason 1 here serves to reinforce reason 2. It is ethnic power sharing that has, over the decades, maintained and even consolidated ethnic identities (and antipathies). Every council post reserved for an Irish American is denied a Pole. Every favor done for an Italian is at the expense of a Latino. Politics doesn't so much revive old ethnic rivalries as create new ones: "An Irishman who came here hating only the Englishmen and Irish Protestants, soon hated Poles, Italians and blacks. A Pole who was free arrived here hating only Jews and Russians, but soon learned to hate the Irish, the Italians and the blacks."[29]

Here we find ourselves faced with a new aspect of the identification between physical, social and political space. The homogenizing instrument in this case is the ward-by-ward election of aldermen by majority vote. The majoritarian principle is implicit in the election rules (50 percent of the vote plus one determines the government) but becomes totalitarian when the system is uninominal and the election serves not only to determine large-scale political choices, but also to decide who is to be placed in charge of the water system. The abstract idea is that one votes for a sanitation commissioner who will be good at the job and have a good sanitation program. The result, in practice, is that a good commissioner, to be elected, must reflect the views of the majority and promise the voters what the majority wants to hear – that even if the sewer system falls to pieces, for example, it will not need to be rebuilt, and so there will be no need for new taxes. The winning criterion thus becomes "I tell you what I think that you think I should think."

---

29 M. Royko, *Boss,* p. 31.

Tocqueville referred to this as the *tyranny of the majority* (which is, nonetheless, a lesser evil than a *tyranny of the minority*).

A deeply rooted school of thought running up to the Trilateral Commission considers democracy to be at heart weak and inefficient: according to Thucydides, as long as twenty-four hundred years ago, Pericles had already argued against this idea – that Sparta was efficient because authoritarian while Athens was faint-hearted because democratic – "not accounting words for a hindrance of action," "but that it is rather a hindrance to action to come without instruction of words before."[30] Tocqueville too regarded the notion of weak democracy as completely false: "In my opinion, the main evil of the present democratic institutions of the United States does not arise, as it is often asserted in Europe, from their weakness, but from their irresistible strength. I am not so much alarmed at the excessive liberty which reigns in that country as at the inadequate securities which one finds there against tyranny." And the wider the range of fields depending on election, the more despotic was the tyranny.

> When an individual or a party is wronged in the United States to whom can he apply for redress? If to public opinion, public opinion constitutes the majority; if to the legislature, it represents the majority and implicitly obeys it; if to the executive power, it is appointed by the majority and serves as a passive tool in its hands. The public force consists of the majority under arms; the jury is the majority invested with the right of hearing judicial cases; and in certain states even the judges are elected by the majority. However iniquitous or absurd the measure of which you complain, you must submit to it as well as you can. [31]

The tyranny of the majority is also the rule in industry, where you can enroll in only one union. It really starts to hit home, though, when you look at ethnic composition. In a community where 40 percent of the inhabitants are Polish and 60 percent Irish, uninominally elected representatives will always be Irish and will procure jobs for the Irish, so that, for example, the neighborhood police officer will be Irish. The Poles are therefore better off regrouping in a neighborhood

---

30 Book II, 40.2, of the *History of the Peloponnesian War*, in Thomas Hobbes's classic translation, *Hobbes's Thucydides*, New Brunswick, N.J.: Rutgers University Press, 1975.

31 A. de Tocqueville, *Democracy in America*, vol. I, part 1, pp. 260–1.

where they hold the majority and can thus elect a Polish alderman who will work for their interests. (When new immigrants cause the ethnic composition of a community to change, the old residents naturally continue for a period of time to hold onto political power. So it was for the Irish upon the arrival of the Italians; so it is today for the Italians in neighborhoods with a majority Hispanic and Black population. These are merely phases of adjustment, however.) Together with housing policy and the criteria for allotment of mortgages, elections also contribute toward shaping the community into a specific homogenous group (in terms of religion, census and ethnicity) located in a particular neighborhood, separating it from other communities and constructing an identity based on segregation from others. In this way, ethnic identities persist in their own right, far from fusing in the melting pot, and perhaps even become reinforced.

Territorial settlement, ethnic composition, relations with the community. We have, of course, already come across an organization with these characteristics: the gang. And if gangs structure themselves in the manner of capitalist businesses and behave like political machines, we can hardly be surprised if political machines are in turn structured along the lines of a gang. This is true in terms of exterior characteristics, for example: in both cases, the leader is called the "Boss." It is true in terms of reputation: in nativist lore, immigrants infected politics with the virus of corruption, just as they contaminated society with their criminality. Just as various ethnic groups have handed on to each other the baton of organized crime, from the Irish street gangs to the Italian Mafia to the Chinese Triads, so too have local political organizations passed the reins of power from one ethno-racial group to another, from white ethnics to Hispanics and Blacks. It is true in terms of values: Park speaks of "fidelity and loyalty" as the virtues most prized by the political Machine; in Sánchez-Jankowski's view, gang leaders are selected for "symbolic loyalty to one's friends" and "loyalty to the community."[32]

A more subtle thread connects the political Machine to the gang, however, and that is the attempt of both to establish themselves without having the necessary capital, or with only nonmonetary resources – what we referred to as "moneyless

---

32 M. Sánchez-Jankowski, *Islands in the Street*, p. 75.

capitalism" in the case of the ghettos. If the Machine is really a "political entrepreneur," it is one that seeks to convert extra-economic resources such as consensus or votes into power and money, just as the gang looks to capitalize its control of the street. While political competition takes place in a world that is slightly less Hobbesian than the ghetto, the Machine too competes to appropriate rare resources for itself: council positions, government and other elected offices. And at a slightly higher level, the Machine is also a *lumpen capitalist* enterprise: hence the contempt real capitalists feel for their half-baked political brethren. While not a single politician has managed to accumulate a sizable fortune through corruption (of the level that would permit entry into the elite club of the *Fortune* 500 list), many businesspeople have done so by corrupting politicians. In this we glimpse an idea that appears to have a glowing future, that the mechanisms of power would be more transparent – the world would be more honest – if they were entirely controlled by economic forces (the logic of the free market) and if political control was in turn restricted to a field as limited as possible.

Not that the men of the Machine were paragons of virtue. Legendary are the corruption of Boston's Jim Curley, the racist greed of Edward Crump, the criminality of Frank Hague (aka "I am the law") in Jersey City, the Chicago Machine's rapport with the Mafia. But if by corruption we mean "abuse of a public role for private benefit in such a way as to break the law,"[33] it has to be said that the Machine's actions were often perfectly legal. Here again, the problem is one of definition, in this case of how *corruption* is actually defined. An activity such as lobbying differs from corruption pure and simple only in that it is licit and (theoretically) permissible by law. This same activity falls under the category of "votes for favors" when practiced not by a large pharmaceuticals company but by the inhabitants of a community; it is then deemed political corruption. Here we see a crucial asymmetry between politics and money: the politicians who use capitalists' money to gain power are regarded as sleazier than the capitalists who use the politicians' power to make money.

We have already seen this banner raised to support "clean hands" in politics – often by anti-immigrant xenophobes. Even more often, though, it has been used

---

33 M. Johnston, *Political Corruption*, p. 8.

to limit the domain of politics (in the sense of the "domain of a mathematical function": the ambit in which it is defined). It is in the name of the battle against corruption that an attempt is made to reduce the public sphere to the private sector's gain and advantage. It is in the name of the battle against corruption that the most antidemocratic counter-revolutions in America's history have succeeded.

While it is true that American society nurtures an absolute faith in the goodness and infallibility of its electoral system, and that it practices a form of electoral frenzy, it is equally true that an incredibly small number of Americans actually vote. In the presidential elections of 2000, the influx at the polling station was around 50 percent; in the legislative elections of 1998, it was only 41.9 percent. Ensuring a majority therefore required the consensus of only 25 percent of those on the electoral register in the first case and 21 percent in the second; the opinion of only one-quarter of the country's inhabitants in the former case and one-fifth in the latter was sufficient to determine its political future. Here we run into a new contradiction: this election frenzy is accompanied by a corresponding electoral disaffection. Americans *may* vote many times, but very few of them actually do so. If the measure of democracy is the number of elected public offices, then, as we said before, America is the most democratic country in the planet's history. But if we measure democracy by the number of citizens who participate in the voting process, then the United States suddenly becomes among the least democratic of electoral regimes.

Things haven't always been this way. Before the great moralizing campaigns of the late nineteenth century, the proportion of voters was extremely high. Between 1840 and 1896, it averaged around 78 percent, never sliding below 69 percent. The Machines had a considerable role in this participation, mobilizing the swelling masses of white immigrants, as well as the now-free Black citizens. Legendary is the case of Philadelphia, however, where the Machine managed in 1902 to send 105 percent (!) of the assignees to the polling stations and get 85.4 percent of them to vote for its candidate.

It was to counter such frauds and corrupt practices, and to defeat the power of the Machine, that the right to vote was restricted: to vote after that, you first had to register, and to do that, you had to demonstrate that (1) you were not illiterate and (2) you paid the kind of taxes that not everyone could afford. In Texas, in the twenty-year period between 1884 and 1904, the voting population plummeted from 80 to 30 percent; throughout the United States, the number of voters at presidential elections fell from 79 percent in 1896 to 49 percent in 1920. Since then, the figure has never again risen above 70 percent. In 1988, the influx was 45 percent, rising slightly to 50 percent in 2000. The crusade against corruption thus transformed itself into a limitation on the practice (if not the right) of voting itself. There is therefore a right-wing vision of corruption, an image of the Machine that every so often once again comes to the fore and is used as an election strategy.[34] What we have to trace, more than a history of corruption, is a history of its image.

It is in fact possible to see corruption not as a disease but as a handy remedy. Not always is the illegal necessarily pernicious. You don't have to go back to Robin Hood to find examples of terrible iniquities that are also legal. By the same measure, as Amartya Sen says, "an illegal and corrupt activity can also be advantageous for the community as a whole."[35] Seen in this light, corruption becomes a form of redistribution of income carried out by semi-legal or illegal means and "benefiting large sectors of society." Without the Machine, its advocates say, the various ethnic groups would never have been able to achieve emancipation. It was thanks to local public sector jobs that millions of Irish, Italian and Polish immigrants were able to escape from the shackles of the slums, of unemployment and crime. What is more, without the Machine and the strong consensus that surrounds it, without its capacity to get citizens to accept higher local taxes, it would never have been possible to carry out any public works or services. Public transportation would still be private, as it was previously. It was a variant of the Machine, with its block of ethnic alliances, that consented the election of a number of Black mayors and that, through local authority jobs, enabled a minority of Blacks to gradually win a place in the sun for themselves among the middle classes: from 1973 to 1997, in fact, the number of Blacks employed in the public sector almost doubled, from 523,000 to 973.000.[36]

---

34 The data in this paragraph are taken from F. Fox Piven and R. A. Cloward, *Why Americans Don't Vote*, pp. 30, 109, 83, respectively; and from Census Bureau, *Statistical Abstract of the United States 1993*, tab. 455.
35 Amartya Sen, "Corruzione e crimine organizzato," in *Politica ed Economia*, July 1993, p. 8.
36 Census Bureau, *Statistical Abstract of the United States 1999*, tab. 537; excluded from these figures are

What continues to prevail is the myth "of machine-as-benefactor, as a sort of extended family providing services for the poor and cutting red tape for business-men. The Boss and his minions are seen not as cynical opportunists but as friends in time of need ... asking only for loyal support in return."[37] Modifications to the Machine brought about by the New Deal reinforced this populist vision. In the 1930s, nearly one of every two American families (between 40 and 45 percent) re-ceived federal aid, and 85 percent of those were pro-Roosevelt. In establishing a solid bond between the voting working classes and the Democratic Party, "among the most important vehicles were the old political Machines that had been nur-tured on funds from federal programs." "Far from rendering the machines obso-lete, Roosevelt reinvigorated them for at least another decade. The most famous instance was the New Deal's relationship with the Chicago machine – initiated in return for Mayor Anton Cermak's support at the 1932 convention – where federal funds made possible the centralization of the fractious ward-based bosses."[38]

Cermak was to pay with his life for this support: on 15 February 1933, while on a visit to Miami together with Roosevelt, he was struck by shots intended for the president, fired by one Giuseppe Zangara. Cermak told Roosevelt, "I'm glad it was me instead of you." He died in the hospital twenty days later. Zangara's last words before he was executed were, "Lousy capitalists."

The second piece of surgery the New Deal performed on the Machine con-cerned trade union relations: the Democratic Party established a strong organiza-tional rapport with the newly formed Congress of Industrial Organizations (CIO). In numerous cities, the unions began to function as local Machines, while their leaders became part of the political Machine. And the same criminalization took place in the unions that had already affected the Machine itself: both were tarred with the same sleaze-soaked brush. In 1968, Norman Mailer wrote, "So Hum-phrey money was there in Chicago for convention frolics, and a special nightclub or cabaret in the Hilton called the Hubaret where you needed a scorecard to sepa-rate the trade-union leaders from the Mafia. ... Every Negro on the take was there as well – some of the slickest, roundest, blackest swingers ever to have contacts in

---

teachers and school staff.
37 M. Johnston, *Political Corruption*, p. 174.
38 F. Fox Piven and R. A. Cloward, *Why Americans Don't Vote*, pp. 131–32.

with everyone from Mayor Daley to the Blackstone Rangers. ... So Hubie
Humphrey came to Chicago with nine-tenths of the organized Democratic Party
– Black support, labor support, Mafia support."[39] This passage has everything,
from the use of the term *slickest* to the train of rot, Mafia / unions / corrupt Blacks
/ Mayor Daley / Blackstone Rangers gang. Thus the loop closes: *gang* had originally been another word for a *work team,* but now a *union of workers* was being
treated like a gang. The claims of the meek, together with their organizations,
have always been regarded as in someway "slick," a judgment that has become a
self-fulfilling prophecy, considering that some American unions, such as Jimmy
Hoffa's celebrated Teamsters, have been involved with the Mafia.

It is Chicago's ethnic makeup, its huge industrial might (and therefore the electoral weight of the workers) and the preeminence of its Mafia that in part go together to explain the extraordinary longevity of that city's Machine (in its classic
form). It's not that the political ground rules and mechanisms have changed
greatly elsewhere – in the 1970s and 1980s, in fact, Blacks were able to win many
mayorships, thanks to the same instruments that fifty years earlier had been used
to elect Italian mayors and, fifty years before that, Irish. But the Machine in other
cities has assumed new forms and is no longer even called a Machine. In Chicago,
by contrast, the old warhorse keeps chugging along. Here, according to Royko, is
how the Chicago way worked during the 1970s under Daley *père:*

> The head of the Janitors' Union was on the police board, the park board, the Public
> Building Commission, and several others. The head of the Plumbers' Union was on
> the Board of Health and ran the St. Patrick's Day parade. The head of Electricians'
> Union was vice-president of Education. The Clothing Workers' Union had a man on
> the library board. The Municipal Employees' Union boss was on the Chicago
> Housing Authority, which runs the city's public housing projects. The head of the
> Chicago Federation of Labor and somebody of the Teamsters' Union were helping
> run the poverty program. And the sons of union officials find the door to City Hall
> open if they decide on a career in politics.[40]

39 Norman Mailer, *Miami and the Siege of Chicago: An Informal History of the American Political
   Conventions of 1968,* New York: Signet Books/New American Library, 1968, pp. 110–11.
40 M. Royko, *Boss,* p. 74.

From this picture one might think that, in some perverse way, the Machine represents the interests of the working classes. If votes are the currency the Machine uses to buy governmental power, however, money is equally a resource that can be used to buy votes. For this reason, the Machine has always been closely allied to the business world. In Chicago, the Republican daily, the *Chicago Tribune*, supported the candidacy of the young Democrat Richard M. Daley for mayor, just as Chicago's Republican ruling class supported his father for twenty years. In part, the money flows to whomever holds power – who decides the allocation of public works, council contracts and building licences. In part, it exploits the Machine's corruptibility to cut through the bureaucratic red tape. Yet in part, its job is also to give real if hidden support to the Machine in carrying out its social role: "Machines often perform a delicate political balancing act over a chasm of class differences, winning votes from the numerous poor and money from the affluent few. These classes often clash over issues of policy, culture, and economic self-interest, but bosses can turn these diverse groups into complementary forces supporting the machine. In the process, machines help dampen potentially serious conflicts."[41] In their constant dealings with the Machine, the owner class know that their bribes pay not only for more rapid contracts, at inflated prices, but also for the maintenance of a social truce. The Machine provides "a method for incorporating working people into politics while keeping their political issues off the electoral agenda."[42]

It is the Machine's underlying corruption that allows the Machine to play this role as a stabilizing force. If the Machine is corrupt, it isn't so much because of the bribes pocketed by its bosses as because of the way it buys the loyalty of entire social groups while satisfying the interests of only a select few of their members. The real corruption lies in this translation of *collective claims into personal concessions*, a bailiff's job here, a subsidy there. Electoral politics becomes *"a politics of the individual*, structured around patronage and selective incentives" (italics mine).[43] So the Machine will provide the leader of this or that union with a more comfortable life, but it will not extend workers' rights; it will help this or that person of an ethnic

---

41 M. Johnston, *Political Corruption*, p. 41.
42 F. Fox Piven and R. A. Cloward, *Why Americans Don't Vote*, p. 74.
43 J. Rast, *Remaking Chicago*, p. 29.

minority find a job, but it will not raise the living standards of the ethnic or racial group as a whole. The Machine will help create a clientelist class of white-collar Blacks even as the situation in the ghettos becomes more and more desperate. Although Black politicians have an important role in the Chicago Machine, they have never managed to pour so much as a glass of water on the inferno of the inner cities. In Johnston's words, as

> to the question of whether or not the machine is a true friend of the poor, if by "'the poor'" we mean the poor *as a class,* the answer has to be no. Machine politicians never intended to lift whole classes of people out of poverty, for poverty and dependency helped secure their hold on power. Political pacification – especially when it extends beyond the machine to other community leaders – makes it most difficult for poor communities to put their political resources to independent use.[44]

Here too, as in the case of the gangs, we see an inversion of perspective. What at first appeared to be a disease reveals itself instead to be a physiological condition of political life; the corruption that seemed to undermine the healthy organism of democracy is shown to be one of the pillars that uphold the status quo. While frequently a target for abuse and an object of unanimous revulsion, the Machine performs vital functions, muffling conflicts and imposing compromise. For this reason, campaigns against corruption and against the Machine in general tend to rage only when the price of social peace becomes too high, when big business is no longer willing to foot the bill in terms of both money and power. When politicians no longer stay in their place, or when the Machine invades others' turf, that is when the knights of the "clean hands" crusade saddle up and sharpen their swords. Once the price returns to normal, everybody goes back to business as usual.

To confirm this cycle, consider how many powerful political heads have really rolled in the United States on account of corruption. The answer is very few. Since the end of the Second World War, the most illustrious victim has been Spiro Agnew (of Greek origin), Nixon's vice-president who faced numerous charges of bribery and was found guilty of tax evasion for a paltry $29,500. But Agnew finally fell in October 1973 at Nixon's last gleaming after the 1972 Watergate scandal,

---

44 M. Johnston, *Political Corruption,* p. 65.

which, it should be noted, was not a case of economic corruption: it was magnetic tape and not money that Nixon was pocketing. Much more devastating for American public life are sex scandals: here we see the hierarchy of sin unveiled in a society that regards the body as more malign than the dollar and where eroticism is more satanic than is egotism, for, as Pastor Conwell said, wealth is to be considered an instrument for the good: "you ought to be rich, and it is your duty to get rich." "Money is power, and you ought to be reasonably ambitious to have it, You ought because you can do more good with it than you could without it."[45]

But that's not all: sex scandals are generally uncovered and reported whenever the social compromise to be safeguarded by the Machine and corruption is placed in jeopardy. Nothing better demonstrates the Machine's conservatism than the way it reacts when something appears to menace the existing order, as was witnessed in the city's splendid parks late one August.

---

45 R. H. Conwell, *Acres of Diamonds,* pp. 18, 20.

23

Prague in Illinois

On 24 August 1968, 250 US Air Force transport planes were on standby at Fort Hood in Texas, Fort Riley in Kansas, Fort Sill in Oklahoma and Fort Carson in Colorado, fueled up and ready to leave for Chicago at a minute's notice. Their destinations were O'Hare airport and the naval air base at Glenview. On board these C-141s were six thousand soldiers trained in antiguerrilla warfare tactics, fully equipped and ready for battle. Senior officers were already at work coordinating preparations at Fort Sheridan, the military base financed in 1886 by the good people of the Chicago bourgeoisie after the Haymarket riots. It was from this same base that the federal troops had marched into Chicago to occupy the city in 1894 during the Pullman strike. Five UH-1 Huey strike helicopters, as used in Vietnam, had been placed at the army's disposal.[1]

The Illinois National Guard had 5,649 soldiers stationed near the center of Chicago, ready to intervene with armored personnel carriers and heavy machine guns. The 11,900 agents of the city police department were in position, each working twelve-hour shifts. To their ranks were added several hundred agents from the state and county police, along with an unspecified number of private police officers and security guards. Never had so many agents of the FBI and the various

---

1 *New York Times*, 25 August 1968.

other government security agencies been seen concentrated in a single city to keep watch on hotels, rooming houses, newspapers and public places.

All of this combined military and police might was assembled to protect the Democratic Party convention, scheduled to begin the following day, 25 August, to select the presidential candidate who would oppose Republican Richard Nixon in the autumn elections. The menu wasn't exactly appealing. The only two candidates who might have had a strong chance of winning the election were both absent. Lyndon Baines Johnson, the outgoing president, had decided not to run for re-election, his popularity battered by the deterioration of the situation in Vietnam. The other missing candidate was Robert Kennedy, who had won five of the six primaries he had run in, the last of which had been in California, where he was shot dead on the night of 5 June.

Under these circumstances, nomination of Johnson's vice president, Hubert Humphrey, was almost a foregone conclusion. Humphrey was a classic Democrat of the Cold War school, who had come to the Chicago convention, as Norman Mailer said, "with nine-tenths of the organized Democratic Party – Black support, labor support, Mafia support ..." Running against him were the intransigent Eugene G. McCarthy of Minnesota, who was in favor of a rapid withdrawal of US troops from Vietnam, and George S. McGovern of South Dakota, another (albeit moderate) peacenik. The one wild card was Teddy Kennedy: was the only surviving Kennedy brother going to be a surprise last-minute addition to the list? (In the end, he ducked out.) It was no contest: three days later, on 28 August, Humprey would receive the Democratic nomination on the first round with 1,761 votes against McCarthy's 601 and McGovern's 146.

But if the game was nearly over before it even began, why was Chicago in a state of siege? Why had the mayor imposed an 11 p.m. curfew in the city's parks? A year before, Richard J. Daley had made it clear that he wanted the convention to take place in his city, where the Democrats hadn't gathered since 1956, and that he wanted the delegates to land at his airport, O'Hare, and the journalists to drive down his urban freeway, the John Kennedy.

But a lot can change in a year. On 30 January 1968, the Vietcong had launched its Tet offensive, and it was then that the United States lost faith in its ability to win the war. That February, pacifist groups came up with the idea of holding a huge antiwar demonstration to take place in Chicago during the August convention. In late March, Johnson retired from the race for the Democratic nomination. A few days later, Martin Luther King Jr. was assassinated in a Memphis motel, triggering an explosion of Black uprisings in every major city in the country. Shops were looted, buildings razed and hundreds of people killed. In Chicago, riots flared on the West Side. That evening, Mayor Daley went on television to make an announcement that left no doubt as to his position (or, for that matter, his syntax): "I said to [the superintendent of police] very emphatically and very definitely that an order be issued by him immediately and under his signature to shoot to kill any arsonist or anyone with a molotov cocktail ... and to issue a police order *to shoot to maim or cripple* anyone looting any stores in our city"[2] (italics mine).

The organizers of the demonstration initially hoped that around 100,000 people would turn up, and both the authorities and the newspapers took them at their word, foreseeing Chicago invaded by a rabble of hippies, beatniks, drifters, homosexuals and communists. The police made their security preparations so evident that, come summer, many of the protest-group leaders were advising their followers to stay home. But the authorities weren't afraid so much of the peace movement as they were of the possible conjunction between the protest against the war in Vietnam and the revolts in the Black ghettos. Mayor Daley must have remembered only too well the march Martin Luther King Jr. had led through Chicago's white suburbs in 1966: for as long as the protest had stayed within the bounds of the slums, it hadn't bothered anyone greatly, but tolerance began to wane fast when the Blacks decided they *would no longer stay put*. Throughout the summer of 1968, Daley went around inaugurating public works for the city's Black residents. On 1 August, he decreed that a long thoroughfare in the south part of the city be renamed Dr. Martin Luther King Drive, after the man Daley couldn't stomach when he was alive.

Meanwhile, TV news bulletins continued to report every day on the growing number of American soldiers killed in Vietnam and on the results of B-52 bomber missions. Four years previously, only 16,000 troops had been stationed in Vietnam. Now, on the orders of General Westmoreland, as many as 543,000 men

---

2   M. Royko, *Boss*, pp. 168–69.

were in the region. But between the war and preparations for the convention, it was the crisis in Czechoslovakia that dominated the news headlines: under Brezhnev's leadership, the Soviet Union was threatening to invade the country to put a stop to the events of the Prague Spring and to Dubcek's attempted reforms. Finally, between the night of 20 August and the early morning of 21 August, Warsaw Pact forces (from bases in the USSR, Poland and East Germany) rolled into Czechoslovakia.

In this heated atmosphere, only a few peaceniks eventually made the trip to Chicago to challenge the combined might of the military and police apparatus: "A defense force of at least twenty-five thousand was in Chicago. Daley had an army that was bigger than that commanded by George Washington. Never before had so many feared so much from so few. At most, five thousand war protesters had come to Chicago."[3] The Walker Commission's report on police violence describes these protesters in tones of self-righteousness verging on disgust:

> There were, of course, the hippies – the long hair and love beads, the calculated unwashedness, the flagrant banners, the open lovemaking and disdain for the constraints of conventional society ... The crowd included Yippies come to "do their thing," youngsters working for a political candidate, professional people with dissenting political views, anarchists and determined revolutionaries, motorcycle gangs, black activists, young thugs, police and secret service undercover agents. There were demonstrators waving the Viet Cong flag and the red flag of revolution and there were the simply curious who came to watch and, in many cases, became willing or unwilling participants.[4]

The protestors chose Lincoln Park as their base. Situated slightly north of the Magnificent Mile, amid lawns, majestic trees and gently sloping hills and hollows, Lincoln Park stretches a little over three miles along the banks of Lake Michigan and encircles a zoo dotted with ponds. The residents of the Gold Coast's luxury condos come here in their designer sweat suits to jog or to take the dog for a run.

---

3 Ibid., p. 182.
4 *Rights in Conflict: Convention Week in Chicago August 25–29, 1968*, a report submitted by Daniel Walker, New York: Dutton, 1968, pp. 3–4.

On weekends and holidays, families from the city's poorer neighborhoods descend in droves with their portable barbecues: Hispanics hang out on the grass alongside groups from the smart set armed with tablecloths and ice buckets. Often the park is invaded by battalions of scouts, choirs, groups of street musicians or picnickers, and on summer nights, people sleep here swaddled in the lake breeze.

For all the youths who had come from afar, Lincoln Park seemed the most logical place to camp out for the night. But Mayor Daley saw things rather differently and maintained his rigid eleven o'clock curfew. At midnight on Sunday, 25 August, Chicago police waded into the thousand or so protesters still in the park, truncheoning whoever fell in their path, including innocent bystanders, women, the elderly, journalists and photographers. The next day, Monday, 26 August, saw further demonstrations and police charges as the park was once again violently emptied of its unwanted guests. One of the protestors' banners read: "Welcome to Prague."

More incursions followed the next day, but the violence reached its peak on Wednesday, 28 August, when police charged demonstrators in Grant Park, in the heart of the city and directly in front of the Hilton Hotel, where key delegates were staying. There on Michigan Avenue, police and soldiers let loose: "Anyone who was in the way of some of the policemen was struck," one witness said. "Police continued to hit people in the back who were running away as fast as possible. I saw one man knocked to the street." According to another witness, police "pursued individual demonstrators for as far as a block. ... In many cases ... when police had finished beating the protesters they were pursuing, they then attacked, indiscriminately, any civilian who happened to be standing nearby."[5] "For no reason that could be immediately determined, the blue-helmeted policemen charged the barriers, crushing the spectators against the windows of the Haymarket Inn, a restaurant in the hotel. Finally the window gave way, sending screaming middle-aged women and children backward through the broken shards of glass."[6]

Journalists and photographers were again chased and manhandled. In that one clash alone, 178 arrests were made. Come midnight, the armored personnel carriers were rolling up and down Michigan Avenue, their heavy machine guns at the

---

5   Ibid., p. 170.
6   *New York Times*, 29 August 1969.

ready. That Wednesday, TV cameras for the first time captured the police attacks – though no worse than before – for a full seventeen minutes. Tens of millions of viewers watched the beatings as, meanwhile, Humphrey obtained the Democratic nomination in the Amphitheater, following the same line as Johnson had: the bombardment of Vietnam was to continue, because "a withdrawal would be totally unrealistic and disastrous."

Many delegates from the conference participated in the following day's march. Again, the march was broken up, and 150 demonstrators (including nine delegates) were arrested. During the night, police searched McCarthy's offices. Humphrey defended Mayor Daley's action. In total, 668 people were arrested during the convention, mostly Chicago residents, a fact that shows that the feared red invasion had not taken place. Injured along with 192 police officers were an unspecified number of demonstrators. Police and newspapers claimed that massive caches of arms had been discovered: in reality, these were mainly bricks, stones and sticks. A rumor went around that some of the protesters had even launched poisonous black widow spiders at police, but most of the missiles had been somewhat less lethal: plastic bags filled with feces and urine. That day, the US Air Force carried out 121 bombing raids on Vietnam. The previous week, the expeditionary force had suffered its heaviest losses since the beginning of the war, with 308 soldiers killed and 1,134 wounded, raising the total number of US war casualties to 27,101 dead and 169,296 wounded.[7]

Between the war in Vietnam, with its mounting death toll, and the scuffle in Chicago, with its minor contusions, there could hardly be a greater disparity. Yet this disparity extended to the situation in Chicago itself, between the plane loads of commandos flown into Fort Sheridan and the ragbag of scruffy kids scattered around Lincoln Park. The same disparity existed between the worldwide media attention given to the beatings of white yippies in Grant Park and the silence surrounding recurrent deaths in the Black uprisings. For when all was said and done, in five days of clashes between protestors and police, not a single fatality had occurred. One Black teenager interviewed by a reporter from the *New York Times* made a point when he said, "I want to see if those National Guardsmen come at

---

7 *New York Times*, 30 August 1968.

Jeeps and baracades during the Democratic convention, Chicago 1968. Courtesy Chicago Historical Society.

them with guns like they did with us."[8]

Yet the images from the Chicago convention were transmitted worldwide and became mentally superimposed upon those equally famous pictures of unarmed Prague dwellers talking to Soviet tank commanders in the shadow of their howitzers, prompting the German newspaper *Die Welt* to comment: "With 300 injured in the streets of Chicago, the Russians can boast that the Democratic convention was perhaps even bloodier than their Prague coup."

The disparity was amplified even further when in September 1969 seven of the protest organizers – Rennie Davis, David Dellinger, John R. Froines, Tom Hayden, Abbie Hoffman, Jerry Rubin and Lee Weiner – were charged with "conspiracy." Also charged, for good measure, was Black Panther leader Bobby Seale. The climate in which the trial took place was unbelievably hostile. The chief pros-

---

8 *New York Times*, 29 August 1968, p. 24.

ecutor described the ideas of the accused as "a freaking fag revolution." Federal Judge Julius Hoffman refused to allow Seale to conduct his own defense, saying that "the complexity of the case makes self-representation inappropriate." To ensure Seale's silence, the judge had him gagged and tied to a chair for the whole of the trial. White prosecutor Tom Foran called Seale the only defendant "who definitely wasn't a fag."[9] Not surprisingly, the Black man, Seale, was the only one of the accused to be given a jail sentence; he was sent down for four years, not on the "conspiracy" count but allegedly for contempt of court. The white defendants were cleared of conspiracy charges and received only light sentences for minor offenses. Not one of them did time.

Conspiracy: this is the crucial term. According to experts in the field, *conspiracy* is an interpretative skeleton key capable of opening every closet in American history. The anarchists conspired in 1886; Eugene Debs and the railway unions conspired in 1894; during the First World War, the Wobblies conspired. The forces of the opposition conspire just as those in power salute their generals. If Palmer and Pullman revered Sheridan, here now was Daley singing the praises of General Westmoreland: "We're honored, our city is honored, to have such a fine and outstanding example of the military of our fine country. We're proud of them and everyone should be proud of them and those who are not proud of them should get out the country if they don't like it."[10]

Behind any threat to the established order lurked the shadow of conspiracy, possibly aided and abetted by foreign agents – in one case the Germans, in another the Soviets or the Vietnamese. And even if they weren't foreigners, the agitators generally came from out of state; the Chicago trial was based on a law somewhat ironically called the Civil Rights Act (1968), designed to punish what it called "outside agitators" held to be responsible for racial disorder. As one Republican from Mississippi had said, "Here we are with one Stokeley Carmichael and one Rap Brown, who among others we find traveling from state to state and from city to city, and in their wake comes conflagration, blood-spilling, wholesale pilfering

---

9   T. Hayden, *Trial*, pp. 36, 43.
10 M. Royko, *Boss*, p. 196.

and the loss of life and property."[11]

Confronted with media protests about his handling of the situation, Daley did not hesitate to play the conspiracy card, explaining to Walter Cronkite of CBS that "[t]he television industry didn't have the information I had. There were reports and intelligence on my desk that certain people planned to assassinate many of the leaders, including myself. So I took the necessary precautions." Nothing more was ever heard of these phantom reports, but the mere mention of them at the time was enough to sway public opinion in Daley's favor.

The protestors also resorted to conspiracy theories, however, to explain the brutal put-down of the Chicago protest (somewhat as Blacks from the ghetto evoke that great white conspiracy known simply as *The Plan*). In Eldridge Cleaver's view, the clashes were part of a conspiracy to ensure Nixon's election by discrediting the Democrats and steering public opinion even further to the right. According to Cleaver, the right's strategy was simply to exaggerate the threat posed by the left in order to stir up fear.[12] For Dick Gregory, on the other hand, the CIA was trying to subvert the country and had been involved in the assassinations of Martin Luther King Jr. and both Kennedy brothers. The conspiracy as a network of hidden causes, then, would appear to be the terrestrial equivalent of Adorno's horoscopes: just as astral projection renders acceptable the inexorable movement of social destiny, so too does conspiracy provide an explanation for the inscrutability of political fortunes.

In this case, though, the conspiracy theory simply isn't plausible – no more so than the Walker Commission's idea that the demonstrators had provoked police into an excessive show of force that eventually exploded in a "spontaneous police riot." Perhaps some of the agents had completely flipped their wigs, but the deeper and more obvious reason for the violence had to do with the wall of incomprehension that stood between the young protestors and the American people (we, the people) represented by the Machine. Daley was the embodiment of generations of white ethnic immigrant workers, police officers and storekeepers who had elbowed their way into society through toil and sacrifice in their fervent

---

11 Cited by J. Anthony Lukas, "The Chicago Conspiracy Trial," in *Britannica Book of the Year 1970*, Chicago, 1971, p. 441.

12 In the introduction to Jerry Rubin's book, *Do It*, New York: Simon and Schuster, 1969.

pursuit of the American Dream. These were the people who had built the urban freeways, airports and skyscrapers of modern America, and they belonged to that ethnic world composed of solidarity, racism, steelworks, wedding parties, blood ties, financial common sense, stubborn pragmatism and deep-rooted superstition. Hence the total incomprehension they felt toward the Blacks, who, they believed, "remain in the slums because they don't do like we do and roll their sleeves up" – and hence their revulsion for the pacifists. To Daley and the Machine (as to the mass of blue-collar workers), the protestors – with their incomprehensible beat poetry by the likes of Allen Ginsberg, their hippie folk songs by Bob Dylan, Pete Seeger and Phil Ochs and their anti-American, pro-Vietnamese banners (in a country where the Stars and Stripes flew proudly from the flagpoles of even the remotest houses) – may as well have been from Pluto. But precisely because of such incomprehension the fear was born of a world completely removed from their horizons. Not surprisingly, an attempt is always made to rationalize this fear of the unknown by attributing it to an alien (foreign) conspiracy. Although the fear the American ruling classes have of their opponents is by all accounts excessive, it does nonetheless carry some small truth: it's the same kind of fear you might experience when faced with some trivial snag, just because it cannot be explained; it's the anxiety that comes from a minor detail that doesn't belong.

It's almost as though some willful and systematic excess of prudence guarantees that even the slightest hint of revolt, the vaguest rumor of subversion, is taken seriously. The might America's capitalists brought to bear on Albert and Lucy Parsons in 1886 was completely out of proportion, as was the fear in 1894 of Eugene Debs's "dictatorship." And there is something comic, something infinitely laughable about deploying the muscle of the US Army against a band of hippies in 1968. It recalls Vincenzo Cuoco, a great Italian writer little known outside his own country, as he recounts – in the heat of the moment and with the kind of passion that only the vanquished can muster – the failed Neapolitan revolution of 1799, referring ironically to the governors of the twin kingdoms of Sicily:

> A number of boisterous young enthusiasts, their heads filled with the latest theories, scoured the pages of periodicals for reports of the events of the French Revolution, which they would then either discuss among themselves or, less profitably, with their sweethearts or barbers. Of no other crime than this were these young men

guilty, nor could they be, having neither rank, nor fortune, nor platform from which to express their opinions. Nevertheless, a bloody tribunal known as the "State Council" was erected to pronounce judgement upon them as though they had already killed the King and overturned the constitution.[13]

Excessive use of repressive force and exaggerated fear are two constants of modern regimes, which tend to behave as though afraid they are about to be deposed, as though deep down they are aware of their own unsuspected fragility. In this overreaction, we catch a glimpse of their true nature, like huge, brawny boys who open their mouths only to reveal that they have squeaky, high-pitched voices.

One is never quite sure whether such overreaction is a result of paranoia or of political wisdom, however. Both the yippies and the hippies, after all, have either disappeared or become yuppies like Jerry Rubin. The protestors of those years are now either wiser, washed-up or dead, while the cogs of the Machine continue to turn. Despite the presence of radical Black fringe groups such as Black Power and the Black Panthers, the Blacks living in the South Side of Chicago that August reacted with almost total indifference to the repression of the protest, widening even further the gap between white activism and Black ghetto unrest.

What is more, despite the many violent scenes Chicago has witnessed in its short history, the 1968 event was the first in which the media and television played a major role. But while images of student clashes with police in Paris's Latin Quarter only a few months before had kindled in the French feelings of nationwide solidarity with the students ("those are our kids they're beating") and set off a general strike, here the TV pictures failed to shock the public. On the contrary, while the violence of the Chicago police enraged public opinion overseas (where indignation is normally at its height when the outrage happens thousands of miles away), the American public fully supported it, as immediate-response surveys showed.

Daley therefore really did represent the feelings of the majority, a majority that may have been silent but was undoubtedly also aggressive. Likewise, the indiscriminate violence against journalists in the long term turned out to be much more forward looking than it at first appeared. The sixties was the last period

---

13 Vincenzo Cuoco, *Saggio storico sulla rivoluzione napoletana del 1799,* Bari: Laterza 1980 (1801), ch. 6, p. 30.

when the press and TV played an effectively critical role, for example, regarding the Vietnam War. It may just be coincidence, but the media has changed decisively since the blows of police truncheons rained down on journalists. You need only think about how the American media reported on the Gulf War of 1991, showing an attitude of compliance that we saw again during Clinton's intervention in Kosovo in 1999. After the beatings meted out by the Chicago police, both press and television returned to the ranks, disciplined once more, just as they had been in 1877 when the *New York Times* had called Chicago a "city in the hands of communists."

This is why the photomontage that at the time became indelibly stamped in the mind of just about everyone – with the image of Russian tanks rolling through Prague overlaying that of the beatings being dealt out by the Chicago police – stands as an index of how mistaken contemporary perceptions can be. At the time, those Soviet tanks transmitted a message of an immense, resolute and irremovable power, whereas the hysterical reaction of the American police, together with military defeat in Southeast Asia, seemed to signal the onset of a major crisis. The Soviet regime and the Warsaw Pact appeared to be invincible, the US in the midst of a full-scale revolt. Today, little more than thirty years later, neither the Warsaw Pact nor the Soviet Union exists any longer, and the Cold War is over – but Richard Daley's son is in the middle of his fourth term in office as mayor of Chicago.

Metacity

Market Missionaries Besieged in Fort Science

"The Cold War is over, and the University of Chicago won it." So ran the encomium published in a 1991 *Washington Post* editorial, following the death of Nobel prize–winning economist George Stigler.[1] Little less than ten years after the end of the Cold War, it seems strange that such a pronouncement could have actually sounded plausible – and not ridiculous – to its author and readers. Could it really be that a group of erudite scholars armed only with dissertations had single-handedly routed the Soviet nuclear arsenal?

Even more disconcerted would be anyone who had actually studied in the stony calm of the university's immense libraries, or had strolled among its neo-Gothic edifices and perfectly manicured lawns, where undergraduates lie in the grassy splendor in spring, elbows propped over a book, or go for a morning jog in the winter, emitting puffs of steamlike breath as they pad along. Nothing could be further from the horrible clangor of war than the cultivated calm of campus. It's hard to imagine that these idyllic, meditative pastures were the formative ground of the Chicago Boys, the group of economists who came to international prominence during the 1970s, when various South American dictatorships began to adopt their economic policies. Looking at the faces of these polite, studious

---

1 George F. Will, *Washington Post*, 8 December 1991, p. C7.

young people, it's almost impossible to convince yourself that they might in a few years' time be acting as advisers to some baby Pinochet.

For me, the doubts began to creep in at the door to the Quadrangle, the pleasantly comfy university club that sits snug at the center of campus. I was leaving the club after lunch with a professor, and I asked him where the nearest subway station was. He replied by advising me not to take the subway, even during the day: wherever I was going, I should always call a taxi. I also had misgivings about the "emergency phone line" installed by the university and connected to the local police station; by calling 134 from the campus and surrounding area, you can have a car sent immediately to pick you up and escort you off the premises.[2] As long as you remain on campus or in the surrounding neighborhood – Hyde Park – however, the feeling of intimidation provoked by so much knowledge surpasses any disquietude these signals may cause.

Under the supervision of 2,000 teaching staff, 12,300 young men and women study here (one instructor for every six students). John D. Rockefeller founded the university, donating $35 million in 1892 and another $10 million in 1910. Here they have everything you could possibly require for study. The campus libraries contain 5.4 million volumes, while the archives hold 7 million documents. Associated with the university is also the Argonne National Laboratory, whose facilities are among the finest in the country. The university's publishing house, the University of Chicago Press, publishes 50 journals and 250 new titles every year and has a backlist of 4,000 titles; more than half the books UCP published during the twentieth century are still in print. On the teaching front, 73 Nobel prize winners have held courses here at one time or another. Everything is available on tap to enable the experts of the future to attain complete mastery of their chosen field.

Chicago is also home to six other universities: Loyola (Catholic), Chicago State and University of Illinois at Chicago (both state institutions), Roosevelt, De Paul, and – with campuses in both Chicago and Evanston – Northwestern. But in the eyes of the world, there is only one University of Chicago – the one where Dewey set up his pedagogical laboratory, where the discipline of urban sociology was born, where Fermi constructed the world's first-ever atomic reactor and where a

---

2 Serge Halimi, "L'Université de Chicago, un petit coin de paradis bien protegé," in *Le monde diplomatique*, April 1994.

school of economics flourishes that has garnered twenty-one Nobel prizes. In his annual address, the president proudly affirms that 63 percent of the students enrolled at the university are drawn from the top 5 percent of high school graduates, while three-quarters come from among the top 10 percent. To study at the University of Chicago, you have to be the best.

Up to this point, we have looked only at the lower end of the American education system, at the public high schools in the projects, where students have to pass through a metal detector as they go in to check that they aren't packing a Glock among their textbooks. These state-run high schools are an example of what Loïc Wacquant calls "America as social dystopia," indicative of a *curve of deterioration* that seems destined to hit Europe in the near future. In the high schools of Chicago's ghettos, three-quarters of the students fail to finish the year, even if they aren't required to take exams to go on to the next class.[3]

By contrast, the University of Chicago expresses that side of American education where excellence flourishes, illustrating that an outstanding elite can emerge even without a widespread base of educational quality. And this is surely the key to understanding whether or not the United States is a nation in a state of decadence: from the evidence of the slums, the inner cities and American apartheid, you are forced to conclude that the country is already halfway down Sunset Boulevard. When you see the amazing wealth of talent and creativity continually churned out by the top universities, however, you are made to believe once more. Indeed, the co-presence of both aspects – the terrible squalor of the ghettos and the innocent spirituality of the campus – is most astonishing.

Here that co-presence becomes a physical fact. The area of Hyde Park, where the University of Chicago is located, is a tiny enclave of privilege literally besieged by some of the city's most derelict Black neighborhoods, with the blasted high-rises of Taylor Homes to the west, the unending acres of ramshackle single-family tract housing to the south. Everywhere you look are gutted houses, abandoned factories, the vacant skulls of burned-out car wrecks. Black windows gape open like toothless mouths; the roads are pitted with craters. Occasionally some Black kids in woolen ski hats break the silence and solitude that reign here, yet they

---

3   L. Wacquant, "De l'Amerique comme utopie à l'envers," in P. Bourdieu et al., *The Weight of the World*.

never venture beyond the invisible line that separates them from the scholars' paradise. No more would the besieged erudites make reckless sorties into the turf of these kids, although they will tell you how they have dared on occasion to cross the inferno of the slums *by bus* in order to get downtown, as though recounting some heroic feat.

Crescat scienta; vita excolatur (the growth of science brings with it a refinement of life), runs the university's motto. But given that a year's study here costs $23,829,[4] the refinement and gentrification of life are obviously the prerogative of the rich. Excellence costs. Even with 32 million people below the poverty line, those in the United States who do have money live (or study or do research) very well indeed.

That's no mean sum – twenty-four thousand dollars – and yet student fees account for only 32 percent of the University of Chicago's income (not counting the revenues generated by the university's clinics and by the Argonne laboratory). If we deduct from these fees the scholarships handed out by the university to the most gifted kids to improve the quality of its intellectual breeding ground, the net fees paid by those who study here amount to only one-fifth of the school's total income. Paradoxically, were the courses to be made free and were selection of applicants based solely on strict entrance exams, the quality would remain at its present level, and the university would lose only 19 percent of its present earnings.[5]

There must be, then, ulterior motives behind such exorbitant fees: (1) as a wealth barrier to block entrance to the middle class and thus guarantee the university prestige as a hothouse for the scions of the ruling class; and (2) to establish and confirm the ideological principle that *knowledge is acquired in the same way one accumulates capital,* that the same laws that govern other fields of human action – the laws of supply and demand, capital and labor – underpin culture and science; that culture and science are, in Kantian terms, *subsumed* under the category of the free market. Consequently, the university is a private enterprise that produces and sells knowledge, with a turnover (including its clinics) approaching $2 billion; furthermore, with eleven thousand staff, it is one of the biggest employers in Illinois.

---

4 For the academic year 1999–2000.
5 Calculations based on the balance for June 1999, excluding hospital revenues, from the Web page adminet.uchicacgo.edu/admincompt/finstatements9899/actstate1.html.

Not surprising, the theory of "human capital" was first formulated in 1964 by one the University of Chicago's own, Gary Becker (Nobel Prize winner for economics in 1992). Knowledge and skills were to be considered forms of capital, because they produced income and even generated higher earnings. They were to be considered *human* capital because, unlike other forms of capital, they could not be separated from the physical person who possessed them. Investing in culture and science would therefore be a rational choice, because it was *good business* to accumulate capital in view of future earnings.

But if education is an investment, it must be weighed in terms of marginal productivity – that is, in terms of whether it yields more than other forms of investment. Is it more profitable for a parent to invest $100,000 in a degree from the University of Chicago for a child, for example, or to buy shares in Du Pont? If the degree is considered to be more profitable, the parent will ask the bank for a university loan to be paid back through the graduate's future earnings. But if human capital becomes devalued because it is too widespread and thus too easily available, the shares might win out. We could even imagine a scenario in which too much culture or science were in circulation, making them no longer profitable (though it would be a strange theory that foresaw an excess of culture!). Investing in human capital is only worthwhile in as far as that capital remains a rare and precious resource; when that is no longer the case, its stock is liable to fall through the floor.

Considering the mess the US education system is in today, together with the appalling resurgence of illiteracy, Richard Freeman's preoccupation with what his 1976 book called *The Overeducated American* cannot but raise a smile. To the relief of the "human capitalists," Reaganism during the 1980s was to bring about sweeping changes. From the early 1970s on, while the real wages of young people who hadn't finished high school decreased by 30 percent while the economic benefits of education soared. This, in Gary Becker's view, would explain why an ever-increasing number of students decided to enroll at private universities despite the fact that fees continued to rise at an alarming rate: "Benefits from college rose even faster than costs."[6]

---

6   Gary Becker, *Human Capital Revisited,* the 1989 Ryerson Lecture, Chicago: University of Chicago Press, 1989, p. 4.

Consequently, market principles govern not only the economy but also the cultural and scientific sphere. Indeed, in the Chicago Boys' view, the market constitutes the *sole* source of rationality; the criteria of this market organize the individual's rational choices in the most disparate fields, from marriage to the family. Such rationalism amounts to a shorthand version of Bentham's nineteenth-century utilitarianism. Not only is each act motivated solely by a quest for benefit, but the generic benefit is restricted to material benefit, which in turn boils down to economic interest, which is finally spelled out as *financial gain*. Everything that escapes the logic of the free market is regarded as irrational and therefore inefficient, whereas the slightest interference with the mechanisms of the market is considered damaging. And because the market itself refers to everything connected with the private sphere, it follows that anything limiting privatization must be irrational and inefficient; whatever intervention the state makes is simply another way of pulling the wool over our eyes.

The theories of the Chicago Boys are thus synonymous with the philosophy of ultraliberalism and laissez-faire economics, the rejection of any state impediment to market values. In this sense, they perpetuate a tradition whose most esteemed exponent in the twentieth century was Friedrich von Hayek. From 1950 to 1962, Hayek was professor of social and moral science at the University of Chicago, where he left an indelible mark. In 1974, he shared the Nobel Prize for economics with Gunnar Myrdal, who in theoretical terms was his polar opposite: the jury had obviously decided to run with the hare and hunt with the hounds.

At least one other city in history has had its name linked with such extremist liberalism and free-market fundamentalism: Manchester. For Engels, Manchester was the ideal city by which to trace the path of the industrial revolution during the nineteenth century (we have already seen how well several of his descriptions fit Chicago). The progenitors of the Chicago Boys were, in fact, the *Manchesterians,* those British crusaders for free trade who included among their ranks the militant James Wilson, founder in 1843 of the weekly magazine *The Economist.* The Manchesterians' stubborn campaign to revoke the notorious Corn Laws, which had imposed a tax on imported grain, anticipated Reagan's policies of deregulation in 1980s America, when the shackles on market competition were loosened and price controls abolished.

The overriding message was this: things would surely improve if only we left them to the free play of market forces. Or, in the words of a celebrated passage from Adam Smith's *Wealth of Nations,* the individual, "[b]y pursuing his own interest ... frequently promotes that of the society more effectually than when he really intends to promote it," because "he intends only his own gain, and he is in this, as in many other cases, led by *an invisible hand* to promote an end which was no part of his intention."[7] In this scenario, we have to imagine billions of single microinterests spinning in the vortex of the economy, colliding with and either neutralizing or reinforcing one another, or entirely avoiding each other's path, behaving like molecules according to the statistical theory of gases. For Smith, this spontaneous statistic of individual self-interest produces the collective good, much more than would any concerted public action (through economic plans or programs). Any obstacle to the free play of individual self-interests would thus constitute a roadblock on the freeway to well-being. This means that the state must reduce to a minimum its sphere of action. From the Manchesterians to the Reaganites, theorists of laissez-faire economics have always desired to "streamline" the state. Here is how Marx sums up the position of Richard Cobden (leader, along with Bright, of the Manchesterians): "Let us reduce the public expenses and we shall be able to reduce also our present taxation!"[8] Sixty years later, Reagan's first act on taking office was to reduce taxes (though not public expenditure).

Underlying the philosophy of liberalism, therefore, is not only a precise idea of what is and what is not rational, but also a very clear notion of the state and its responsibilities – of a "night watchman state," or what Nozick calls the "minimal state" – reduced to its policing function, ensuring only the individual's personal safety and the integrity of individual property. In this scenario, the state has no obligation to guarantee either health care, schools or infrastructure (roads, bridges, communications).

Such an idea of the state's role implies a particular vision of institutions and therefore of rights. Even the concept of justice is here subsumed by the economy,

7   A. Smith, *An Inquiry into the Wealth of Nations,* p. 456.
8   In the article "Parliament. Vote of November 26. Disraeli's Budget" in the *New York Daily Tribune,* 28 December 1852, no. 3650, in *Marx and Engels Collected Works,* London: Lawrence and Wishart, 1979, vol. II, p. 464.

while its criteria become the laws of the market. This school of thought, founded by the Chicagoan Ronald Coase (yet another Nobel prize winner), is known as Law and Economics. Here the interpretation of the law begins to have an influence on the law itself: when Reagan nominated two of the school's exponents, Robert Bork and Douglas Ginsburg, as Supreme Court judges, what had been merely a theoretical current suddenly became a position of judicial and legislative power, whose pronouncements would thereafter define what could be considered licit or just. If that didn't include redistributing resources between the privileged and disadvantaged classes, then it followed that the state was not obligated to provide assistance for the poor, because such an action, even though undertaken with the best intentions, would in the end have only negative effects.

Here we encounter again the power of "perversity," that rhetorical figure so dear to reactionary discourse, for whom any progressive policy would inevitably be counterproductive: "Attempts to reach for liberty will make society sink into slavery, the quest for democracy will produce oligarchy and tyranny, and social welfare programs will create more, rather than less, poverty. *Everything backfires*."[9] So it was that the idea began to get around in the United States in the 1980s that the welfare state was damaging to the nation's health. In a 1984 book criticizing welfare (which enjoyed considerable success),[10] Charles Murray maintained that the system did more harm than good, creating a culture of welfare dependence in which assistance became habit forming. (Again, we see the use of the word "culture." Earlier, it was "culture of poverty"; now it's "welfare culture.") The message was clear: we mustn't help the poor, because receiving help becomes a habit for them. And if it is not the state's task to help the poor, then the state has even less business trying to relaunch the economy in times of recession.

But the Chicago Boys' toughest battle (which they appear to have won for now) was against those who believed that the state must intervene to create jobs in periods when unemployment is rife, that it is the state's job to right the private sector when it begins to list. In this sense, the Chicago Boys' real enemy was John Maynard Keynes and Keynesian economics in general, which favors state intervention and increased public spending as a way of pulling the economy out of re-

---

9 A. Hirschman, *The Rhetoric of Reaction*, p. 12.
10 Charles Murray, *Losing Ground: America's Social Policy, 1950–1980*, New York: Basic Books, 1984.

cession. Against Keynesianism, Milton Friedman (another of Chicago's Nobelity) has advocated monetarism. If the free market is able to right itself, as the Chicago Boys believe, then capitalism is inherently stable; if, on the other hand, state intervention is required to surmount economic crisis, as Keynes maintained, then the implicit conclusion is that capitalism is unstable. Friedman, on the other hand, argues that "government action itself destabilizes and that the self-corrective process of the free market ought to be allowed to operate with a minimum of government involvement."[11]

The only intervention that Friedman concedes to the government, in fact, is its monetary policy. Here we have another version of the state as police, in this case policing money, ensuring that a certain quantity of the stuff is allowed to circulate – and not a penny more nor a penny less. This is what economists call the "minimal state." Such a vision offers little room for the notion of public service, because services can be exchanged only in the form of commodities. Thus Friedman suggests that the state should no longer provide schools, but instead should distribute vouchers enabling individual parents to purchase the type of school they want for their children.

In question here is the very notion of the public sphere. In the works of the Chicago School economists, "social control increasingly was depicted as ineffective and unnecessary, and as standing in the way of the establishment of a more perfect economy; that is to say, a competitive one. … [T]heir works define collective goods more and more narrowly, thus assigning to the private arena a broader category of economic activities."[12]

Even the social costs of a business – its so-called neighborhood effects, or external diseconomies – are as far as possible removed from the field of collective action to that of private contracts. Ronald Coase went so far as to extend the concept of transaction to include the buying and selling of *damage rights*.[13] This is no mere abstract theory: as we have seen, pollution rights and futures through which companies buy the right to emit toxic substances are among the commodities traded on

---

11 W. Carl Biven, *Who Killed John Maynard Keynes? Conflicts in the Evolution of Economic Policy*, Homewood, Ill.: Dow Jones-Irwin, 1989, p. 59.
12 Edythe S. Miller, "Economics for What? Economic Folklore and Social Realities," *Journal of Economic Issues*, June 1989, p. 349.
13 Ronald H. Coase, "The Problem of Social Cost," *Journal of Law and Economics*, 1960, no. 3, pp. 1–44.

the Chicago stock exchange. Then there are the futures quoted on such rights. Not by chance, the illustrious personage called upon to inaugurate the new Chicago Board of Trade building was none other than Milton Friedman himself.

Against the Chicago Boys, one could level the classic criticism deployed against other theories of laissez-faire economics, which Schumpeter summarizes as follows: that, in reality, such theories *recommend* what they purport to *describe*.[14] By insisting on the need to remove all power from the public sphere and to transfer all activity to the private sector, the Chicago Boys are in effect recommending that we take the process that has already come to dominate large portions of our daily life during the last century to its logical conclusion. Travel – moving from place to place – used to be a public act (using public transportation, walking on the public road) but has become a private act made within the sealed-off private *compartment* of one's own property, in this case the car. Increasingly, the town square as a place of public assembly and entertainment is being replaced by huge malls and shopping centers, which are similar to squares in every respect except that, being privately owned spaces, they "close" at a given hour. Likewise, an increasing portion of public diversion has become a matter of private consumption. In the past, you could not listen to music without the presence of musicians, which meant venturing into a public space. Today, music can be enjoyed in solitude: on the radio, on Walkman headphones or on CD players. Music is possessed in the form of commodities, such as CDs and tapes, leading to the interpenetration of the two aspects of the private sphere: private property on one hand, privacy on the other. Theater and cinema, once an important part of public life, have been replaced by television. The spectator no longer has to go to the arena to watch modern sports. The city itself, as we have seen, is increasingly structured along the lines of a private community, with its own private constitution and its own police, with the concept of democracy becoming streamlined to the point where it coincides with what is decided at the monthly residents' meeting. As its semantic field continues to grow, the word *private* acquires new meaning, taking in an ever-larger part of the world, while the word *public,* by contrast, falls into decline.

This expansionism of the private, the way it increasingly comes to pervade and

14 Joseph Alois Schumpeter, *History of Economic Analysis* (1954), New York: Oxford University Press, 1986, p. 888.

impoverish the experience of the world, is possible only because it is founded on a symmetrical omnipotence of the individual. The private can triumph only if "the self-governing individual constitutes the ultimate unit of the social sciences," that is, and "all social phenomena resolve themselves into decisions and actions of individuals that need not or cannot be further analyzed in terms of superindividual factors."[15]

The individual is thus the subject of "rational decisions," for which the only legitimate motive would be the person's own interests. This individual constitutes the exclusive subject of history, divested of every possible social determination, bleached of every historical inheritance, removed from any possible belonging, literally abstract, whose only motive is to secure individual *property*, which is both a means to well-being and an aim in itself.

Paraphrasing Asterix, we might say, at this point, "These Chicago Boys are completely nuts." How can they even think such a thing? If only they would poke their noses off campus, or take a walk across the street, they'd see just how much general well-being their free play of self-interests has produced. Is it possible that a brief visit to Taylor Homes wouldn't raise even the slightest sliver of doubt in their minds? How can they even talk about market efficiency after having witnessed the horrors of the ghetto? And how can those Chicago Boys think there's an abstract individual out there, when the only people who live in this city are Blacks, Hispanics or white ethnics, when everywhere you look you see nothing but ethnicities and castes? When all these various social groups, identities and cultural heritages affirm themselves by giving each other a wide body-swerve, when they determine every aspect of their members' lives down to their zip code? Indeed, the refutation of the Chicago Boys' hypothesis becomes even more withering when you consider that what has produced this society divided into castes and stratified in ethnicities and races is precisely their hallowed logic of individual gain. The structuring of society – in terms of predefined groups and social destinies from which the individual cannot escape (a person may become rich and famous but will always remain Black or Hispanic or Italian) – is the result not of traditional

---

15 Ibid.

precapitalism but of the individualist capitalism that has historically organized American society into communities.

So many Nobel winners can't all be mad. In terms of their opulence, the campus and the surrounding neighborhood of Hyde Park would appear to confirm the most extreme forms of liberalism, in fact. Here, as Lewis Mumford would say, "one might live and die without marring the image of an *innocent world*. ... [H]ere individuality could prosper oblivious of the pervasive regimentation beyond." Here, in fact, state power really was streamlined down to the perfect anorexic figure of the "minimum state" when, to prevent the neighborhood from falling into decline, a private association was delegated the right to expel and expropriate residents and knock down buildings. The Hyde Park Kenwood Community was 70 percent financed by the university, while its director just happened to be the rector's brother. As a result, between 1960 and 1970, the area's overall population of fell by 26 percent, the Black population by 40 percent.

And that's not all. Here on the campus and in its vicinity, you can already see signs of what Nozick has termed "the ultraminimal state," for whom the "minimal" or police state would be still too generous (because in the police state, the taxes of *some* pay for the physical protection of *all*). Through police activities, this means, resources are actually (horror of horrors!) redistributed. Instead, "an ultraminimal state maintains a monopoly over all use of force except that necessary in immediate self-defence, and so excludes private (or agency) retaliation ... but it provides protection and enforcement services *only* to those who purchase its protection and enforcement policies. People who don't buy a protection contract from the monopoly don't get protected."[16] If you get mugged on the street and you haven't had the foresight to buy a public protection policy, the police are unlikely to come to your aid. The criteria for security are the same as those of a private health care system where only those who pay get treated.

The University of Chicago pays, all right. It pays for a private police force with thirteen squad cars (all to cover an area of less than two square miles) with all the power of the regular police and responsible for 80 percent of the arrests made in the area. Naturally, this neighborhood counts only one or two homicides and

---

16 R. Nozick, *Anarchy, the State and Utopia*, pp. 26–27.

about a dozen break-ins per year, whereas "out there," in the ghettos just beyond the invisible borderline, homicides run well into the double figures, assaults into the hundreds, break-ins into the thousands. How, one might ask, is it possible to live like this, with the anxiety of being in a perpetual state of siege, always primed to call the police, always careful not to step over the line that separates you from hell on Earth, enclosed in your own colony, barricaded inside a fortress under attack from all quarters? Who knows what notion of culture can come from such a situation. It's enough to make you stop *believing* in the market.

But, in fact, belief is the key. Although you would think it out of place in relation to such by-the-book rationalism, *belief* is in fact the word most often used to describe the Chicago Boys' zealous enthusiasm and trust in the benevolence of laissez-faire economics: "fierce belief in the organizing power and efficiency of a free market economy ... singular in the intensity of its commitment to the efficiency of market interaction."[17] This is the irrational hocus-pocus logic to which Edythe S. Miller refers in her ironic summary of the Chicago Boys' thesis:

> The Competitive Economy is accepted as both ideal state and achievable reality, if only unnatural impediments (that is, a governmental presence) were removed. Thus today, for example, deregulation regularly is equated with competition, whatever the industry and market realities. The magic exercised is the assignment of a benign potency to the essential attributes of that system: private property, free contract, and free exchange. ... Regulation is portrayed as ineffective, corrupt, and, in any event, unnecessary. Private enterprise is exalted as pristine, efficient and ever a textbook case of competition. ... The only institution admitted into analysis is the market that, in conformance with the folklore, is posited as a neutral, if not benign, allocational and distributional mechanism. The individual is accepted as the only reality.[18]

Sarcasm aside, Edythe Miller captures here the age-old argument whereby any form of fundamentalism chooses to refuse the evidence of its own eyes: if the miracle doesn't happen, it is for the simple reason that we haven't prayed enough; if communism didn't work, it was because there wasn't enough communism; if the

---

17 W. C. Biven, *Who Killed John Maynard Keynes?* p. 53.
18 E. S. Miller, Economics for What?" pp. 353–54.

market economy is rampant with misery, it's not because of any inherent fault in the system itself, but because there are still too many obstacles blocking the way to the perfect realization of pure, transparent, immaculate competition. The recipe for any form of fundamentalism is *"Encore un effort."* If the market doesn't work properly, then we need more market. Again, we see how reductionism and extreme positivism go hand in hand with fideism and fundamentalism. Were the unsung Iranian scribe to write his *Persian Letters* today, he would no doubt define the Chicago Boys as "ayatollahs of capital," confirming Adorno's thesis: "The bourgeois form of rationality has always needed irrational supplements, in order to maintain itself as what it is, continuing injustice through justice."[19]

In the gospel according to Chicago, then, state intervention is the devil incarnate, whose corruption is contagious. This is why fighting against political corruption, rather than striving to improve the political system, tends to reduce and suppress the political altogether in favor of market transaction. If outside the campus is a world of untold misery, the state's inefficiency is to blame. Thus the horror that surrounds the University of Chicago is actually proof of the market's validity. Oppression and exploitation are born from the legendary corruption of Cook County. Urban desolation is worsened by the waste and inefficiency that are rife in the public sector. That capitalists are easily convinced of this is obvious. As George Stigler once noted, "A lecturer denouncing cannibalism naturally must view the applause of vegetarians as equivocal evidence of his eloquence." What is more extraordinary, public opinion the world over believes this to be true, to the point of making the philosophy their own. It is now considered plain *common sense* to see anything marked "public" as inevitably more inefficient and corrupt than anything marked "private," just as it is common sense to view the market as being more transparent than politics, and thus the power of capital as being less iniquitous than political power. It is this overturning of public sentiment that marks the real victory of the Chicago Boys, a victory that goes well beyond winning the Cold War to conversion of a large section of Western public opinion to their way of thinking.

---

19 Theodor W. Adorno, *Jargon der Eigentlichkeit. Zur deutschen Ideologie*, Frankfurt am Main: Suhrkamp Verlag, 1964. Eng. trans. *The Jargon of Authenticity*, Evanston, Ill.: Northwestern University Press, 1973, p. 47.

Now these millions of people can't all be dupes of the all-powerful ideological apparatuses of TV, radio and newspapers, even if these undoubtedly play a major role. Without having to resort to anarchist utopia, to a society without the state, or to the "dismantling of the state" pursued by Marxism, what we find at stake in the antistate argument is a persuasive preoccupation with personal freedom, of the kind that fueled political protests such as the Civil Rights struggle and that informs Thoreau's Civil Disobedience, which begins: "I heartily accept the motto, – 'That government is best which governs least'; and I should like to see it acted up to more rapidly and systematically. Carried out, it finally amounts to this, which also I believe, – 'That government is best which governs not at all.'"[20]

The first political battle, as we have seen, is to take possession of political definitions (of the type "I am a *leader*, you are a *boss*"). In this, the market system has won its battle by seizing hold of the definition of *freedom*, which is why we refer to the "free" market, "free" trade and so on. For a large part of humanity, the experience of state power has been, and is, one of daily tyranny. One of the reasons (other than poverty) so many waves of people have poured into the United States has been to escape such tyranny. The strength of their conviction lies in the idea that the laws of the market (of supply and demand) are ubiquitous, that they are the same for everybody – whereas state justice is more just to some than to others. The market, then, is supposedly the only system that gives everybody an equal chance, and thus it contains an idea of democracy (embodied in the notion of the "self-made man"): "The decisive advantage of market systems is that they decentralize power away from the Washingtons of the world and toward individual businessmen, workers and consumers."[21]

Such belief in the market's palingenetic virtues has a long history. Back in the nineteenth century, the Manchesterians felt that the market enhanced moral virtues by tempering human indolence and making the individual strong – indeed, the market ensured that only the strong would survive (again, we see the specter of social Darwinism): "*Laissez-faire* puts iron into a man's character. If it doesn't,

---

20 Henry David Thoreau, "Civil Disobedience" (1849), in *Walden and Other Writings* (1849–1862), New York: Bantam Books, 1981, p. 85.
21 Gary Becker, in *Business Week*, 30 December 1991, p. 22.

and he perishes, he presumably hasn't a character worth putting iron into."[22] Nowadays, students refer to the University of Chicago campus as the "monastery." Along the main thoroughfare of Hyde Park, there isn't a single place you can get a beer, not one store that sells liquor.

A good number of the Manchesterians were pacifists: "They believed that free trade would give buyers and sellers all over the world so strong an economic interest in peace that they would prevent their governments from making war."[23] Even today, as Benedict Anderson observes, there prevails the idea "that there is some inscrutable connection between capitalism and peace," such that "'free market' is instinctively juxtaposed not merely to the command economy but to war."[24]

It's incredible the things we humans build our hopes on. In the same period, another group of Utopian freethinkers, the St. Simonists, believed that the advent of trains and railroads would bring different peoples to know each other better and would thus end war. They failed to consider that railways would also enable the more rapid transportation of troops and artillery to the front.

There is something almost moving, even pathetic, in the trust that so many people place in the equanimity of the market, a system whose iniquities cry vengeance to the heavens. But this talent for self-delusion is in fact an irresistible force, a force that is able to move mountains (and, as we have seen, also banks), to reshape human geography, to shake entire continents. Here we again find ourselves faced with that duplicity we have so often encountered, in this case the duplicitous game of freedom: on one hand, we have the myriad people who aspire to the mere *freedom to exist,* while on the other is capital itself, which insists on a *free hand* and demands that it not be bound by any power over and above its own.

It's a Saturday afternoon in July. Bathed in the chill of its air-conditioning, the Joseph Regenstein library lies almost deserted. Each of its five stories is split into two sections; on one side, the reading room is equipped with chairs, desks and computer on the other, endless rows of close-standing shelves in the windowless book

---

22 William D. Grampp, *The Manchester School of Economics*, Stanford, Calif.: Stanford University Press, 1960, p. 80.

23 Ibid., p. 7.

24 Benedict Anderson, "The New World Disorder," *New Left Review,* May–June 1992, no. 193 , p. 6.

depository house hundreds of thousands of volumes on each floor. Having worked out the shelf location of a particular title on the computer, the reader is left to venture into the forest of shelves to find the volume in question. One shortly becomes disoriented amid these walls of paper, whose fantastic accumulation renders each volume indistinguishable from the next. In the echoing silence, the depository seems like some vast cemetery of human thought whose bones lie piled up in the apartment-block style of the modern necropolis. Like tombs that no one will ever visit, innumerable volumes shall no doubt lie in the cool dark, unopened for all time. Owing to the library's energy conservation policy, in fact, the lights go off after a few minutes, leaving you suddenly blind, alone and helpless (murder in the library?), imagining that someone may find you one day, all shriveled and wizened, like a book that crumbles to dust in the reader's hands.

Epilogue

Human Tides Again

Outside the packed stadium, the city is in the grip of February chill; inside, it's hot enough to roast a hog. The home team, the Chicago Bulls, hits the basketball court. The players, in their vests and long baggy shorts, are nearly all Black. Tall as lampposts, they display a feline grace and agility whenever they spring for a slam-dunk. In a film of a few years ago about a street basketball team of young LA ne'er-do-wells, called *White Men Can't Jump,* the word *jump* was also a synonym for sexual prowess.

On the edge of the court, busty cheerleaders in short sequin dresses show acres of leg as they chant in time with the flurried attacks of the Bulls. Up in the stands, amid thousands of cheering spectators, a group of girls in Islamic head scarves add their frenzied screams of support to the deafening roar. The daughters of Muslim immigrants, they are all students at the University of Illinois in Chicago. What strikes you isn't so much their religious origin, however, as the contradictory image they embody, almost as though, right there in the bedlam of the stadium under the electric floodlights, you had the snapshot of a human paradox. Belying the tightly wrapped head scarves worn in respect to Islamic tradition is what Koranic scholars would no doubt call the frenzied applause of females at the sight of half-nude men. Just as McDonald's has gone to Mecca, so too the chador has now come to the ball game.

It's midday, and the sun is going full blast. It's the Fourth of July, Independence Day. In the parks that run for miles along the shores of Lake Michigan, from Lincoln to Belmont and on up to Foster, tens of thousands of people recline on the grass, countless clans of families out for picnics. With the fingertips of her right hand, a Punjabi woman makes the distinctive motion of rolling her rice, vegetables and dhal into a ball; elsewhere, a megafamily of Mexicans crowds around a spread of tacos and burritos; a swarm of Vietnamese children, spring rolls in hand, chase a kite across the grass. All have their origins in their mouths, yet all are so American. Few speak English, yet they already collectively bear the stigmata of the Yankee: you find it in their passion for ice cubes; in their huge portable fridges; in the deluge of sauces, each in its color-coded plastic bottle; in the way they endlessly chomp on potato chips, popcorn, snacks of all shapes and sizes. Taking pride of place in the center of each group, like an altar to the Penates, is the barbecue, where the young Maghrebans immolate a chicken, Black teenagers offer their hot dogs to the gods, and a stern-looking Parsi prepares a leg of lamb for the sacrifice.

These are small signs of two huge phenomena. First: immigration, which has begun to flow once again in the direction of the United States and has once more burst on its shores, is leading to a shake-up in human geography as profound as that caused by the immigrant waves of the nineteenth and early twentieth centuries. A hundred years later, the migration of entire peoples, the fabled *Völkerwanderung,* has recommenced. Second: it is now possible to be at the same time American and Vietnamese, or Sikh or Iranian – that is to say, there is a new way of being American.

In March 1999, 26.5 million of America's residents were foreign born. (The Immigration and Naturalization Service [INS] estimated around 5 million illegal aliens as well, yielding a total immigrant population of around 32 million people.) Of these, 17.2 million had been admitted in the last twenty years, since 1980; 9.3 million have entered the country in the last ten years alone, more than the number of entries in the period between 1900 and 1910 (8.8 million) – indeed, more than in any other single decade in US history. Moreover, more immigrants entered the United States between 1990 and 1999 than in the forty years between 1931 and 1970. The novelty lies in the fact that no longer are the vast majority of these entries from Europe. Between 1981 and 1997, out of 14.3 million legal immigrants, only 1.7 million came from Europe (including 240,000 from Poland and 456,000 from the ex–Soviet Union), whereas 5 million were from Asia and 7 million from elsewhere in the Americas, 3.5 million of whom were from Mexico alone (Mexico also accounts for more than half of all US illegal aliens: 2.7 million out of 5 million).[1]

The immigrant waves of old are now being submerged by new human tides from Latin America, Asia, the Middle East, even Africa (450,000 from 1981 to 1997). For the first time – *pace* Tocqueville – African people now live in the United States who came to the country of their own free will rather than as slaves. This new America is ceasing to be a Western nation built by Europeans and populated by European immigrants, a white civilization created by white ethnics (cruel and hostile toward Black, African alterity) and has become instead a multiracial and multiracist realm of Arabs, Cambodians, Iranians, Koreans …

In the shaping of this new human geography, the notion of the West disappears, what from Helenic civilization on would be bundled together under the concept of the New, the New World, or (in Vico's terms) the "young peoples": the Greeks were young compared to the tribes of Asia, America was dubbed the New World, the United States is a *young nation*. (Nobody, however, would dream of calling Germany a "young nation," even though the German state was formed more recently than the United States.) After prehistoric times, the flow of migrants seemed to be entirely one-way, from east to west: first the Indo-Europeans and Mongols moving to Europe and the Europeans and deported Africans to the United States, then the Americans themselves pushing to the far west of the continent. Now, however, we find the Chinese and peoples of the Far East on the *West* Coast of the United States. The influx of migrants from Asia to America constitutes an *eastward* movement.

It is now a long time since the immigrants from the Old World ceased to be Europeans and became Americans, while all the time remaining Westerners. Now, as new patterns of migration overlap with old, the United States, with its unprecedented hybrids of Irish and Sikh, Chinese and Neapolitan, Lebanese and Mexican,

---

1   Census Bureau, *Statistical Abstract of the United States 1999*, tab. 5, 8; and *Current Population Survey, March 1999*, which can be consulted on the Web page , Internet release date: 12 September 2000; US Immigration and Naturalization Service, *Statistical Yearbook of Immigration and Naturalization Service 1998*, Washington, DC: US Government Printing Office, 2000, p. 239.

can no longer be considered a Western nation. Likewise, the traditional ethnic partition of Chicago has begun to look somewhat long in the tooth, a relic of the old America, altered by now beyond all recognition.

In the chasm of Colorado's Grand Canyon, millions of years of history can be read in the geological stratification of different rocks, each with its own color and consistency. Likewise, in Chicago's main thoroughfares you can read the stratification of a century and a half of immigration. "For 23 and 1/2 miles from Evanston on the north to Blue Island on the south, Western Avenue – the longest street in Chicago – runs through neighborhoods with Russians, Indians, Pakistanis, Poles, Germans, Arabs, Lithuanians, Ukrainians, Croats, Italians, Puerto Ricans, Mexicans, Vietnamese; Irish, Blacks and Jews – 'the avenue is a sociologist's dream and a Census taker's nightmare,'" recounted a recent *USA Today* cover story.[2] Hardly a single zone is now inhabited by the immigrant group suggested by its name. You might think that Pilsen was a Czech neighborhood. Wrong: it's the Mexican barrio. You venture into the Lithuanian neighborhood and find the same thing you find in the Hungarian neighborhood of Cleveland: namely, that the "Lithuanians" here, like the Cleveland Hungarians, are all dark skinned and for the most part have fleshy lips and fuzzy hair. Further north, on Clark Avenue, you find the Swedish cemetery, because the area was once a Scandinavian stronghold. Now its inhabitants are mainly Arabs. On Milwaukee Avenue, a few writings in Polish recall a past now blanked out, if not completely erased, by advertisements in Spanish: the Poles, meanwhile, have shifted north to "Jackowo" (named after a church) on Avondale between Central Park and Pulaski, where you feel like you're in downtown Krakov: everything is Polish, from the street signs to the newspapers to the food on sale in the drugstores. On North Broadway, you run into a recently established Vietnamese neighborhood, where the rents have gone up; before the Asian order moved in, the area had been run by the Hispanic Mafia, who in turn had taken control of it from the Scandinavians. Again, to the north, up on Lincoln Avenue at the intersection with Bryn Mawr, next to the old Bohemian cemetery, you come to where the Latin alphabet ends as the neighborhood suddenly turns Korean; even further north, on Devon between Rockwell and Western, is a re-

---

2   *USA Today,* 12 April 2000.

cently established Indo-Pakistani community.

In the early years of the twentieth century, the various ethnic communities lay side by side, each with its own Main Street, huddled around the Chicago Loop. "To the north of the Loop was Germany. To the northwest, Poland. To the west were Italy and Israel. To the southwest were Bohemia and Lithuania. And to the south was Ireland."[3] Then the Blacks arrived from the South, and after them the Hispanics, whose numbers quadrupled between 1960 and 1980, reaching 546,000 in 1990. (Counting those in the metropolitan area, the Latino population now stands at 1.2 million.) This was followed in the 1970s and 1980s by the Asian invasion, and now, with the end of the Cold War, the Poles are back again, engaged in a no-holds-barred struggle for the lower end of the job market, offering their services at rates even more rock-bottom than those paid to Mexican *indocumentados*. And with the influx of new arrivals comes a corresponding exodus to the suburbs by old white ethnics, so that, according to the last census, Blacks and Hispanics account for 58.7 percent of the city's population, but only 32.9 percent of the population of the surrounding area.

The Irish have in part abandoned Bridgeport, shifting further south toward Mt. Greenwood, Ashburn and Beverly. While the poorer Poles reside in Jackowo, their more affluent co-nationals now populate the suburbs of Jefferson Park, Norwood and Edison. The moneyed Italian community has for decades dwelt in River Forest, Melrose Park, Riverside and Oak Park.

From this, two impressions result. First: history repeats itself. The new waves of immigration from Asia and Latin America are going through the same processes that Europeans went through in the nineteenth century. After a phase of digestion, America has once again begun to take up and ingest populations, engulfing new sources of human energy from new continents. The same logic of capital that a century ago attracted such a huge workforce (enabling the bosses to keep the cost of labor to a minimum) exists today. Not by chance did the most recent period of large-scale migration (1980–1990) coincide with the Reagan era, as well as with – to borrow an expression from the nineteenth-century *New York Times* – some of the most resounding workers' defeats in the "battle between capital and labor." Just as furious competition between Blacks and white ethnics in the

3   M. Royko, *Boss*, p. 30.

job market could be glimpsed in embryo in the 1919 Chicago race riots, so too have the LA riots of 1992 been seen as the explosion of a new hostility between Blacks and Hispanics. The October 1992 *Atlantic Monthly* ran the title story "Blacks vs Browns" (where "Browns" stood for Hispanics).[4] As *La Prensa San Diego* wrote on 15 May 1992, in interpreting the riots according to the Blacks-versus-whites scenario, the media had missed the crucial point: "The riots were not carried out against Blacks and Whites, they were carried out against the Latino and the Asian communities by the Blacks! Faced with nearly a million and half Latinos taking over the inner city, Blacks revolted, rioted and looted."[5] Today, as a century ago, we are witnessing the shift of millions of people, swept up this time by the forces of the global market, a market that its advocates imagine, in the words of Benedict Anderson, "as a force for peace and order, but all modern history shows to be the most deeply subversive institution we know."[6] Now, just as in the nineteenth century, the logic of capital ensures that migrants leave as individuals but arrive as peoples, that the class struggle continues to generate racial conflict.

The second impression that one gets, however, is that beneath this apparent continuity, the styles of migration are changing; we are witnessing, in fact, a mutation of the very meaning of the word *migrate*.

Today's immigrants are different before they have even packed their bags. For a start, their perception of their own poverty is more painfully acute than that of their forebears. "The difference between the masses of the Third World countries today and a century ago is that, while they are still poor, they now know, through the marvels of modern communication, that they are poor and that other people are not."[7] Wealth and poverty these days are much closer bedfellows than they once were. Every day, the luxury and excess of the Northern Hemisphere is displayed on the televisions of African bidonvilles. (Contrariwise, Third World misery has become a spectacle for affluent families whose lavish dinners are nowadays accompanied by TV images of starving children from Bangladesh or

4 Jack Miles, "Blacks vs Browns: Immigration and the New American Dilemma," *Atlantic Monthly*, vol. 270, October 1992, pp. 41–68.
5 Cited in J. Miles, "Blacks vs Browns," p. 51.
6 B. Anderson, "The New World Disorder," p. 8.
7 W. C. Biven, *Who Killed John Maynard Keynes?*, p. 193.

the Sudan. Through the media, the specter of poverty so often hovers at the window of people's homes that they are no longer bothered by the real thing when they step out the door.)

Modern migrants are also different in the way they depart: for the most part, by plane. The revolution brought about by air transportation is often underestimated. The airliner annuls distance more radically than did either train or ship. Once again, we encounter the need for "the annihilation of space by time,"[8] which, according to Marx, was what generated modern mass communications. Once more, a quantitative mutation (of speed) has had qualitative effects. The same logic of fixed costs that applied to a single continent for railroad companies applies on a global scale for today's air carriers. Migrating to the most far-off lands is no longer a question of time or money, or even of discomfort. Distance has become irrelevant. Filipinos emigrate to places on the other side of the globe, such as Italy, as easily as do Ethiopians, who are much closer. The travel factor has become secondary in determining both geographical provenance and the number of emigrants.

What is more, the airliner is more egalitarian than the ship: compare the scenes at the international flight terminals at O'Hare or Kennedy Airports with photos from the beginning of the century depicting immigrants from Europe as they disembarked en masse on Ellis Island; the difference is that between a group of people and a herd of cattle. This greater equality also derives from the influence of tourism. Until the Second World War, foreigners who *disembarked* in the United States were for the most part immigrants.[9] Since 1945, by contrast, foreigners *landing* in the United States have mainly been tourists: between 1990 and 1998, the number of *nonimmigrant* foreign nationals admitted to the United States was 204 million, compared to 9.1 million legal immigrants – twenty-two times less.[10] Air

---

8 Karl Marx, *Grundrisse der Kritik der politischen Ökonomie* (1857–1858 Engl. trans. *Grundrisse: Foundations of the Critique of Political Economy*, New York: Vintage Books, 1973, pp. 524, 534.
9 The 1920s saw 4.1 million immigrants land in the United States, compared to 719,000 visitors. In the following decade, with restrictions on immigration in place, there were a mere 528,000 immgrants, compared to 775,000 visitors. From Census Bureau, *Historical Statistics of the United States*, vol. I, tab. C89-101, H941-951.
10 Data calculated by Census Bureau, *Statistical Abstract of the United States 1999*, tab. 5, 7; US Immigration and Naturalization Service, *Statistical Yearbook of Immigration and Naturalization Service, 1998*, tab. 1, 37.

travel has made intercontinental tourism possible for hundreds of millions of people, not only because it is cheap, but above all because it requires much less time, the modern-day worker's most precious and sparse resource. Travel by ship, by contrast, required the luxury of having a lot of time and considerable means on one's hands.

Tourism is in fact connected to immigration in three ways:

1. Tourism enables illegal immigrants to enter the country. Don't be deceived by all those heart-rending images of Vietnamese boat people, or of Mexicans piled into the back of a truck, hidden under a consignment of watermelons: a large number of illegal immigrants step over the border these days in the guise of tourists, with money in their pockets and a return ticket they will never use, as they remain in the country well beyond the expiration date on their temporary visas. The difficulty of distinguishing these fake tourists from the real ones is in part responsible for the rise in immigration compared to a century ago.

2. Tourism permits a preliminary inspection of a territory. The would-be migrant can go to another country, see how co-nationals who have already emigrated are fixed and decide if the streets there really are paved with gold. Such a reconnaissance trip would have been unthinkable for the Sicilian or Bavarian peasant of a century ago.

3. Tourism's greatest influence is that it allows people to return home frequently and offers relatives who have remained in their home country a chance to visit the immigrant (thus triggering further migration). In the age of sea travel, returning to Europe was much more rare, often occurring toward the end of the emigrant's life after retirement, by which time the person had become a stranger in the native land and would return only to find that land transformed. Hence the feeling of sorrowful rupture, of definitive abandonment, the irrevocable severing of ties to one's past that once haunted the overseas emigrant. For today's migrants, returning from the United States to Korea, for example, is no more difficult than it would be for a Neapolitan bricklayer living in Germany to spend Christmas with his relatives in the Mediterranean. Consequently, when the emigrant leaves today, he doesn't salute his homeland for the last time.

In addition, while away, the emigrant stays "on line," not only by radio, but by telephone, fax, TV and e-mail. With the telephone, one can easily keep in touch, compared to the old system of laborious and infrequent epistles written in a quavering hand. The telephone rings in a Filipino woman's New York one-room apartment, and from thousands of miles away, those in her native community from Cebu rush into her home to wish her good morning or good evening, or perhaps she simply hears from old friends who have decided to call on a whim. The connection is as effortless as that between a Parisian mother and her daughter in Lyon, two cities in the *same* country.

Television, meanwhile, ensures that you don't forget your mother tongue and keeps you informed about the political events in your part of the world. Through satellite TV, an Indian emigrant can follow the fortunes of the Bharatya Janata Party, whereas the white ethnics of yesteryear tended to receive less and less news, very little of which concerned them: people who lived abroad would gradually cease to take interest in the sport of their own country and, after a while, would begin to follow that of the host nation. This says nothing of today's mountains of faxes that fly from continent to continent, or of the e-mail that connects different bank accounts in real time, thus bringing together a family's bank statements. In this sense, the family has become a *lumpen multinational*, with its different branches spread over various countries.

All of this explains why American sociologists, in defining contemporary migration patterns, speak in terms of *transnational communities*: it is no longer a case of a Mexican village on one hand and a neighborhood in Chicago on the other. A single community connects these two places, a "binational entity"[11] that is neither Mexican nor Chicagoan but something new. At one time, immigrants sought to preserve their original identity, defending it from the surrounding forces that besieged them. It was in this way that communities such as "Little Italy," "Little Odessa" or "Chinatown" took root overseas, enclaves of Italianness, Russianness, Chineseness that were separated by an ocean from their respective motherlands and that, in closing themselves to the outside world, discovered the obduracy that would enable them to keep the Italian (or Russian, or Chinese) flag flying.

Today the Mexican barrio of Pilsen is in all respects (cash flow, customs, entertainments, cuisine, social life, marriage arrangements and so on) closer to

11 Douglas S. Massey et al., *Return to Aztlan: The Social Process of International Migration from Western Mexico*, Berkeley: University of California Press, 1990, p. 7.

Michoacán or to any other Mexican town than it is to Evanston or Park Forest. What we see here is a doubling of space. On one hand, the community is concentrated in a single place, a *neighborhood* (such as the Chicago barrio); on the other, the space becomes abstract, detached from the physical limits imposed by its surroundings and, like a hyperspace, linked with other sites distant from itself (Guadalajara and Chicago, Cebu and Rome, Amritsar and Vancouver).

The community, therefore, becomes independent from its own land and can grant itself Italianness without the need of a Mediterranean, Indianness without a Ganges. Uprooted from its native soil, identity takes on a new meaning: being Parisian without the Seine is a form of unprecedented otherness, as is being a Tuareg in the absence of the Sahara. (What is remarkable here is not so much the shift in meaning, as the fact that identity persists at all.) With identity detached from its cradle, the idea of belonging becomes a more abstract matter. This is not to say that the community's ties are loosened: on the contrary, reduced to its nucleus, the community may even become more cohesive, as often happens with nomadic peoples or gypsies, as happened in the Jewish Diaspora (the first case in history of a transnational community). A new type of community results, one that is perhaps more immaterial, though certainly no less sanguinary in its hatreds, a community held together by electromagnetic waves, fiber optic cables, telephone wires, jet turbines.

Being Tamil in Melbourne or Chinese in San Francisco is no longer a natural fact of birthright. It has become a differential of semantics: "Human bodies, though caught up in the vortex of the market, are not merely another form of commodity. As they follow in the wake of grain and gold, rubber and textiles, petrochemicals and silicon chips, they carry with them memories and customs, beliefs and eating habits, music and sexual desires. And these human characteristics, which, in their places of origin, are usually borne lightly and unselfconsciously, assume quickly a drastically different salience in the diasporas of modern life."[12]

Wearing the veil in Tlemcen is natural, whereas donning it in a high school in Sarcelles in the Paris banlieue is forbidden. In the stadium of the Chicago Bulls, an Islamic head scarf sends a message completely different from the one it transmits in Esfahan. What was formerly natural becomes deliberate; habit becomes choice.

---

12 B. Anderson, "The New World Disorder," p. 8.

This is the sense that Benedict Anderson intended when he coined the term "imagined communities" to describe modern nationalisms, not because they are unreal (on the contrary, they are real enough to kill or die for), but because they have come into existence through being thought or imagined; they constitute "cultural artifacts of a particular kind."[13]

Building up an actual living community means endowing it with a past, thinking of it in the primordial terms of originary destiny. One is Italian by fate – but what does it actually mean to be Italian? Nationality is regarded as innate, in the manner of Platonic ideas. Just as knowledge for Platonism is a question of remembrance, so too the ethnic group or nation is conceived in a specific way to recount it "as late awakening from sleep" (of national or ethnic consciousness).[14] In history text-books, when you get to the nineteenth century, you always find a chapter on the subject of the "resurgence of national identity," even though it was only during that time that the various nationalisms first arose. Among the examples cited by Anderson, none is more striking than Indonesian nationalism: Indonesia is a rela-tively recent entity, composed of 13,000 islands whose myriad peoples speak more than three hundred different languages and, until a century ago, completely ig-nored each other's existences. One might therefore ask, In what does this originary Indonesian consist? What lies behind this national pride for which so many people are willing to kill or die? Curiously, the borders of Indonesia match those of the old Dutch empire. If the Dutch had conquered Malaysia, would that mean that the citizens of Kuala Lumpur would also now be *Indonesian by fate*?

Benedict Anderson's book is one of a number of studies that have analyzed the "creation of the past"; another of these is the collection of essays edited by Hobsbawm and Ranger, *The Invention of Tradition*. One of the essays in this collec-tion reveals the myth behind the idea that the Scots have since time immemorial worn kilts, with different tartans for each clan, noting that the kilt "far from being a traditional Highland dress … was invented by an Englishman after the Union of 1707; and the differentiated 'clan tartans' are an even later invention."[15]

---

13 Benedict Anderson, *Imagined Communities* (1983), London: Verso, 1992, p. 4.
14 Ibid., p. 195.
15 Hugh Trevor-Roper, in Eric Hobsbawm, ed., *The Invention of Tradition*, Cambridge: Cambridge University Press, 1983, p. 19.

We have also witnessed the birth of traditions, some short-lived (such as the "Dawn of Liberty," the anniversary of the Paris communes, which the anarchists of Chicago celebrated for thirty-seven years), others of longer duration (such as May Day, which became a "Workers' Easter holiday." In a different field, in his classic study *Orientalism* Edward Said explicitly stated that he wished to research how the category of the Orient had been constructed, saying that "The Orient was almost a European invention."[16]

It's interesting to note how such studies on the "creation of the past" first became widespread during the early 1980s, at a time when (1) the unprecedented character of new migration trends had become evident; (2) the 1960s had already seen the advent of the "Black is beautiful" model of African American empowerment, as well as the literal invention on the part of several Black leaders of an originary Islamic identity (the Black Muslims' story of Yacub); (3) in the wake of the Black (and feminist) movements during the 1970s, white ethnics had begun to express traits of what Gunnar Myrdal called "romantic ethnicity":

> Ethnic writers have concentrated on an abstract craving for historical identity, but they have not clarified by intensive study what cultural traits are implied, who wants this identity, who should want it, and why, and how it should and could come about. I am afraid, therefore, one must characterize this movement as an upper-class intellectual romanticism.[17]

Myrdal underestimated the strength of this *ethnic romanticism,* whose roots were much deeper than any elite intellectualism. Throughout this book, I have written many times that at a particular time in the United States there were X Blacks, Y Hispanics and Z descendants of German immigrants. The United States publishes extremely precise and detailed statistics on the ethnic and racial origin of its inhabitants. And yet – as we have seen – even the highly important Black category is genetically illusory, because the census defines as Black whoever has even "one drop of Negro blood."

Here we come to a key point that is, once again, connected to the power of

16 Edward W. Said, *Orientalism,* New York: Vintage Books, 1979, p. 1.
17 Gunnar Myrdal, "The Case against Romantic Ethnicity," *Center Magazine,* 1974, p. 30. Cited by S. Steinberg, *The Ethnic Myth,* p. 50.

naming: the simple act of naming something (whether it be an apple, an ethnicity or a type of wood) generates the thing named and makes it real, or else modifies its reality in some way. Here the power to name is that exercised by the Bureau of the Census. Benedict Anderson has pointed out the vital role censuses play in producing "imagined communities." The census expects to be able to subdivide the population into categories that do not overlap (no one belongs to two different categories) and that are sufficient to define all the nation's inhabitants (no one is exempt from categorization) – into what in abstract algebra we call the division of a set.

The only problem is that not all sets can be clearly divided. "The fiction of the census is that everyone is in it, and that everyone has one – and only one – extremely clear place. No fractions."[18] To avoid gray areas, the census has had the brilliant idea of inventing the category "Other" (occasionally labeled "Miscellaneous"), which gathers together all those who remain outside its general taxonomy. Once the population has been subdivided, these categories are then recorded in job application forms, medical and school records, work papers and police files. They can therefore effectively change an individual's life: gradually "giving real social life to the state's earlier fantasies."[19] Nothing expresses this more clearly than the categories employed by the US Bureau of the Census. "The concept of race the Census Bureau uses reflects self-identification; that is, the individual's perception of his/her racial identity."[20] This means that people declare the race they *think* they belong to. There are five racial categories to choose from: American Indian or Alaska Native; Asian; Black or African American; Native Hawaiian or Other Pacific Islander; and White. The subdivision is already deeply offensive: the category "Asian," for example, blends together in a single race peoples of Indo-European (Indians), Dravidian (Tamils), Mongoloid (Chinese), and Malay origin, racial groups that are completely different from one another.

The incredible part, though, is that for over a century, up to the 2000 census, each individual *was forced to choose* which race he or she wished to belong to. Even someone with a Chinese mother and a white father, say, could "enroll" in only

---

18 B. Anderson, *Imagined Communities*, p. 166.
19 Ibid., p. 169.
20 Census Bureau, *Statistical Abstract of the United States 1999*, p. 4.

one of these two races. In 1997, when the Office of Management and Budget (OMB) decided to finally put an end to this taxonomic coercion (which was becoming a scandal) resistance led to rejection of the proposal to insert a "Mixed Race" category as an alternative to the existing five racial subdivisions. Chosen instead was a system of almost baroque complexity, symptomatic of what Anderson calls "bureaucratic delirium." Instead of "Mixed Race," a sixth category was added, a mysterious "Other Race," and applicants were also permitted to declare more than one race, so that "for Census 2000 63 possible combinations of the six basic racial categories exist, including six categories for those who report exactly one race, and 57 categories for those who report two or more races."[21]

As a result, the United States now finds itself faced with the prospect of a combinatorial delirium, because future statistics will report as many as sixty-three different races! It is a figure that demonstrates once more what Luca Cavalli Sforza has never ceased to remind us of, that race has no genetic foundation, that there is in fact no such thing as this or that race, only diverse populations. Any form of racial classification is thus purely arbitrary: "For instance, we don't know the answer to the question: 'How many races exist on Earth?'"[22] But even if most of us don't know the answer, you can be sure the Bureau of the Census does: there are in fact sixty-three races on Earth – no more, no less.

Yet the forces of coercion that encourage racial self-imprisonment are so deeply ingrained in American society that only a very few US citizens have seized the opportunity to define themselves as either multiracial or "Other Race." Although the definitive figures for the 2000 Census were not yet available at press time, sample data showed that only 2 percent of respondents reported being multiracial or "Other Race," an incredibly small number considering the multiracial presence in the United States today.[23] Everybody, it seems, *wants to belong to one race, one ethnicity.* If we look at children's death records between the years 1983 and 1985, we see a noticeable discrepancy between the ethnic origin declared on

21 Census Bureau, Population Division, Special Population Staff, "Racial and Ethnic Classifications Used in Census 2000 and Beyond," issued 12 April 2000; available at www.census.gov/population/www/socdemo/race/racefactcb.html.

22 Luca and Francesco Cavalli Sforza, *Chi siamo: La storia della diversità umana*, Milan: Mondadori, 1993, p. 333.

23 "Census Race Question Has Limited Impact: Survey Finds That About 2% of Respondents Report Having Mixed Heritage," *Washington Post*, 30 July 2000.

birth certificates and that recorded on death certificates. The very fact that the parents had declared different origins shows a *desire* to belong to an ethnicity. The Census creates and encourages an ethnic consciousness, whose status is, to say the least, problematic.

This sense of willingness is even more glaring in the case of race: 6 percent of those who declare themselves to be Black appear to their interviewers to be white, while one-third of those who define themselves as Asian might pass for either Black or white. Such incongruence is the very basis of the system of definition, however. As far as US statistics are concerned, since at least 1973 (when a federal committee established the new racial taxonomy[24]), humanity has been split into two basic groups: one of *Hispanic origin*, the other of *non-Hispanic origin*. One could imagine a surreal exchange along the lines of "So what are you?" "Me? Oh, I'm non-Hispanic." And nothing manifests the absurdity of this division more than the category of Hispanic or Latino itself. *Hispanic,* in fact, includes Bolivian Indios, white Chileans, black Caribbeans and Portuguese-speaking peoples such as the Brazilians. It is neither a race nor an ethnicity nor even a language. And yet, in the end, it begins to *function* like a seventh race to add to all the others, because, thanks to it, a blond, blue-eyed Argentinean isn't counted as white, or an Indio from the Yucatán considered native, or a dark-skinned Haitian considered Black.

The extraordinary thing is that these categories become interiorized and eventually come to define a new community. We already saw an example of this when *La Prensa de San Diego* trumpeted the cause of the *Latino community*, condemning Black assaults on Latinos, even though many of these Latinos were themselves empirically Black. Another case is that of the American Indians, whose population between 1960 and 1990 grew from half a million to almost 2 million (a demographically impossible increase of 250 percent): at a certain point, it must have become cool to go Native. But it isn't simply a question of taste. Money is also involved.

Indeed, signing up for membership with a well-defined minority group has its own (poor) advantages. Through positive discrimination, a number of federal contributions and public jobs are assigned to each of the various minorities on the basis of quotas. Consequently, being Native American or Asian or Hispanic can

---

24 Ibid., p. 50.

have its financial rewards. This has gotten to the point where, nowadays, Arab immigrants complain about being assimilated into the white category when they would prefer to have their own race of Arabic peoples, with its due quota of public jobs and contributions. The Arabs would like to be recognized as a legitimate caste and, in this way, to obtain, for example, a seat in Congress.

So there we have it: one begins with the arbitrary category of Latino or Native, which has no precise racial or ethnic content to begin with but which soon acquires its own interests and advantages and finally begins to boast of its Hispanic or Native pride. At this point, you suddenly have *real* Latinos, *authentic* Natives, white supremacists. The individual goes in search of an *original* identity, tries to rediscover his or her roots. The more uncertain or ambiguous the origin is, the more frenetic the search, resulting in an all-American "passion for genealogy."[25] It's true: everywhere you go in America, you run into the difficult question of origins. The first thing one university professor told me was of his anxiety about going to Russia to trace his forebears, Volga Germans. And then there is the risk that you might be sorely disappointed by your origins, as happened to a journalist who felt a sense of disillusion on visiting the town of Stettino, from whence his forebears had set off fifty years previously.

An even greater sense of bitterness was that felt by Black soldiers who formed part of an American expeditionary force sent to Somalia in 1992 for an operation somewhat blusteringly code-named *Restore Hope*. There, on coming into contact with the Somalians, the soldiers' sense of African American identity was brought brutally into question. As Black Americans who were American through and through, they had virtually nothing in common with the Somalians. Yet back in the United States, this African American identity, founded on white oppression and segregation, is a real and tangible thing.

It's amazing how, despite the fact that virtually no Black is truly black, and despite the abyss that separates modern Black America from Africa – an abyss wider than any ocean – American society has managed to construct an authentic Black, African American identity. Here we witness the process of the "construction of authenticity." Maybe this wasn't exactly the way Martin Heidegger intended to

---

25 E. Hobsbawm, in the *Invention of Tradition*, p. 292. Hobsbawm traces this back to the 1890s for families who wished to establish the purity of their WASP origins.

arrive at the concepts of *authentic* and *inauthentic,* on which his thought was grounded; it cannot be denied, however, that he too nurtured a nostalgic desire for "origins" and venerated "a priceless, age-old rootedness in the Alemanian Swabian territory" of the Black Forest.[26] And it is symptomatic that the question of origins was to mark the horizon of reactionary modernism, the "conservative revolution" in whose ambit Heidegger was working.

The modernity of such a procedure lies in the fact that the supposed origin has never been originary, that its primordial essence is a modern invention. An anxiety over the future manifests itself as regret for the lost past, a *desire for nostalgia.* A corollary to this is the fact that the duplicity implicit in creating the past has the effect of reshuffling the political cards of right and left. The left, wishing to help emancipate minorities, supports positive discrimination initiatives and is thus bound to maintain existing ethnic definitions (consider the furor over political correctness in education). Meanwhile, the right, against affirmative action because it wants to shake off the burden placed on the state by the concept, sincerely hopes to do away with ethno-racial categories altogether, maintaining inequality by making everybody more equal. This reshuffling of values has led to an American version of what happened to the communist movement when its focus shifted from Marx's proletarian internationalism to Lenin's national liberation front – when nationalism, once considered a tool of bourgeois oppression, was suddenly being trumpeted as the masses' means of emancipation from imperialism.

In July 2000 in North Carolina, eighteen people of either Lebanese or Lebanese-American provenance were arrested and accused of funding the Hezbollah through cigarette trafficking.[27] In August of that same year, "the parents of an Israeli-American teenager killed in a 1996 terrorist attack in Jerusalem filed a $600 million lawsuit in Chicago against several charities and nonprofit groups contending that they were raising money to finance terrorism."[28] The American press is by now full of such episodes. Back in 1993, two Americans of Palestinian descent

---

26 Martin Heidegger, "Warum bleiben wir in der Provinz" ("Why Do We Remain in the Province?"), *Der Alemane,* March 1934; quoted by Pierre Bourdieu in *L'ontologie politique de Martin Heidegger* (1975). Eng. trans. *The Political Ontology of Martin Heidegger,* Cambridge: Polity, 1991, p. 51.
27 *New York Times,* 22 July 2000.
28 Ibid., 13 August 2000.

from the Chicago area were arrested in Jerusalem by the Shin Beth – the Israeli secret police – and accused of financing the Islamic fundamentalist terrorist outfit
Hamas, even though the money had been destined for charity according to the editor of *Al Bustan,* one of Chicago's many Arabic-language newspapers. Many in
Chicago's Arab community, now numbering 150,000 people, turned out for a
massive demonstration in support of the second Palestinian Intifada in the winter
of 2000.[29] Thus it's not simply that the chador cheers on the Bulls.

A real political battle is being waged on the shores of Lake Michigan for control
of the Gaza strip – and it's not just among Palestinian emigrants. One of the clear
signs of our times is what Benedict Anderson calls "long-distance nationalism."[30]
It's a nationalism exacerbated by distance and taken to extremes in its attempts to
affirm an endangered identity. Many Punjabi supporters of an independent
Kahlistan live in Chicago, just as many Sikhs support their compatriots from their
homes in Vancouver, while American Tamils can participate long distance in their
guerrilla war campaigns through Tamilnet. To finance the campaign that led to
the destruction of a mosque in Ayodha, the Vishwa Hindu Parishad – the world
Hindu council – collected sizable donations from its members in North America
and Britain.[31] Meanwhile, Chicago's Croatian community certainly didn't skimp
on the funds, arms and men they sent to support their compatriots' cause in Europe: here, too, religion is the binding factor. Just as many of Chicago's Palestinians gather around the Mosque Foundation, so too do the Croats flock to the
Franciscan monks, the Serbs to the Orthodox church.

When you consider that Cleveland is now the biggest Slovenian city in the
world (larger even than Lubljiana), so much so that in 1991 the city's financial support for the newly proclaimed republic of Slovenia helped play a determining role,
you begin to realize the extent to which part of the war in the former Yugoslavia
was fought between the states of Ohio and Illinois, a fact that has some curious implications. The bishop of a Serbian Orthodox church, for example, who also happens to be president of the local Chetnik association, freely admitted that

29 *Chicago Tribune,* 29 December 2000
30 Title of a chapter in Benedict Anderson's book *The Spectre of Comparisons: Nationalism, Southeast Asia
    and the World,* London: Verso, 1998, pp. 58–74.
31 Reported in Praful Bidwal, "Bringing Down the Temple: Democracy at Risk in India," *Nation,* 25
    January 1993, p. 86.

Chicago's Serbs had sent volunteers to fight in Yugoslavia. Not only that, but the Serbs had bought up the mobile field hospitals the US Army had used during the 1991 Gulf War and operating theaters on a tour of the theaters of war from Iraq to Bosnia.

Nothing new in that, you might say. The century-old support of Chicago's Irish community for Irish independence and then, during the postwar period, for the IRA's campaigns in Ulster is by now legendary. Even the walls of the bar in Chicago's Hilton Hotel are plastered with Provisional IRA banners and slogans. There is a crucial difference, however: Irish descendents feel themselves to be Americans with Irish roots, while the backers of Hamas arrested in Israel or the Serb or Croat volunteers consider themselves Palestinians, Serbs and Croats, only in America "right now."

Black academics who support political correctness in education may search for their roots in African culture and history so as to *act now,* yet for no reason would they voluntarily go and live in South Africa, nor would they consider themselves Zairian, Tanzanian or Senegalese. By contrast, the volunteers who leave for southern Europe or the Gaza Strip consider themselves Croat or Palestinian in the *present tense.* In this sense, they are the reverse of emigrants: Croats of American origin or US-born Palestinians, like the Sikhs of Canadian or the Tamils of Australian origin. Here we see a "shift from, say, American through Armenian-*American* through *Armenian*-American,"[32] with the stress sliding from American to Armenian (or Sikh).

While the surnames of politicians in the Americas such as Eisenhower, Galtieri and Trudeau once bespoke their immigrant origins, we see now an inverted diaspora: politicians now emigrate from the United States back to their country of origin. The first sensational case of this was that of Andreas Papandreu, who started his life as a Greek citizen, then became an American citizen and then, opportunely summoned by the motherland, returned to Greece once more as a Greek citizen, where he went on to become prime minister. In the 1990s, the Canadian computer systems baron Stanislaw Tyminski stood in the Polish elections against Lech Walesa, while Rein Taagepera, a professor at the University of California at Irvine, was defeated in the Estonian presidential campaign. A retired US Army colonel,

---

32 B. Anderson, "Long-Distance Nationalism," in *The Spectre of Comparisons*, p. 72.

Alexander Einseln, who had emigrated to the United States at the age of eighteen, returned to his native and newly independent Estonia, where he was made chief of staff. Milan Pani, another US citizen, has served as the Serbian prime minister, while Mohammad Sacirbey has been Bosnian ambassador to the United Nations. Moheen Qureshi, former vice-president of the World Bank, became interim president of Pakistan while holding a US green card. And when Long Beach millionaire Kim Kethavi stood in the 1993 Kampuchean presidential elections, his party's office was awash with the red, white and blue. The *New York Times* of 17 February commented that, in the unlikely event that Kethavi won, "he would *probably* have had to renounce his American citizenship" under US law.

Yet another splitting exists: though new nationalisms continue to erupt everywhere, the actual ties of nationality are loosening as the idea of nation shifts away from a sense of permanent belonging. One could in fact compare *amor patrio* to the idea of marital fidelity, the bonds of nationality to those of wedlock. While other civilizations have endorsed *synchronic* polygamy, the idea of having several partners at the same time, ours has replaced monogamy with a form of *diachronic* polygamy: at any one moment, the individual has only one marriage partner, but over the course of a life, a person may, diachronically speaking, have several. In the case of nationality, the migrations of the nineteenth century constituted a divorce from the immigrant's country of origin followed by remarriage, through assimilation, to the newly adopted homeland: the immigrant was a citizen of two different nations over the course of a life but belonged to only one at any particular moment. And when an immigrant refused to divorce the old country, as the Germans did until the outbreak of the First World War, that contumacy was roundly condemned, as though it were the patriotic version of adultery. By contrast, in terms of nationality, today's migration reestablishes synchronic polygamy, though in a way that is diatopic (occurring in different places). That is to say, the individual belongs to more than one nation at the same time, but in different places and, above all, in a way that is reversible. This reversibility, linked to the dream of a "circular migration," is possible only insofar as the individual's assimilation remains partial, however.

Compared to only a few decades ago, the immigrant's attitude toward integration has been completely overturned. Once immigrants bowed to the decree "you will become like us whether you want to or not"; today they spurn assimilation or, at most, accept the bare minimum as an inevitable part of moving to a new country. In this, they represent the defeat of what could be called the French model of complete assimilation and erasure of origins embodied in the figure of the *citoyen*, whereby the Armenian-born Charles Aznavour and the Italians Yves Montand and Leo Ferré became the archetypal French crooners.

And being the bearer of a dual or multiple nationality is much easier than it sounds. In Chicago, the phenomenon is particularly evident. The Korean who sends the kids to summer school in Seoul wants them to "be American but at the same time not forget *their own* country": these children will be American, to be sure, but "their country" will continue to be Korea – the Korea of a street in Chicago. Overlaid upon their American-ness will be a veil of Korean nationalism. So it is that you can be both Yankee and Palestinian, much in the same way that the team that wins the NBA championships will be declared "world" basketball champions, when the world, of course, means America. It is a place where the nation of the United States is your life's horizon, while the Palestinian (or Croat or Tamil) nation is the identity you aspire to.

In blowing millions of human lives from one continent to another, the tornado of capitalism, the "most subversive force we have ever known," has also reshaped the very concept of nationhood. The human destinies it sweeps up clutch at distant identities, reasons for living that would be laughable were these humans not also ready to die for them.

"Reasons for living," "death." Benedict Anderson comments on that peculiar monument, the emblem of modern nationalism, "The Tomb of the Unknown Soldier." Cultures other than ours have erected cenotaphs, of course, but the identity of the deceased has been well known in such cases; all that was missing was the body. But here – No. The idea of filling the tomb with a body or even attributing a name to it would be sacrilege. In that tomb, the absent body is the nation itself: in Rome, the unknown soldier is the Italian, while in Paris, under the Arc de Triomphe, it is Frenchness that fills the void. "The cultural significance of such monuments becomes even clearer if one tries to imagine, say, a Tomb of the Unknown Marxist or a cenotaph for fallen Liberals."[33]

---

33 B. Anderson, *Imagined Communities*, pp. 9–10.

Precisely insofar as it is imagined, and thus experienced as a destiny, as a primordial and immutable fact, national identity attaches itself to meaning and to death, questions that "all evolutionary/progressive styles of thought, not excluding Marxism" respond to "with *impatient silence*"[34] (italics mine). By his actions, the nationalist must answer his dead. Indeed, the nation is the very thing that transforms the dead into "our dead," just as the Vice Lords spill a mouthful of bourbon in memory of *their* fallen comrades.

So it is, in the streets of Chicago, that all people carry within themselves their own fragments of meaning, of the underworld and the beyond. The vacated city disperses into endless tracts of single-family suburbia but also becomes dislocated in inner worlds of myriad patriotisms, diasporas of belief, with a Sheridan Avenue in Ho Chi Min City, a Lincoln Avenue in Seoul, a Humboldt Park in Guadalajara. You meet somebody whose next-door neighbor lives in Belgrade, and then immediately somebody else who is talking mental long-distance to Calcutta. It appears to you that the Chicago street map traces a precarious web of lives suspended in silence, floating in a cosmic void of ungraspable meanings. No country like the United States – and no city like Chicago – conveys such an intense feeling of the metaphysical, here where even the slaughterhouses once emitted the *hogsqueal of the universe*.

What exacerbates this sense of the metaphysical is the contrast between positivism and the rational market–led choices of the Chicago Boys on one hand and the senseless brow-mopping, work-till-you-drop ethic of the city's inhabitants on the other. It's greed soaked in belief, vanity of vanities, wind thirst in the Windy City. Wounding is the intensity with which each fights his own individual struggle and does his duty, free-falling through clouds of nothingness. Between State and Superior, in front of the Holy Name Cathedral, in the elegant heart of the city, a ragged old gray-haired woman sweeps the parvis steps with a broom. She's there every afternoon, tirelessly sprucing up each step, the sweep of her thoughts extending no further than the broom's sorghum bristles. She performs this task as though the planet's equilibrium depended upon it, which perhaps explains why, in Indian cosmology, Siva Nataraja cannot stop dancing even for a moment, since his graceful movements sustain the enormous weight of the universe. The immense

---

34 Ibid.

responsibility on this woman's shoulders, along with her hard and lonely labor, have the effect of placing an opaque wall between her and the world outside, which prevents the values and opinions of others from reaching her. The scraping of her broom is like a scream that reduces all else to silence.

And yet, on a calm summer's night, they come in tides to see the Fourth of July fireworks, torrents of dark bodies from the South Side, pale faces from the front lawns of the North, spiky groups of Indios. The almond eyed and the hook nosed, Indian irises black as embers and blue-eyed she-devils. They come from the far-off suburbs, from Cicero and Calumet, Gary and Evanston, and they pour into Grant Park, on the shores of Lake Michigan opposite the Art Institute, beneath the giant silhouettes of skyscrapers. Fantastic flowers of multicolored light burst into bloom in the night sky, and an immense wave of heat emanates from the crowd, from these millions of human beings who are gathered here *together,* conveying the feeling of stubbornly cheerful hope, intense participation, enormous pride or simply satisfaction in being here, and filling you with an inexplicably moving sense of faith in the future.

Postscript

One More Blues, and Then ...

There's a smoke-filled club on Halsted Avenue, a noted venue in the story of the blues, called, aptly enough, simply *Blues*. Here is where we say good-bye, after our long wanderings through Chicago. Next to the bar with its glass menagerie of liquor bottles is the club's stage, where the Black singers, trumpet players and drummers perform, gray-haired old-timers who play to an all-white audience. The rough-hewn phrases of the blues jar heavily with the tapping of the long, red fingernails of elegant ladies whose hairdos are similarly lacquered to suburban perfection. They come from the provinces of the great central plains, which spread out from the city once dubbed by nineteenth-century columnists "a seat of empire."

It's strange to think that only eighty years ago, the blues was young people's music played by Blacks for Blacks. But that was another era, another America, another Chicago, when cotton pickers from Alabama, Mississippi and Louisiana flooded onto the shores of Lake Michigan like it was the promised land. So it was that the trains of the Illinois Central brought the great jazz and blues players – from Louis Armstrong to Bessie Smith – up from Memphis and New Orleans to play in clubs the likes of Lamb's café or in dance halls such as the Trianon. It was in Chicago that the first Black record label was launched, and for more than half a century, the city was the capital of blues, its biggest annual festival held in the city's parks in the first week of June. In the meantime, the Blacks were being shut up in their ghettos, in the "Black belt," while musically, Chicago became "a place where 'white boy met horn.'"[1] It isn't for nothing that John Belushi and the Blues Brothers are so deeply Chicagoan and so deeply white.

The sound of the blues thus evokes a Chicago that is no more: the Chicago that grew up under the logic of fixed costs and "railroad" capital, the Chicago of slaughterhouses, of the lumber and cereal-crop trade, the white ethnic Chicago with its Teutonic substratum, the city of Irish mayors (Daley, Kelly), Polish shopkeepers and Italian gangsters (Al Capone, Sam Giancana).

Chicago presents itself as exemplary, as the faithful representation of real America: a city that describes itself as *necessary,* the "inevitable metropolis" of the Midwest, in the words of Parton. To observe Chicagoland means to recount the myriad layers of its stratified urban and human geography. The city's history, both architectural and industrial, becomes an archeology of capital, a dig amid the rubble that capital has left in its wake, the vast armies of human lives it has shifted and thrown in at the deep end of the American Dream, the inventions it has instituted, from the balloon-frame house to the skyscraper, the mechanical combine harvester to the refrigerated meat wagon, up to the mercantile exchange where options are traded on the bacon of the future.

Of this history, as brief as it is swollen, not even the effigies remain. The stockyards lie deserted, Grand Central Station razed to the ground, Haymarket Square reduced to an overpass. Hobohemia has undergone regentrification, while the only thing that swings in Bronzeville nowadays is the wrecking ball. Both Lamb's café and the Trianon have been demolished: an entire book of photos shows images of this "lost Chicago," as though it were some latter-day Atlantis.[2] The Calumet Steelworks rusts in peace, the Stewart-Warner factory has been turned into a gated city. Whole ghettos have vanished, cleared away to make room for tracts of cute little townhomes. Blown away are the anarchists, the Panthers, Debs and his union crowd, the lumberjacks who hacked the white pine from this land, the railroads, the hobos. All have been swept from the stage of history, or perhaps buried in a cemetery à la Spoon-River (Edgar Lee Masters, another of Chicago's sons). In

---

1   Eric Hobsbawm, *The Jazz Scene* (1959), rev. ed. New York: Pantheon, 1993, p. 94.
2   David Lowe, *Lost Chicago*, Boston: Houghton, Mifflin, 1975. Reprinted, New York: Wings, 1993.

a few years, the ruined, fire-blackened towers of Taylor Homes and Cabrini-Green will also haunt the pages of *Lost Chicago,* a myth in the back roads of the city's memory, just like the ecstatic frenzy in the pits of the Chicago Board of Trade and the Mercantile Exchange.

An archaeology we have, then, but an archaeology of the future – because this kind of self-destruction and self-consumption, this constant leveling and rebuilding, is what it means to be modern. As Marx and Engels wrote in their *Communist Manifesto,* "all that is solid melts into air,"[3] a phrase taken by Marshall Berman for the title of his book on what he calls "the experience of modernity." What only yesterday shaped and built Chicago, what made it a great city, has already gone – just as the city we see today is likewise destined to evaporate. What doesn't change, though, is the process of dissolution itself, the way the city lives its perpetual dying, autophagy as a means of growth. Chicago seems to ceaselessly practice upon itself the process that Schumpeter saw as the principal feature of capitalism: "creative destruction."[4] But while it may be true that everything "melts into air," through this process, as Marx completes his reflection, "man is at least compelled to face with sober senses, his real condition of life, and his relations with his kind."

As you, the reader, will no doubt have gathered by now, I am not a specialist in American Studies, no more than this book has the right to sit on that particular shelf, to say nothing of its questionable status as a "history" of Chicago. Indeed, you'll probably have noticed how I've tried to maintain my outsider's gaze, the incredulity of the foreigner, the "European": in Germany or in France, I am obliged to feel *Italian,* but once I came to America, I was forced to regard myself as *European* and to ask myself, as Wolfgang Schivelbusch had done, when exactly it was that "we became them."

It isn't true that we are the architects or engineers of our books, demiurges who first outline a project and then actuate it. Generally speaking, anyone who writes a book first *bumps into* it, just as I stumbled across Chicago, a city that nothing in my training (either as a physicist or as a Francophone sociology student) or in my pro-

---

3 *The Communist Manifesto* (1848), London: Verso, 1998, pp. 38–39.
4 Joseph Alois Schumpeter, *Capitalism, Socialism and Democracy* (1946), London: George Allen and Unwin, 1954, part II, ch. 7.

fessional experience had prepared me for. The city stood before me like an ordering factor, capable of weaving sense out of an array of preoccupations I had
regarding the experience and nature of modernity, a series of questions that,
though separate, were at the same time connected in some jumbled up way and
that my mind continued to ravel and unravel. My senses perceived the city as
though it were a character in a novel, a subject that would enable me to transform
an essay into a story, a study into a narrative.

Perhaps it had something to do with the particular moment in my life when I
encountered the city, but immediately I sensed what I can only call its *stink,* which
was the *stink of modernity.* As anyone who travels knows, if you live too long in a
city, you no longer perceive its odors: on returning after a long interval, however,
no matter how clean the streets are kept, each city welcomes you with its own
uniquely powerful smell, which, though it may be unbearable, is at the same time
strangely *familiar.* Now Chicago stinks of the modern. It's not a subtle aroma: it's a
mighty stench, and it perhaps explains what Nelson Algren perceived as "the paradox that Europeans are more concerned about the city than ourselves."[5]

Even after having lived here from the autumn of 1992 to the spring of 1993, it
would take me another two years of study and additional field trips to master the
concepts and instruments that were themselves barely sufficient to bring to light
elements of modernity: the only thing of which I knew was their smell. Only over
the course of this endeavor have I come to understand how it is that so many of
modernity's key episodes – the birth of the skyscraper, the standardization of flavors, the rise of urban sociology, the first atomic reactor, the Chicago Boys' school
of economics – have taken place here on the shores of Lake Michigan.

It would be pointless to reiterate here the salient traits of modernity that we've
managed to pull from the rubble: the power of naming, the question of authenticity, the gradual spread of the private sphere, the social mechanism whose input of
class conflict leads to an output of racial antagonism. More than anything else,
Chicago's continuing ability to astonish lies in the revolutionary and subversive
power of capitalism, which is still a long way from exhaustion.

What comes to the fore are the masses of human lives caught up in the perma-

---

5   Nelson Algren, *Chicago: City on the Make* (1951), Chicago: University of Chicago Press, 1983, p. 87.

nent revolution of capitalism, shaken and uprooted by its vortex, the millions of disinherited and impoverished dragged from one continent to another, each clinging stubbornly to the hope of a better life. On the shores of Lake Michigan, 170 years ago, were only the tepees of American Indians and the odd fur trapper's station. Today the Vietnamese community here celebrates its new year, the Tet, while Arabs pray in the city's mosques. Just 170 years ago, buffalo populated the prairie, and Chicago wasn't even a village. Now, at the dawn of the third millennium, this megalopolis of 8 million inhabitants has completed the cycle of modernity. The question now is whether the city, in its already wizened maturity – as an urban way of life and civilization – is unraveling into a reticular, multicentric sprawl, a muddled middle ground that is neither fully town nor country: whether the city too melts into air.

To measure the abyss that separates then from now, an abyss dug in just 160 years, it's enough to compare the Manchester slums described by Engels and the ghettos of Chicago. While they may be identical in terms of their squalor, filth and desolation, three enormous differences remain: (1) Engels's slum dwellers were *white*, whereas the inhabitants of today's Chicago ghettos are all *of color;* (2) the former were *factory workers*, whereas the latter are *unemployed;* and (3) on the streets of Manchester was a *bustling crowd*, whereas what strikes you in Chicago is the silence and *solitude* of the nearly deserted streets.

In Chicago, the subversive logic of capital was able to unfold without impediment, without being slowed down either by government (as in France), by a landed aristocracy (as in Britain) or by the church (as in Italy). Capitalism got to the United States first and thus imposed itself in a more extreme form than in Europe. This is why many of the situations and configurations we have encountered in the United States are only now beginning to make their appearance on the Old Continent, or are at a very early stage in their development. It is in this sense that the study of Chicago constitutes an archaeology of the future – the future of Europe, the future conceived as a general trend that is not necessarily positive (Wacquant even goes so far as to speak of "America as social dystopia").

In the early 1900s, visitors from Europe (among them Sombart and twenty-three English trade-union secretaries, the so-called Mosely expedition of 1902) consistently reported back that American workers were better off than their

European counterparts, that American houses were nicer, the food eaten there infinitely superior, the women workers, as Sombart said, more "elegant."[6] Today, an American union leader would probably say the same thing about workers in Germany: in the United States, worker well-being has grown and declined in advance of Europe. But not only the large-scale trends are so ominous. Equally telling are the smaller, less noticeable signs: the French old guard has stopped wearing their *casquettes* and now play *boules* in baseball caps. Dapper Italian gents now venture out in (fabulously expensive) warm-ups and tennis shoes: in Europe's cities, the homeless have begun setting up box in the center next to opulent thoroughfares.

Slightly more hidden is another characteristic of Chicago that prefigures the modernity of other cities, and that is its being, at the same time, both *provincial* and *global*. It was Saskia Sassen who introduced the concept of the "global city": in a delocalized global economy, services must be concentrated, and "global cities" become necessary, because "they concentrate the infrastructure" and institute "global control." "The latter is essential if geographic dispersal of economic activity – whether factories, offices, or financial markets – is to take place under continued concentration of ownership and profit appropriation."[7] As the cradle of the futures market, Chicago is the global city *par excellence,* and yet – as David Moberg notes – it is so in a provincial way. "Chicago lacks some of the typical attributes of the 'world city.' Despite its airport, it does not have a great port linking to the wider world. Although its influence in the arts, theater, literature and intellectual life has grown in recent decades, it comes nowhere near Los Angeles, with its film and television production, or New York, with its varied broadcast, publishing and fashion industries, as a center of mass cultural or ideological influence (The *Chicago Tribune*, for example, although extremely profitable and locally influential, does not have the international stature of the *New York Times, Wall Street Journal*,

---

6 W. Sombart, *Why Is There No Socialism in the United States?*, p. 97. On the subject of food, "In his eating habits the American worker is much closer to the better sections of the German middle class than to the German wage-labouring class. He does not merely eat, but dines."

7 Saskia Sassen, *Cities in a Global Economy* (1994), Thousands Oaks: Pine Forge Press, 2000, p. 85.

or *Los Angeles Times*)."⁸ A city of the global economy it may be, but Chicago is at the same time profoundly Midwestern, betraying a dislocated rootedness that foreshadows the existential horizons of the peoples of the future.

In this bedlam that is at once *cosmopolitan* and *provincial*, the daily encounters between Poles and Filipinos, Russians and Sikhs, prefigure a world where identities will be constructed and *imagined* in a wholly different way. Flipping the dial through Chicago's radio stations is like choosing from a catalog of language courses. It makes you reflect on how life must have been in Babel. Maybe it wasn't that bad after all – not so much a living hell of tongues in collision as a form of purgatory that, though cacophonic, was at least bearable, where different idioms slid over one another like rustlings that you hear but choose not to listen to. Maybe you could have lived there, you think, after we shake hands and part company at the end of an evening stroll down Halsted Avenue, just as you could live here, in Chicago. One more blues, and then ...

This book has been contaminated by its subject. Like Chicago itself, it has in its various lives undergone incessant and often sudden transformation. Hot on the heels of the city's perpetual autophagy, the book first appeared in Italy in November 1995 and already had to be revised for the third Italian edition in 1996. In the meantime, the many faces of Chicago went under the knife, statistics changed, new studies were published and couldn't be ignored. And so the book was once again revised for the German translation (hardcover 1996, paperback 1998) and for the Italian paperback edition (1999). Now, for the English edition (2002), it has been subjected to an even more radical process of "creative destruction." My only regret is that I was not able to make use of the conclusive data from Census 2000. The updating of statistics, along with various rewritings and additions, has of course augmented the number of people I am indebted to – which was already a pretty long list – who in various ways and in varying measure enabled me to undertake this project and bring it to conclusion, and who have corrected various errors and inaccuracies, who have therefore helped this book make at least some headway in the world. It would be too long and te-

---

8   D. Moberg, "Chicago: To Be or Not to Be a Global City," cited on p. 80. The fact that in 2000 the *Chicago Tribune* became proprietor of the much more influential *Los Angeles Times* is just another demonstration of Chicago's global power and its concurrent provincialism.

dious to specify the assistance that each gave. But certainly the following people know the reasons for my gratitude: Tariq Ali, Guido Ambrosino, Benedict Anderson, Joel Bleifuss, Pierre Bourdieu, Franco Carlini, Manuela and Bruno Cartosio, Francesco Cataluccio, Deborah Cole, William Cronon, Mike Davis, Giulio and Luce d'Eramo, Micaela Di Leonardo, Valerio Evangelisti, Carlo Feltrinelli, Adelin Fiorato, Marina Forti, Roberta and Larry Garner, Maria-Grazia Giannichedda, Jane Hindle, Charles Hoch, Leo Kadanoff, Linda Grace Kobas, Ann Lovell, Corinne Lucas, Giulia Maldifassi, Ornella Mangione, Beth Maschinot, David Moberg, Franco Moretti, Anna Nadotti, the Nnoberavez family, Alessandra Orsi, Antonella Palombo, Giorgio Parisi, Valentino Parlato, Luigi Pintor, Alessandro Portelli, Teresa Prado, Saskia Sassen, Marie-Ange Schiltz, Wolfgang Schivelbusch, Erik Schneider, Maria Concetta Straccamore, Anna Maria Testa, Graeme Thomson, Fabrizio Tonello, Lietta Tornabuoni, Fernando Vianello, Susan Watkins, James Weinstein and the kind staff of the Harold Washington, Newberry and Regenstein Libraries and of the Chicago Historical Society.

Bibliography

Listed here are only those works whose texts I have directly cited or from which I have taken specific information. I have therefore excluded works that, though they were useful for my research, I have not referred to explicitly. Also excluded are articles taken from daily newspapers or weekly or fortnightly magazines.

Adorno, Theodor W. *The Stars Down to Earth: "The Los Angeles Times" Astrology Column: A Study on Secondary Superstition*, in *Soziologische Schriften II*. Frankfurt am Main: Suhrkamp Verlag. Eng. trans. *The Stars Down to Earth and Other Essays on the Irrational in Culture*. London: Routledge, 1994

——. *Jargon der Eigentlichkeit: Zur deutschen Ideologie*. Frankfurt am Main: Suhrkamp Verlag 1964. Eng trans. *The Jargon of Authenticity*. Evanston, Ill.: Northwestern Univ. Press, 1973.

Adelman, William J. *Haymarket Revisited*. Chicago: Illinois Labor History Society, 1976.

Algren, Nelson. *Chicago, City on the Make* (1951). Chicago: Univ. of Chicago Press, 1983.

Althusser, Louis. *Positions*. Paris: Editions Sociales, 1976.

——. "Ideology and Ideological State Apparatuses," in Slavoj Zizek (ed.). *Mapping Ideology*. London: Verso, 1994.

Anderson, Benedict. *Imagined Commmunities: Reflection on the Origin and Spread of Nationalism*, 2nd edn. London: Verso 1992.

——. "The New World Disorder," *New Left Review*, ser. I, no. 93 (May/June 1992): pp. 3–14.

——. "Exodus," lecture at the University of Chicago, April 1993, manuscript.

——. *The Spectre of Comparisons: Nationalism, Southeast Asia and the World*, London: Verso, 1998.

Anderson, Nels. *The Hobo: The Sociology of the Homeless Man* (1923). Chicago: Univ. of Chicago Press, 1961.

Auerbach, Erich. *Mimesis: Dargestellte Wirklichkeit in der abendländischen Literatur*. Bern: A. Francke, 1946. Eng. trans. *Mimesis: The Representation of Reality in Western Literature* (1953). Princeton, N.J.: Princeton Univ. Press, 1968.

Barthes. Roland. *Mythologies*. Paris: Seuil, 1957. Eng. trans. *Mythologies*, London: Jonathan Cape, 1972.

Beatty, William K. "When Cholera Scoured Chicago." *Chicago History*, vol. 11, no. 1, (Spring 1982): pp. 1–13.

Becker, Gary. *Human Capital Revisited*. Chicago: Univ. of Chicago Press, 1989.

Benjamin, Walter. *Das Kunstwerk im Zeitalter seiner technischen Reproduzierbarkeit* (1936), originally in *Zeischrift für Sozialforschung*, reprinted in *Schriften*, Frankfurt am Main: Suhrkamp Verlag, 1955. Engl. trans. "The Work of Art in the Age of Mechanical Reproduction," in *Illuminations*. London: Fontana (1973) 1992.

Berman, Marshall. *All That Is Solid Melts into Air: The Experience of Modernity*, New York: Simon & Schuster, 1982.

Biven, W. Carl. *Who Killed John Maynard Keynes? Conflicts in the Evolution of Economic Policy*. Homewood, Ill.: Dow Jones-Irwin, 1989.

Blakeley, Edward J., and Mary Gail Snyder. *Fortress America: Gated Communities in the United States*. Washington, D.C.: Brookings Institution Press, 1997.

Bourdieu, Pierre. *L'ontologie politique de Martin Heidegger* (1975). Paris: Seuil, 1988. Eng. trans. *The Political Ontology of Martin Heidegger*. Cambridge, Mass.: Polity Press, 1991.

——. "Effets de lieu," in Pierre Bourdieu et al., *La misère du monde*, Paris: Seuil, 1993, pp. 159–67. Eng trans. "Site-Effects," in *The Weight of the World: Social Suffering in Contemporary Society*. Cambridge, Mass.: Polity Press, 1999.

Bourgeois, Philippe. "Une nuit dans une 'shooting gallery': Enquête sur le commerce de la drogue à East Harlem," *Actes de la recherche en sciences sociales*, no. 94 (Sept. 1992): pp. 59–78.

Boyer, Paul. *When Time Shall Be No More: Prophecy Belief in Modern American Culture*. Cambridge, Mass.: Harvard Univ. Press, 1992.

Brecher, Jeremy. *Strike!* San Francisco: Straight Arrow Books, 1972.

Bryce, James. *The American Commonwealth*, 2 vols (1893). New York: Macmillan, 1917.

Cartosio, Bruno. *Lavoratori negli Stati Uniti: Storie e culture politiche dalla schiavitù all'I.W.W.* Milan: Arcipelago Ed., 1989.

——. *Anni inquieti: Società media ideologie negli Stati Uniti da Truman a Kennedy*, Rome: Editori Riuniti, 1992.

Castel, Robert. "La 'guerre à la pauvreté' aux Etas Unis," *Actes de la recherche en sciences sociales*, no. 19 (Jan. 1978): pp. 47–60.

Cavalli-Sforza, Luca, and Francesco Cavalli-Sforza. *Chi siamo: La storia della diversità umana*. Milan: Mondadori, 1993.

Chamberlain, Leslie. *Nietzsche in Turin: The End of the Future*. London: Quartet Books, 1996.

Chernow, Ron. *The House of Morgan: An American Banking Dynasty and the Rise of Modern Finance*. New York: Simon & Schuster, 1990.

Coase, Ronald. "The Problem of Social Cost." *Journal of Law and Economics*, no. 3, 1960.

Conwell, Russell Herman. *Acres of Diamonds*, New York: Harper Brothers, 1915.

Coulon, Alain. *L'école de Chicago* (1987). Paris: Presses Universitaires de France, coll. "Que-sais-je?" 1993.

Cronon, William. *Nature's Metropolis: Chicago and the Great West*. New York: Norton, 1991.

Cuoco, Vincenzo. *Saggio storico sulla rivoluzione napoletana del 1799* (1801). Bari: Laterza, 1980.

Cutler, Irving. *Chicago, Metropolis of the Mid-Continent*. Dubuque, Iowa: Geographical Society of Chicago 1973; Kendall/Hunt, 1982.

Davis, Mike. *City of Quartz*. London: Verso 1991.

Dawkins, Richard. *The Blind Watchmaker: Why the Evidence of Evolution Reveals a Universe Without Design*. London: Norton, 1987.

Derluguian, Georgi. "A Tale of Two Cities." *New Left Review*, ser. II, no. 9 (May/June 2000), pp 47–71.

Dewey, John. *Logic: The Theory of Inquiry*. New York: Henry Holt, 1948.

Dostoevsky, Fyodor. *Crime and Punishment*. London: Penguin, 1992.

Draper, Theodor. *The Roots of American Communism*. New York: Viking Press, 1956.

Dumont, Louis. *Homo Aequalis: Genèse et épanoissement de l'idéologie économique,* Paris: Gallimard, 1977.

Durand, Jacques. "Rhétorique du nombre," in the special issue "Recherches rhétoriques" of *Communications*, no. 16 (1970): pp. 125–32.

Engels, Friedrich. *The Condition of the Working Class in England in 1844*, Chicago: Academy Chicago Publishers, 1993.

Evangelisti, Valerio. *Sinistre eretiche dalla banda Bonnot al sandinismo*. Milan: Sugarco, 1985.

Faris, Robert E. L. *Chicago Sociology, 1920–1932* (1967). Chicago: Univ. of Chicago Press, 1979.

Foner, Philip S. *History of the Labor Movement in the United States*, 9 vols. New York: International Publishers, 1955.

Foucault, Michel. *Surveiller et punir: Naissance de la prison.* Paris: Gallimard, 1975. Eng. trans. *Discipline and Punish.* New York: Vintage, 1979

Fraser, Russell. "John Peter Altgeld: Governor of the People," in *American Radicals,* New York: Monthly Review Press, 1965, pp. 127–44.

Freeman, Richard. *The Overeducated American.* New York: Academic Press, 1976.

Fremon, David K. *Chicago Politics Ward by Ward.* Bloomington, Ind.: Indiana Univ. Press, 1987.

Fried, Albert (ed.). *Socialism in America from the Shakers to the Third International: A Documentary History.* New York: Columbia Univ. Press, 1970.

Friedan, Betty. *The Feminine Mystique.* New York: Bantam Doubleday Dell, 1963.

Frommer's Guides, *USA '93–'94,* New York: Prentice Hall Travel, 1993.

Gabaccia, Donna R. *We Are What We Eat: Ethnic Food and the Making of America,* Cambridge, Mass.: Harvard Univ. Press, 1998.

Gallino, Luciano. *Dizionario di sociologia.* Turin: Utet, 1978.

Garreau, Joel. *Edge City: Life on the New Frontier.* New York: Doubleday, 1989.

Goethe, Wolfgang. *Goethes Werke,* Band 1,12 neubarb. Aufl. Munich: Verlag C.H. Beck, 1981 ("Hamburger Ausgabe").

Graham, Taylor. "An Epidemic of Strikes in Chicago," *The Survey,* vol. 42 (August 2, 1919): pp. 645–64.

Grampp, William D. *The Manchester School of Economics,* Stanford, Calif.: Stanford Univ. Press, 1960.

Grossman, James R. *Land of Hope: Chicago, Black Southerners, and the Great Migration.* Chicago: Univ. of Chicago Press, 1989.

Hagwood, John A. *The Tragedy of German America: The Germans in the U.S. of America During the Nineteenth Century and After.* New York: G. P. Putnam Sons, 1940.

Halimi, Serge. "L'université de Chicago: Un petit coin de paradis bien protégé." *Le monde diplomatique,* April 1994.

Harrington, Michael. *The Other America: Poverty in the United States* (1962), New York: Penguin, 1981.

Hayden, Tom. *Trial.* New York: Holt and Winston, 1970.

Hayner, Don, and Tom McNamee. *Streetwise Chicago: A History of Chicago Street Names.* Chicago: Loyola Univ. Press, 1988.

Heenan, David A. *The New Corporate Frontier: The Big Move to Small Town, U.S.A.* New York: McGraw-Hill, 1991.

Heidenheimer, Arnold, et al. *Political Corruption: A Handbook.* New Brunswick, N.J.: Transaction, 1989.

Hirschman, Albert. *Exit, Voice, Loyalty.* Cambridge, Mass.: Harvard Univ. Press, 1970.

——. *The Rhetoric of Reaction: Perversity, Futility, Jeopardy.* Cambridge, Mass.: The Belknap Press of Harvard Univ. Press, 1991.

Hobbes, Thomas. *Leviathan* (1651). New York: Liberal Arts Press, 1958.

Hobsbawm, Eric [Francis Newton, pseud.]. *The Jazz Scene* (1961). rev. ed. New York : Pantheon, 1993.

Hobsbawm, Eric et al. *The Invention of Tradition*. Cambridge: Cambridge Univ. Press, 1983.

Hoch, Charles, and Robert H. Slayton. *New Homeless and Old: Community and the Skid Row Hotel*. Philadelphia: Temple Univ. Press, 1989.

Hofmeister, Rudolph A. *The Germans of Chicago*. Champaign, Ill.: Stipes Publishing Co., 1976.

Jackson, Kenneth T. *Crabgrass Frontier: The Suburbanization of the United States*. New York: Oxford Univ. Press, 1985.

Jacobson, Julius (ed.). *The Negro and the American Labor Movement*. Garden City, N.Y.: Doubleday Anchor, 1968.

Johnston, Michael. *Political Corruption and Public Policy in America*. Monterey, Calif.: Brooks/Cole, 1982.

Josephson, Matthew J. *Robber Barons: The Great American Capitalists, 1861–1901*. New York: Harcourt, 1934.

Kapp, Yvonne. *Eleanor Marx: The Crowded Years*, 2 vols. London: Virago 1979.

Katz, Michael B. *The Undeserving Poor: From the War to Poverty to the War on Welfare*. New York: Pantheon, 1989.

Kepel, Gilles. *À l'ouest d'Allah*, Paris: Seuil, 1994; Eng. trans. *Allah in the West: Islamic Movements in America and in Europe*. Stanford, Calif.: Stanford Univ. Press, 1997.

La Bruyère, Jean de. *Caractères* (1688). Eng. trans. *Characters*. London: Penguin, 1970.

Landes, David S. *Revolution in Time*. Cambridge, Mass.: Harvard Univ. Press, 1983.

La Vergata, Antonello. *Nonostante Malthus: Fecondità, popolazioni e armonia della natura, 1700–1900*. Turin: Bollati Boringhieri, 1990.

Leech, Harper, and John Charles Carroll. *Armour and His Times*. New York: Appleton-Century, 1938.

Leibniz, Georg Wilhelm. *Monadology* (1714). Engl. trans. in *Discourses on Metaphysics and Other Essays*. Indianapolis, Ind. & Cambridge: Hackett, 1991.

Lewis, Oscar. *La Vida: A Puerto Rican Family in the Culture of Poverty–San Juan and New York*. New York: Random House, 1966.

Lindberg, Richard C. *Ethnic Chicago*. Lincolnwood, Ill.: Passport, 1994.

Lindsay, Almont. *The Pullman Strike: The Story of a Unique Experiment and of a Great Labor Upheaval*. Chicago: Univ. of Chicago Press, 1942.

Lowe, David. *Lost Chicago*. New York: Houghton, Mifflin 1975. Reprint. New York: Wings Books, 1993.

Luebke, Frederick C. *Bonds of Loyalty: German Americans and World War I*. Dekalb, Ill.: Northern Illinois Univ. Press, 1974.

Lukas, Anthony. "The Chicago Conspiracy Trial," in *Britannica Book of the Year 1970*, Chicago, 1971.

Madison, James. *Notes on Debates in the Federal Convention of 1787*. Athens, Ohio: Ohio Univ. Press, 1984.

Mailer, Norman. *Miami and the Siege of Chicago: An Informal History of the American Political Conventions of 1968*. London: Weidenfeld & Nicholson, 1968.

Malcolmson, Scott L. *One Drop of Blood: The American Misadventure of Race*. New York: Farrar Strauss Giroux, 2000.

Malcom X. *Autobiography of Malcom X*, with Alex Haley. New York: Grove, 1965.

Malinowski, Bronislav. *Argonauts of the Western Pacific* (1922). Prospect Heights, Ill.: Waveland, 1984.

Marx, Karl. *Grundrisse del Kritik der politischen Ökonomie* (1857–1858). Berlin: Dietz Verlag 1953. Eng. trans: *Grundrisse: Foundations of the Critique of Political Economy*, New York: Vintage, 1973.

Marx, Karl, and Friedrich Engels. *Marx & Engels Collected Works*. London: Lawrence & Wishart, 1979, vol. 2.

——. *Manifest der Kommunistischen Partei* (1848). Eng. trans. *The Communist Manifesto*. London: Verso, 1998.

Massey, Douglas S., and Nancy A. Denton. *American Apartheid: Segregation and the Making of the Underclass*. Cambridge, Mass.: Harvard Univ. Press, 1993.

Massey, Douglas, et al. *Return to Aztlán: The Social Process of International Migration from Western Mexico*. Berkeley: Univ. of California Press, 1990.

McKenzie, Evan. *Privatopia: Homeowner Associations and the Rise of Residential Private Government*. New Haven: Yale Univ. Press, 1994.

——. "Trouble in Privatopia." *The Progressive* (Oct. 1993): pp. 30–34.

Mead, Frank S. *Handbook of Denominations in the United States*. Nashville, Tenn.: Abingdon Press, 1961, 1990.

Miller, Edythe S. "Economics for What? Economic Folklore and Social Realities." *Journal of Economic Issues* (June 1989): pp. 339–56.

Moberg, David. "Chicago: To Be or Not to Be a Global City." *World Policy Journal*, vol 14, no. 1 (Spring 1997): pp. 71–86.

Moretti, Franco. *Signs Taken for Wonders* (1983). London: Verso, 3d. edn. 1997.

Mumford, Lewis. *The City in History*. New York: Harcourt, 1961.

Myrdal, Gunnar. *An American Dilemma: The Negro Problem and Modern Democracy*. New York: Harper, 1944.

——. *Value in Social Theory*. New York: Harper, 1958.

Nelli, Humbert S. *Italians in Chicago: A Study in Ethnic Mobility*. New York: Oxford Univ. Press, 1970.

Nelson, Bruce C. *Beyond the Martyrs: A Social History of Chicago's Anarchists 1870–1900*. New Brunswick, N.J.: Rutgers Univ. Press, 1988.

——. "Anarchism: 'The Movement Behind the Martyrs,'" in the special issue on Haymarket, *Chicago History*, vol. 15, no. 2 (Summer 1986).

Nozick, Robert. *Anarchy, the State and Utopia.* New York: Basic Books, 1974.

O'Connor, Richard. *The German-Americans: An Informal History.* Boston: Little, Brown & Co., 1968.

Offe, Claus. "L'utopia dell'opzione zero," in *Ecologia politica.* Milan: Feltrinelli, 1987, pp. 41–72.

Pacyga, Dominic A., and Ellen Skerret. *Chicago, City of Neighbohroods.* Chicago: Loyola Univ. Press, 1986.

Paretsky, Sara. *Burn Marks.* New York: Bantam Doubleday Dell, 1990.

Park, Robert E. "Sociology," in Wilson Gee (ed.). *Research in Social Sciences.* New York: Macmillan, 1929.

——. "Human Migration and the Marginal Man," in *The American Journal of Sociology,* vol. 33, no. 6 (March 1928): pp. 881–93.

Park, Robert E., Ernest W. Burgess and Roderick McKenzie. *The City* (1925). Chicago: Univ. of Chicago Press, 1967.

Parton, James. "Chicago." *Atlantic Monthly,* no. 19 (1867): pp. 325–45.

Patillo-McCoy, Mary. *Black Picket Fences: Privilege and Peril Among the Black Middle Class.* Chicago: Univ. of Chicago Press, 1999.

Pierce, Bessie Louise. *A History of Chicago,* 3 vols. New York: Knopff, vol. 1, 1937; vol. 2, 1940; vol. 3, 1957.

Piven, Frances Fox, and Richard A. Cloward. *Regulating the Poor: The Functions of the Welfare State.* New York: Vintage, 1971.

——. *Why Americans Don't Vote.* New York: Pantheon, 1988.

Portelli, Alessandro. *La linea del colore: Saggi sulla cultura afroamericana.* Rome: Manifestolibri, 1994.

Rast, Joel. *Remaking Chicago: The Political Origins of Urban Industrial Change.* DeKalb, Ill.: Northern Illinois Univ. Press, 1999.

Rein, Martin. "Problems in the Definition and Measurement of Poverty," in *The Concept of Poverty.* Peter Townsend (ed.). London: Heinemann, 1970.

Renshaw, Patrick. *The Wobblies: The Story of Syndicalism in the United States.* New York: Anchor, 1968.

Rosenberg, Nathan. *Perspectives on Technology.* Cambridge: Cambridge Univ. Press, 1976.

Rowsome, Frank. *Trolley Car Treasury: A Century of American Street Cars.* New York: McGraw & Hill., 1956.

Royko, Mike. *Boss: Richard J. Daley of Chicago* (1971). New York: Penguin, 1976.

Sade, Comte Donatien-Alphonse-François de. *La philosophie dans le boudoir* (1795). Eng. trans. in *Justine, Philosophy in the Bedroom, and Other Writings.* New York: Grove, 1990.

Said, Edward W. *Orientalism.* New York: Vintage, 1979.

Sánchez-Jankowski, Martín. *Islands in the Street: Gangs and American Urban Society,*

Berkeley: Univ. of California Press, 1991.

Sassen, Saskia. *Cities in a Global Economy* (1994). Thousand Oaks, Calif.: Pine Forge Press, 2000.

Sawyers, June Skinner. *Chicago Portraits*. Chicago: Loyola Univ. Press, 1991.

Schivelbusch, Wolfgang. *Geschichte der Eisenbahnreise*, Munich: Carl Hanser Verlag, Wien 1977. Eng. trans. *The Railway Journey: The Industrialization of Time and Space in the Nineteenth Century*. Berkeley: Univ. of California Press, 1986.

——. *Lichtblicke: Zur Geschichte der Künstlichen Helligkeit im 19. Jahrhundert*. Munich: Carl Hanser Verlag, 1983. Eng. trans. *Disenchanted Night: The Industrialization of Light in the Nineteenth Century*. Berkeley: Univ. of California Press, 1988.

Schor, Juliet B. *The Overspent American* (1998). New York: HarperCollins, 1999.

Schumpeter, Joseph Alois. *History of Economic Analysis*. Oxford: Oxford Univ. Press, 1954.

——. *Capitalism, Socialism and Democracy* (1946). London: Allen and Unwin, 1954.

Seale, Bobby. *Seize the Time*. New York: Random House 1970.

Seely, Bruce, and Jonathan Gifford. "To Build a Nation: America's Infrastructure," in *The Wilson Quarterly* (Winter 1993): pp. 18–49.

Sen, Amartya. "Corruzione e crimine organizzato." *Politica ed Economia* (July 1993).

Sinclair, Upton. *The Jungle* (1906). New York: Airmont, 1965.

Singer, Charles (ed.). *The Age of Steel*, 1850-1900, vol. 5 of *A History of Technology*. Oxford: Clarendon Press, 1954–58.

Slayton, Robert A. *Back of the Yards: The Making of a Local Community*. Chicago: Univ. of Chicago Press, 1986.

Smith, Adam. *An Inquiry into the Nature and Cause of the Wealth of the Nations* (1776). Oxford: Clarendon Press, 1979.

Sombart, Werner. *Warum gibt es in den Vereinigten Staaten keinen Sozialismus?* (1906). Eng. trans. *Why Is There No Socialism in the United States?* White Plains, N.Y.: International Arts and Sciences Press, 1975.

Squires, Gregory D. et al. *Chicago: Race, Class, and the Response to Urban Decline*. Philadelphia: Temple Univ. Press, 1987.

Stead, William T. *If Christ Came to Chicago: What Would He Do?* Chicago: Laird & Lee Publishers, 1894. Reprint. Evanston, Ill.: Chicago Historical Bookworks, 1990.

Steinberg, Stephen. *The Ethnic Myth: Race, Ethnicity and Class in America* (1981). Boston: Beacon Press, 1989.

Stover, John F. *American Railroads*. Chicago: Univ. of Chicago Press, 1961.

Suttles, Gerald D. *The Social Order in the Slum: Ethnicity and Territory in the Inner City*. Chicago: Univ. of Chicago Press, 1968.

Thompson, Edward P. *The Sykaos Papers*. London: Bloomsbury, 1988.

Thoreau, Henry David. *Walden and Other Writings*. New York: Bantam, 1981.

Thucidides. *History of the Peloponnesian War*, in Thomas Hobbes' classic translation:

Hobbes's Thucydides, New Brunswick, N.J.: Rutgers Univ. Press, 1975.

Thurow, Lester. *Head to Head: The Coming Economic Battle Among Japan, Europe, and America*. New York: William Morrow, 1992.

Tocqueville, Alexis Clérel de. *De la démocratie en Amérique* (1835). Eng. Trans. *Democracy in America*. New York: Knopf, 1994, 2 vols.

Todorov, Tzvetan. *La conquête de l'Amérique: La question de l'autre*. Paris: Seuil, 1982. Eng. trans. *The Conquest of America: The Question of the Other*. New York: Harper & Row, 1985.

Townsend, Andrew Jack. "The Germans of Chicago." Doctoral thesis, Univ. of Chicago. Reprinted in *Jahrbuch der deutschen-amerikanischen historischen Gesellschaft von Illinois*, 1932.

Townsend, Joseph. *A Dissertation on the Poor Laws, by a Well-wisher to Mankind* (1786). Berkeley: Univ. of California Press, 1971.

Townsend, Peter (ed.). *The Concept of Poverty*. London: Heinemann, 1970.

Tuttle, William M. Jr. *Race Riot: Chicago in the Red Summer of 1919*. New York: Atheneum, 1970.

US Bureau of the Census. *Statistical Abstract of the Unites States 1992, 1993, 1999*, Washington, D.C.: Government Printing Office; each issue is published twelve months after the given year.

——. *Historical Statistics of the United States, Colonial Times to 1970*. Washington, D.C.: Government Printing Office, 1975.

US Immigration Commission. *Immigrants and Crime*. Washington, D.C.: Government Printing Office, 1911.

US Immigration and Naturalization Service. *Statistical Yearbook of Immigration and Naturalization Service 1998*. Washington, D.C.: Government Printing Office, 2000.

Wacquant, Loïc J. D. "Le gang comme prédateur collectif," *Actes de la recherche en science sociales*, no. 101/102 (March 1994): pp. 88–100.

——. "In 'The Zone,'" in Pierre Bourdieu et al. *The Weight of the World: Social Suffering in Contemporary Society*. Cambridge, Mass.: Polity Press, 1999.

Wade, Louise Carroll. *Chicago's Pride: The Stockyards, Packingtown, and Environs in the Nineteenth Century*. Urbana and Chicago: Univ. of Illinois Press, 1987.

Wade, Richard C. "The Enduring Chicago Machine," *Chicago History* (Spring 1986).

Walker, Daniel. *Rights in Conflict: Convention Week in Chicago, August 25–29, 1968*. New York: E. P. Dutton, 1968.

Wallis, Allan D. *Wheel Estate: The Rise and Decline of Mobile Homes*. New York: Oxford Univ. Press, 1991.

Weber, Max. *Die protestantische Ethik und der Geist des Kapitalismus* (1920). Eng. trans. *The Protestant Ethic and the Spirit of Capitalism*. New York: Routledge 1993.

Weinstein, James. *Ambigous Legacy: The Left in American Politics*. New York: Franklin Watts, 1975.

———. *The Decline of Socialism in America: 1912–1925.* New York: Monthly Review Press, 1967; rev. ed. New Brunswick, N.J.: Rutgers Univ. Press, 1984.

Whitaker, David T. *Cabrini-Green in Words and Pictures.* Chicago: W3 Chicago, 2000.

Williams, Michael. *Americans & Their Forests: A Historical Geography.* Cambridge: Cambridge Univ. Press, 1989.

Wilson, William Julius. *The Declining Significance of Race.* Chicago: Univ. of Chicago Press, 1978.

———. *The Truly Disadvantaged: The Inner City, the Underclass, and Public Policy.* Chicago: Univ. of Chicago Press, 1987.

Young, David. *Chicago Transit: An Illustrated History.* DeKalb, Ill.: Northern Illinois Univ. Press, 1998.

Index